The Autobiography
of a
Painter-Etcher

Photo Bob Herrick

Michael Blaker

The Autobiography of a
Painter-Etcher

Beresford House Press

© Michael Blaker
Published By
The Beresford House Press
16 Ross Street
Rochester
0634 407127

First Published 1986

ISBN no. 0948 322 02 0

We acknowledge the kind permission by Hutchinson Century to reprint some relevant passages from "Leaves from my unwritten diary" by Sir Harry Preston.

Type set and printed in Great Britain by The Devonshire Press Ltd., Torquay

Introduction

An autobiography of an etcher should, properly, concern itself only with the exigencies of biting the plates, with the formulae of acids, the mixing of resistants, the technique of needling, and other apparently inexplicable matters. These items—hopefully to be explained convincingly and without the obscurity they may suggest—will indeed be touched upon; but there is, as well, that illuminating subject, the development of the artist. Upon this, with a full exposition of his successes, disappointments, achievements and follies, the writer may digress with some enjoyment—followed, let us hope, with equal enjoyment by the captive (or perhaps, at the least, captivated) reader.

★ ★ ★ ★ ★

Chapter 1

An etching should, of course, traditionally, be in black and white. It "always has been," and to the mind there at once leaps the image of a thin black frame enclosing a vast white mount in which the print—ideally rather small—sits enshrined with rather more of authority about it than an old master drawing. There is, and always has been, as Sickert inferred, *something about an etching*. Today, at the time of writing, we are all *printmakers*. The term is usually connoted with size—that is, large size—and colour (invariably rather bright). But these new etchings of the late Twentieth Century are not to be dismissed. There is no point in working archaically. I collect, avidly yet with a discrimination which is essential in such a one-time oversubscribed mode, the magical sepia and black etchings of the Twenties and Thirties; but my own prints of the day and hour must have a flavour at least of the period of their production. For instance, I add tints today—with a wash of watercolour only, it is true—but I subscribe in that degree to the new movement. My peers of the craft take a good deal more trouble. Trained more recently, their technical expertise knows no bound, and their results are on almost a computerised level in stream-lined efficiency. They superimpose three or four plates on the paper, in a hand version of the old three-colour half-tone block method of commercial printing; or, indeed, the modern photolitho, that has made colour printing so much cheaper and more available for exhibition catalogues and art magazines.

Although I have painted numerous oils as well as being an etcher, it was, from the beginning, the magazine and the comic paper, the black and white political cartoon and the apparently cheap and vulgar toning of the mechanical tint colouring that essentially fascinated me. As a small boy, my father's newsagent's shop was a treasure house to the imagination—a feast of comics

1

and annuals to which I had full access. I could take away whatever I wished to read provided that it was returned in pristine condition. This shop, with its two bay windows flanking a central door hung with brightly Mickey-Moused tin pails, and both wooden and dangerously sharp iron spades and shrimping nets, was only five minutes away from the Hove beaches, and full of aesthetic interest for an embryo artist. Basically, the images were of outline and flat tint in overlapping areas. The decorative titles of the *Rainbow*, *Playbox*, *Tiger Tim's*, *Chicks' Own*, were brilliant drawings involving various animals in striped trousers or hats and jackets disporting themselves in and about the lettering, which in the Xmas numbers was topped with snow, like custard on a pudding. Endless cartoon symbols were to be learnt from these publications—expressions, angles and hands and feet, radiating lines to denote frustration or embarrassment, and of course the disposition of balloons in which the actual words gave an even greater life, like the gilded ribbons of Gothic script that flow from the lips of saints in a Mediaeval painting.

There were some comics that were black and white only, such as *Film Fun*, which relied on the celebrity of real actors reduced to cartoon form; and a cheaper kind of production such as *Chips*, printed on a pink or green pulp paper that in fact produced an extremely satisfying effect—an excellent lesson for the potential artist, that all one needs is black and one colour, and that expensive polychrome is not necessarily an essential. There were postcards, as well: Bonzo, Granpop—an elderly orang-utan—and Mabel Lucy Attwell, whose drawings also illustrated (for the most part too whimsically) a contemporary edition of *Peter Pan*. A worrying artist, whose thick-legged children seemed an omnipresent institution. There was the *Happy Mag*, often with a William Brown colour cover by Thomas Henry—and the *Strand Magazine*; but the latter's kind of three-dimensional modelled realism went (paradoxically) beyond my sense of what was real. It was perhaps too real, and therefore, with no scope for the imagination, lacked reality. The cartoon outline figure was Truth—it was how life looked; and the shadowless landscape backgrounds gave one a method of seeing nature itself, by synthesism. Uncomprehended Reality is in itself too much for a child.

Apart from the British comics in the shop, I also discovered the wonderful world of American comics; a more developed form of the art, aimed at the adult, which was why perhaps they were the more fascinating. With their mysterious phraseology and meaningless (to an English child in the mid-Thirties) allusions they presented a world similar but different to one's own, with an extra exoticism. The Katzenjammer Kids were a semi-satire of, presumably, German immigration; Oakey Doaks a Mediaeval Knight of naïve and engaging aspect, and Little Orphan Annie sermonised to "Daddy" Warbucks, her war-profiteer guardian . . . these were to be found in the comic section of the *Journal American* which I came upon at the age of ten by finding a boy at school reading it, buying it from him, and regarding it subsequently as perhaps some would their first sight of the Sistine ceiling.

2

I made my first drawings in emulation of this art form, but a pencil seemed not to capture the sparkle of my exemplars. My mother, who drew well and had attended the Brighton Art School, took me to Mr. Boast's little art materials and framing shop in Ship Street, Brighton—a famous meeting-place for artists—and I was fitted up with a small watercolour box (which I observe, looking up from this manuscript to my drawing materials six inches away, I am still using) and a bottle of Indian Ink, the Elixir of Art. From the moment of first using this (as with Pear's soap) all doubt and lack of faith in one's medium disappeared. Here was the dense black of the comic papers; the subsequent colour served only to give atmosphere. One had no need to model form—it was inherent in the line. This simple principle was at once apparent; perhaps it is the one most essential. One can, always, with a little hatching, turn a contour; but the secret is to start with, refer to and rely upon the line; not to work up to it later. Of course, here lies the difference between the illustrator and the painter—the draughtsman and the brushman. My own painting relies on line; and much as I may admire the furry out-of-focus of Renoir, or Titian, it is not a manner that is natural to myself, despite being incredibly short-sighted from birth and basically living—if I take off my spectacles—in an Impressionist fog. Perhaps for that reason it is the almost painful sharpness of a cubist angle that gives me pleasure and inspiration; or the finer-than-fine quality of a Durer line-engraving. It may indeed reflect that happy moment at the start of each day, when one's spectacles are put on, and all the mist resolves itself reassuringly into Pre-Raphaelite clarity.

The first attempts at Indian ink at the age of eight or nine were, unfortunately, disastrous. Previously, I had made pencil drawings of Kings, Ancient Britons, and all the characters in *Treasure Island*; together with some delicate interpretations of ghosts rising from graves that had quite terrified me. But now the Indian ink was to give body (so to speak) to such phantoms. A dip into the bottle, however, and over it went, covering me with streams of blackness that striped my knees and arms like a zebra, before proceeding to the carpet. However, after some initial authoritarian displeasure a fresh bottle was acquired, and art proceeded, with a scene of Judge Jeffreys presiding at court.

As an experience of great interest to my developing potential in black and white, my mother took me to visit an acquaintance who had a little glass-roofed Victorian conservatory extension that she used as a studio. It was attached to a first-floor flat behind what was at that period a store—Plummer's—on the Western Road. The building had once been a Victorian Gothic villa, and above the facade of the store was an octagon turret and battlements—and are there yet if you look above the shop-windows. The tenant of the little studio was a young woman in her twenties who in fact drew a great many of the strips featuring personalised toys (the models stood about the room) portrayed in round-cornered rectangles for the comic *Tiny Tots*. Here was indeed an immediate eye-opener to me as to how such work was achieved. White card, not paper, and the drawing made much larger, to sharpen up in reproduction when

3

reduced. Behind the toys she drew, and their speech-balloons, was a solid black Beardsley-like slab as a background.

I much admired the political cartoons of this period—Strube, and his "Little Man" who appeared in the *Daily Express*. I puzzled a good deal over the meanings of these pictures. What *was* the Locarno Pact? And: "If to me you would be loyal, put a ban on Musso's oil" comes to mind still. And a broom with Leon Blum's face, and moustache: "The new Blum—will it sweep clean?" And ever and anon the figure labelled "Popular Front." One I particularly liked was of a crowd of top-hatted figures on a raft, oars shipped, in a mountainous sea—"Conference to decide whether we should all pull together." This one may have been by Low. I liked his drawings, but they were more evidently drawn with a brush; I could think only with a pen. . . .

With the new advanced theories of education of the early Thirties, I was encouraged at my kindergarten school to make objects, animals, figures, anything, from a box of assorted cotton reels, bits of wire and other trivia that each child was obliged to collect together. We cut out cardboard figures to people the indoor sand-pit, and when spring came round we borrowed a toad each from the school pond, and with it before us in a jam-jar of water, made studies from life. In the autumn, with a more Victorian approach, we copied the tints, with watercolour, of a fallen sycamore leaf. Apart from art and literature, I found other subjects somewhat tedious; but when discovered illicitly in one class at work upon a vista of crocodiles, I was requested to reproduce it as a large picture—this was followed by scenes of elephants and other animals, and they began to appear on the walls of the school, hung for all to see.

Regrettably, however, I did not see too well myself. Though realised neither as yet to myself or others, but only in hindsight (as one might say) I could not see in focus. In a race on sports day—the rhododendron-bordered lawn scattered with panama- and straw-hatted old buffers with white moustaches, and the eager young women who were our mothers, I raced in the lead, towards—what? Hesitant to penetrate the blurred cloud of formless tone before me I paused; a burst of laughter from the audience greeted my defeat as the field swept past me. As in general I was not much concerned with distance, the disability was only discovered one sunny picnic day on Portsdown Hill, when—with packed trunk strapped to the rear bumper of the square Morris 12—we were en route to our annual holiday in the New Forest. I could not see the ships out in the shimmering sea, and obliged to wear glasses ever after. Shortly before being fitted with these spectacles, and before I had gone out from the opticians' into a glass-splinter-sharp world whose first image (Palmeira Square) I still recollect clearly, our school had made a visit to a puppet-show demonstration. As I could see nothing of it, I assumed it must have been a *puppy*-show, and wrote my subsequent obligatory essay on that theme. This, considered to be an unfortunate attempt at humour, was crushed with typical tutorial irony. Perhaps as some sort of consequence of the sense of the deprivation of potential inspiration on this occasion I have, subsequently, always liked the macabre element of the art; the directly carved and over-modelled emphatic faces of Punch and Judy I find likeable for their terror-attraction—a lingering element of the Sublime in art, perhaps.

When one is obliged from childhood to think about one's glasses—to avoid breaking them, to leave them in a shoe when you go swimming, to be wary of scuffling about and fighting, it would seem to lead towards an extra self-consciousness, and an extra carefulness regarding possessions. This perhaps leads on to collecting in general, and then to specified connoisseurship. It is all a far cry from those days of being sent out to find the time from the blurred school clock, and then hanging about rather than go back to confess one's inadequacy; an object of contempt to other masters, who pass you in the corridor and assume you have been sent out for misbehaviour. However, in addition to the hazard of short sight (or perhaps because of it) I was often subjected to various accidents of a near fatal nature. At three, I was all but drowned in a dew-pond—sinister tarns that used to be a feature of the South Downs in the ubiquitous sheep days. I was pulled from below the water by my uncle, who (rather unkindly) was not allowed back in the car on the drive home, but—wet-trousered—had to stand on the running-board outside, with his damp socks fluttering from the windows in an attempt to dry them. Subsequently, on another day, I leant against the unlocked door of the car as it bounced along unmetalled chalk and flint on another idyllic downland day, and was thrown out. I was discovered unconscious, to be permanently scarred in lip and limbs. "He can always grow a moustache," the doctor consoled my mother.

In the St. Anne's Wells Gardens, where the elderly, still in black Victorian dress, sat about the bandstand in a timeless Edwardia, I picked up broken glass by accident, and cut my wrist. My father projected me within seconds to the fortuitously adjacent children's hospital, where—with an almost Eighteenth Century approach—a pad of wool soaked in ether was jammed on my face until I subsided. Spinning wheels of fire having gradually converged, I awoke centuries later, extremely slowly, with the image of a Scottie dog on a nearby calendar seeming to have filled the universe for ever—and with my wound sewed up.

We had a puppy—a wire-haired fox terrier—but this poor animal was pursued by inescapable fate. Having somehow survived puppy distemper in an era presumably without injections for immunity, he was taken out at last to the Downs for his first country run. This went to his head, and he began to froth at the mouth, pant and fall over, and eventually collapsed into a fit. At this precise moment there appeared the fateful deus-ex-machina; or, rather the inescapable Diable. He might have been anywhere else in the world at that time, but, no, here he was, propelled by what agency?—a man with a shotgun, and all the (very possibly suspect) worldly-wise air of the old countryman. My parents, thinking the puppy rabid, voiced their fears.

"Bitten by an adder. Kindest put 'im out 'is mis'ry." This outback sage seemed infallible, and our noisy little rough-haired entity, with his bristly whiskered face, was in a moment no longer a part of my experience—or, in fact, its own. Sitting in the back of the car on the way home one felt a flat detachment, as if this was the way things might possibly always go—wrong, if you took any step at all: the sense of being unable to control events that occurs in dreams. It was obvious in life that you had to go very very slowly and quietly, with a great attention to caution. Perhaps this sense of detachment could be a genesis for aesthetic perception, which necessitates an absence of participation in the objective approach: you don't like a painting of a spring wood because you like bluebells, but because you like the quality of the painting.

I was invariably ill as a child. When my sister was being born I was sent to relations, who took me down to the beach for a long heatwave day. I forgot my sun-hat, and having only a thin cloud of blonde curls, got sunstroke, and for some days hovered fitfully in a limbo of dreadful nightmares. These were in the style of the Disney "Silly Symphony," such as the skeleton dance—old witches, bat-like black shapes rushing about. . . . even Mickey Mouse himself, with his sable ears, and his black pin-limbs always on the move, has a certain quality of terror-image. The moment when the skeletons in that cartoon film remove their heads, and all sink down into a pile of bones, has always stayed with me; and black shapes, shrieking across the canvas, have continued to appear in my imaginative canvases. No doubt the dread terrors of childhood are significant factors in the evolution of later artistic production—to that extent I suppose they have their uses, but it seems a hard school.

I discovered that it was possible to hire a complete Micky Mouse fancy dress—head, gloves, boots, complete with tail. Being invited to a fancy dress party at the Grand Hotel on the sea-front (a friend's father was the manager) I succeeded in persuading my parents to order this coveted suit. At last, the day of the party, it arrived; but to my horror and dismay, they had sent Minnie Mouse—a polka-dot black and orange skirt in place of the pants. I had to go in it, but being too embarrassed to take off the head, had to forego all the cakes and ice-cream. However, my own identity remained undiscovered.

I observed and appreciated the colours and decor of our house—pale blue, yellow and grey rugs and carpeting; and in the large front bay-windowed first-floor parlour over the shop, yellow walls and an orange carpet, that was once obscured when a torrent of soot fell unexpectedly down the chimney upon us. In the children's bed-room was an apparently sacred corner where hung

reproductions of Watts' *Sir Galahad*, with the white head of the horse in the picture, and Waterhouse's *Hylas among the Nymphs*; both of which I have always liked, despite their going in and out of fashion, back and forth, over the decades, to a quite remarkable extent. Apart from cartoons and late Pre-Raphaelitism, the somewhat macabre tableaux of the natural history museums were a prime inspiration towards the conceiving of the world in terms of art, or as transmogrified into art. There would seem to be an essential requirement of our pysche to trap the world into a box or frame—and also to enjoy a story. Of course, television combines both. Perhaps the need of the primitive man to catch his prey—or even the wolf-puppy to become his dog—by constructing some attractive box with a deadfall may have had something to do with it. Nonetheless, we throng the galleries to see anything encapsulated four-square. Even the cubist phases of our recent culture are presented in Rococo gold-leafed extravagance; and for all Seurat's conception of a flat frame pointillistically enhanced, the Monet sketch is usually found in a frame more suitable for the chiaroscuro of a Baroque altar-piece.

Brighton was rich in natural history collections in the Thirties. Indeed, until a recent curator swept away the great animal and bird room at the museum, one could still study and draw these specimens. The one-time skeleton room always impressed me; the black and white effect had a direct link with pen drawing, and the bones were displayed against black-backed cases that gave a Beardsley effect. The long-armed ape stood next to a human, the fragile tree-shrew clasped a twig in cold semblance of its natural position, and high above against the glass roof hung the skeleton of a whale. It was a fairly small whale; but I had in fact seen it lying stranded on the Palace Pier beach one long-ago Thirties morning, with its tail curled beneath it, a mournful little group of spectators around. My father had taken me down before school to see it. He also took me to see the Palmeira Stores when it caught fire early one morning, and we watched the hosing of the top story, the fireman up on ladders from the picturesque old fire-engines one now sees in museums only. Fires have devastated several individual buildings of one's early inspiration. I watched the great swoops of red flame engulf the upper part of the old Bedford Hotel one day in the Sixties, while firemen unconcernedly walked in and out of the ground floor entrance. I had many times drawn the portico; Dickens stayed there, and set scenes of *Dombey & Son* in the building. I had danced there on many a New Year's Eve. I saw Waterhouse's Hove Town Hall burn down some time later, with the famous carillon hanging half out of the tower—the interesting mechanism that had so many tunes to its lyre, playing selections at mid-day, and a special programme at Xmas.

The animal room at Brighton featured numbers of tropical and predictably highly-coloured birds, a great python and other sensational creatures; but my own favourites were the smaller British rodents, a shelf of star-nosed moles, and a young hedgehog preserved in a jar of spirit. Over the thirty years that I knew this temple, the level of the spirit perhaps fell a quarter of an inch, and some of the rodents' fur grew paler; but the room was always there—the atmosphere always still and church-like, and you picked up your thoughts from the time of your last visit. The real museum-goer does not want change. The seasoned National Gallery dwellers hated it when the apparently permanent settings of their favourites came to be altered, and you could no longer march your friends through the rooms directly to the Bellini Doge. One will not linger upon that other lost facet, the glazes of time and varnish that, once removed, took away also the romance of the old master; and in place of depth upon depth of glowing chestnut variations of tint and tone we have the underpaint in a scrubbed pale pink wash, as if put in by the caretaker. But then, it probably wasn't by Durer, anyway—nor even a portrait of his father after all, either. The sky of Titian's *Bacchus and Ariadne* became an electric blue; the Ariosto portrait (discovered not to be Ariosto) became grey-blue, from its previous Burne-Jones sea-green. But at least, if we are lucky, some of us still have one or two of the old postcard reproductions of them from the Golden Age. They will probably be exhibited one day; but I doubt the Gallery has any left.

However, Brighton has—or had until recently—one museum still unaltered—a fascinating manifestation of those increasingly stranger Victorians: the Booth Bird Museum. Conceive today of an enthusiast armed with punt and gun, and weapons of every bore and function, who spends his life collecting and preserving, in enormous cases, a sample or more of every avine species available to his marksmanship. Cormorant and gulls nest on apparently genuine cliff-edges—you see them before you. Eagles on crags gorge upon dying blood-streaked lambs. A crow perches on the back of a stuffed sheep (a favourite, this, with everyone). Picture after three-dimensional picture—plus a back-drop. Perhaps one should have become a sculptor—or a theatrical impresario—with such an early series of examples. Perhaps some of the canvases I painted many years later, of angels arranged on a roof-top, or madonnas and attendants set squarely in a garden, originated from the puffins on the ledges, and the cormorants on the cliffs.

To move to yet another, even more bizarre—yet almost deliberately bizarre—establishment, there was also the Potter Museum at nearby Bramber, the mecca of a weekend drive out from Brighton, to be combined with a cottage tea—cream and scones and boiled eggs—at one of the lattice-windowed Shoppes that satisfactorily speckled the Sussex countryside. Sixpence gained admission to a narrow building that housed the Potter collection. This manifested a quite extraordinary devotion to the unusual and exotic. Five-legged kittens, two-faced lambs; tableaux with all the clothes and accoutrements carefully made in scale, with stuffed young animals playing the parts: the story of Cock Robin (Potter's first masterpiece as a sixteen-year old son of the innkeeper); The Rabbit's Village School—Potter made all the slates and pencils; a village band (Potter cast all the instruments); Lower Five with carousing low life rats and a companion case with Upper Ten squirrels playing cards in a club room. This marvellous and unique social document of the manners and customs of the times, not to say of village art, was apparently privately owned, and so eventually sold; it appeared for a while as a peep-show in one of the Brighton under-promenade arches; but in the Seventies found, I believe, a permanent home in Arundel, where I hope new generations will continue to be fascinated. Why it is not in the V&A or Museum of Ethnology one does not know; but how can anyone evaluate culturally what would appear to be totally unique as a phenomenon? At least no one has staked their reputation in trying.

The Thirties, as an era, was remarkable in the sense that all one's friends' fathers had the same element about them—almost a mystic bond between them, which wives and children could not enter: they had all been in the War; and they had each been the only one of dozens of their companions-in-arms to have survived. They all seemed permanently pre-occupied. They were, perhaps, all in a state of shock, and would always be so. At least, they seemed very different to the younger men who had just missed participation. They were relaxed at once among themselves. Two men would talk at a petrol pump—and it would immediately be of France "Where were you?" "What lot were you with?" I went with my father to an Armistice Day service outdoors, at the Memorial in Hove's Grand Avenue. All the veterans were young, in 1932. The very sunshine seemed holy. Religion, to me as a child, only seemed real when applied to the War. The Eleven O'clock Silence on November 11th was the important, mystic, moment in the year, as a few second's thought for all the lost, and was felt to be so. When the *day* was changed, later (!!!) they were lost indeed, for all time. One did not talk to that generation about the War. They talked to each other about it, not us. We regarded their experiences as some unmentionable weight that would always be on them. Which it was.

. . . . . .

My artistic life continued in the making of animals out of nut shells and plasticene, of constructing books with story and illustration somewhat in the Beatrix Potter format, and in constructing painted boot-box houses for a model village laid out on the spare-room floor. But the most intriguing visual scene that I knew was my grand-parents' restaurant on the lower promenade of Brighton sea-front. Once across the Boundary line into Brighton—marked by a dark green bronze angel on a plinth, known as the Peace Statue—and the excitement commenced. The first item of interest was the Victorian Band Stand, a delicate and lacy image, and some fifty or so old bathing machines, wheels and all, carefully kept by but no longer used. No modest matron of the Thirties requested one; and although the horses still turned the capstans with a long pole through the top, the bathing machines seemed to have gone beyond the point of having a horse set between the shafts. The Twenties had initiated a new way of beach life, and everyone changed on the beach, although even the men's costumes possessed a kind of modest skirt and a vest-like top. I attempted a perspective memory view of the bathing machines—the lines vanishing to a point were very marked—and drew the donkeys by the Peace Statue as part of the picture. These aspects of beach life—brass band in the band-stand, horses winching pleasure boats, flags everywhere, the piers gleaming white and silver, sunshine, the newness of life, sweet cigarettes with Disney character cards, ha'penny novelty sweets in kiosks, liquorice sticks, fish, men fishing, ice-green waves fresh in the morning, have always remained favourite subjects for me, even when most no longer exist. There were paddlesteamers until the early Sixties—intermittently, at least—but in the Thirties you could set your watch by them. Curiously, relatively few painters made much of the Brighton subject round about this period. Spencer Gore painted a very true canvas of the pier and gardens in 1912; Sickert of course didn't miss the chance, yet seems not to have been so taken with the Palace Pier as with the more conventional choice of St. Mark's at Venice. That fine painter—one of my favourite artists—Jacques-Emile Blanche, and Conder (seemingly from memory) both immortalised the atmosphere and seaside attributes convincingly and sensitively, as if they loved the place—which indeed they did; and the etcher Robert Goff—perhaps one of its greatest devotees—made many an evocative plate, including a summer sunset effect on the promenade which only a resident really knows, with the curious effects of shadows and silhouetted pier. Incredibly difficult subjects, these, with all the bits and pieces of cast-iron lamps and promenades, with perspective everywhere as a further hazard, and slopes to the beach and shelters and kiosks abounding. It is hardly surprising that many artists and etchers found it all too much of a muddle, and preferred the sleek serenity of Kipling's whale-backed downs, or the meadows of mid-Sussex. And then, of course, not everyone can endure working on the spot in the centre of the inevitable throng that collects at once as at a sideshow. Once, in the Fifties, I set up my easel on the Hove lawns to paint a brilliant late-summer sun and shadow evening effect; two people stopped, then two more, until there were fifty or sixty, and others began to run towards the scene from far away, as to an accident. Having painted the view, I took another canvas, turned the easel round and commenced the view from the opposite direction. The by now huge audience then slowly moved round as well, so as to be once more behind me as spectators.

The West Pier itself was a diversion to—or extension of—the promenade. One might walk out to the end and observe the anglers, or look at the ancient slot-machines that enacted various morbid incidents—the Hanging, and the Haunted House. There was an escape artist who every afternoon hurled himself into the sea while locked into ropes and chains—sometimes on a bicycle as an extra frisson, as if one were needed—and emerged to cheers and coins. A sand-modeller would spend all day creating giant crocodiles on the beach beneath this great minarretted cat-walk; and towards the fish-market were the flag-decked pleasure boats (fishing-boats plus ribbons), old fishermen knitting nets, booths of shellfish, little plates of cockles and whelks and mussels. Fat women with huge purpled arms and hands served up these delicacies, and with the massed crowds on the beach it was all like a mad party, with the echoing cries "moderboat just going round the bay—moderboat going—moderboat going." Others proclaimed the fare available at the restaurants in the arches, and our walk—or my mother's, for I would have been on a small blue tricycle all the way—concluded at the Élite Cafe, where Fred, a doleful ginger-moustached figure in a straw hat and a white coat, recited endlessly, in a kind of singing monotone, the magic phrases: "Fishanchips—Oysters—Crabteas— Lobster Salad"—Boards propped at angles chalked with prices—windows patterned with varied shellfish on a ground of artificial green grass made of rafia; and inside the rows of white tables, the player-piano, and my grandmother and my aunts all round a table at the end looking at a great book of steel-engraved views of Switzerland.

My mother's parents were both Swiss and had come to England in the Nineties. My grandmother, whom I have drawn, etched and painted many times, would always subtly jerk untidily placed articles and ornaments into a right-angled pattern as she passed by, so that her progress through a room was marked by an increased sense of order. She had come from Poschiavo, in the Italian canton of Switzerland, in 1894, at the age of sixteen, to work in her aunt's restaurant in Margate. They did not get on. A few months at loggerheads with her relative sent my grandmother running away to an uncle at Bournemouth, where she was encouraged by him to marry—with the inducement that he would set them up in a restaurant in Brighton—my grandfather Victor Lanfranchi. Victor had been born in Florence, but his father dying early, his mother returned to her home town of Poschiavo and re-married. Victor was sent to Amiens to be apprenticed in a pâtisserie, and learn the profession of cakes and pastries and chocolate. He made his mark by being the only person in a safe area to volunteer as a conveyor of bread and food supplies to a part of the town isolated with cholera. For the remainder of his life he was always welcome there, and would depart for France in the Brighton off-season loaded with his expensive rifles in order to hunt and shoot with his many friends there.

The Lanfranchi are a family quite remarkable for historical interest. They were one of the powerful families of Pisa in the Renaissance. But like many of the great families of those times, their reputation was not unsullied.

Dante, in Canto 33 of the *Inferno* tells of meeting a Lanfranchi in Hell. This related to 1288, when Pisa was divided into three. The Guelfs, who supported the Pope (as opposed to the Ghibellines who were for the Emperor) were divided into two parties, one led by Ugolino della Gherardesca, the other by his grandson, Nino Visconti. The leading Ghibelline at the time was the then archbishop of Pisa, Ubaldini, who was supported by the Lanfranchi family. When Ugolino expelled his grandson's faction, weakening his own side, the Archbishop, with Lanfranchi, Sismondi and Gualandi to support him, arrested Ugolino and his family. They were imprisoned in a tower for some months, then, the keys were thrown into the Arno and the inmates left to starve. Their prison-tomb was subsequently known as the Torre della Fame. Dante, it would seem, had no doubt as to the eventual destination of the Lanfranchi family. They were in fact, subsequently banished from Pisa.

A distinguished earlier member of the family was a crusader, Ubaldo Lanfranchi, Archbishop of Pisa. In 1203 he conceived the idea of bringing back fifty-three ship-loads of earth from Golgotha, and created the Campo Santo behind the Cathedral from it, so that Pisans could be buried in earth from beneath the cross. The arcades later erected (in 1278) around the graveyard were to be painted with the marvellous formalised murals by Orcagna and others, the greatest artists of the period, whose work is simple and essential, far removed from the pitfalls of the chiaroscuro to come and the photographic style, predictable and impersonal, of the post-Caravaggio Baroque.

Considering that painting was eventually given a new direction in the Nineteenth Century by the Pre-Raphaelite Brotherhood's enthusiasm for the engravings by Lasanio after the Pisan frescoes, one might say that without Ubaldo the P.R.B. might never have existed; nor, perhaps would they ever have found it necessary to invent themselves.

In 1350 another Lanfranchi, Benedetto "one of the first families in Pisa" tried to lead a revolt against the current Tuscan tyrant (according to Machiavelli in "The Prince," that 16th century handbook for Kings) but unwisely tried to influence two Florentines in the scheme. He was betrayed and beheaded; but around 1650 a more fortunate member of the family, the architect Francesco Lanfranchi designed the cathedral at Turin.

My grandmother was a Giuliani, and her grandfather a Longhi from Lombardy—was he a Carbonari who came to Switzerland after some unexplained incident and never returned home to Italy? My grandmother always prefaced a drink with the toast: "Viva la Carbonari, e viva la Liberta!" "I don't know what it means," she said, "but he always said it."

Pietro Longhi is, of course, the famous artist of the family, whose painting is unique and individual. His delight in showmen and street entertainers is one I share myself; also his aesthetic pleasure in the black notes in a composition made by hats and masks. His sense of the macabre mirrors my own, and his love of including a dog in a corner if possible. In self-portraits it is obvious that I share with him the "Family Face." I was interested to come upon his picture of a number of characters grouped across a canvas with his favourite black mask motif creating an underlying pattern of echoing shapes that holds the composition together like a rosary of black beads. It is the same device that I used in my first large picture—a mural at Brighton College of Art—when I employed the same construction, using the pattern of black top hats, which I painted in first, as if they had been thrown across the surface of the picture. Reading about him, he appears to have been one of the first artists to paint the amusing, everyday aspects of life; also one of the first to have plates engraved of his pictures and to market the prints. One letter complains that someone has not yet returned the tube that held the rolled engravings. All printmakers know the value we place on these convenient cylinders.

My grandmother's brothers mostly emigrated from the small valley of Poschiavo. In the Eighties, some went to Canaan, Connecticut, to farm. Two uncles travelled to Australia, where one was lost in a quicksand while out swimming. Another uncle (by marriage) penetrated into the outback prospecting, and spent ten years in lone company with a Chinese goldminer. As neither could comprehend the other's language, they evolved a mutual tongue that both understood. Having presumably gained something by their toil, they eventually each returned to their respective homes; but my grandmother's uncle could now speak only his new patois, and for the remainder of his life he stamped around Poschiavo furiously, continually misunderstood, and always known as "The Chinaman."

My Blaker ancestors can be traced back on a family tree to 1560, and always seem to have lived in Sussex—principally around Cuckfield, Lewes, Brighton and Shoreham, and have been, in the main, grocers and shopkeepers and of an individual and uncompromising burgher integrity.

My grandfather Fred and his brother John were mayors of Brighton turn and turn about in the Edwardian period, although Fred died young, after a lively start. Apprenticed to his grandfather, he ran away from the grocery to become a bookmaker's runner, but returned to trade and eventually owned half a dozen shops, which unfortunately at his sudden death were at once sold. When I was nineteen, an avid burrower among the treasures of the open market, I saw a canvas leaning against a stall. It seemed to beckon me from a long way off. I turned the portrait around: "Portrait of John Blaker, of 100 Church Street, Brighton"—and his dates; the label all but detached, the picture about to disintegrate from its stretcher. This was my great-great-grandfather, aged 52 at the time. Certainly, by the end of the morning it would have been swept away among the rubbish at the close of the market. I had the necessary sixpence—I restored and cleaned the portrait. At 100 Church Street, nearby, the shop still stood. Beneath modern repainting on the sign I could distinguish the raised paint of the original inscription—"Blaker." I have always kept this picture in my studio. When I was nineteen he seemed very aged—now he appears fairly youthful.

In the parish registers of Hove old church we find plenty of Tudor John Blakers. The family has persisted, also the name. One of the Blakers was known as the "Cuckfield Giant," and was of the entourage of "Butcher" Cumberland.

Together with his brother John, my grandfather Fred formed a trio with Sir Harry Preston, the noted Brighton character, breeder of bull terriers, and proprietor of the Royal Albion Hotel on the sea-front. In Harry Preston's book of memoirs *Leaves from my unwritten diary* he describes the origin of the long road along the sea front from the Palace Pier to Black Rock, laid down as the earliest tarmac motor-racing track, where they hoped to achieve speeds of over 70 m.p.h. Under the auspices of the Royal Automobile Club, Sir Harry says: "I had gone to the Mayor, who at that time was Mr. Fred Blaker . . . a man of enterprise and vision. He was enthusiastic"—Fred later officiated at the opening of another unique Brighton institution, the famed but short-lived—owing to its destruction in a gale—"Daddy-long-legs," a double-decked car on high struts; the wheels running on an under-water track that stretched from Black Rock to Rottingdean, the power being electricity, from a cable above. This was an invention of the famed Volk, whose little electric railway (still in operation) between Black Rock and the Aquarium was the earliest electric-powered line to run. The demise of the Daddy-long-legs was greeted with joy by the Pre-Raphaelite painter Sir Edward Burne-Jones, who lived at Rottingdean and obviously did not consider such innovations Arthurian.

The square concrete blocks that held the rails of this incredible invention could still be seen in my youth, and when the sea was far out of a summer evening, and one was pottering among the rock pools, looking at prawns and sea-anemones, the light of the summer evening would gild the surfaces, so that this glowing golden path of giant's stepping stones flowed magically into the hazy distance of the setting sun, with the silhouettes of the piers faint in the far distance like fairy palaces. One would think that very suitable for Burne-Jones. What more could he want? Surely, it was just up his Pre-Raphaelite street.

In the Thirties, the Volk's railway ran at certain points over the sea itself. The beach has today filled up the space to the level of the tracks; but the lashing waves below, as one hung out of the open sided cars, were yet another exciting contribution to life in Brighton, which still possessed a great deal of the almost child-like desire for novelty on the part of the (unknown-to-them) television-starved Edwardians. Another boy's enjoyment, at the Hove end of the promenade, was on a good rough day to wait for a giant wave to hit the promenade wall, and then as the water hung poised twenty to thirty feet in the air to run along the fifty or so yards beneath before it crashed down. If it caught you, it swamped you thoroughly, or bowled you over; the railings of course preventing your being hauled back into the sea as the wave retreated.

"One of the first friends I made in Brighton," Sir Harry says, "was Sir John Blaker, shrewd and wise. By astute foresight he had amassed a fortune, mainly in real estate operations. He believed in Brighton and its future, and he quietly bought land; whatever he bought seemed bound to increase in value. He achieved a baronetcy, the chief magistracy of Brighton, an unassailable local reputation, and an almost national celebrity for terse, common-sense maxims from the Bench. He was a good friend to me." Sir John was the only magistrate licenced to carry a revolver, and had been known personally to arrest a malefactor.

My father, born in 1895, was sent to Petworth to learn the grocery business, but while there fell foul of the omnipotent Lord Leconfield—"Old Lecky," king of the area. Riding in his carriage one day, he commanded my father to open a gate for him. "Open it yourself," replied the fearless but tactless boy. "Right-ho! I know *you*, young Blaker! You'll be out of this town by tomorrow." And he was. Returning to the shop, the manager told him: "Old Lecky's been here. Pack your bags." There were three grades of wine sold at the grocery—the most expensive came up in a specially cobwebbed bottle. All were filled from the same casks. My father went to London, where he enjoyed a happy period frequenting all the theatres and music-halls and amassed a voluminous repertoire of music-hall songs that he could recall and sing endlessly almost without repetition. Enlisting with the Middlesex Regiment at the outbreak of war in 1914 he was sent to France, and after their return home was about to be sent out again for a fresh offensive. The troops of that volunteer army were, incidentally, extremely offended by being sent to the Front in uncleaned cattle trucks as if they had been prisoners, or were of no consequence; and their dislike of the local villagers, who would charge them for glasses of water, was intense. The day before embarking once again for the Front, the battalion played the Scots at football. My father heard several of the opposing side murmuring about him; and in a concerted attack he was bowled over and carried off the field with a broken leg. The battalion proceeded to the Front to be decimated, and my father went to hospital. In convalescence he would visit the Conan Doyles for tea, as they lived nearby, and took an interest in the recovering casualties. While in France, my father's detachment had been bombed by the German air ace von Richthofen's "Flying Circus"—Hermann Goering was one of the pilots.

"Move up, Jack," cried another soldier, leaping into the trench where the troops were sheltering. My father did so, and a missile landed directly on the newcomer. My father went from hospital out to Mesopotamia; where, as a signaller, he laid communication wires in the No Man's Land between the Lines; on one occasion being led almost into the Turkish trenches by a confused sergeant, who had persevered in his own opinion despite my father's warnings. My father boxed for the battalion, and seems to have been the local Regimental champion; but he hung up his gloves and refused to fight again after a man knocked unconscious took several days to revive. Despite threats of courtmartial if he did not represent the battalion in the next tournament, my father remained adamant; and after a conversation with the Colonel—mainly about cricket—was sent home to be commissioned. Emerging as a junior subaltern, he found the War over; returned to work in one of his uncle's Brighton groceries, and shortly afterwards set up a small newsagent's shop in Prince Albert Street, where he was the first to announce the end of the General Strike some years later, having got hold of the news and been earliest to the station to collect the London paper deliveries. Marrying my mother in 1925, he took a larger shop in Hove, where he employed three assistants, a boy of all work—inevitably "Albert"—a fleet of delivery boys, a washerwoman, and ordered a pair of trade bicycles with his name painted across the advertising board beneath the crossbar. The ladies who served in the shop would sit for their tea-break by the wide open range in the back-room, and in the wash-house beyond old Mrs. Robinson would stir the clothes about in the copper, while I hung about talking and bothering them. I had a live-in nanny, an Australian girl called Nurse May; and there was a cook called Edith, and a succession of uniformed maids. My mother spent her mornings with friends, and enjoyed coffee with them to the sounds of a light orchestra in the palm-strewn restaurants of the larger Brighton Stores. She attended Health and Beauty classes—a kind of early Yoga, in a sense—and the rising-sun wireless played Henry Hall and the Savoy Orpheans (with Carrol Gibbons). Radio Luxembourg, the arrival of a vacuum-cleaner—always carefully replaced in its

Our Summer and Winter Oysters
are of the best quality at
reasonable prices.

Our

Fish Dinners and Suppers

*are Cooked Fresh for
each customer.*

All Eels are killed and Jellied
on the premises.

All kinds of Shell Fish,
Lobsters, Crabs, Prawns, Mussels
and Cockles
when in season and obtainable.

mahogany box (except when the cat selected it as the receptable for a large number of kittens) and the wonder of a telephone like a black flower on its stand, with a winding handle for connecting with the shop down below, were keynotes to this existence.

My grandparents' restaurant in Brighton presented, as I observed earlier, a very different atmosphere, none the less attractive. My grandmother had about her the archaic quality of all the images of the past, which seem to fuse into one, prior to our advanced era. She spoke of going to the chemist's for "a jar of leeches;" and a sick person was "yellow as a guinea."

My grandfather always had a dog somewhere about; he would sit up all night with them if they were sick. A whistle from him, and a dog would come running on the instant. For many years he kept a large semi-wild cat he had taken from a nest in a tree, climbing up in the absence of the mother to secure one of the kittens. Known as "Tiger," I recall it as an enormous old creature, its head carried on a permanent slant, due to a brick once thrown by some beach vandal. In my time, my grandfather had the one dog, a springer spaniel, "Caesar" named after Edward VII's dog. As Fred Blaker always said, in the phrase of the times: "If it's good enough for Teddy, it's good enough for me." Victor had once owned, also, a pair of white bull terriers, pedigree dogs bred at the Royal Albert by Sir Harry Preston. Sir Harry's own dogs would invariably attack the Brighton tramps, but my grandfather Lanfranchi, who always had hot soup ready in the winter to ladle out to any passing unfortunate, would keep a cupboard of old pairs of trousers always at hand. The tramps would arrive in torn (or dog-bitten) clothes, with the familiar : "Spare pair, Guv'nor? spare pair guv'nor?"

My father, as a boy, enjoyed helping his mother on to a tram or a horse-bus at one end of the Kemp Town, and then running through the streets to race it; finally at Brighton's Castle Square helping her off on her arrival.

My Swiss grandfather, when I knew him, had become an enigmatic character, with large moustache and yachting cap. I once asked him if he had ever been a sea-captain, and he seemed to give this suggestion much thought. His accent was so marked that I found it difficult to understand him; but I used to sit in his sunshine-filled office with him, reading books from a kind of treasure cave at the back of the arch—a dark place running directly under the main promenade road above. The ceiling was vaulted like a kind of bee's hive, the bricks whitewashed, and at the top a round man-hole cover, and a few ferns poking out from where they had taken root. Down below, I would be poking about among the rows of bookshelves—Zola and Marie Corelli, all in French, and strange French children's books, the stories and illustrations rather cruel—the heads of animals were not cut off in the comic strip children's books that *I* knew. All this made a visit to my grandfather exotic to say the least. Musical instruments—a mandolin, a violin—boxes, trunks, pictures . . . a mint condition framed Caton Woodville print with the pattern on the frame being the embossed name of the product that had sent it out on the receipt of a hundred labels, and still in the box in which it had been delivered. Keep it, it will be valuable, my grandmother had said. Curiously enough, against all the odds (which is usually the case) it would have been, had it survived to its collectable era; but then the destruction of the thousand is always the reason for the desirability of the one.

My grandfather, bent over his roll-top desk; the arch of the window, the *Skylark* serene on the beach below . . . "Go and make yourself an ice-cream cornet—"

I would go down through the dark corners of the restaurant and its connecting passages—great brown-glazed jars of water in which floated curls of butter—other jars full of bread rolls; the ice-cream making apparatus, with a lining for ice and salt. Up the steps to the ice-cream parlour, a spike on the wall for knocking the glass marbles down into the lemonade bottles to open them, and both large and small cornets ready to be filled. Reaching down, blinking in the sunshine, to the chill contrast of the ice-cream tub when the lid was removed. Returning with a well-filled cornet, and never so stupid as to leave the lid off.

On the beach, just across the tarmac sizzling in the sunshine, and throwing up wriggling mirages, were the aforesaid *Skylark* pleasure boats, with the large and sturdy redfaced Captain Collins the Second standing by. These great ships—the largest with a great white bird figure-head, beneath which I used to stand looking up at it—were later to be lost at Dunkirk, having set off across the Channel one sunny June morning from this beach. They were loaded with food for the troops they hoped to collect—my grandmother and uncle had emptied the restaurant larders to help fit them out, but it was to be their last trip across the flat mirror-bright sea. "What happened to the chaps who took them?" I once asked. "Oh yes—young so-and so—yes, didn't see him about again, now you mention it . . ."

The engravings in the Swiss books of mountain village views—probably wood in the text, and steel for the plates—were to me an introduction to a different kind of linear art, where the lines massed together made a cobweb of greyness through which the Alpine passes and chasms loomed—or, in a more reassuring vein, created pine-flanked vistas peopled with ox-drawn wagons and black-garbed workers. I responded to this monochromatic world of cross-hatching; but I did not see it as something that could actually be done by the hand of man—or myself. One could emulate with pen and Indian ink the newspaper cartoon, but these engraved pictures were not technically comprehensible. The Victorian era of illustration, linked with the Élite Cafe, the sense of going into the past that a visit into Brighton always provoked, created in my mind a sense of greater reality in the past than in the present; consequently pictures and drawings of the Nineteenth Century seemed more real than those of the present day. The fascination of Tenniel's *Alice* pictures was enlarged by a kind of terror attraction in them—they were too real, more solid than the cosy symbols for reality produced by the more kindly era of the Thirties. The

Tenniels, one felt, might actually leap from the paper and get at you—one hardly dared open the book. It seems few people have actually *liked* them, as children. Too nightmarish a quality emanates from these albeit masterpieces of illustration.

As regards dreams and nightmares themselves, I soon progressed to the point while dreaming at which one could comfort oneself with the knowledge that it was only a dream; but nonetheless I still wandered—and have continued to do so—through an unpeopled mansion of total and unknown—as it is unseen—Terror. This is no doubt a common enough dream-image, this house without windows, but only huge rooms, deserted like the Marie Celeste, with staircases either end, and no corridors but connecting doors. Perhaps such a sense of lurking fear is a useful element in giving a grain of magical terror to a work of art, to stimulate and worry those who look at it, and make the images memorable if only for the irritation in the mind that they provoke; it has been analysed by Burke in his enquiry into the Sublime, but the painters of that period used it perhaps too obviously and too theatrically. There should always be a frisson somewhere, but it must be well concealed.

On Bonfire nights, we drove along the promenade into Brighton—the piers, spotlit pink and blue, reflecting in the black water with a dream impression of the Arabian nights, Dulac and Rackham. The dark black wings of the Peace Statute rose in silhouette against the oriental bandstand, and black Callot-figures danced on the beaches before their orange bonfires. The Brighton Level was a turmoil of people hurling their unwanted possessions into the yellow flames. On a quiet part of the beach we lit our own gold- and silver-rain and occasional Jack-in-the-box—a banger—and admired the enthusiasm of the Catherine Wheels once we got them started.

Before the birth of my sister (when I was three) I was one of those fortunate children whose parents do not let their advent circumvent usual expeditions. If my parents went anywhere, I went with them. I was a quiet observer, not desiring the limelight—unwilling, in fact, to have notice taken of me. We used to run up to town of an evening to the theatre—as they used to say—enjoying refreshments at the curtain-windowed lamplit tables on the Brighton Belle; and then there was the atmosphere of the theatre auditorium, and the intense blinding light from the stage. The Colosseum—White Horse Inn—the images remain; and the subsequent exhaustion when one fell asleep on the train home. The Hippodrome at Brighton was a favourite with the residents—all the operas of the annual Carl Rosa season; Gilbert and Sullivan; Lilac Time, all the regulars; Lord George Sanger's Circus—also seen under canvas in the New Forest—and pantomimes in which once legendary figures of the music-hall took part—Sandy Powell, Harry Tate Junior, Nellie Wallace—living reminders and memories of my father's youth, still there before him—and all the comedians who had survived into the Thirties. A little later, when I was nine or so, I joined the autograph-hunting bands of children who hung around the stage door, and we would chat to the sympathetic and friendly celebrities such as Billy Cotton. "You want to ask *him* for his autograph," said Arthur Askey to me, after inserting a flourishing inscription in my book, and pointing to Richard Murdoch—"he's *Famous*."

I commenced as a pupil at the Brighton, Hove and Sussex Grammar School in September 1935, at the age of seven. This school had been created by a group of Brighton burghers as a company electing a board of governors. My father's brother Fred, killed on the Somme in 1916, had been a pupil. My eye would stray at prayers to his name on the oak Roll of Honour on the wall. These ubiquitous memorials to the War met one's eye at every point. They were, as I say, Religion. In every village, one read the list—soon to have the next war lists added on. But in the Thirties, we were still bathed in halcyon sunshine—days on the beach—ghost-images of small children, white sun-hats glittering on the retina in the intense morning heat. Not for the South the slump of the times, but the permanent holiday of the seaside town; flags fluttering, and only the grey-faced dole queue, shamefaced outside the labour exchange in their ill-fitting second-hand clothes, to suggest another view of the era. For the poor were still with us—only they didn't go on the beach.

A new element now came into one's life—the image of the Distinguished Old Boys of the School. One such was the painter Louis Ginnett. Some of his most remarkable canvases were the giant achievements that formed the mural decorations around the great hall of the Grammar School. These portrayed the history of Man in Sussex, from the wild barbarians in the Hollingbury camp on the nearby Downs to the archaeologists of the Thirties discovering their haunts on the same site, now a golf course, with a panorama landscape of Brighton in the background, creeping ever nearer over the horizon. I recall the official unveiling of this canvas and the other final one of the series—the Prince Regent in the grounds of the Royal Pavilion. These were involved compositions, with the figures life-sized and close-up, the back view of a footman like a heraldic motif. I have always admired these works; perhaps in shape and conception they may owe something to Madox Brown at Manchester, but the type of figure and portraiture has always seemed to me basically very original, given that they belong to a certain era: they are *academic* art of the Thirties as opposed to the avant-garde style of those times. Louis Ginnett himself stood by, as a huge blue curtain was pulled away from each picture, and tributes and speeches of course followed. I had imagined that the artist would be dressed in a beret and an orange smock; but he was in a suit, like a doctor or banker, with glasses and a moustache, and seemed both confident and assured in manner. I have seen other pictures by him since; and he was especially good at small landscape pochades made on wood panels in the traditional way, direct from nature.

Another distinguished Old Boy was Aubrey Beardsley, whose work was often spoken of when I was a pupil. One day in the Fifties, when I was in fact about twenty-eight, I was walking along the sea-front when an ancient car stopped, and an elderly man driving it rather surprisingly offered me a lift. I was not far from home, but we got to talking, and I climbed in. Discovering in a moment that I had been a pupil at the Grammar School, he declared he had also been one; naturally, I asked him about Beardsley—"He was a bit older than I; but he and Charles Cochrane—you know, he became a great theatre impresario—they were thick as thieves. They used to put on shows together, school productions. Beardsley did the music, of course. They were always planning to run away to America, but were caught before they reached the boat when they tried it. Cochrane tried it again on his own, later, and succeeded. Got clear away." Other anecdotes followed. I record the occurrence as an odd one.

We wrote at school with brass "Saxon" nibs—long ones, imitative of a quill—and we wrote copperplate style, from examples. The "Relief" short nib was regarded with a scathing horror, and if caught using this, or—more obscene still—a fountain pen, severe wrath would follow. Such innovations savoured of *America*; whose speech, accent, comics and films (despite their universal popularity) were not considered fit examples to follow. Having always had a fascination for all aspects of American history, writing, illustration, literature and social development, I took no notice of this kind of stricture. However, the copperplate pen was to my taste—it was excellent for drawing; and in the Eighties I am now down to my last two nibs; and I have used these for fifteen years, carefully sandpapering them back to sharpness when blunted.

I walked to school each morning, after an hour or so spent delivering newspapers—in this way I earned additional pocket money, and continued at intervals to work in our shop in this way all my schooldays. I included in my rounds the house where Lord Alfred Douglas spent his retirement far from the glitter of Oscar; but I suppose not so far from Worthing, which seemed to mean so much to the latter, if only to get away from the former. There were indeed, many hints of Edwardia still in that world. Horse-troughs still stood and were used. The Hanningtons Removal wagon was a vast horse-drawn caravan that moved at about two miles an hour, and drinking-fountains for men as well as horses stood in the squares and parks; although one was forbidden (as carefully-brought-up children) to drink from the steel cups chained to these press-button fountains. The lamp-lighter switched on his lamps with a long boat-hook, circling from side to side of the road on his bicycle in a figure of eight movement, lunging at the lamps like a knight at the quintain. For tea, there might be winkles, with beside each plate a clean needle with which to prise off the cap and corkscrew the succulent delicacy from its shell. Such unusual food now almost belongs to the past. My mother spoke of the larks arriving from abroad when she was a child—not singing migrants but preserved, each in silver paper, side by side in a tasteful wooden box. The famed Sussex wheatears were of course totally decimated by the Victorians for food, being caught in tunnels of plaited straw culminating in a kind of crabpot, into which they obligingly threw themselves by the lemming-like hundreds. We did indeed shrimp; and later on (as an adult) using a four-foot wide net, I was to catch large quantities to cook of an evening.

Opposite our house, across the road, the breadshop had a giant loaf painted on the wall, on a blue background, where the corner turned down Brunswick Street West; and the fishmonger next door received great blue blocks of ice every morning from a horse-drawn wagon, the ice packed with straw between the blocks. Why did it not melt in the sunshine? An old tramp sat all day smoking cigarette-ends as they were thrown away by others; flies were everywhere; and the breeze tidied the dust on the pavement into little heaps.

Late Monday afternoon, we sung in the school hall with Mr. John Greenwood, the music master—just the one form of about twenty boys in the vastness of the hall falling away into a grey and misty obscurity as the November twilight settled. The Ginnett murals seemed almost to move and come alive in the pale light—the Brangwynesque galleons returning from sinking the Armada were more than real. Mr. Greenwood, his brow convoluted and tense, encouraged us through "Blow, blow, thou wintry wind"—. The whole scene had a kind of pathos about it—rather like Mr. Mell and his flute. But our master was not merely our teacher. He was a composer of some regard, and wrote music for films of distinction. When Robert Flaherty's *Elephant Boy* came to Brighton, the school went in a body officially to see it, and to appreciate John Greenwood's soundtrack. He resided in Ditchling (as did Ginnett) that nearby village of art and culture where Eric Gill, Edward Johnston, Brangwyn, Charles Knight and many others lived or had lived. Mr. Pratt, the tall white-maned taxidermist of Cranbourne Street in Brighton was a Ditchling resident, and the window of his shop was a picture in itself; a kind of collage of books, eggs, glass eyes, scalpels, stick insects for sale, birds set up in cases—a fascinating over-crowding of images. Sometimes we walked over the Downs from Brighton, past the gypsy encampment, descending from the steepness of the Beacon into the village for tea. On a Sunday afternoon we might drive there to feed the ducks in the pond and look yet again at the strange architecture of Anne of Cleve's cottage. I have always known Ditchling—it is a Brighton excursion.

Another favourite day out was to take the small railway to the Dyke. This has long ago disappeared and the track taken up; but one may still walk the empty cutting, past deserted platforms where the decorative shrubs have become giant trees. At the Dyke, where a hotel stood, there were the bones of mammoths, or dinosaurs, to be seen as an attraction in the gardens; and once a cable car had spanned the Dyke Valley, and a funicula descended into Edburton and Poynings, the Wealden villages below.

Photography became of permanent and paramount importance to me from the moment of acquiring my 620 Popular Brownie box camera in 1938. This was held against the chest—which means that all snapshots of that period have a different character, and different level, to the subsequent pictures focussed from eye-height. Disliking people as a subject, I took buildings, churches, animals and Inn-signs—a successful one being "The Trusty Servant" at Minstead in Hampshire, with his padlocked pig-snout. The New Forest inspired me photographically—the Rufus Stone (I made drawings of the Walter

Tyrrell accident) and other immoveable subjects such as statues and tombs. I tried insects and small creatures, using a portrait attachment; and in some ways only *saw*, as a photographer. Perhaps the viewer acted as an extra lens for my eyes. Churches as subjects interested me, although I was wary and fearful of religion as such, and kept well away from it, although I attended the Union Church Sunday School at Castle Square, Brighton, which was in fact full of images. Once a month we attended the church proper, where the preacher would jerk in his pulpit like a puppet, finally collapsing over the edge to hang head downwards, like Punch—an eerie and terrifying performance, all among the Victorian Gothic stone and woodwork. The news that it was possible to partake cannibalistically (albeit symbolically) of the gentle meek and mild one we were encouraged to adore surprised me into abhorrence, and a further confusion between the terms saviour and savoury did not help this conception. However, there was a romanticism about it all, and the church occasions— evening services with the glow of the hot-chestnut stall outside afterwards; and people emerging as black shapes against the light from the inside. Also there were theatrical events in which one sometimes participated.

As a small child in the Kindergarten, I had been required at times to present, in velvet suit and lace, a bouquet to the Headmistress or other personalities on speech days and such occasions; and I had already appeared in a production of the *Wind in the Willows* as one of the Field-mice carollers, with a cardboard mouse head. Now, in the performance in the Union Church Crypt, I was a converted Heathen. My legs were covered by my sister's long brown stockings; and with a grass skirt and upper parts obscured with cocoa and milk I was a South Seas Islander, until caught and made to see the Light of Truth. Later, as a member of the audience, I was more than impressed by an apparent realisation of Frank Bramley's *Hopeless Dawn*—except that the lost fishermen son came back . . . in a white sheet, while the old mother still sat by the guttering candle peering out of the latticed window at the great grey waves. I was pleasantly terrified.

We spent Easter Holidays—and summer week-ends—at the village of Fittleworth, near Petworth. Constable considered this area one of the finest possible painting grounds.

At the Swan Inn the still-narrow approach road from the South permitted an ivy-covered sign-bearing beam across the lane, that framed the view of the village. The Swan had always been a favoured centre for artist sketching parties. Academicians brought their students to stay, and in the traditional way left a small painting. These were built into the panelling of the Inn and remain there today, darkening reminders of another age, as the cars flash by outside on the widened road. In the Thirties I sat on the wall watching the hounds meet on the green, and at evening service in the church up the lane—a Samuel Palmer lane of close-walled cottages and trees enveloping—the flaring candles, lights and organ music pulsated in one's half-asleep mind.

The candles rose like torches and one had to leave and drift back down the lane in the silence of warm grey-blue mist—all out of Helen Allingham or Fred Walker, or the book of Sussex watercolours by Wilfred Ball. True evocations these, with a kind of watermeadow sadness over them so different to the objective optimism of a French Impressionist. Of course there is no sublimity to Sussex except on some Downland views at odd moments—there is no Lakeland grandeur. It is all bits of elder tree and kitchen gardens, and pigs and poultry and a sense of approaching teatime.

Petworth House, nearby, has the kind of comforting quality of having remained the same for fifty years—possibly three hundred—and the things—happily—don't seem to have been moved, and are still in their right places, so that the great sculpture room still feels like the Eighteenth Century, and the Turners hang on walls a few feet away from where they were painted, with the same views by their side out of the window. To echo the availability of visits to houses such as Petworth and Parham, there was the other potential availability of the country cottage. This could be rented for a few shillings a week, or even purchased for a few pounds, but no one bothered to do that, of course. Beams, old range, kitchen gardens overgrown, trees and the jungle advancing—help yourself. Family friends had rented one of these picturesque dwellings for summer stays, and we spent happy days there making hay-huts, or climbing to an owl's nest to take out a chick, scratching and furious, all white fluff and talons. Very fortunately, the mother bird wasn't there at the time.

In Hove, it was every day on the beach, unless there were South-West gales, with the rolling grey breakers unbelievably high, crashing and smashing against the supports of the pier, as one looked down excitedly through the ironwork. No steamers, or anglers at the end on those days. On other days, the tide comes up, the tide goes down—you move up the beach, you move down. You huddle against the breakwater out of the draught—"where shall be go then? Up against the wall?" The sea goes far out, and we expand—little black figures tumble or wander against the reflected glow of the sand. My mother goes racing across the beach one morning, straw hat bowling along the pebbles behind her, to rescue a small child drowning face downwards in the pool of water it has just created round a sand-castle. High tide, and we swim in the swell off-shore, to eat apples afterwards, broken in half by my father's hands.

We were each encouraged to give a lecture to the other members of the class during the school year; having succeeded in avoiding this for some time, I was surprised when the master's eye alighted on me, and I was summoned out. "You esteem yourself an artist. Right—I'll take your place"—he sat down at my desk—"and you can take *mine*. Tell us about *art*. Take the chalk, and draw on the blackboard, as you do when I'm not in the room." With this unusual encouragement, I produced a great fresco—in temporary form—representing a gun battle in a Western saloon. This subject was of course familiar to everyone via the films. The magic element of the Thirties was in the cinema. Hardly an opiate. More of a life-creator—you didn't want to miss what was on next week—you had to keep well enough to go, even if you snuffled all through the performance. "What's on at the Academy, the Regent, the Savoy, the Curzon, the Tivoli?" Evocative and exotic, the absurd names! There were dozens of the places. On the outskirts of town, a hoarding: "Site for proposed cinema"—the sign was there for years—all through the Second War. It never was built. No week was complete without a couple of afternoons or evenings in the relaxing darkness. The organist, coming up in a cage of illuminated stained glass, trailers, news . . . you came or left as you pleased—"I think this was where we came in"—You evolved a way of enjoying and comprehending the story the wrong way round, even saw the whole show twice over—stayed all afternoon and evening. The merest child could afford the price of entrance.

"Looks like a picture afternoon," my father would say, and we would drive off, well equipped with bags of sweets, stumbling to our seats, blind "until your eyes got used to it."

I chose a small handcranked projector for a Xmas present when I was nine; Felix the Cat films were provided, and although the film inevitably ceased to wind up, and when the lights came up the floor was a mass of celluloid toad-spawn (as it were) the strange mobility of the cartoon figures inspired one to essay a similar series. *War in the Hive* was one for which I made thirty or more frames; but it was too involved a business, obviously. Each picture almost the same, but just a little different—rather like an edition of etchings? But I was still an animal cartoonist, and had created an animal city in my mind and drawings, where law and order were enforced by the White Mouse Brigade and the Woodland Rangers; and of these I made a large number of drawings, intensively and endlessly.

Perhaps these subjects were suggested by the approaching war. We were equipped with gasmasks in cardboard boxes in 1938, and carried them with us everywhere for years. No one was ever without this item slung from a shoulder either in a leatherette case or a tin cylinder—although these were considered unreliable, as they could be dented and the respirator wedged. After Munich the respirators were put away—usually in cupboards in overwarm places where the rubber tended to perish. However, one carried them from 1939 onwards, more in fear of infringing the regulations than any faith in their capacities—indeed, the only positive result from them in my experience—and this a tragic one—was the fact that an adventurous boy I knew at school tried to sleep in his as an experiment and was discovered defunct the next morning, a severe shock to all.

My family moved to a newer, art-deco style house just before the war. The main feature was the presence of black and white or pale green decorative glass in every room. Mantelpieces were cubist blocks of black glass irregularly placed—bath-room and facilities were variegated glass from floor to ceiling, and simulations of black and white chequered floors in a rubber substitute greeted one in the spacious hall. The walls were a roughcast stone, and the staircase widened and curved as one descended, to culminate in a lamp in the form of an olympic torch, the glass shade being intended to represent smoke, though I always assumed it was a pineapple.

My mother's piano stood in the front parlour. She excelled at sight-reading all music from operetta to the popular songsheets of the day, so I was brought up singing. Thirties music, with its plaintive sentimentality, and elaborate charm. As Noel Coward said.

My sister and I had already commenced piano lessons with a kindly elderly lady, one of a trio of instructors who formed a small music school in Brighton. This house and its ambience represented to me inspiration in every way. The house, one of a Regency terrace that surprisingly formed a circle around an interior mutual garden—or park—was named Park Crescent. It seemed to symbolise the atmosphere of Brighton of those times, with the Victorian sensation increasing the deeper you went into the town. The houses were still miniature Mentmores, treasure palaces of charm—the sofas and pictures and china and statuettes still where they had been placed sixty years before. It's not just the articles that create the sense of a period—it's the space they occupy—how they were arranged by the original owners—the way they were *seen*. The auction room is of course the grave—but so is the museum reconstruction, and even the educational exhibition, however well done. Only the picture still unmoved from its hook after ninety years is really still alive.

No. 11, Park Crescent. Firstly, a bus took you along the Western Road to the Clock Tower (with its enamelled inset portraits of Queen Victoria and Prince Albert) down North Street to Castle Square, and along the London Road to the market. Here, a blacksmith still had his forge. We walked up a misty gaslit street where ragged children—some occasionally with bare feet—slipped in and out of the lamp's glare. Fascinating shops packed with sweets and pathetic cheap toys beckoned the coins from our pockets. At the end of this street loomed the Salvation Army Hostel, and ill-looking men, shambling along, began to be a feature of the twilight. The railings glimmering wetly. We approached No. 11 and rang the bell.

The house was crammed with pictures and steel engravings, and the sound of piano lessons from behind shut doors down long passages was a consciously romantic sensation to linger over while climbing the grey-papered staircase—the house seemed all in monochrome—to the attic room where our teacher presided. In summer, the corridor leading from the front door culminated in a light green rectangle, as the door to the park was kept open, like the gate to a looking-glass world or magic garden; but in winter the corridor was dark, although the gas lamps bubbled and hissed in their mantles. Miss Houghton's room was a Phiz illustration to one's delighted eye. Over the piano, close to the gas bracket whose flicker seemed to give it a breathing movement, was a ferocious portrait of Beethoven, glowering down at you, if you ever dared look up from the music.

"Wherever you are in the room, his eyes are looking at you," I was informed. One might have therefore assumed that the total mission in life of this malevolent god had been to make music as difficult as possible for the discomfort of pupils, and to take pleasure in this. But I rather enjoyed the presence of such a Power standing by, as it were. It seemed rather in the nature of a compliment to one that he deigned to recognise your presence by this everpresent eye of his. Miss Houghton also taught us theory and composition, for we attended a weekly class; and furthermore, she lent us the works of E. Nesbit, with their inspiring illustrations by H. R. Millar, atmospherically vignetted like late Whistler etchings.

— MOUNTING GUARD
OVER MOUSE-TRAPS —

CHAPTER 2

By 1939 I was in the upper school, and drawing cartoons endlessly; inventing more animal characters, and writing stories about them. I particularly wanted to publish a comic paper myself, and my mother, an inevitable store of good ideas, suggested a printing jelly, that she recollected from her days as a teacher for the multiplication of exam papers. We went down to a bookbinding and stationery suppliers in Duke Street, and purchased a zinc tray, inks, and the crystals for the Hectographic Composition. These last were melted over the gas-ring in a saucepan, and poured into the tray. When set, a drawing, made with the special inks, was laid face down on it; and when removed, would give the impression back to other pieces of clean paper pressed upon the surface. What could be simpler? For added colours, one remelted the jelly, and drew with a different coloured ink; after which you added this second overprinting to the first proofs. You were limited to line; and the balloons of words had to be written in reverse—a good training for a future etcher. I made an eight-page comic paper, printed in colours, both sides, with strip-cartoon adventures. The registration could be worked out with accuracy, and I still have a copy, the ink unfaded. With an edition of thirty copies, it was feasible to tint some areas in with watercolour. I sold these comics at school at one penny each, although this was not really the point of the enterprise.

In the fateful September we were holidaying in Cornwall; and being greatly taken with some old books of ghost and Cornish pixie stories, with engraved illustrations, I was attempting the weird rather than the comic. On a fishing-boat trip one evening on a rather choppy sea a huge cloud seemed to take on the form of a threatening giant against the red sunset, while a smaller seemed to represent the bravery of a resistant pixie. I commenced telling a story about this, as the boat rose and fell among the grey waves, and the clouds obligingly altered to fit the tale. This was commenced basically for the benefit of my sister, but I found after a while that the other children had all quieted down as well, leaving me a rather unwilling centre of attention. However, on reaching land I scampered for my drawing materials—which went everywhere with me—and made a large wash drawing of the whole scene—perhaps my first picture actually inspired by nature rather than imagination.

With the approaching war, I had not hesitated to create scenes of tin-hatted mice in the trenches; but it seemed a good deal more serious when we cut short our stay to come home in time to hear Mr. Chamberlain announce that "this country was now at war," and the words will always give one a sick feeling in the stomach. The sirens at once sounded, for some misplaced reason—or perhaps someone was emotionally carried away, or even just leant against the handle—and all windows were filled at once by people craning out to look for enemy aircraft—they learnt better later—in the assumption that Armageddon was upon us, so well had German propaganda films (shown regularly on our newsreels) convinced us of the millions of planes and tanks possessed by the invincible enemy. Gas-masks were taken from the cupboards once more. Soon the rear end of the school-field was criss-crossed with trenches lined with corrugated iron—somebody's recollection of the Western Front. In the event, no one ever had time to get to them in any emergency. The siren usually went off (in contrast to its first burst of efficiency) about ten minutes after a small pack of planes had shot out of the sun from across the Channel (this was after the fall of France) and had fled back after leaving a blown-up house or so—or, more tragically, the Kemp Town cinema filled with a Saturday morning Mickey Mouse Club audience.

The siren came as an anti-climax on such occasions, causing ironic merriment. The greater part of the school field was given over to a battery of giant anti-aircraft guns—really heavy stuff; and at least some of the football matches were curtailed. As I could neither see without glasses, nor play without getting them broken, and also had a double rupture—hernias which I pushed back as they came out when I ran, but had not yet told anyone about, games were something I viewed with more than a lack of enthusiasm; being always bowled out at once in cricket by being quite blind to the presence of the ball—and unwilling to move in close while fielding for the same reasons.

Before Dunkirk, when Brighton was considered a safe refuge from possible aerial attacks on London, we were inundated with evacuees, and for a year or so Selhurst Grammar School from Croydon (not exactly a million miles away!) shared our building, so that we only went to school for an hour or so in the afternoons, to be taught by unfortunate octogenerians—recalled from retirement, and not destined to last long. Most of the younger masters had been called up, and the whole period was of course a field-day for the boys. I personally would never have missed a day at school—there were too many entertaining moments, despite the overall tedium.

The beaches were now covered with barbed wire and unmarked mines (which caused difficulties later on) as were the seafront lawns, where my mother had once walked along as a child, in those village-like days of Edwardia, to see the King sitting there quietly of a morning during a convalescent stay in

Hove. Now, great concrete blocks were to be set along the promenade, a Bofors or similar light anti-aircraft gun between each one. Holes were blown in the accesses to the main pier fabrics, and the destruction of the old seafront atmosphere was complete. My now widowed grandmother had, after Dunkirk, to abandon the Élite Cafe at a moment's notice, leaving it to the defenders to loot and to smash all the plates. It seemed a long time since we used to sit on the beach and laugh as the boat with "Wake up England" painted on its sail used to cruise back and forth among the swimmers in the sparkling afternoon sea.

My father, whose wartime work was a Special Police Sergeant, was in fact aware that no one was ever going to fight on the beaches despite all the official encouragement. In the event of invasion, it seemed, all armed personnel were to form a new line on the North Downs, and defend it Western Front Style (some real oldtime enthusiasts must have been still somewhere about), abandoning the encumbrances of non-combatants left in the path of the enemy—who would by now presumably have come up the beaches, undeterred by the holes in the piers. Family friends in Westmorland suggested my sister and I might like to stay there for the duration of this emergency (or possible cataclysm) and one June morning we set off.

We crossed London in our taxi, passing again and again smoking gaps in the streets where last night had been houses and shops, while firemen, police and ambulances stood by, blocking the roads, and workmen tried to dig out the injured. But eventually we got through all the glass and brickstrewn streets to the relevant station; and by teatime were in a pre-war world, with a salmon-mould tea, in a town without an anti-aircraft gun in sight. My mother returned to Brighton after some adventures—arriving late at night to a lightless London in the middle of an air-raid, with the problem of crossing it to get to Victoria Station. She came upon a daring taxi-driver who said he would have a try, and for some hours they cruised about, trying to thread a way not only through the Stygian blackness lit by explosions, but finding their way blocked time and again by bombed and destroyed streets. "No good—we'll have to try another way"—What an experience! At Victoria at last—the taxi drove off—the station seemingly closed, huge and black—ferocious sounds of bombs and shellfire from all over the city. Suddenly a porter—"come with me . . . in here, quick"—A train was lurking, full of people, not a light. Interminable time went by; then, in the lull that had to occur, it crept out, and by stopping and hiding in tunnels at intervals, at last got to Brighton Station; the place deserted except for my father chatting to a lone policeman, having waited for most of the night.

But we in Kendal were having a glorious time—by comparison. I did not live with my sister, in the house of my parents' friends, but in a curious establishment on the Windermere Road, just on the outskirts of town. Here, at the age of twelve, I had freedom to do just what I pleased. My room was like a small study, with desk and dormer window looking across to fields and rocky outcrops on the Heights. The house was owned by a youngish woman whose husband was in the army; two other rooms were occupied by two refugees from the Manchester bombing, an old lady and her rather older daughter who looked after her. They never said anything, and one scarcely ever saw them. They looked terrified, and perhaps they had been and still were. I at once began a series of black and white strip cartoons for a potential giant comic paper that I had in mind. I was sent almost immediately, however, to Heversham School—near the village of Milnethorpe, some six miles away by a specially chartered vehicle from a small bus firm in Kendal. It was a square-cabined, long-bonneted antique that went very slowly, and got us to school in time to have missed most of the first period. There were about a dozen pupils who lived in Kendal, and with these I made good friends—although not until after the almost imminent summer vacation. Consequently, I spent a good deal of that summer on my own in the town, and developed a certain degree of introspection that has perhaps subsequently been something of an advantage for artistic detachment. I was able to cook my own breakfast, and set off by stars and moonlight to walk into town of a morning, descending the House of Correction Hill, until I got to the corner by the old Surgery. Slowly, the boys would congregate. A shop would open—a square of yellow light in the greyness. A wireless would play—"You'd be far better off in a home. . . ."

At school on my first day I was chased around the playground by the massed Northerners, finally spreadeagled against a wall, and made to repeat my name again and again to yells of jeering laughter at my funny accent. We were made to play Rugby here, which was an additional impossibility; however, soon no one minded if I turned up or not, thankfully. There was also an embryo cadet force being formed, basically on the existence of an indoor rifle range. Being country boys, they knew how to shoot. Regrettably, I broke a window with my first and consequently only shot—which does not say much for the organisers' safety drill. However, I felt this as a sad loss of cast, and determined to become one day an expert shot, if nothing else. The masters seemed aged—high-collared, Victorian and moustached. A sad shock to their comfortable ways, it must have been—but when we returned for the Autumn term, they had all been called up. For a while there was an engrossing void. "Was the schoolboy's dream to come true?" said the School Magazine: "A school without masters?" but no: within days "a whole new gaggle" had arrived. Some of these were too old; some were strangely young, and must have been unfit rejects from the armed forces. There was even one who had—by a curious coincidence!—been a master at the Brighton Grammar School the previous term. Old "Bunny" Mason, the School Chips, was the only one of the originals left. Even the Head was new—about twenty-five—and there was a beautiful lady art teacher, just out of College, who took me up and encouraged my work with special paper and materials, in the intervals of being squired about by the unfit young masters. The prefects were allowed to wear trilby hats and smoke pipes and put their hands in their pockets.

I added considerably to my American comic collection by spending most of my money weekly in Woolworth's on a whole stack of 1929 editions—mostly featuring Harold Teen, Somebody's Stenog, and Moon Mullins. My father sent me each week the comic sections of the *Toronto Star* and the *Montreal Standard*, which were ferried over as ballast, defying the U-Boats; and I also received *Men Only, London Opinion* and *Lilliput*, for the fine work in black and white by the leading cartoonists that appeared in them; though the Kendal ladies were predictably disgusted at the sending of magazines with nude photographs to a "young boy." An artist who interested me greatly was Louis Raemaekers, a volume of whose savage propaganda work of the 14–18 war was in the house bookshelves. The savagery was lost on me, but I liked the technique—although I did not see how he did them.

I saw in Kendal my first newspaper printing works, and was shown the making of line-blocks—the final pieces being taken out manually. At once, all was clear to me—I saw how it was done, and how the black ink line was to be used. Later, I also saw the lead being melted for the casting of the day's printing sheet from the paper matrix; which led one into the thought of modelling and casting sculpture.

Together with my school friends, I made fireworks—the new chemistry master had given us the secret of gunpowder, and by carefully purchasing the ingredients at different shops—for medicinal reasons—we were enabled always to keep a store of it about. I also played an endless war game in the evenings at one of them's house. We built on the old billiards table in his basement a complete battlefield with hills and defences, using toy soldiers and cannon, taking shots at each other's territory by turns and registering scores and hits. During the long summer holiday, I sometimes spent the time with my eight-year old sister. We scaled the Heights, ledge by ledge—we were given sandwiches and told to take bicycles and not come back until evening—we climbed onto the tops of high walls made of loose rocks, far out in the moors, and taunted and screamed at a ring-nosed bull furiously blowing smoke-clouds of aggravated breath at us, two feet below.

On one walk we came upon a field that contained possibly all the signposts in the North of England (carefully removed in case of invasion). Hundreds of these informative boards and finger indications were surrealistically stacked in heaps, some semi-hidden under tarpaulins in this obscure corner of Westmorland. For years after the war no traveller was ever to find his way easily; it is possible that no records were ever kept of the whereabouts of these articles.

We swum at a lyrical creek, straight out of Claude, called Cold Harbour, where you could jump from a leaf-screened rocky promontory twenty feet down into a deep pool of water—if you were lucky enough to avoid the rocks. Of course, you were out of your depth all the time—we would have scorned it otherwise. We swum also near Heversham, in the tidal race opposite Grange, which comes in and out with so much speed that you are whirled along, and have to grasp an overhanging tussock to get out at all. The rougher Heversham boys patronised the minute sweetshop of an even more minute old lady in Heversham village, and thought it clever to all crowd into the shop shouting for various items, so that in her confusion others among them could steal what they wished. Every lunchtime the cry would go up "The Milnethorpe Loonies are coming!" and along the road, with two warders, would come a platoon of shambling unfortunates from the Asylum, in their worn-out secondhand and old grey clothes and caps, some grinning foolishly as if to try and answer the jeers and taunts of the boys. Well, they were the lucky ones; they weren't in the army, and the boys soon would be.

One of my eight-year-old sister's letters home includes the laconic remark: "It is very nice in Kendal but there is a lot of rain. When you next send me a letter, please tell me if Brighton station was bombed . . ." A letter of my own enquiries: "Have any more bombs dropped? It seems funny there are no sirens up here." An interesting slant on the times reads (from another of my letters): " . . . a man up here was fined £15, and 14 days, because (I think he was drunk) he was yelling in the street about 'Hitler will win the war' Hooray." etc.,—etc." A time-bomb was in fact dropped near Kendal in a rare raid, and all "went to see the crater."

. . . . . .

As additional interests I discovered the fret-saw, and made dogs and huntsmen with moveable legs and arms axled with old hairpins. I also cut out a frieze of drawings of the enemy leaders I had made in emulation of my favourite newspaper artists, with whom these characters were of course a regular standby. I also discovered Mark Twain and read *Tom Sawyer* and *Huckleberry Finn*—the first all in one night. These books gave me a new dimension; I was eager to camp out on islands with tent and rifle and fishing-line. I had read *Swallows and Amazons*, but the American material was Real. My other great new interest was in Natural History and Taxidermy, although I had collected insects for some time already. A year or so previously, before the war, we had all been taken on a school excursion—first to the paste factory at Chichester, where succulent poultry were reduced to a giant pinkish toothpaste, and then to Tangmere aerodrome, where I photographed the fighter planes—bi-planes, Gauntlets and Furies, I imagine. We concluded with a tour of the Victory.

I won the resulting annual essay prize for a description of this event, and was enabled to select my prize in books from Combridges of Hove. The manager, Mr. Freddy Cook, was a famous figure who wrote books on Sussex that he published from the bookshop. These were illustrated in line with Sussex scenes from the pens of well-known Sussex artists, including Louis Ginnett. I had also won the general knowledge prize, so was well known to Mr. Cook, and my choice of text-books on British Beetles, Moths and other insects was an expected one.

I now found, one day, while waiting for a bus at Levens Bridge—where we used to throw up sticks to bring the walnuts down from the fine tree there—the perfectly cleaned skull of a sparrow. Then, the lady with whom I lived read me two news items. One: "Herstmonceux vicar breeds green mouse," which seemed an unusual preoccupation for a rector in the bomb-torn South, was highly fascinating. The other item was the macabre tale of a boy who had bred a whole collection of white mice whose skins he had cured in order to make his mother a handbag. I certainly didn't want to do this; but I thought I would have a try if I came upon a rodent who had died naturally; and subsequently, finding a young dead rat I set about trying to skin it, with no knowledge of either the art or of anatomy. The time for school came and went—I callously ignored, on that occasion, such an interruption. The result was very inexpert, but I soon got myself some surgical scalpels and forceps, and a Victorian treatise by Montague Browne F.Z.S. and proceeded, mixing preservative powders, curing the skin, and boiling and cleaning the skulls and skeletons to set them up in cases—although, as I concentrated on small rodents found dead on the roads, this was very difficult. Subsequently, I began to collect natural history books of all sorts, preferably Nineteenth Century, and combed the shelves of second-hand establishments for such volumes. My interest in all branches of natural history consequently became all-absorbing. A letter remarks: "I am writing this with a quill pen I made myself from a swan's feather . . ." and, while climbing a mountain: "We couldn't see anything but blank cloud. . . . I found a sheep's skeleton. I kept a tooth as a souvenir." I continued, as well, to collect beetles, in the Victorian manner, and was allowed to kill them in the science laboratory (with chloroform) and to set them up on boards.

. . . . . .

By 1941 the Invasion scare was over. I left Heversham and returned once more to Brighton Grammar School and my friends there, with whom I had continued to keep up a regular correspondence. Once more, however, the nights were regularly interrupted—at about ten p.m. when the enemy planes went over, and at about one a.m. when they came back having discharged their loads. The night air was filled with the sound of these fleets of throbbing engines. All this was accompanied by a tremendous noise that you felt would bring the roof down, as all the guns on the promenade about two hundred yards away, and the big guns on the school field to the North all went off at once like a mad shooting gallery. Searchlights skimmed paths of light across the black sky, and any bomb still on board was at once jettisoned. I hadn't been home for more than a week or so when a five storey Victorian house and shop around the corner—about five houses up the street, was absolutely blown away. I was woken in fact by the sound of hoses; and my father and I dressed and went round to look at the gaping smokey space where yesterday there had been a huge house of flats, and a shop below that used to sell candied violets and speciality chocolates, in the days when you could buy such sweets and delicacies. Firemen and hoses were all about, and an air-raid warden in shorts came over and chatted to us. Part of the road was also blown away, and a wood-block section from it had embedded itself in our lawn, four gardens down from the crater. Fortunately, it had not gone down through the roof. The bomb had been a real blockbuster; and if it had not taken itself deep into the basement and sent the blast upwards, it could have brought down all the houses round about. We usually got up and went downstairs to a relatively more sheltered room during these occasions, if the siren sounded. One night, in the very middle of what seemed a grand Wagnerian Finale (by the sound) my mother suddenly got up, deadly bored, and said, "Well, I can't be bothered to stay up any longer. They can do what they like!," and went off to bed, leaving the rest of us feeling rather ridiculous. One morning at school a boy who had been staring out of the window at a plane cried "Look out!" and jumped under his desk. We all followed suit. He had seen the bomb fall. We went down at lunchtime to see the wreckage of the house not far away. Oddly, it was the house of a schoolfriend of my sister's; but fortunately no one was in at the time. Cycling along to Portslade to see a friend one morning I decided to go a different way, and a few minutes later was off my bike and taking shelter in a doorway. A column of smoke from around the corner denoted a house or so had been demolished on my usual route; but it was not the kind of incident that one seemed able to convey to anyone at the time, being almost impossible to describe as a humorous anecdote. Immediately after any plane was brought down (which I think was a fairly infrequent occurence) it would be surrounded at once by souvenir-hunters, who would tear it to pieces if not prevented. The same thing would happen if it had been a British plane. There was a mania for this kind of collecting, and after any gunfire everyone had pockets full of shrapnel from the streets, wickedly jagged pieces of iron.

I myself had a large collection of military ephemera; but in fact it was the more lyrical world of the countryside that meant most to my aesthetic sense, and during the Easter Holidays of 1941, soon after my return from the North, I went to stay with a friend whose father farmed in the nearby Sussex Weald. Here I saw the last of the old Nineteenth—or indeed of any century's—country ways. I had discovered Thomas Miller's *Country Year Book*, with delicate vignettes by Birket Foster, and I saw the country around me through their eyes. We harvested with a horse-drawn reaper and binder, stood the shocks of wheat up in stooks to dry, and later pitchforked the sheaves on to the great wagons to take for threshing. The old men wore black waistcoats and white collarless shirts, with a battered old trilby, and we all stood by as the reaper reduced the standing corn to a small square. A pause, and then the rabbits came out, to be pursued and pulled down by the collies. "That's the way you do it," said one man, taking a rabbit from me—I had been given its limp form by a dog—and dispatching it with a practiced and merciful downward chop.

We roamed around the countryside, looking at birds, nests, animals. I always travelled with collecting boxes ready for specimens, with my reference books, and my taxidermy equipment; and, of course, drawing materials, notebooks and paper for writing. I had become an increasingly avid essay-writer at school—it being my best subject—and was writing a short novel about the animals in a cornfield. On one memorable day I was sent off from the farm on one of the giant cart-horses—there were two, Nobby and Prince—with directions to take him to the blacksmith, and also to deliver two live hens. I had these with their legs tied together and with a connecting rope. They were draped either side of the horse just in front of where the saddle would have been, except that I was riding bareback. "Best way to learn to ride," said my friend's farmer father; "you can't fall off a cart-horse." I felt very grand riding out of the yard, along the track, and out on to the open road. Fortunately, traffic was a rarity in those petrol-starved times. We were just coming up to the crossroads by the church in the village centre when the horse decided to pull down and eat a lilac tree in a nearby garden, and he took little notice of me until I had got down and eventually pulled him off. As I couldn't get up again on my own I had to lead him to the blacksmith. "Wouldn't trust you on him, then, wouldn't they?" he remarked.

The great feature of our youth was the omnipresent bicycle. We were out in the country at all times, at all hours—often helping ourselves along by hanging on to the backs of passing lorries, when they slowed down for some reason or other and could be grabbed. It was important to take the left side, as otherwise the driver would see you, and slow down suddenly so that you ran into him and got shaken off and capsized. This of course was strictly forbidden—the hanging-on, that is—and not feasible after a mirror on the left side of the lorry became also a legal requirement. An excellent place for great crested newts was a lonely dewpond on the very top of the Downs; and the stream through the watermeadows below Lancing College, by the Sussex Pad Inn, was a favourite dredging haunt of mine for water-beetles.

I took yet more magazines weekly—*Pond Life* and *Fur and Feather*. I had made a tough net in the shape of a smallish shrimping net, but constructed of perforated zinc, which was ideal. With all these implements, jars and so on hung from the handlebars, my bicycle was, I felt, a real collector's vehicle.

I bought a good deal of collecting and preserving equipment from Mr. Pratt's shop—glass eyes and the like, and spent much time after school on a regular circuit that included the book shops, the junk shops, Mr. Pratt, and the pet shop in North Road run by a kindly but not too communicative couple called Jack and Lil Wilson. I stood for hours simply staring at what was in the windows of all these establishments. It was a great event when somebody brought in a dead fox or a huge pike to be stuffed by Mr. Pratt—the fish tipped out from an old sack; the silver of the scales, bright with reflections of its recent pond, luminous on the dark counter. I had begun to breed mice—black and white were my favourite varieties. I sold these at school or to Jack and Lil Wilson for threepence each. The back of the garage at home held several large glass battery jars that were available cheap and made fine aquariums where I kept the newts and water-beetles, and small fish such as roach and rudd, small carp, and goldfish. They were useful for drawing from also, as the creatures would hang poised before you on the other side of the glass. The water-beetles

(*Dytiscus Marginalis*) were fed by suspending a small piece of raw meat from a cork with a length of cotton.

In the garden, in the shed, I kept yet another collection of animals—cages and hutches were everywhere. I built a brick and cement frog and toad pit. I kept grass-snakes, lizards, hedgehogs, ferrets, guinea-pigs, mice, rats, dormice and voles. I would dig voles from their nests on the downs—they become tame in a moment if enclosed in the hand for a minute or so until their memory is effaced. In my room, pictures, guns, preserved curiosities caught the eye. Stuffed owls hung on strings from the ceiling, together with squirrels I had shot and preserved. We usually ate the flesh—as boys in this wartime period we lived a strangely primitive life. As regarded the collecting of moths and beetles, any chemist would make you a "killing-bottle," if you took in a glass jar with a screw-top; and he would fill it one third full with a mixture of plaster of paris and cyanide, for a few pence.

Unsupervised by the usual abundance of grim adults, we roamed the countryside, shooting and rabbitting. Officially, the Downs were prohibited to the public, and fenced off with barbed wire and kept as training grounds for the army. Where once picnickers and nature-lovers had roamed was now an abandoned wilderness of unexploded mortar bombs it was best to ignore; but foxes, partridges and pheasants abounded. As boys, we lived a lyrical Eighteenth Century kind of country life, in effect. With long poles we poked the adult squirrels from their nests in the thickets, and climbed up to get the young, which we reared on a bottle. Nonetheless, this was difficult, as wild animals are so infected with worms that get to the lungs, that few reach maturity. My grandmother arrived one morning with three baby rabbits she had found in a field in mid-Sussex. I successfully reared one of them, who was certainly a survivor—exceptionally large and wild, and strong enough to keep digging until finally he got under the wire of his pen and returned to the open

country. Fields and woods seemingly were a vast private territory for exploration. It was Huckleberry Finn come true.

. . . . . .

As the school specialist on creatures living and dead, I was the recipient of any defunct animal or bird found by anyone on his way to school or during the weekend; the message would be passed to me—"there's a large dead stoat over on the school field by the air-raid shelters" and I would go and take a professional look at it and decide if it was sufficiently fresh for skinning. I would mount a fox-tail or head on a shield for some sporting sixth-former—or possible unsporting—and my box of geometry instruments had been transformed into a case for scalpels, tweezers, dissecting instruments and glass eyes. My desk was full of manuals on taxidermy and natural history. In fact, I lived a totally dissimilar life to the others, passionately studying my own subjects, and reading my favourite authors. I discovered *Wuthering Heights* while in a detention class. I had been told to open the desk I was sitting at and read the set book of the class in whose room the detention was being held. I was so absorbed by this—the atmosphere, the passion of non-attainment, and the odd construction, that I had to get back to the detention the following week in order to find the name of the book, which I had forgotten to note. Increasingly I found that writing was a delightful enjoyment in which I could lose all track of time and myself. My main objects of emulation were Dickens and Kipling; and the influence of the remarkable imagery of *Treasure Island*, the first book I every read.

We sometimes went out ferreting with a famous Sussex character—one Stan Anscombe. With nets and dog, and sack of ferrets, we would go through the woods to a likely warren. "Old dog'll tell you," Mr. Anscombe would mutter. The ferrets would be put in; silence; then the rabbits would be out like rockets, to bowl over in the net, nearly taking the peg from the ground. They would be dispatched and gutted at once and laid by—a remarkable addition to the tiny meat ration of the day. The rabbits and fish that we caught were valuable moneywise or for our own table. Sometimes the ferret would seem not to want to emerge. "She's laid up against a rabbit in the warm," said Stan, and the long digging-out would begin, with Stan taking over when we got near to her. The ferrets were not meant to attack the rabbits, and were often muzzled. We were taught how to pick them up without being bitten, as they can turn in their skin, a technical impossibility, but a practical fact. Mr. Anscombe bred not only ferrets and rabbits but cage birds, and his house was surrounded by aviaries. The front garden was full of giant lifesize sculptures, painted, of bears and suchlike exotic beasts. His recreation was to go up to the London Zoo, study the large creatures, have a huge block of Portland Stone delivered, and then carve it direct, from memory. He was always head beater, when we beat for a shoot, and all the farmers stayed out in the open, firing, as we drove through the woods driving out the quarry to them.

All this imagery was reflected in my drawings and watercolours, and I could scarcely endure the school hours with patience until the evenings and weekends enabled me to be away on my cycle with guns, traps, collecting boxes, devoting the time to what I thought was some useful and practical purpose.

The inspiration, literary, aesthetic, artistic, that I found in the Sussex country scene lasted until the influence of Van Gogh moved in upon me with its drums and tambourines, its shrilly accented tints, its palette too bright for a highlight to make its effect; in fact, for a *solitary* note to be heard. Strange, this, from so lonely an artist as he. And yet, it was only under Van Gogh's tutelage, as it were, that I first began to be able to represent the countryside at all to my satisfaction in oil paint; although I had always been content enough with the watercolour drawings I made of it.

I had joined the Scouts, in succession to my period as a Wolf Cub, but I wasn't very successful at either. In the Scouts, I bent to observe the woodchopping for the fire, and was caught over the eye by the backward swipe of the axe. Coming to, I lay under a tree all afternoon, very sick, until the time came to cycle the twelve miles home from the day camp.

At this point my state of health had finally been correctly analysed, and my situation of being in more or less constant pain and discomfort was to be corrected. Over the next year and a half I had three operations for my hernia conditions, with the subsequent convalescences of not being allowed to run but only to walk slowly—in fact, having to learn to walk again each time, as after a long period in bed one lost the sense of balance on two legs and simply fell over. I missed a good deal of school, and got rid of most of my menagerie, except the voles and the ferrets, which my mother and sister were kind enough to look after, although they regarded them—the ferrets particularly—as ravening beasts. Once, shortly after an operation, a plane tore through the sky, followed by a deafening salvo as the seafront guns delightedly started up. It was curious not to be able to move out of bed, or get away from the window. In the event, it was one our ours; and unfortunately it was one of the few they ever succeeded in bringing down.

Post-operation condition meant that I no longer had to bother to cross my name off the games lists on the school board and move up the reserve—my usual practice. Now, I did as I pleased even more, and of course my own interests came first; I spent a great deal of time at the cinema, as I was supposed to rest a great deal anyway. When finally well I joined the School Cadet Corps., and enjoyed firing on the rifle range and being one of the House shooting team. Indeed, the musket and star badge that the First Class Shots wore on their uniforms was a coveted distinction that I enjoyed possessing, though it all went back to Mark Twain and the Mid-West. Collecting guns, pistols, cartridges and military equipment was a passion with every one; boys would arrive at school with perhaps a Sten gun under their jacket. With so many of the masters being elderly, liberties were often taken. Once we shot the glass out of the form-room clock with an air pistol; after which, by one boy standing on another's shoulders, the minute hand could be altered at will, so that before the master came in it was put on ten minutes, and pointed out to him, with significant coughs, that the period should have ended. "Dear me—it's gone by very quickly . . ." We took a Mills hand-grenade from the military stores on the school field; as we attended lectures on the construction of all these articles we knew all about them. I took off the top, and emptied the T.N.T. out onto a desk, then threw a match into it, creating a column of white fire, which certainly made the others jump. With such-like pranks we amused ourselves, until the authorities made a rule that even the possession of a single live round would lead to immediate expulsion; but of course it never did. I created a pistol by sawing down an old shotgun and getting the breech bored out; but this unfortunately being discovered I was brought up before the local magistrate, who held the article in the air tentatively, and before confiscating it and dismissing the case as trivial, remarked "what a fiendish invention!" This was afterwards reported by the local press, as "schoolboy invents diabolical weapon." For one day of every week, each class was obliged to spend a day working on the land; weeding or singling sugar-beet. We were put under the authority of a captured Italian prisoner of war, with a great patch on his jacket to denote his status. He, like others, moved freely about the farm and countryside, living in a local cottage. To observe this enemy soldier trying to explain to our form-master what he should do to "single" beet successfully, and eventually falling back into impatience and vituperation when his pupil failed to comprehend, was a great pleasure to us all.

The wartime atmosphere had strange unrealities to it. A day in London—the recognised treat above all others for a Brightonian—was heralded by the silver glow of the barrage balloons as they caught the morning sunlight. But it was, however, as well to catch an early train home before the night raids on the city began, although you had of course missed the possibility of the mid-morning hit-and-run in Brighton, if it was bright and sunny. One might have thought that we would have looked back to the Thirties continually, to that time of unlimited sweets and chocolates and biscuits; but we were quite happy swapping our limited number of sweet coupons with one another, and we hardly took much notice of the Front Line promenade of barbed wire and cannons at the end of the street, having become used to it over the years. Nonetheless we were constantly wary—there was always the apprehension of what the next air-raid warning might bring, and the careless sense of relief at the All-clear. Recently called-up boys would occasionally drop in, looking very grand in their officers' uniforms; but at morning prayers the head read out the names of the latest ex-pupils to have been killed. Sometimes this had a very personal meaning, as when the news went round that so-and-so's brother, who had recently left, and whom all knew well, had been "lost over Germany last night"; and an eerie sensation spread over the school.

The cinemas would announce the occurrence of a raid by flashing on the screen the disturbing slogan "The air-raid warning has sounded. If you wish to leave the building you may do so"—or something of that sort. There would be a groan, but no one ever left. Nevertheless, it was difficult to concentrate on the film, which suddenly went two-dimensional, as you kept straining to hear if anything else was approaching. I was in a sea-front cinema watching *Henry V* when this occurred. The cinema was half-empty, and as the famous charge commenced, all the sea-front guns opened up at the same time—the noise was extraordinary, with the music of the famous sound-track as well.

Our street leading down to the sea-front was now filled mainly with Canadian soldiers; many of the large Victorian houses opposite having been requisitioned. One night, oblivious to the blackout regulations, they seemed to be having a party. I watched from my window as they sang and danced and capered about—black figures against the lights from the doorways and the lamps they had even brought out in the street. The drinks flowed; the music played—it went on for hours. Next morning the street was surprisingly empty and deserted. They had all gone off to raid Dieppe. It had certainly been their last party. Previous to this they had been deadly bored in Brighton, and were often seen fighting each other in the Brighton streets, sometimes throwing each other against the plate glass shop windows until the glass trembled and shook in a terrifying way. Later, the street was again occupied; American soldiers sunbathed all day in the garden next door, and soon, the Guards armoured division arrived. The top of the street was barricaded with barbed wire, and one had to get a pass and see the sentry to get home. Tanks and their crews lined the pavements, the weapons laid out for inspection every morning. One had to ask them to move a tank to get the car out of the garage. All was set for the invasion, and when they began to move off this time the roaring of the engines and the streams of military equipment along the promenade to the ports went on endlessly. There was a tremendous excitement in the air—nothing had been announced officially; but all who lived in the middle of all this preparation could see that "something was up."

At school, we were astonished one day when the daylight raids began—the other way, this time. A light roaring in the sky commenced; then it grew louder and louder . . . the lesson stopped. We all went to the windows. The whole dome of the sky, as far as you could see, was full of Flying Fortresses. It was incredible—there were millions of them. Where had they come from? It didn't seem believable. We hung from the windows, cheering. Was the tide really beginning to turn? Was something going to *happen*? After that, we became used to the frequency of these chequer-board formations passing over; but nothing can equal that unbelievable first sight.

In the light of history and retrospect the seemingly quite unnecessary savagery they were going to inflict on places that would one day again be havens for happy holidays and on people that were one's own mirror selves seems totally deplorable. But things were different then—and what would have happened otherwise?

And then, of course, we were still at the mercy of the doodle-bug flying bombs. Sunbathing in the garden—an old motor-bike kind of sound—and then, not that far up, there comes along this dustbin-coloured thing, put-putting along, rather too slowly for comfort. All hope that it won't cut out just yet—let someone else be on the receiving-end! . . . it goes over, and the sound dies away, thank goodness. Fortunately, they seldom fell on Brighton, being timed to get well clear of the coastline and up country a bit first.

I was now in the Sixth Form, having got through the School Certificate examinations. The English Language paper had been interrupted by a daylight raid in the middle of my essay—a story about a dealer in old spears and weapons, the historical original owners of which had come alive in the shop in order to repel thieving intruders—and one had to lie flat in the corridors outside the exam room, in case of flying glass or blast or worse, while yet another nearby house was hit and the huge guns on the field made their customary devastating noises, as if the whole world was coming to an end. They were, after all, only a few hundred yards away from us. A few minutes after this, we returned back to the strict conditions of the exam room to finish our essays: "Come on, settle down now, stop mucking about." The drowsy sound of summer bees floating in through the open windows recommenced, the blue sky twinkling outside. . . . we had really thought the exam rooms at the end of the corridor had been hit this time, by the sound; and I had thought it annoying not to have been allowed to finish my story.

I had never wanted to become a painter, precisely. There were some pictures that I liked. I always went into the school through the Junior entrance because I enjoyed looking at the reproduction of the Van Eyck *Arnolfini* hung on the staircase—I looked and looked; I still couldn't seen how it was done. The Holbein Hanseatic merchant in his office, surrounded by meticulous pieces of technical still-life, was another reproduction of interest; and then the blue-grey emptiness of Whistler's *Cremorne Lights*—why was it so empty? Was it intended as a kind of joke, to have painted a picture out of nothing at all? My re-actions were quite Nineteenth Century—or at least, Pre-Raphaelite. I was introduced to the National Gallery by my mother when I was sixteen: "It's time you saw some paintings"—and shown her own favourites—the *Doge Loredano*, and the *Virgin of the Rocks*. I was then led through the galleries unerringly to the *Fighting Temeraire*. The scale of the real pictures surprised me after the reproductions, and the freedom of handling—even in the Arnolfini—after the reproductive condensing. I have never wavered in my admiration for these first canvases and panels shown to me; my mother still had the catalogue of the great Italian exhibition of the Thirties; and I often asked to look at this, with the beautiful and masterly drawing of the portraits. I had always regarded with most respect so far the black and white men, and those little masters of the final state (as one might say) the Victorian taxidermists, who in their semi-sculptural spatial arrangements had—paradoxically—more feeling for life in their pictorial cases than many a painter stubbing away at his canvas in order to perpetuate the possibly inflated conception of his own personality . . . however, I now began to move over into this field myself. My parents had some idea that it would suit my liking for animals to train as a veterinary surgeon. I needed, however, one more subject—or at least, a credit level rather than a pass, in Latin. I had enjoyed this language—particularly for the personality of our excellent master, who gave it life. When Laocoon thrust his spear at the Trojan horse, Mr. White cried: "do you hear that word—*Stet*! The choice of that particular word is the genius of Virgil. No other word would have done—you can hear the spear still vibrating—."

I spent my last year at school taking Latin only; but despite my pleasure in the letters of Pliny the Younger and the activities of Pallas Athene, they were replaced for this next year by the duller works of Martial and Livy; and I had meanwhile discovered new interests, neglected to attain the required level in Latin, and to my satisfaction was released from the unappealing veterinary prospect.

In fact, the Art master, Mr. Daines, had suddenly taken an interest in my work—being first amused by my School Certificate effort (which did not earn me high marks) of a design for a St. George and Dragon inn sign. In an attempt to be different, I had made a ferocious face of the Saint in close-up, in the act of strangling the dragon with unmailed hands. For ten years, Mr. Daines had patiently taught us perspective, repeat-patterns and free composition; and, most valuable of all, the laying of a watercolour wash. Hour upon hour have I added one more drop of water to the mixture in the dish—one for each subsequent brush-line added to the wash—all the time keeping the puddle of colour along the line. This endless practice was to be of inestimable value to me. It was not the kind of technique one would be taught at art college, but what better preparation for a watercolourist could one have? That is precisely what the craft is all about. Mr. Daines now became interested in my inspired suggestion to him that I might spend some of my time in the art room—in fact I asked if I might have the spare long room at the end—with the best windows, giving a wide vista of playground and school field—as a studio. He assented to this, and then was kind enough to assist my enthusiasm with private lessons in the intervals of the other classes. Consequently I worked away, producing large landscape views from memory of country scenes that had impressed me, and gradually filling the studio walls with these images. As there were so many, Mr. Daines began to hang them in the art room proper, until there was a permanent exhibition covering all the walls. He then set me to still-life painting in watercolour, from groups of bottles and violins and shoes and hats. It was excellent training; and I painted my first landscape from life—a view from the window. As the war now approached its conclusion I drew a regular series of cartoons depicting the state of the current situation, which I pinned up for all to inspect—concluding with the meeting of the East and West forces in the ruins of the Third Reich. I was well up in the news as I read the papers each morning as I delivered them, hurling them into doorways from the front basket of the trade bike as I sped down the pavements. (Of course, on wet mornings they had to go through the letterboxes; but one can get quite expert at spinning a folded paper through the air so that it lands where you want it, and avoids the corner drain in a basement, or the milk-bottle on a sill. Not that one hasn't had one's failures . . .)

A friend and I spent a week cycling through Sussex and Hampshire. We put up at pubs and bed and breakfast houses—looking for the sign C.T.C. recommended—and sketched and drew the paddle-steamer ferry to the Isle of Wight at Lymington. We also visited the island and I made my first beach watercolours. At Salisbury I drew the White Hart Hotel and made an elaborate study of the Cathedral; being rather put off by a member of the clergy who reprimanded me for riding my bicycle down one of the paths: "Don't you know there are people buried under there?" Nonetheless, the long hard twenty-mile pull from Blandford had been worth it to see the spire suddenly appearing above the hills.

Back at school in my studio I painted many Turner-inspired sunsets and twilight scenes, employing images seen the previous day or evening on fishing expeditions. Turner seemed to have anticipated in his seascapes my subsequent experiences off Brighton in a dinghy. The marvellous calm of his summer evenings by the Chain Pier, with the reflected light of after-sunset making the surface pale gold, made me see again my latest evening fishing trip, the Palace Pier now taking the place of the Chain Pier, but all else the same, after all. In the Tate Gallery there is a wall of long Turner seascape sketches that are perhaps the best pictures of Brighton ever painted—even better than the Constable beach scenes.

During the war, my parents had bought a small dinghy, which had sat for four or five years upside down in the garden, optimistically awaiting resurrection when the beaches should be cleared. Now, with the occupation of Europe and the freeing of France, the beaches were being cleared with mine-detectors, and the guns removed; the concrete blocks resounded all day with pneumatic drills, and you could walk along the promenade once again. There were the familiar old railings from one's distant childhood, and the framed map of the town still on its stand, the barbed wire wound around it having being cut away. The foxes were driven out of the six-feet high grass of the lawns, and the turf returned to bowling-green perfection. The Piers still stood gaunt and unpainted, with no work done on the iron supports all these years; but they were of Victorian construction, so had not fallen to the onslaught of the gales. With the cessation of the fishing industry in the recent years, they had become breeding grounds for fish, particularly the succulent black bream and the bass, those favourites of Brighton anglers that yet seldom appear in the shops. Several of us at school had dinghies, and we formed a small group whose activities centred on coastal fishing and camping up the rivers. We fished for both sea and river fish, and swam like fish wherever we were, weaving underwater through the waving green weeds, far down, eyes open, looking and peering like otters, playing in the waterfalls. On the beach, when the sea was occasionally calm and clear enough, one could swim down to the sand, and following the sea-bed, chase a flat-fish as it skimmed ahead of your nose, making furrowed smoky tracks in the sand. Above, the sea was silver like mercury, and you could sing and shout to each other under water, mouth open, provided you didn't thoughtlessly take a breath, of course. When we saw water on our cycle rides, we would at once swim, without costumes, drying ourselves on our vests, and tying the vest on the handlebars to dry as we continued our rides. We had access to the school changing room, as we were entrusted with the key, and would run a mile round the school field in our gym shorts, every day winter and summer after school, even in the snow. At seventeen, one feels a strength not manifested later.

Apart from the advantage of being also given the key of the art materials cupboard so that I had unlimited paper and materials, I formed, with one of my friends, the Economic Sixth. An aged accountant, Mr. Jones, with glasses thick as the base of a bottle, was appointed to teach us book-keeping and short-hand. This offer had been made to the Sixth as a whole but only we two had responded. The introduction to these arts—particularly the former, as we never made much headway with the latter—has certainly been of inestimable value, in one's career as a free-lance artist; and encouraged by my father, I began to keep books of my in and out-goings, and have found it an interest ever since.

Finally, the last day of the War approached—not unexpectedly but with predictable inevitability. We listened to the announcement of peace in the same room, to the same wireless, in the same place—exactly as we had heard the declaration when we were children. Everything appeared different, immediately. There was a lack of urgency, at once. It was all in the past. We walked along the sea-front into Brighton. It was a quiet warm evening, tinted with the pale yellow glow of an old Brighton aquatint. We seemed to be back in the Thirties when there was no lurking danger from the skies. No one around us said anything. There was no cheering. Everything was, merely, as it *was*.

The houses across the street, once full of exuberant soldiery, now contained semi-convalescent South Africans recently released from prison-camps. Skeleton-thin, they slowly wavered and tottered up and down to the sea-front, like elderly men—almost like the ghosts of those who had occupied the houses before them.

. . . . . .

School holidays were as usual spent camping out. Loading up our dinghies, we set off in a convoy along the coast that summer, spinners out for the odd mackerel. Entering Shoreham harbour, we progressed swiftly, under the old wooden bridge—the very pattern of the ones in Whistler's Thames etchings— and up the picturesque Adur river. The narrow church of St. Botolph's and the fresco-filled chapel of Combes, burrowing its Twelfth Century self into the hillside, came and went, the bumpy fields below the elms denoting the remains beneath of a once highly-populated area. In the times of the tin trade, this had been the harbour and collection point; and only a chance decision had made London and the Thames, and not Shoreham and the Adur, the great port of England to be developed. Up past the favourite of Sussex villages, Bramber, and then we carry the boats and provisions overland to a great old quarry, now derelict, filled with water, and picturesquely ringed with trees and woods, at Smalldole. This discovery of ours was more or less unknown to the general public; though the occasional visitor appeared—including six boys who set up a tent, and then as we watched the flames run up the back, all shot out double-quick, stood around the smouldering remains sorrowfully, and then walked off, heads bowed, only twenty minutes after their arrival. But we were not so stupid as to light fires under canvas. We constructed a dock for the dinghies from the great beams that lay about from wrecked workings. We knew old chalk pits in Sussex that were likewise abandoned, like ghost towns in a Western; wrecked offices and shacks—and we often went to the village of Standean, requisitioned (and wrecked) as a training ground deep in the forbidden Downs where we so often ventured. The largest house had an almost bottomless well in the front garden, a great open affair on which they had presumably all depended. I was sitting on the edge and only discovered the depth by dislodging a brick, which seemed to descend for ever.

At our camp by the quarry we made a fortification with more beams on a kind of overlooking ledge, and here set the tents and the fire. We cut mud bricks to make an enclosed clay oven; and with flour and water made pastry for fruit tarts and pies: an old overgrown orchard of plum and apple—remnant of a house now gone—abutted to our very camp. We spent hours rowing about the lakes, fishing from the boats, or shooting with our .22 rifle. We ate fish, and even tried a coot; although this bird, though popular in earlier centuries, is too oily to eat unless well soaked in salt water for a day or so. Packet soup, tinned pilchards—these were our regular fare—and flour dampers. These were all unrationed; and we carried plenty of powdered egg, from which to make fried pancakes. We spent days like this, but when the wet weather set in we packed up camp and set off down river once more—first checking our tide charts. These cards, sold at all fishing-tackle shops for a few pence, were invaluable. With the right direction of the water, you simply held the tiller, and were swept happily downstream—sometimes even up on to a sandbank in mid-river. Stopping to cross the road to a wayside cafe—an old place of corrugated iron and rusty tin advertisements—we discovered the war had ended; the Bomb had been dropped. It didn't give anyone much sense of guilt—in fact, none at all. No one seemed to think that nothing would ever be the same again. And had it gone on we and our friends would all have been involved, and it would have continued for ever, jungle by jungle, island by island.

At this period we were in the position regarding the other side of the channel of our counterparts in the Napoleonic era. We knew nothing of what art had recently developed there. In fact, we were not to know for another half a dozen years what the younger artists were really up to; but it was considered vital enough for the sake of culture that the newsworthy enfants terrible of the Thirties—good old Picasso and Matisse—should have their latest canvases brought over (we were not as yet permitted to travel abroad ourselves) and put on exhibition at the V. &. A. The general public knew nothing of these aged artists, and thought their style a total innovation; and the Philistine journalism of the times made much capital in fostering a total hatred for these, admittedly rather dreary, scruffily executed and incomprehensible canvases. A school-friend and myself went up to see them, joined the extensive queue, and looked in silence with the other confused visitors, whose reaction basically was not of derision at all, but boredom. The pictures in fact weren't interesting, that was what was really wrong with them. I have often thought, that with the freedom modern and abstract artists have demanded and won for their approaches, they have done surprisingly little with it on the whole in the shape of masterpieces. Apart perhaps from Boccioni; but then it is all a matter of taste, after all. And perhaps we were still happy Philistines ourselves in those days, with blind eyes. We were all basically aeromodellers, and made 1/72 scale model from plans of aircraft ranging from Gloster Gladiators to Mosquitoes. And of course, with the opening to the public of the Shoreham and Newhaven jetties, we fished even more, passing hours on the end of the East Pier at Newhaven, with rods and lines baited for the elusive additions to one's menu. The great ambition of all was to land a really large bass. A specimen about three feet long was regarded as the ideal catch, and would make a feast for all one's friend's and relations—if one didn't sell it to the fishmonger first. A small and not very practised angler, fishing a little nearer the shore than the others, did on one occasion hook such a monster. Frantically excited, it was splashing away down below among the struts of the pier. Everyone abandoned their own lines to run over to see the excitement. "Don't lose it!" "You'll never reel it in—you'll break the line—" Eventually I offered to climb down the structure of the pier with a net, and get the fish into it. Those above then hauled the huge bass up. The flapping giant was tipped out onto the concrete deck of the pier, where it lay still and eyed its captor malevolently.

"Well, go on," said everyone to the successful angler, encouragingly, as if to a timid gladiator—"go on and break its neck."

The successful angler hesitated, looking a little sick.

"Put it out of its misery!" said everyone, begining to side with the fish.

The giant bass looked fiercer than ever. The angler timorously approached the fish—the fish flapped—the angler jumped back.

"I don't know how!" He could no more kill it than he could have throttled a dog.

"Put a bit of stick in its mouth, hold the neck, and pull the head back," said a tall man in a knitted balaclava. "Here! I'll show you!"

He leapt upon the fish. There was a flurry, and the catch, no longer a personality but a dead and edible article, was jerking convulsively. The timid angler bore it off with a murmur of thanks, but was never again seen among us.

Although the Brighton piers had not yet been repaired, and the public were not officially allowed on them, several of us would launch our dinghies out from the beach, row out to the piers, tie up, and fish all day from the abandoned Victorian iron-work. The piers were breeding-grounds for pigeons, also, and their eggs and young were everywhere. I would select pigeons about to fly, take them home and rear them. One particular bird liked to accompany me everywhere on cycling and sailing expeditions. He would fly off, then return, gliding in to land neatly on the handle-bars, or to alight on the bows—although sometimes missing and falling in the sea, when one had to dive overboard to the rescue and dry him out on a towel. Sometimes, when fishing, a mackerel would take the bait, swimming down between the struts of the pier, to tangle the line round and about some rusty bar. Then, it would be necessary to undress, dive down into the green water, and with one arm hooked to the bar, unwind the line, with the mackerel whirling round one's head in a frenzy.

The West Pier at Brighton, when one had climbed up the corroded steps of the jetty, was a sad sight indeed. The huge old brass bell that had warned people of the approach or departure of steamers was still in place, and we used (I am sorry to say) to fire at it from our boats with air-pistols and register a hit by the ring. But the once-familiar woodwork of the Pier fabric was rotting away; the theatre was intact, but in sorry condition; and some occupying troops or other had taken a store of rolls of tickets and thrown them as streamers from the balconies; so that the whole auditorium was draped with yellow and blue and red, like the sides of the *Queen Mary* in the Thirties, when we used to go and see her off from Southampton almost as if she was travelling to outer space.

Sometimes we rowed through the avenues of criss-crossed struts under the pier, from end to end of it; being obliged to lie down in the boat to pull ourselves through. If there was any sort of swell, the boat would be swung upwards and wedge, and you had to bounce it down and then bale out the shipped water. Under the Palace pier it was darker, and more gloomy, but the scale was larger, and the threading through from end to end easier. My preference, though, was for the West Pier, a place I have known for so long and seen through so many vicissitudes. It was soon over-hauled, restored, re-painted, and brought back, incredibly, to its former flag-flying glory; and Harry Groombridge and his light orchestra played in the coffee-lounge of a morning as if the war years had never been. Even the steamers started up again in the Fifties; but things went from bad to worse; the Pier lost money, changed hands, and fell eventually once more into disrepair. The jetty collapsed, and the famous bell—you could see it even from the beach—fell to the bottom of the sea, where she lies still, one must assume. The pier was closed down, section by section; and only the extremely gallant efforts of the West Pier Society and its dedicated Secretary John Lloyd have kept the battle going to save it against all odds, organising fund-raising schemes and applying for and receiving local and government grants. Already the shops at the shore end have been re-opened, and one day the bell may yet ring the steamers in once again.

It was always a mark of respect in our school, and a great competition, as to who had swum in the sea earliest in the season. One February day I rowed two friends out—they dived in, swum to shore, then took me out. I dived in, and knew nothing more until I was crawling up the beach. Continuing our passion for adventures, the three of us set out one cool March morning, in a sailing dinghy loaded with tents, supplies and kitbags, for a trip to Littlehampton, whose tropic-like sand-dunes and wide beaches were a favourite place of ours. By a land approach, a little ferryman, his neck twisted and knotted with the repetiton of his regular pull to the right to allow for the current, would take us over to the wilder, grass-topped stretches—miles of sandy beaches. On this particular morning, the wind became too fresh from the West, so we turned about to let it take us towards Newhaven instead. We should have known that this was the fore-warning of a South-West gale; the waves rose higher, becoming white horses with foaming crests—in a moment we were all but swamped, the little dinghy wallowing nearly a mile off shore, Brighton front lost to sight, the end of the Palace Pier a distant blur through the rain and spray. We tumbled aft, and the open bows, having dipped below water twice, miraculously forebore to go down again. Somehow we bailed the brimming boat, which was only eight feet long, yet carried three of us, kitbags and gear; and by some miracle just kept her afloat by a hair's-breadth. We headed out to sea, being obliged to face the great waves, climb their oncoming slope, hit the crest with an explosion of foam, and slide down the other side into the trough, being almost perpendicularly suspended each way. Fortunately, the South-West wind kept us going fast, close-hauled as we were; we had to hit each wave squarely—to have been struck broadside would have swamped us. The boy at the tiller (who had built the boat himself) had his elbow in the water the whole time; but imperturbably, as each roller appeared, he would swing us round to face it, while we hung on, with bailers at the ready for immediate use.

After heading South-East into mid-channel for half our journey (which took us five hours or so) we turned about so as to head towards Newhaven with the waves now at our back. We surfed forward on each wave is it caught us up and threw us onward. Around us, were the huge black curving shapes of the porpoises that had accompanied us all the way, shiny and sleek like slugs against the grey-green and white of the sea. Later, I made a painting of this effect. Porpoises are friendly, concerned creatures. They behave as if they are your dog, and obviously wanted to keep a friendly eye upon us.

When we entered the harbour at Newhaven (and its extraordinary contrast of calm water), customs and dock officials ran to greet us and hand us cigarettes (a contemporary custom implying respect and congratulations). They had watched our passage for some time through telescopes and had several times given up their belief in our chances, as we disappeared from view in the enormous waves. Indeed, from deep in the troughs, even the lighthouses had been lost to view. The customs found it difficult to believe we had survived such a sea, and had assumed we were entering the country illegally from

France—no travel being permitted—and were astonished to find we had sailed from Brighton.

Later, up the river at Piddinghoe, we made camp, left our clothes to dry by the fire, and went to the village inn wrapped in blankets. The next day, the village children from the school came down to watch P. making repairs to his boat, while I drew a watercolour of the scene.

The largest porpoise I ever saw raised itself from the sea one day when we were fishing from my dinghy for whiting—these fish come along in shoals in October–November, and you have to discover where they are feeding and row quietly into the middle. Once discovered, you can go back the next day to the same place, and follow them as they move very slowly along. There was a sudden flurry of water—I looked directly into an unbelievably huge face peering into mine, two feet across, four feet high—a strange, ugly nose and mouth, little eyes. He looked long and interestedly; then, with a long sad blowing sigh, sank beneath the surface, like a visitant from another world—which, in a way, he was.

One afternoon, we saw a huge mine floating off-shore, some way out—evidently broken loose from its chain and escaped the attentions of those busy clearing such areas. It was a cold day, not too calm, and no one on the beach. As the armed forces had not yet been demobilised, there were not a great many people about those days. We pushed off, and eventually got to a point about six feet from it—a huge object it seemed, with all the horns sticking out. We only had to bump one off, and up it would go. It was difficult getting close, yet keeping away—like a yo-yo. We sheered off after a while, and the mine went drifting through the waves towards the pier, missed it by a few yards, then went out to sea, probably to come ashore under the cliffs the other side of Seaford. Presumably it did so, as we heard no more of it.

Chapter 3

Encouraged by the advocacy of Mr. Daines, it was decided that I should attend Brighton Art School. This seemed a natural solution to all my interests and preoccupations. I had commenced oil painting already, having produced a still-life of fish and rods and tackle on a large piece of board that had formed a blackout panel on our French windows, and which was happily no longer required. I had no real intention of becoming an artist as such; happily my intentions were to write books and illustrate them with black and white cartoons; but I was quite happy to go to the art school, despite no particular enthusiasm. I preferred working on my own, basically; but I was to learn that such a course would have borne no comparison to the amount we learnt, and were obliged to learn, at the art school of this period. Probably, a better syllabus never existed before or since. I was even able to learn life-drawing under Louis Ginnett himself—for one term only, as tragically he died quite suddenly. He wasn't, it had soon appeared, the quiet and monk-like type—at least, not to us. He was definite, terse, emphatic—an excellent teacher. You got away with nothing. "Why are you holding your pencil like that?" he cried, wrenching it from my fingers—"it's not a pen!" With this (had we known it, fore-runner of an etching-needle, for me) he demonstrated how to proceed—standing well back from the paper—great broad sweeping movements, as if it were a palette knife—"Draw like a *painter!*" Again and again he voiced his Velasquez dictum: "If you can paint two eggs on a plate, you can paint anything!"

Breadth—no minuteness—that was the approach. George Hooper, another master of great influence and character, did indeed wear a coloured neck-scarf, and red shirts. He would show us drawings in red conte by Meninsky, and work on the side of our paper until the point tore up the surface. To see the reality of a great drawing like the Meninsky, full size, was invaluable—I have never forgotten it, which proves the point. The reproduction gives only an equivalent—you have to learn from them, but you can't learn sufficient. "Why are you shading her knee like that?" George Hooper asked me. "I'm modelling the high-light." "High-lights aren't *form*! High-lights are incidentals. Ignore them."

Our course gave one a training to be a High Renaissance painter of frescoes, portrait and landscape. What better, even if we were only going to design a Magazine advertisement? It was very hard work, the kind that leaves you blank, exhausted, ready to sleep and delighted to begin again the next morning. For two years, we worked from 9.30 in the morning to 9 at night, and every moment was a constant satisfaction, with no time wasted.

We drew real bones and skulls in varying positions, and consulted and drew from *Gray's Anatomy*—in a country churchyard, as we irreverently termed it. For the Intermediate examination, one had to be able to draw a figure with its skeleton, shaded and modelled in the third dimension, in action and with all the bones correct to the number of ribs, and labelled. Also, a similar figure with the muscles on, also labelled. Practically, our course was what a Fifteenth Century apprentice might have been required to learn, less the knowledge of grinding colours, preparing panels and mixing varnishes. All that was to be absorbed in the next two years, in the painting course.

I continued to work privately with oils, and made a small portrait full-length of a student friend in his boxing gear. But out-of-door painting of landscape was my next aim, and I found it very difficult to attain any results that were at all satisfactory. I made a study of a farm wagon and some small country scenes; but I had not yet found a style that seemed natural to me. The sketches I began to make in pen and watercolour of streets and harbours, or skeletons in the museum—the long evenings of life drawing and anatomy were all preliminaries, but for what? I felt no particular interest in the people around me, as pictorial inspiration. I didn't at this point want to portray my friends, or ask the girl students to sit. They had no pictorial quality for me as they were to have a little later, when I was old enough to see them at a distance, as it were. In addition, it was still the Forties, and Beauty was suspect, in art and life. People didn't emphasise their *own* looks. They imitated film stars, to their own deteriment. The Forties worshipped the cinema like a church. The crowds in the audience had no conception that they could, if they had desired it, have been more attractive, more characterful, more beautiful as individuals than the exaggerated made-up features of the stars of the screen. Mainly, however, they didn't want to. It was the cinema that kept them going through the years of utility and drabness and war, and they liked to think of it as a corner of heaven that was theirs for one and ninepence, and the movie actresses the resident goddesses that made them forget their own unsatisfactory lives, surroundings, and appearances.

We modelled in clay from our life drawings in the sculpture class; subsequently casting the figure in plaster of Paris. This was under the guidance of James Woodford, R.A.—an archetypal figure, solid, taciturn and chain-smoking, who would work over our attempts, adding bulk and solidity by the application of a series of small clay pellets. He was later celebrated for his series of large Heraldic creatures—the Queen's Beasts, made originally for the Coronation, I believe. His later work had something of the Maillol influence, though I have seen work of his as a young man that has the flowing Art Nouveau style of bronze cast from modelled clay. Woodford encouraged me to specialise in sculpture and take my diploma in it, but I still had black and white work firmly in my mind. I wished, in any case, to leave the art school without taking the final teaching year, as I had no wish to become qualified, in case events forced me to use such a qualification. If I had no permit to teach, I reasoned, nothing could make me a teacher; and I was set on making a living from the actual crafts I had come to study. I learnt silversmithing with Dunstan Pruden—I have always liked working with metal. Mr. Pruden was an Eric Gill disciple from the Guild of St. Joseph and St. Dominic, and he taught a favoured few how to transform a sheet of gilding metal into an engraved porringer or spoon. We were only favoured because chance had set our names down for this craft; but I found the soldering, and the making of bowls, cigarette boxes, hammered-out spoons, planishing and polishing, a very congenial occupation.

．　．　．　．　．　．

At this period, 1945, I was fortunate in being given an art training denied later students, because we were able to enjoy the last year of official countenance by the education authorities of antique drawing from the casts of the famous Greek and Roman masterpieces of sculpture that had helped train so many artists of the past. One wonders what the Ministry of Education knew about it, to remove such a feature from the syllabus. These works had inspired the Renaissance; drawn the world out of the dark ages; helped save the world from the barbarians; all the knowledge and power in them was to be had for the looking, and drawing was the best way of looking. As to the expense of education, all that was needed were pencils and paper and application. For the first year, we drew these great casts in the evenings, learning to perceive in them the bones and muscles we had studied assiduously in the anatomy classes. This long tradition of cast drawing in no way invalidated the potential achievements of several centuries of students—rather the other way about—who had been instructed in drawing the casts of the pensive Lorenzo de Medici, the modest Venus, or the straining Discobolus. These casts filled the life room that did duty as a painting room also. But a distant official had decided that this was too archaic a way of learning to draw—it is just as good, if not better, than most ways—and so began the long slow reorganisation of art teaching presumably intended to result in a total training to become an abstract artist. One might say that this was perhaps no less valid than training to become a Renaissance artist—or just as unprofitable if there was no real living for 90% of the students in either, and if you were going to teach art both aspects are useful; but this tendency seems to have culminated in art schools ceasing to include life drawing even, and banning figure work in toto, so that every art school should became a miniature Bauhaus—out of date enough in its way, as well. I have known many artists who have lamented the absence of knowledge that they missed as students in the uncompromising rethinking of the Sixties, and am glad that I trained earlier—even, though, curiously enough, I took myself through a period of rigid cubist-futurism, culminating in abstraction in 1950, that would not have been approved of by the art school at the time, and which I left in order to pursue my ideas privately. So where are we? But then, I did have the life drawing and anatomy as a ballast.

My interest in cartoon drawing—again, perhaps rightly from that point of view, frowned upon by the teachers of the Forties—caused me to be invited by the older students in charge of the Xmas festivities to make a series of caricatures to be shown through the epidiascope at the annual party. I sat at the back in comfortable anonymity, while the drawings—flatteringly enlarged to life-size proportions—presented the images of our august teachers in various situations—Charles Knight, the eminent watercolourist, standing up to his waist in water as he painted a view of his favourite Rockford Falls—Dunstan Pruden planishing a large silver bowl while inside it, leaning out over the edge. This kind of work gave me a chance to make use of my cartoon tendency, and I also contributed a large number of cartoons to the Rag Magazines, sold in the town each year for charities in connection with the annual Rag Day. The Xmas party concluded, in those innocent days, by the presenting of a relevant gift to each member of the staff; and by some semi-satirical songs: "Bless you, for seeing that angle—just when it seemed, perspective was not for me—."

As we sat drawing away at our compositions—either in the front bay-window of the Art School annexe (one of the Regency houses fronting the gardens and the statue of Queen Victoria set up by my great-uncle John on the occasion of her visit to the town) or by the cosy coal fire in one of the lower rooms, the comforting sound reverberated in our ears of the workmen's drills dismantling the air-raid shelter at the corner. Certainly, at the moment one entered this new existence, a different era had commenced.

During the years of the Intermediate course I spent much time drawing on Wednesday, Saturday and Sunday afternoon excursions with a fellow-student friend. We favoured pen and wash as a medium, and followed the careful incisive perception employed by Whistler in the Thames etchings; a precise, on-the-spot approach that would capture all the spirit of the moment, albeit with a technique of Pre-Raphaelite minuteness. We admired Ruskin, another forgotten prophet, whose works could be found, beautifully bound, on every bookstall in the penny to threepence shelf. In the gentle post-war sunlight, the gems of high Victoriana, awaiting the kiss of life that would bring them back into fashion, slumbered at the back of the antique shops of Brighton, or were sold for nothing in the open market in Upper Gardner Street on Saturday morning. This was a favoured haunt, where we could buy engravings and Victorian watercolours for sixpence or less. The masterpieces that we let go by for want of a little more money were remarkable. We scoured the stalls of the open market as one has scoured such stalls ever since. In later years the vendors became of antique shop status; but in these days they owned junk shops—everything was, to the eyes of the times, rubbish—but the kind of rubbish that today in the Eighties would be eagerly acquired—the very treasures of kings, or at least of Queen Victoria. But the gilt as well as the dross of the Victorian age was there for the taking—it was considered laughable, and worth nothing; consequently for those—basically of the artist world—who were the harbingers of the later swing round in taste, these years were full of pleasure and wonder that so much could be collected (as one might say) for so little. Today the Boot Fair has become a universal attraction, and we are all stall-owners and all collectors—there is not even a social stigma distinguishing us any more. All sell their unwanted articles from the back of their car, shamelessly, on Sunday mornings or Saturday afternoons in the summer. It is all basically rubbish that, curiously, would once have seemed the unbelievable luxuries of an H. G. Wells future—cassettes and L.P.s and Videos—but among the plastic one may find an antique—a genuine Bakelite ashtray of the Thirties, perhaps, redolent of Gold Flake, Black Cat, and the times when Art Deco was an innovation rather than a revival.

Alone among our contemporaries, student or teachers, A. and myself were devotees and admirers of the much-derided Pre-Raphaelites. The mere mention of Millais was enough to make those around us split their sides. And as for Ruskin! Yet, even then, the relatively minute prices charged for Landseer, Burne-Jones and others were still beyond our pocket. We were told of a Landseer going for seven pounds, that had once been in the thousands range. But seven pounds would have taken one on a two weeks holiday. Who had seven pounds to spare? We dealt in sixpences at the markets. A shilling—a mere five new pence—was an outside price.

Some pictures—as with the portrait of my great-great grandfather that I found (or that found me) about this time, would seem almost to select their purchasers: a portrait I bought was that of Thomas Frederick Burney (1765–85, as a gold label on the back of the stretcher informed one). I ignored the portraits of his parents, not having *three* sixpences to spare. Applying to the National Portrait Gallery, the late Kingsley Adams suggested I write to Miss Phyllis Mann, who had made considerable researches into the history of the Burney family. Thomas Frederick, it appeared, was the cousin of Fanny Burney, nephew of Dr. Burney, the musician, and brother of the painter Edward Francesco Burney. Miss Mann kindly sent me a concise biography from her archives. Thomas Frederick was "a youth of the most amiable qualities, intermixed with so much drollery and good humour, that his society was always a delight." The curious fact emerged that he was a fine pen and ink artist; unfortunately, after an attack of influenza, his lungs were permanently affected, and tuberculosis set in. Although he went to London to study as an engraver he was obliged to return home where a fall from a horse precipitated his demise. It was somewhat extraordinary to learn so much about the subject of this portrait, at first a stranger, and now like a friend whose history is familiar. But the odd point was that his interests and ambitions had been so much like my own. However, I have always kept these portraits by me in the studio, and can only hope they derive some satisfaction from the atmosphere in which one must suppose they particularly desired to be. . . . .

One likes to elaborate the mystical element of coincidences. Yet, any part of the past that comes alive to one is slightly fantastic; and it is only through art that we can experience the past vicariously. That actual canvas must have been admired by Fanny Burney, no doubt—one can see Edward Francesco (who is presumed to have painted it) saying, "Come and see Tom's picture; I've caught him to the life—" Tom smiling modestly, and nobody realising they were to lose him so soon; or perhaps they knew, and kept up a front. . . .

I also have a smaller oil from the market barrows—a little portrait of a Victorian girl of seventeen or so. There is nothing quite like an original, after all; and not only are they of *their* past, but after a while they belong to one's own, as well.

As students, A. and I would walk whole lengths of the Sussex coast, clambering over the rocks on the wild beaches between Seaford and Cuckmere Haven—making certain, with a tide-chart, that we would not be cut off. Here were subjects for one's pictures: Turneresque effects of light upon water, and pink evening hazes over the long low tides and the rocks—cormorants flying by as if following a constant, immoveable horizontal string, or standing for hours on the stumps of old jetties at Newhaven, their heads turning in a different direction every ten minutes or so. Broken and rotting boats and all the traditional foreground clutter of an English watercolour characterised these beaches where no one ever walked—it could be a three hour race with the incoming water—and the dull silver duralamin of the pieces of wrecked aircraft washed up gave a Paul Nash addition to the ephemera of Clarkson Stanfield. There were occasional tunnels some twelve feet up the cliffs, if you could climb to them—evidently dug out at some period by fishermen as emergency bolt-holes. Stooping, you followed your candle some thirty feet into a wood-lined cabin, a chair and table, all unused for many years. The fascination of the wild beaches with their great chalk boulders streaked with seaweed and algae, was particularly in their potentiality for beachcombing—a perennial Brighton habit, particularly after storms. I have seen the Palace Pier beaches littered with thousands of oranges—none still edible; and on another occasion a huge number of dead cuttle-fish, the Brighton octopus, with its great staring

eyes, oddly human. You could un-pop the horny beak from these rotting creatures, like a plastic addition that had been added to them by hand; and once they had decomposed in the sea the clean white cuttle-fish bone, glinting against the newly washed pebbles on a fine morning, was eagerly collected for canaries to peck at for grit, or by artists to use for rubbing down their canvases, as it is the finest of gentle abrasives. Once, as a child, we were all removed from the beach as a dead man came floating in among the bathers; and I have seen a great black ship wallowing off shore, wrecked at Hove, while we stood on the promenade in a tremendous gale, and the ship rose and fell in those unbelievably immense breakers that again no one ever sees but the residents.

Under the cliffs we would come across bones—a human femur, a jaw-bone—remnants of what tragedy? It all comes ashore in the end. An old fisherman told me once that everyone was searching the beaches for someone lost out Worthing way . . . "I knew where he'd be. I waited, then I took a walk down . . . There he was, lying on the sand in the Bight of the Cuckmere." Shades of Steerforth.

We collected winkles from the rocks, boiled them in sea-water in old cans over fires made with driftwood and lumps of tar, and sat smoking in the blue dusk as the evening slowly descended (the reflecting sea holds the light a long time) and immensified the cliffs and boulders, and emphasised the loneliness and space. Then we would walk on, turn up the river and wait for a Southdown bus to loom up at Exceat Bridge and whirl us along the coast road; its reassuring yellow-lit green presence returning us at last to Pool Valley, and the coach station that had once been full of horse-drawn stage-coaches—they did indeed run to London and back until about 1925, it would appear. The Old Bun Shoppe at Pool Valley, with its black glazed bricks (that in fact are, apparently, hung tiles) was made even more real to us by a famous watercolour drawing by our teacher Charles Knight, who had rendered these tiles with extraordinary and inspired expertise. One afternoon, coming down a cliff path at Newhaven I lost my footing, found myself running instead of walking, and eventually was propelled so fast that I began to progress in cartwheels, unable to stop myself. Spectacles and sketching materials flew from me, and I tumbled at last onto the beach, flat on my back, at the foot of a group of people who had been watching my wild descent. I was too winded to get up for a while, but when at last I did, I found that a tin box of watercolours in my hip pocket had been entirely crumpled in its useful protecting of me.

At Berwick, a village some miles north of Cuckmere, were the famous decorations by Duncan Grant and Vanessa Bell. A. and I would make this the goal of a pilgrimage; but be nonetheless surprised at the oddly academic intentions of such proud sophisticates. One would have thought that a Matisse-like approach would have been dearer to the heart of even a parochialised Bloomsburyite. Sentimental (and even patriotic) to a fault, they were nevertheless part of our adventures, and we had a fondness for their in some ways charming naïveté. We combined all our Wednesday and Saturday afternoon—and all-day Sunday—walking or cycling expeditions with endless sketching, employing very fine mapping pens with sepia or watered-down Indian ink. We used small Whatman's drawing blocks of rough-surfaced paper that gave a resistance to the pens. Fired by Ruskin and the etchings of Whistler as examples, we worked with a minuteness and accuracy upon the details of church architecture and ruined farm buildings; seldom adding more than a monochromatic wash of colour.

I was influenced also by the etchings and aquatints of old Brighton—Regency productions—that at this period were still to be acquired cheaply from folders of prints and drawings in the markets; although even then they were becoming more expensive. Most of the seafront vistas portrayed were as yet little altered; and the faint yellow glow over the prints was romantically and atmospherically appealing. One could still see with Regency eyes, when going down to the fish market to sketch among the capstans and boats, or discover the details of classical architecture—made real to us via our art school studies—as we drew the old Hotels, Harry Preston's Albion, or the grandly porticoed Bedford. The illustrations of Phiz—particularly in his Betsey Trotwood at the Copperfields' cottage, and the frontispiece showing the upturned boat house of the Peggotty's, also influenceed me towards the finest of line work. The microcosmic world of illustration linked up with one's childhood appreciation of Dickens—Copperfield and the Dombeys were my favourites—and the influence not only of the pictures, but of his own illuminating optimism and seething confidence—the multiplicity of characters and images—led one also to a careful observation of the world. I always liked that quality of the book and the print which makes it available to all: there *is* no original—every copy is original. This universal availability, so removed from the one-only oil, always attracted me; as did Beardsley's use of the line-block as his medium, with the drawing for reproduction geared to the process first and foremost, a blueprint merely for the final result.

Burne-Jones, like Beardsley, seemed a local, particular possession. His windows at Rottingdean church would glimmer through the rainy mist of a winter's night as you stood in the churchyard, the glowing blue-draped madonnas lit from within. And stained glass is always different, every time you go to look—it changes with the sky. All over Sussex was marvellous Victorian glass—usually apologised for by the rectors in the foxed and fly-specked guide slowly rotting for twopence at the entrance. The angels at Rotherfield—beautiful pieces of drawing—the world has woken up now to these treasures, fine as the Renaissance counterparts they lean towards through their Victorian Gothic leadings.

Our expeditions took us from church to Sussex church. We drew in Hamsey, near Lewes—first knocking at a cottage door to get the key, which hung on a hook in the porch—and climbed the birds'-nest-strewn winding steps in the tower to achieve the belfry; where we spent hours seated among the beams drawing the capstan-like construction and the great green copper bell.

61

"William Hull made mee," it said informatively, on the side, with a Seventeenth Century date. Our paper blocks slipped easily into a pocket—ink, pens, minute water-colour box, or even a match-box with a cake or so of colour in it. A paste-pot jar, perhaps, and water from the waterbutt, or even tea from a teacup in a cafe.

We made many and regular expeditions to wander around London, that Mecca for Brightonians on a day out. Ice cream had become available again by now, and we consumed huge quantities, standing outside the newly re-stocked Fortes' and Gizzi's and perhaps eating a dozen wafers in succession. At the Art School, a short break between sessions left time for a walk across the Pavilion gardens to the North Street "Joe" Lyons—as it was familiarly called by all. These cafeterias—suavely innovative in the Thirties, where a favourite aunt would treat me to Banana Splits—were now steamy venues for the poor and aged who could spend a winter afternoon there for the price of a cup of tea. The green gaslights on the way across glowed through the pale evening and the domes and minarets of the seaside palace, the pup of St. Paul, silhouetted themselves against the afterglow reflecting from the sea. Baked beans were the style at Joe Lyons; and the poor all about—and the poor at this period looked poor—sat, stolid, their faces over-red or over-grey, or sickly yellow. We laughed and joked, and threw our high spirits about; everything was a joke—we laughed with the girls serving or cleaning the tables with a greasy cloth; and the aged sat there, cigarettes burning between the lips, while we noted their positions or even sketched them for our compositions. We were encouraged in this kind of observation by our teacher, the eminent watercolourist Dorothy Coke, R.W.S., whose enthusiasm and kindness was unstinted. Her own watercolour drawings—particularly one in the Brighton Art Gallery of an undercliff scene, with those very green streaked chalk boulders beautifully rendered with an economy of means and selection, was a real inspiration. Her tiny sketchbooks, full of pencil observations of cows and people, were masterly examples of selection, which is perhaps the whole story of art.

We usually looked into Brighton Art Gallery on our way back from North Street. This was before the days when every successive director of a museum (as previously observed) turns it—possibly with justification—upside down. In these days the museum was permanent and predictable; and fathers took their children to see the same preserved animals and pictures, in the same places, that their fathers had shown them. Lamorna Birch's great pine-treed lane with flashes of white remarkably in tone—yet *out of tone* as well, as snow in a landscape is, I looked at again and again. *Lingering Snow*, it was, but it was not allowed to linger for ever in its long-accustomed place. A new regime a decade or so on had it to the cellar in no time. The Cornish School was out, and the art deco revival in. I did not see the Larmorna Birch again until very recently, when in the early Eighties it was included in a tribute re-assessment, at the Barbican gallery, of the Newlyn period. To stand once more before the unchanged painting after nearly forty years was an eerie experience. Some pictures alter for one; the memory of an early impression is fallible—but this hadn't . . . unless it had merely come back into fashion, as it were, and therefore seemed satisfactory to one's vision.

I had liked from childhood another masterpiece: Arthur Hacker's *Flare and Flutter, Piccadilly Circus*—not a blue-grey evening this time, like the conventional Whistler coolness of appeal, but an umber, sepia and transparent golden ochre-glazed yellow fog, through whose exciting obscurity came the head-lights of now archaic cars and vehicles. One cannot underestimate the effect of these early pictorial experiences upon one. They do not need to be by Rembrandt; one takes in so much by regular looking, and one can learn to paint from a Victorian just as well as from a Florentine. Then there was the watercolour room—another permanancy, with its series of microcosms. This was perhaps nearer to our own preoccupations with architectural drawing. One got to know Clarkson Stanfield by heart; and Turner, Cox and the others; even though there was one elaborate work in which the water appeared to have *collected* in the *hollows* of the waves. This amused our critical eyes; and another picture in the hallway—a huge Impressionist picture purchased from the first showing of such works in England. They had a try-out first in Brighton, and it had inspired my mother and her art school generation with a passion for broken pure colour, which they rendered with pastels, in still-life studies. This huge fountain and swan canvas was by Gaston La Touche; and the broken touch would have been more advantageously seen at the end of the great picture Hall. But this was still full of old masters; and the upper level was hung with immense and dark canvases of men o'war fighting confused and tangled sea-battles. "He had la Touche," we would say, as we left the gallery with a final look at the fountain and swan.

On our London days, A. and I would catch the cheap workers' train at 6.30—four shillings and sixpence day return—and sit surrounded by a dismal crew all half-asleep and puffing at the perennial cigarette until the air was thick and the windows running with condensation. There were some who played cards all the time in an endless game that went on every day, securing seats for their club of friends; but most of the passengers endured the endless clickety-clack until they tumbled out into the raw air at Victoria. For us, it would be straight into Joe Lyons and more cigarette smoke; then perhaps a stroll through the chill air to the Monument; and then to the National Gallery, ready for the doors being opened at ten.

In this era the floors were uncarpeted, and the rooms seldom full. Heavy wooden throne-like seats held slumbering tramps, and the pictures had yet to be cleaned. Advantageously, the lights were seldom put on; so that you could enjoy a painting under all light effects; and it is amazing how some gain, and some lose, and some are seen at their very best in the weird light before a thunderstorm.

One has been, it seems, wandering around the National Gallery all one's life. The exhibits are old acquaintances—one has seen them rearranged, rehung, taken down, cleaned, become begrimed all over again, or looked fresher than ever in loan exhibitions . . . . in over thirty years of knowing them several cracks have appeared, too. . .

Still pausing for hour-long—or more—sketching interludes, A. and I toured the British Museum, or the Tate. Later, we proceeded to Speaker's Corner; and some of my earliest oils were attempts to portray from memory the groups and characters of these fascinating days of incident.

"I have news for you all!" a bearded old banner-waving orator proclaimed. "Have you got a 'News of the World'?" cried somebody, sniggering. "I have news of *another* world, brother!"

Back to the puffing steam locomotives waiting at Victoria, the drivers fussing about them like mahouts, wiping the brass with oily rags, listening to the steam gauges, poking about with the levers. It was always something to do if too early—"Shall we go up and look at the engine?"

Drawing at Newhaven, we sketched the old dredger as it came and went with its moving chain of scoops—the "Foremost Prince" it was somewhat romantically named. Once, sketching an old high-funnelled tramp steamer we were invited on board for refreshments and shown around. It was all out of W. W. Jacobs; the Captain and the Mate, and all predictably wry and humorous. The pleasure in all these times was not because they were in the past, but because *we* were; that is to say, in our own past, our formative period, when all is new, both to discover and to *draw*.

Our architecture master was another enthusiast, who made us look at the drawings of Ingres; and not just his form, but his characterisation. "You can just tell that the Cavendish-Bentincks are English, even before you read the caption—." We were taught perspective by that great etcher R. T. Cowern, and learnt how to construct a building on our sheet of cartridge paper in three dimensional accurate perspective merely from given information, first making a plan and raising it from this preliminary. We also learnt a building from each period of architecture; so that we could, in an exam. room draw plan, elevation and perspective view accurately, and from memory. I knew in detail the Paris Opera house, the Petit Trianon, the Erechtheum, the Mansion House, the Parthenon—all the details, numbers of columns, plan, rooms, everything. It was extraordinarily useful for drawing buildings from life, as so many of the styles have been welded together, used and resurrected, and influenced each other in every street and townscape vista; and then there is the pleasure of actually visiting on some subsequent occasion a building that you know so well yet have not previously seen.

Wherever we found ourselves, we sat down and sketched; which is the only way to improve, after all—and the growing into one's surroundings that this entails is of great value. It's as if you own that piece of street—you see people go out—come back—you chat to them, or they to you; they accept you as part of the landscape itself.

A year or so ago, I was painting a view of the Blatchington windmill, at Hove, when a lady emerged from the nearest house—rather an imposing place, with lawns and a drive: "Would you care for your tea out here, or indoors?" I decided on where I was, as it wouldn't interrupt my work. It was brought out on a silver tray, with cakes, bread and butter and biscuits. I ate it all with a pleasing sense of wonder and benevolent gods and angels.

One morning in the open market A. bought a metal Victorian model of a classic portico. He hammered the columns together, tied a string around them, and attached a label: "Architectural masters are not to assume that when the string is cut the columns will immediately straighten themselves." This was wrapped up in a number of pieces of paper and given to our tutor, whose main aim in life was always to impress us with the quality of classic sculpture. Banister Fletcher's History of Architecture was our constant bible and textbook, and we would consult it for knowledge and details, from the Temple of Khons at Kharnak to the Choragic Monument of Lysicrates.

We cycled (and sketched) from Arundel to Amberley. At Shoreham, across the old Toll-bridge, the road (once out of Worthing) was as yet unwidened, and huge valleys—now filled in—and heights—now levelled—gave variety to the road. In the opposite direction out of Brighton, we were fond of Lewes. We climbed to the top of the castle—where A. photographed me mounted on a penny-farthing we found there—and sketched the steep lanes that run down from the High Street. We were invited in to look at the ovens built into the brickwork of the wall by old Penfold, the Huguenot baker. "Goes back a long way," he told us. "Right back to the Sixteenth Century," said A. Once, a composer invited us in to see his picture collection, and then, with his eyes dreamily on the Downscape view from his window, insisted on playing us a very long composition of his own. Bonfire night at Lewes, when rival Bonfire Societies crushed into the streets, traditionally parading in opposing different directions, was a pictorially vital experience. Red Indians, cowboys, soldiers, cavaliers—fancy dress everywhere, and all carrying a lethal lighted torch of blazing tow and tar on a stick. We followed them to the hill outside the town, where an effigy of the Pope is traditionally burnt, while huge crowds jeer and throw fireworks at it.

.   .   .   .   .   .

I found that my long interest in taxidermy and dissection had given me a good knowledge of animal—and hence human—construction for drawing; and that I could look as it were through a creature, just as an architect looks through a building.

Eventually A., as with others of my old school friends, was called up for National Service. This interruption to further education was to continue until the late Fifties, curiously enough; and although deferment could be applied for, most young men preferred to go in and get it over. The period of enlistment could last for nearly three years, so that the students had virtually to start again on returning to art school. I was called up for a medical, and with my interest in boats had put down for the Navy. It was realised, however, that my eyesight was too poor to enable me to be of much use to anyone, as I could only read the largest type (without spectacles) from an inch away. "Good god," the doctor cried as he followed my progress towards this card through the length of the hall. "Take off your glasses and walk down until you can read the largest word," he had said. I had groped through the fog past bays of doctors examining the potential conscripts. Together with my history of operations, this eyesight deficiency caused my rejection and classification of a Grade III health status—although, in company with my school friends, I had always aimed (somewhat unsuccessfully in comparison) towards what we called the "bruiser" status at school.

"Blaker?" the old doctor went on. "Hmm. No relation I suppose to my old chum Freddy Blaker, one time Mayor of Brighton?" I assented. "Good god! Freddy's grandson! No, you don't want to waste your time in the Forces. War's over. What are you doing?"

"At the Art School."

"Good, good. Well! Freddy's grandson! We shan't need you!"

Towards the end of the Intermediate course of art, before one specialised in painting, sculpture or whatever one fancied (most people, it seemed, were

seeking a teaching diploma) a competition was held for a design for a mural to be painted in the hall of the art school. I made a careful and elaborate plan, and was permitted to square up the wall and commence my twenty by twelve foot picture. A scaffolding was put up for me, and I was able to paint away undisturbed, the students passing to and fro beneath me like symbols of impermanence while the images of the mural grew stronger day by day. The theme was Brighton, and included all the Regency motifs, the capstans I had drawn, and historical details from favourite old prints. For those weeks of early summer I enjoyed the pleasure of working on a large scale—the intoxication, rather, one should say. The artist who paints a work of these dimensions learns so much that he can turn back to smaller paintings with the greatest ease. It is perhaps the secret of the high standard of the painters of the Renaissance—-that great experience of constant fresco work.

The etching room was directly beneath my scaffolding, and the busy scene below, the great press wheel being turned, inspired me so much that at last I had to climb down and ask R. T. Cowern, the master, if I might join the class. I was under age, but permitted in. My first etching was from the drawing of the belfrey at Hamsey, where A. and I had sketched.

I soon began, however, to work direct on my plates from nature, remaining on a convenient site (such as the top of the cliff above Brighton Station) for the whole day if necessary for completing the needling-in. It seemed important not to stop once started; to attain a kind of dream trance state while working, oblivious to time—one's mind involved in the view below, while the etching needle delicately skated about the plate, piercing the black smoked-wax ground on the copper. It was an exacting occupation, and the more attractive because of it. One had to avoid the inclination to merely suggest, and remember to keep *drawing*; exactness of transcription was the only reason for working, and any more flamboyant expression of the subject would leave one annoyed afterwards and regretful at wasted hours. Or at least, that was my aesthetic and method at the time.

The Art School hall was formed of round arches over the doors of each room or workshop, one of which was in the centre of my mural, and led into the siversmithing room. The one opposite was that of the etching room. The Art School was an interesting building, much liked by successive generations of students, but eventually, being considered too small for the potentially immense numbers of students created by closing down all the regional art schools round about, it was pulled down in the Sixties. Unlike many subsequent buildings that prided themselves on their modernity of design while either letting in too much light or none at all, the old Art School was well-planned window-wise, so that light seemed to flow in from all sides, cutting through apertures, and around corners, so that even on the sunniest days, it never got in so as to dazzle your eyes. Planned to the site, the function, and the prevailing daylight of winter and summer, the Art School had attended to all these points as a matter of course. The Victorian approach seemed different to more contemporary constructions, that often make a feature in their plans and models of all these points, but in the event may ignore them in the economic cutting of excessive expenses that have inevitably overtaken the original estimates possibly geared down to acquire the tender in the first place.

At the end of the war, a large number of American soldiers had been disposed of, so to speak, by making them Brighton art students. They were just leaving when I arrived, so that there were in fact only seven students in our class the first year. Within eighteeen months, the called-up students were fast being replaced by demobilised war veterans on grants, and the classes were packed full to the point of inconvenience—and continued to be—so that a larger art school did in fact come to be a necessary preoccupation. Perhaps it would have been better if they could have merely added more space to the original building, for the site was available. In a later era, conservation consciousness might have secured the permanence of the original building for future generations.

The new students, being a good deal older than the traditional school-leaver age, seemed to alter the old traditions. Adults, used to their pipes and pints of beer in the pubs, they swept away the old world of teenagers. Many of the ex-service students had wives and families, and wished mainly to achieve a diploma and a teaching job as soon as possible. However, as one of the few remaining younger students, I was fortunately detached from these kind of preoccupations.

I was very inspired by Rembrandt's direct views of Amsterdam, and his plates of mills and cottages; and for sparkling black notes and the stop-watch accuracy of the biting-in of the finest lines, I admired the early Whistler, and Meryon. The very atmosphere of the etching room, with the white dishes of dangerous green acid, the procedure of damping down the best rag paper, of smoking the beeswax ground—the air of devoted, monastic dedication, seemed archaic, Reformation period. We lived for the Friday all-day sessions, and I spent a great deal of time studying the history and methods of my new interest. From that moment when I had looked through the fanlight from my scaffolding and seen the etching-room at work I had known by divine intuition that it was to be my selected way of life. Nevertheless, I was still involved, and was to continue to be so—we are, after all, essentially, *Painter*-Etchers; which means that one of the strings to our bow always strengthens the other—with painting, modelling and sculpture. Whistler—Rembrandt—Goya—Samuel Palmer— many of the greatest etchers are also major painters; although one might say (again) that Meryon was great *because* he did not dissipate himself in any other direction.

After the *Hamsey Bell* and the *Railway yards*, I made a plate of a horse in the rain; sketching it in very quickly on the spot, in the course of sheltering from the weather while walking over the Downs from Pyecombe to Hurstpierpoint, where I had worked in the harvest fields as a boy. The fields of stooks were still with us, and the horses and wagons, and I made both paintings and drawings of these subjects. The sparseness of the *Horse in the Rain* was to me daring—albeit relating to Rembrandt's *Six's Bridge*—in that it took but a few minutes. Copper plates were expensive—I was always selling my best books, and I had sold my collection of model aeroplanes piece by piece from my father's shop window in order to buy these sheets of planed copper. We were trained to take the greatest care of them, work and work over them, and be satisfied only after many corrections and consideration of the proofs of each state. I studied the volumes of *Fine Prints of the Year* in the Reference Library of Brighton Museum—a wonderful selection from which to learn one's craft. I had no knowledge that the etching market had collapsed in 1929, and that the etchings of the period I most admired had gone out of commercial favour and were to remain so until the revival of the Seventies. But then, my interests were not with selling etchings or buying and selling them, but with making them. I admired particularly the prints of the members of the Royal Society of Painter-Etchers and Engravers, and I took the reproductions of their work in *Fine Prints of the Year* even though the series ceased publication in the early Thirties, as examples.

My mural had of course included a portrait of the Prince Regent (over the door), Martha Gunn, and "Smoaker" Miles—the Gunns and the Rolfes were still the main Brighton fishing families and fish-shop proprietors. Many an evening when out night fishing in my dinghy on a warm flat sea I would run into a circle of Brighton fishing boats, lamps twinkling from the masts: "Get out of the way of the trawl!" they would shout—"and where's your light?" (After the first admonition in that direction we fitted one up on our mast—a necessary addition we had previously thoughtlessly omitted; dangerous, as you might be run down.) Other historical Brighton figures from the Regency era peopled my mural, together with details of architecture taken from my outdoor drawings, and items such as "Mahomet's Hot, Cold and Vapour Baths" taken from books on old Brighton. The staff of the Art School complimented the work, and said it should stay there. It was reproduced in the local paper, and in effect did stay for a further thirteen years; until a group of distinguished British painters who now represented the new trend of art education visited the school in the early Sixties with a view to establishing the new tuition of non-figurative basic abstract design. "They stopped short in horror when they came in and saw your picture," the caretaker told me. "And one says—whatever is *that?*" They went to then Principal," he went on, "and said to him: 'Get rid of it!' And *that's* why I've got this bucket of whitewash here!" I had called into the College (as it had somewhat self-consciously renamed itself by then) at that very moment of my mural's abolition, after a short period away from Brighton—I had kept up a long association with the art school, as I shall recount.

However, in 1947 I felt quite pleased with my progress. The architecture master had shown me how to square up the wall with a length of string dipped in red paint, and then to pluck it like a guitar string against the wall, leaving a red line, so that the whole wall could be squared up for transference from your sketch (also squared up to scale). I learnt the basic rules of art from this huge picture—my first, and my largest—as I went along. "You don't need to paint everything bit by bit," my tutor told me, "—fill in the large flat shapes, then add a bit of line, or dark shadow, or light, at an edge, and the whole form will stand there for you. The observer's own eye will fill up the modelling. And remember that the thin black mast of a ship is equivalent to a grey one twice as wide—and the grey one looks *right*—and narrower."

We were now permitted to cross the Channel and visit Europe; so in that July of 1947 my family set off for Switzerland, to visit at last the ancestral village of my Swiss forbears. Crossing Paris by taxi from station to station one saw only grey and seemingly deserted streets, except for the occasional lonely dismal figure at a corner. All was grey, drab and depressive; this seemed strange, to one now accustomed to the rehabilitation of Brighton seafront—though it is true that London was equally black and unkempt. But one side of Basle station—the French side—was like a coal-cellar. Through a doorway, past the customs into Switzerland—merely the other side of the platform—and we blinked. A different world! Here all was white, clean, relaxed; in opposition to what we had just left—pinched, poor, hungry, economically bankrupt. Here, there were stores full of sweets, chocolates—unbelievable luxury abounded. I have never been able to walk round a supermarket, even in the Eighties, without still having the same sensation from this first impression that it is still all too good to be true; and how odd it is that one may actually *buy* all this!

We travelled by mountain railway higher and higher into the Alps; this was after a stay in Zurich where I did a good deal of drawing in pen and watercolours on my blocks of Whatman paper. Below the railway line we travelled upon we could see, far beneath, the bridge traversed earlier; and beneath that, yet another. The scale was incredible—whole towns perched on mountain plateaux above and below. At last, we slid down into the valley of Poschaiavo, and the family's favourite hotel, Alta Villa, of legendary recall.

I at once went out and began to draw; and it was here that I first gained a confidence and I think a manner that prepared me for elaborate etchings. I seemed to see the way, here—congenial subjects were all around—wagons, cattle, boys with goats in the shade of groves of trees, old people in black, women in black and grey vertically striped skirts. It was Breughel, rather than Van Gogh—it seemed that art was indeed a matter of shapes, black and crisp, that brought meaning to the more diaphanous and atmospheric parts of a composition. It was here that I was given a vision of a kind of subject I might paint that was in some way personal to myself, apart from my essays in pen and ink and etching, or the more free Impressionist oil landscape style. The mountains and scenery, the pine trees and rocks of Switzerland were surprising in their monumentality. One could note fragments of landscape that recalled the masters, and see here a Corot, a Courbet, and perhaps a Caspar David Friedrich or even Claude.

My room at the hotel was composed entirely of bare wood planks—floors, wall and ceiling. The effect was of an interestingly terrifying one—with a claustrophobic inevitability of impersonal tragedy imminent. The Kafka atmosphere of this room inspired me. It was the first item out of real life that had seemed as if perceived by I alone (like Van Gogh and his yellow chair, I thought). The sketches and etchings I had been producing, even my mural, had seemed to me quite similar to what other artists had produced; indeed, I had hoped that much of my work would not be unworthy of the Whistler tradition, as I admired the Master unreservedly. But this packing-case of a room, that nailed one into planked darkness, was a discovery unique to myself. I went out into the pale blue warmth of evening, and down a deserted narrow side street. There was a clatter and a rumble, and round the corner came an ox-cart, with three peasants in black, their heads bowed, following. A long box, covered with a black drape, lay on the rough wood of the mediaeval wagon. Their son had died earlier that week by jumping into the freezing water of a mountain waterfall to cool himself. They disappeared towards the church where he was to lie in state, while I pondered this phantom apparition, knowing I had something more to paint, something that would at the right moment demand painting, that would in fact paint itself. . . .

One day, in the main square, there appeared a lugubrious group of peasants—or farmers, as they really were. After all, they were not serfs, but in fact land-owning people; however, peasants is a term generally used to describe a certain kind of archaic figure in a traditional landscape. The day was actually one of national celebration—a balloon-man stood surrounded by presumably impecunious or economically minded children—for none had a balloon—and a band was playing. I glanced across the crowd, and saw a head that in one second's glance gave me the direction I was to take in painting for the next few years. Being young, I did not see beauty in youth, but in *age*; this head belonged to an ancient, yellowing old woman, whose face was slabbed into rocky planes—Cezanne could have created her—her eyes were distant sparks

71

glowing from under craggy brows. An expression of wolfish malevolence was expressed by these features; it was certainly not a transient emotion, but a habitual mind-state. I had no sketchbook, as the quick sketch never did anything for me but replace the sharp visionary quality of life with a scribbled cliché; and in any case, I could learn her face better by looking hard instead. With the enthusiasm of a dedicated naturalist discovering a new variety of the species, I hovered near, circling and staring. When she turned her head to glower at me it was like a primitive painted wood statue moving . . . . she wore a black blouse, and the traditional grey and black striped dress. This garb was in itself an aesthetic joy; it fitted so well into any composition.

Back in my packing-case at the hotel, I was soon drawing this cubist head, re-creating these planes and shapes. Somehow, she seemed to have given me eyes. After her, I discovered all kinds of sudden visions, super-perceived images about me, as carefully drawn by nature as she. An old man beating out a scythe blade, sitting with legs outstretched either side of his portable anvil: a symbolic motif of archaic timelessness. Another scythe man, with a great basket (hurla) on his back, striding across the hillside. Aged black garbed figures filled my view. A one-legged cripple with a flowing old coat—ox-drawn wagons of crops. When I wasn't outdoors making careful factual pen drawings of buildings I was at the hotel drawing from memory, in a sculptural solid way, the figures of old women, ox-carts and scythers. I had found not only a range of subjects, but a way of expressing them, in a simplified, patterned style—not flowing and Japanese, but angular; as Gothic-spiked as the terrifying carved wood group in the village church, of Christ being nailed to the cross, half-life-size. There was a morbid, death-inevitable Middle Ages sense in the valley that belied the Van Gogh fields, the giant green grasshoppers and sunshine. I found it infinitely attractive: the memento mori not beneath the surface, but everywhere apparent. The little temple behind the church, for instance, with its shelves of skulls—removed one by one from the restricted space of the graveyard, as others came to fill it. A clumsy skull and crossbones of painted tin was wired to the iron railings that protected these souvenirs of past time. It seemed significant and typical of these black figures to have erected such a sombre sepulchre.

My mother had visited the valley as a child, in the winter of 1908; at this time the railway did not descend into the valley, but the final part of the journey was taken by sleigh, bells ringing to warn all of the inevitably silent approach. (The arrival of the post vehicle was to this day of 1947 accompanied by a continual warning as it circled the steep descents.)

During the course of that stay, my grandmother and mother attempted to cross a snow-filled waste to visit a friend's farm. But the distance and depth of snow proved illusive—eventually my mother became unconscious from cold and exhaustion, and they were only saved from extinction as evening came on by the merest chance encounter of help.

There were numerous other stories and tales recalled of past Lanfranchi,

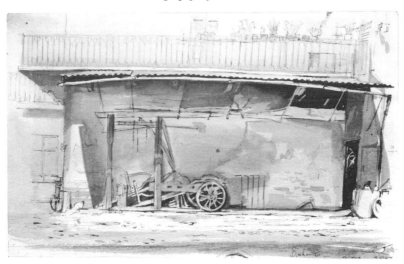

Giuliani and Longhi ancestors. My great-grandfather Giuliani had been killed by a fall of rocks from the building of the new railway near by his house. He had sat watching from the porch, waiting for the whistle that would denote the cessation of work, and of waste rock being tipped down the mountain. The whistle sounded. He got up, went across to fetch a fine log for the fire. Above, they threw down one more load—he was, of course, beneath. A gentle man, who would not have hurt a fly, said my grandmother. He couldn't even kill a pig, she added: my great-grandmother, who had no such squeamish nerves, was quite happy to attend to such matters. The family applied for compensation from the railway because of my great-grandfather's death, but it was refused—they said he was old anyway. "So," my great-grandmother Teresa Longhi replied, "because he is old you have to kill him."

I took many photographs as I roamed about on my drawing expeditions, and drew portraits of my great-uncle Silvio, who lived above his farm, set on uneven levels. A trap-door pulled up directly under the floor by the front door revealed the backs of the beautifully-coloured—pale warm raw umber and milk—Swiss cattle in the cowshed beneath. An extraordinary character, Silvio was out all day at work in his fields or on the other farm up in the mountains, a precipitous kind of sloping field. Goats were everywhere. The ceiling of Silvio's house—the walls, floor and ceiling were all bare boards—was ribboned with poles ringed with hard circles of bread. We smashed them on the table before putting them in the soup, and drank wine and ate home-made salami. I drew a portrait of my uncle, and of my cousin Agnesia, and made another drawing of a man, stooping and short yet broadshouldered, advancing crablike up the lane with a huge round bundle resting on his bowed neck. It turned out to be Silvio carrying a

small haystack. I also drew one of the old men with a goitre—it was still a Swiss valley affliction.

My grandmother, as a child in Poschiavo, had lost her mother at birth; consequently she was suckled by a goat. It was a red goat, my grandmother said, and when she went out into the yard the goat would run up to her and raise a leg ready to be sucked. "What happened to the goat in the end?" I asked, imagining that it would have been pensioned off and cherished subsequently, as in an English storybook: "I expect it was killed."

In those hard days, when most youths emigrated on adulthood, as there was little for them in the valley, the children were sent out to kill frogs, and take young birds from nests to add to the polenta. They enjoyed skinning the frogs by cutting them across and "taking down their trousers." Life in such basic terms was a long way from the books in the Hove Children's Library, let alone the English sense of kindness to animals, conservation of species, R.S.P.C.A. and humanity of approach. But then we ferreted for rabbits in Britain, and hunted, so what really was the difference? Merely a convention, with an aura of picturesque romanticism to hide the inherent savagery and to sweeten its concomitant literature.

As a child of eight or nine, I had watched a local hunt digging at a set on the Downs just above Hove. The terriers were put in, to withdraw hot and furious after baiting the animal below. At last a hush fell . . . "he's coming out"—the pink-coated riders gathered eagerly. I was standing just by the hole—with a rush, out it came—a large badger, and shot down the hill, the slope of which was almost too steep for horses. I shot after it, and was the first to reach the scene at the foot of the hill, where amidst the most terrific growling and roaring, the badger was being torn to bits. A girl rider and a huntsman came up. "Clear out of the way, *you!*" bellowed the huntsman, trying to ride me down, if I hadn't leapt aside. He then, with an apparent barbarism more suited to a South Sea Islander (of the archaic period) picked up a piece of the badger, and smeared the girl's face with blood. Well, it was an honour, I was told, as I retreated, in a fury at the whole incident, and somewhat disconcerted still at the way the horse's hooves had been directed to knock me over.

We made a day's trip into Italy, crossing the custom point at the end of the valley. Again, here we were once more in an era of utility and drab poverty. A group of men sitting under an arch by a cafe was however the very image of Whistler's etching *La Traghetto*. I continued to make drawings all about the valley of Poschiavo, spending four or five hours at a sitting, drawing as slowly and carefully and accurately as possible. I drew a detailed study of a wooden ox-wagon, and worked at a picture of men and women working in the fields with such picturesque implements. I climbed up the mountain and drew the house where my great-grandmother had lived—stone and cement, flat stones from the river on the roof, and beams and poles creating different levels of flatness from the mountain slopes. I sat on a hillside above a strange railway halt, the building with a typically huge snow protective roof, and made a drawing that took all day. This was on the plateaux above the valley, and only an occasional train stopped. When at last one came to punctuate the endless lonely silence of the immensity of pines and mountain ranges about me, a man leant out and shouted—could he see the picture? I held it in the air, and he at once got out and climbed up the slope to look more closely. Another followed; and then the whole train emptied, as people clambered out and began to run up the hill. The driver and guard were the last to abandon their vehicle—very properly. At last, after much discussion and talk, the driver inferred that they had better get on, and with waves and handshakes, the passengers returned, waving from the windows as they moved off, and leaving me once more with the somewhat oppressive sense of silence.

I walked up towards what seemed a four foot wall of ice, on another day—the edge of a glacier; but after an hour or more of walking, and leaping from rocks in the apparent stream which became a torrent, I came at last to the glacier to find, even on this summer day, that it was a great forty-foot cliff of dripping ice, stretching away up a cleft between the mountains.

Chapter 4

Back at the Art School for the autumn term, I entered the Illustration course, with the idea of being trained to earn a living in my old ambition of black and white work; another incentive was that in the painting group I should not have been permitted to continue with etching. In addition, I was not really interested in painting in the deepest sense, and had no wish to spend days seeking out volume by hours of life-painting from a model I had already drawn a hundred times. I had progressed in life-drawing from a 4b pencil—as advocated by Ginnett—to a 4H, of which he definitely would not have approved! But, heading for etching, and in any case finding a pencil an unattractive medium for me, I soon progressed to pen and ink for life work; and my examination drawing was a huge and dynamic affair spattered with blots and scratches in its freedom of approach.

My master had said to me: "Go ahead and use ink, boldly. When they mark the drawings, they go first to what they can *see*—MAKE IT STAND OUT."

The current style of painting taught at the Art School was a cross between Puvis de Chavannes and an academic Cezannism; it went, understandably, for form and breadth, but not *detail*; and detail in art—and interest of subject—was what interested me. I didn't care for form—except in sculpture where it belonged—and I thought, rather modernly, that painting should be interesting for its calligraphic handling, not its conscientiousness; rather, in its flat decorative elements, and its freshness and sparkle. I painted at home, slowly progressing, and never over-painting or even giving a picture a second session. It belonged to the hours when it was being painted, was my creed. Premier coup; and when you come to yourself and think: "Now what else does it need?" it means that it's finished.

I was much inspired at this period by a touring exhibition that came to Brighton Art Gallery, of the work of the Belgian James Ensor. I didn't care for the etchings, although I liked the fish and the masks and skeleton paintings (apart from the technique); but what did impress me were the early palette-knife pictures—the young miner, for instance. This use of bold thick paint went further even than the Manet glasses of beer in our much admired café scene in the National Gallery, before which A. and I had stood talking for hours. (We would stand for an equal time before the Arnolfini, talking and gesticulating, until a guard pulled my arm away with the disapproving caution: "These things are valuable, you know.") However, I awaited the time when I should possess the courage to plunge at my canvas, knife in hand and with presumably an equal amount of paint to spare. I early decided to employ only ordinary white undercoat for my whites—it gave a convenient flow when required—and as a medium for mixing with other colours for tints. This procedure I have always followed, sometimes also using flake white to accent required passages; and paintings now forty years old show no signs of deterioration—except (as I shall relate later, when I attempted the use of pure white lead). In etching, apart from the Rembrandt, Meryon, Whistler and R.E. approaches (which are all linked) I liked Tiepolo, who is quite different, and achieves a marvellous silvery transparency and solidity without working up his darks at all. Durer's engravings I much admired, and bought a facsimile book of them in Switzerland (in a bookshop at St. Moritz). I tried making copies in fine pen and ink of these, including the skull on the shield; the knowledge one immediately gains from this kind of study is immeasurable. It linked to the way of seeing in terms of cross-hatched and variegated fine pen line that had begun for me with the steel engravings of the countryside after Birket Foster, and the Phiz etchings on steel in Dickens; and, as a perennial influence, the plates of my master, R. T. Cowern, mounted on swinging panels on the first floor hall of the art school, outside the Principal's office. These wonderful etchings—the cabbages of *Garden in Winter* in particular, with their unerring attention to detail, and the minutest of background biting, were something to consider as a height that could never be equalled. This, an excellent thing in a master's work, ensures that a student keeps trying. To watch R. T. Cowern print a plate was an object lesson in technique—polishing up the bloom on the plate surface using the gently waving edge of his palm, like the fins of a goldfish keeping static in a tank, was a lesson never to be forgotten. The disquisition after the blankets were flipped back and the proof expertly peeled off generally had one result, as we all gathered round—it was never good enough, needed strength. Bite it again, scrape, burnish. Time means nothing! Grind more ink, add more red, more French Black—no, we don't use tube ink here, or canned ink, with its dull greyness in the plate tones. Rembrandt didn't use tube ink. "While there is copper there is hope," was Cowern's dictum. There seemed a whole world waiting—as indeed there was (and always is: just go out in the nearest car-park with your needle and plate, if you like: there's a real problem for you! Rembrandt never had the chance of that subject).

The Principal of the Art School, Sallis Benney, an eminent watercolourist who specialised in beech trees, individually drawn and often tinted in monochrome blue, was most friendly and encouraging. At Xmas a group of us would carol-sing round the town to end up at his house for coffee and mince-pies, in those somewhat village-like days. We were still young. My room at my parents' house still possessed—somewhat enriched, or more crowded, with the numerous etchings and paintings—much of its original museum-like aura: stuffed owls still hanging down on strings from the ceiling, preserved and mounted squirrels, fox masks, weapons, Landseer engravings of dogs, two woodcarvings, one a hedgehog, the other a crouching figure, and cases of insects. I used these last items as still-life subjects, and made a drypoint—my first incursion into this wonderful medium—from a stag-beetle in my collection. I had once come upon a remarkable sight in a lane near Bramber castle. A battalion of stag-beetles had all emerged from their five-year pupal period at the same precise time; and the ground was covered with this impressive and unusual creature in the plural—usually only occasionally seen, and then glimpsed as an individual flying solemnly and grandly Concord-like ten feet up on summer evenings. Moreover, they were all battling away, though apparently without mutual injuries. Some, however, lay dead—perhaps from defeated pride, and these I had taken away and set up.

I had made the two wood-carvings at the end of the previous summer term, in the intervals of those two extremes of scale, mural-painting and etching. A. J. J. Ayres had been my teacher, and I had been instructed to make a clay model and carve from it as a pattern. A different approach perhaps to the direct carving of Gill, but the right way for a student to work. I enjoyed carving, and casting from a modelled figure, and have always intermittently practiced those arts; but with all the other departments of art beckoning, it has had to take a secondary place. I continued with drypoint, working direct in the Life room, and once made a plate of a group of lions, working directly on the ungrounded metal in the lion house of the London Zoo. Later that afternoon I had wandered into some obscure corner to draw an ostrich, when, slowly, the zoo became quieter, a peaceful hush settled over the scene—the animals gave up grunting and growling, and rolled over listlessly in their cages in the warmth of evening. The place had closed. I put away my completed work, and set out to look for human company. All was deserted. I was locked in; every gate barred and chained. It was a strange experience. The animals still awake looked reproachfully at me as I crept by. Eventually, climbing a ten foot fence, I dropped down the other side into the path of a policeman. Fortunately, he accepted my explanation, upon my producing all my perhaps incomprehensible copper plates.

As an illustration student, one's earlier preoccupations in art as taught—supposedly the realisation of life and atmosphere for those attributes' own sake—now became replaced with *effect* as the main consideration. A printed page was not a painting, and was to be viewed from a foot away, not half a gallery's distance. Consequently, one was taught to catch the eye, but only with the intention of leading it at once into the text. Surely the worst training for an aesthetically inspired artist dreaming of grand and personal pictures? But it seemed to do no harm; rather the opposite. And as one of our tutors remarked, after an impassioned discussion re. aesthetics—why were we in the department at all if we didn't want to learn a living drawing double-spreads, with the girl's face on the right and with eyes the same size as her mouth so that a prospective purchaser would see her as he flipped through the magazine on the railway bookstall? (Remember, you only have five seconds to catch his attention.) Some of us had thought more in terms of high class book illustration when we decided on the course—possibly of being approached by the Folio Society, or the Golden Cockerel?—"You're so *green!*" our tutor laughed. "But you'll find out! You'll come down with a bump!" Well, anything you learn is useful in the end, somewhere; and it was all of interest.

We were not only taught the baser methods of catching fish. After two days a week of commercial training, we did indulge in two days of real illustration. Leslie Cole, our master, was an energetic wasp whose acid comments kept us busy at our work. Small, dark, curling beard, flashing of eye, straight from many and varied campaigns where he had been official War Artist—had I realised what he had experienced, I should never have expected him to be interested in *my* petty opinions. But the War was a thousand years away, by now, and ex-service experiences were all around one, and hardly mentioned. I painted (unasked) a pen and gouache picture of Van Gogh, mortally self-wounded and leaning against a tree in a cornfield, his black crows filling the sky. "Poor old Van Gogh," said Mr. Cole, in rather an unfeeling way. "Couldn't do anything right, could he? Couldn't even shoot himself properly—."

This insult to the Saint brought a sharp defence from me at which Mr. Cole laughed heartily. His own preference as a teacher was for *shapes*—silhouetted areas in different colours and texture. We were to reduce form, figures and objects to essential geometric areas that we cut out, using the void as a stencil, solid or spattered. On this we built with pen, ink, wax, gouache—anything to hand, including collage with printed materials, patterned scraps of cloth, silver paper . . . an excellent training for picture-making, taking one away at once from that curious tradition which still persists: the sacrosanctity of oil painting. Strangely—but perhaps inevitably—Leslie Cole's own work was far less extreme in this direction than his teaching. He was, however, included in the exhibitions with other artists of the time whose paintings and drawings—always with a certain quality about them still of the vision of the English watercolourist, however contemporary in feeling and approach—Turner has much to answer for—were considered vital. Interestingly, just as I was writing this, I found that the Imperial War Museum had staged an exhibition of Cole's war paintings. He told me once that, like myself, he had at times kept odd animals as pets. "Rabbits, dogs, mice, rats, guinea-pigs—got a wife, now," he said, grinning, his eyes flashing. "Ah yes," he recalled, when we re-established contact at a later date—"you're the chap who always refused to do lettering." It was true I had always demurred from participating in this sphere; considering (with considerable judgement) that almost anyone could accomplish it better than myself. This whole new set of artists to which Cole belonged had strong graphic elements and delighted in and practiced the new illustration—an illustration light-years away from the double-spreads of the women's magazines.

Foremost in influence were the paintings and drawings of John Minton. But the free and flowing style of Topolski was influential; and specifically for illustrations the work in line and freely applied wash approach of Anthony Gross, as exemplified in his subsequent lithograph decorations for the "Forsyte Saga." His work—war artist drawings of the desert campaigns, or troops—including Montgomery himself—portrayed in the lyrical orchards of Normandy, were to be seen in touring exhibitions and in the modern collection of the Brighton Art Gallery. All this had a new and stimulating effect, taking one away for a while from a devotion to the 1930 Painter-Etcher School. We admired, as well, the vital and considerable amount of black and white work being created for *Lilliput* magazine, *Radio Times*, the re-designed *Strand*, and for the more sophisticated press in general. James Holland, Pearl Falconer, Edward Ardizzone—these were people whose best drawings, vignettes, tailpieces, we collected for our interest. After all, you can make your illustration collection with a pair of scissors. We felt we were part of the living art of the times in our emulations. But then, all modern art is basically graphic art, from the Cubists and the Expressionists (almost from the Symbolistes of the Nineties, whom nobody as yet knew about in England) and is not painting at all, in the old sense.

James Boswell was an illustrator of the day—similar in style to James Fitton, who carried the approach over into large paintings—who was art editor of one of the pocket magazines of the day. He wrote an interesting book called *The Artist's Dilemma*—one of the King Penguin style of publication, small but hardbacked, that were a feature of the era. I went to see him bearing a portfolio of my work in black and white. I considered it was never too early to commence bothering people with it, although you would usually meet another young artist exiting from a gallery or publisher as you entered, and the celebrities within were remarkably generous with their time and advice, in retrospect. I remembered always one point in Boswell's book, to the effect that the reason you see the occasional artist around, apparently surviving on his work, is because he never gave in. . . I went up to the Arts Council to talk to the Director, but saw Gabriel White, then the deputy. He was kind enough to give me sensible advice. He said it did a young artist very little good to have a one-man show; it was much better to have one picture in every show—every gallery and summer show you could get into; you would then hang with celebrated artists and receive more attention from critics and public. I have always remembered this sensible opinion.

We did not neglect the study of the past, in our admiration of the new school, and were perhaps some of the first to re-evaluate the Pre-Raphaelites, whom the painting department would still have none of. To us, they were great illustrators. (They would have made a fortune as double-spread artists.) In fact, of course, they had been great illustrators, and *Illustrators of the Sixties* was a favoured Illustrator's Bible. Millais, Rossetti—we stood in astonishment at the modern quality of Millais' remarkable drawing in the Tate: *The Exhumation of Queen Matilda*—in a curious formalised style which regrettably he did not develop—and learnt a great deal also from the condensed detail of Rossetti's *St Cecilia*, with the elaborate townscape in the background. Was it he who lamented the cutting down of a square inch off a block, and said "I could have got a whole city in that?" It doesn't who matter who said it—it is the right lesson for the illustrator whose preoccupation is the using of the space on the page, not the elbowing of others out of the way on the walls of the Royal Academy.

Charles Keene was the God of all of them—but Du Maurier, Linley Sambourne, and all the *Punch* draughtsmen contributed equally to our vision. Drawing was in fact all—and the drawing of details, getting facts correct, historical costume, machinery—everything. We were encouraged to build up collections of sketchbooks for reference by drawing everything we saw, all the time, wherever we were. Tenniel's political cartoons for *Punch* were a considerable influence on my paintings and drawings, from the time I picked up a huge volume for sixpence from a Brighton bookshop. I had always checked over the stock of all these places (mostly now gone) from Combridge's in Hove to Sexton's in Ship Street. I amassed a large collection of Victorian biographies of artists and illustrators (always massive and comprehensive works that no one wanted) packed full with anecdote and information, and creating a cross-section of people and personalities of the era rather like a re-creation of Balzac's inter-connecting characters that people his pages, so that you can hardly open one of his books without coming upon Étienne Lousteau, Nathan, or Rastignac, among the crew of journalists and self-seekers.

We visited the Pre-Raphaelite exhibition at the Tate—the first re-evaluation of the period for many years. It was much laughed at. All about people were screaming with laughter—there was still supposed to be something hilarious about a *subject* in a picture—and any suggestion of sentiment embarrassed the visitors terribly. The long hair of the girls repulsed the public of the time; there was still a sort of Thirties, post-World War I fear-of-lice way of thinking about, and as for women being portrayed as gentle, delicate—even beautiful! Such an idea was repellent to an age whose image was the brassy nylon-peroxidism aseptic theatrical apparently-sexy but in reality Victorian-prudishness of the Betty Grable era, where Make-Up is the woman. It was a strange contrast to some twenty five years later, when these same pictures—that one has known all one's life, as a kind of religion indeed, and stood gazing at their ever-fresh quality for forty years—evoked from a different generation a worshipping silence similar to that which might be given to Van Eyck and Van der Weyden. In fact, if one thinks of Hunt and Rossetti's early visit to see the pictures in Belgium, and their ignorance of pre-Raphael painting other than in engraved reproduction, it is probable that their own real aesthetic and technical awakening was inspired by the Flemish school.

Bewick and Beardsley, of course, figured high in our study; and we were advantaged all through our course that, unlike the painters, who could only study properly before a real canvas that might be inaccessible, an illustrator can look at the intended end result of the masters in any book. It is useful to see an original drawing, of course; but with an engraved Victorian block, of course, it has disappeared with the engraving, and we admired the Dalziells as did their own contemporaries. Besides etching, we learnt and practised lithography on stone, being taught by a printer from the local paper who had actually experienced professional working in this craft, and you can't do better than that, if you want to be instructed. We studied Heraldry, History of Costume, and learnt the details of all methods of Reproduction, from the Wood-cut to Photogravure and Collotype, so that we could describe them in the examination room in a special question paper. It was all very technical.

While the painting group were still studying to be artists of the High Renaissance, we were being given the potential outlook of Caxton or William Morris. The great Type designers—Bodoni, Baskerville, Gill—were all familiar to us, and the work that came from inspired private presses and created such fine title-pages, design and production were put before us in lecture and example. It was a comprehensive course, and I was pleased I had learnt many things that I would use if ever I had the time.

A new figure appeared to teach us, as more and more ex-service enlarged the classes. This was Robin Jacques, whose delicate cross-hatched drawings were well-known to us from his *Man in the Moonlight* illustrations, *Radio Times* drawings, and a tribute to him in the excellent *Alphabet and Image* magazine that treated of the best in the field of contemporary illustration and typography. I still have a drawing he made on the top of my worksheet, of Magwitch accosting Pip in the churchyard. This was the time of the great Ealing films, and we were highly conscious of David Lean's film images. We also drew Fagin, after studying both Cruikshank and Alec Guinness. *A Place of One's Own* was another memorable film, with its Rex Whistler inspired images. That artist had a link with Brighton because of the painting of the Prince Regent

Awakening the spirit of Brighton that he had created on the wall-paper of a requisitioned Brighton house during his billetment here immediately prior to the Invasion. An additional tragic poignancy was given to the work by his being killed in action very shortly afterwards. With an almost incredible piece of civic sensibility, the house next door was somehow acquired, and the wall demolished from that side, leaving first the lath and plaster, and then the wall-paper. This was then backed by a canvas, and taken off to the Royal Pavilion, where it was hung in state, in the very palace of the person whom it was goodnaturedly satirising.

Robin Jacques, with his controlled technique, was an immense influence on us. He worked same size, it appeared, without the advantages of refinement that reduction gives—one normally draws a third up. He left quite soon to become art editor of the *Strand* Magazine; but his example lingered and lingers still. We drew from the clothed model, now, to learn the fall and flow of different drapery, and employed varying techniques each session. We might be restricted to the fine pen hatching approach, or use pen and wash in two colours only. We were given lectures on lay-out by a surviving veteran of the war with Japan, who, as he told us, had been "one of the unfortunate British Coolies who built the Burma Road." But all around were war veterans. Pipes and beards proliferated more and more, where once there had been only adolescents. Nearly all of these had now taken their place in the Services. My fellow-students were sometimes older than their teachers, and spoke to them with adult equality. I became older than nineteen years, evolved into a heavy smoker, and gave up shaving. "All good artists grow beards," Sallis Benney said to me, with kind encouragement.

. . . . . .

I bought an old copy of *Trilby* on a barrow one market-day, and found both the story, Du Maurier's personality and his illustrations so appealing that I felt it imperative to have a studio. With three other students—the only ones still left of my own age—I rented a large upstairs room in the Lewes Road, picturesquely near the Viaduct. This had been bombed in the war, and a huge drawing by Muirhead Bone, of the scene under reconstruction, hung in the Brighton Art Gallery. Nearby was a Monumental Mason's yard full of various stones; a junk shop, and small shops opposite—it was very Nineteenth Century. The room had a fireplace, so we always had a good fire going. We furnished it with various items from the Élite Cafe, which we conveyed on a barrow borrowed from an uncle who was a wholesaler in the fruit market behind the Art School. We gave the studio more than a touch of Du Maurier's period with some comfortable upholstered chairs, small tables, and a huge horsehair sofa with a sweeping mahogany back. This cost nine shillings and sixpence from the junk shop next door. The room was twelve and sixpence a week, and £5 furnished it. Here we drew and etched, made studies of the old shops from the window, and painted the occasional portrait from one of the girl students who didn't mind sitting for us. We played my collection of old records from the Thirties—I had been given a gramophone for passing the School Certificate—and the sounds of the Savoy Orpheans accompanied our work.

I etched an elaborate plate from a combination of drawings made in Switzerland; and another, in situ, of the Brighton Fish Market in the early morning, with the light glinting on the cobbles as they were hosed down, and the barrows of fish with the pier and boats just visible through the mist. I had a great liking for the one or two Buhot etchings I'd seen in reproduction—though not in the original—and I liked his treatment of weather. In effect, it wasn't much like mine; but the work of a master can lead you to seeing your own subjects afresh. I had seen this market subject many times as I walked to the Art School along the sea front of a morning. Together with the *Railway Yards* and the Swiss plate, I submitted this to the Sussex Artists exhibition in the Brighton Art Gallery—an annual affair in which our masters and all the notables in the area were hung—and also the Royal Academy. They were accepted by the former, but became the first of a long series of rejects from the R.A. I found (as have many young artists) that it was very difficult to have one's work accepted by a jury for an exhibition. However, taking the etchings up to hand them in at the back of Burlington House (there was no entry fee in those days) led me wandering across to Cork Street and Bond Street. I early discovered, in fact, the London galleries, which have always been a source of interest to me. I have visited them regularly for thirty-nine years and watched the careers of dealers span lifetimes, and the same pictures turn up again and again. It is an interesting occupation—purely the onlooker—rather like natural history. But as a side-issue to this academic connoisseur outlook, I also decided to be a participant from the point of view of the artist, and to take some of my work to the Redfern, Roland, Browse and Delbanco and/or others as soon as possible.

By the following spring, in my twentieth year, I found that my approach in pen and wash was becoming a little more free; and that I had moved quite away from the precise quality that I still felt was essential for copper plates, even when executed quickly and sketchily. I had not felt sufficiently confident to try versions of my cross-hatched drawings of Swiss characters on a plate, and so the time went by, as my style had changed, and they never were done. There are so many avenues to explore as a student (or perhaps always) that many ideas are shelved for later development, and the moment goes by for them, and they are never achieved. An exhibition of new French techniques of gravure—really Thirties techniques, but new to Britain (except for an informed sophisticated field of connoisseurs) and certainly new to art schools—arrived at Brighton Art Gallery. The Arts Council did excellent work in this era in bringing all kinds of inspiring ideas to towns outside London who would never otherwise have had the chance to study it properly, particularly in the student field. We all experimented with these approaches, with the enthusiastic help of R. T.

Cowern. Sugar-process aquatint was the main discovery—as with the Picasso plates to Buffon's natural history. There was also a white-line woodcut, the separate areas to be handcoloured. It was a stimulating show, and perhaps the first to prophecy the eventual new school of etching and engraving that resulted in the great print revival of the Seventies onwards.

A large Chagall show was held at the Tate also, about this time. This was full of most wonderful images—the birthday picture with his wife flying through the air, the remarkable black and white patterned Rabbi. I didn't like the etchings—I didn't think the ideas suited the medium—and I thought the late paintings too free and sugary, and the lack of drawing unnecessary; but the early canvases, with their imaginative use of cubism, gave me the kind of impetus that I needed; although the effect lay dormant for some years, having to wait until I had got through various other manners first.

By now we had given up the studio as I, as treasurer, had found it almost impossible to collect the weekly rent from some of the others. It was felt we no longer had a use for it. The Victorian furniture would have made high prices (and perhaps did if it survived) thirty years later. It was sold back to the junk shop, however, for a few shillings; my co-tenants departed for the armed forces, and I went off (in the Easter vacation) on a sketching and walking tour of Cornwall, in the traditional manner, with an older student, G. We spent an enjoyable time walking, hitchhiking and sketching along the North Coast, from the Pebble Ridge at Bideford to Land's End. This was an interesting contrast to a slightly earlier expedition with another friend, when we had cycled to London, and stayed at the Youth Hostel. Half of this was still unusable from bomb damage, so that you had to be careful not to walk the length of the upstairs corridor in the dark, or you would have walked off the broken timbers. We sketched the new bridge and the Shot Tower from the Embankment at Cleopatra's Needle. This was before the Festival of Britain had erased that Whistlerian view with the first of the new Bankside complex, or the Hayward Gallery had come into being.

In Cornwall various adventures came our way, as they will immediately one sets in movement any course of action. Walking from Bideford we were assured of a lift from one of the few cars or lorries that came along. A small sports car, rather new and smart, drew to a halt to our questing thumb.

"What do you think of this machine?" the driver enquired, after a while. "Cost me nothing—nothing at all. I was at this lady's house, fixing the electric switches, and she says '—you want a car? You can have the one in the garage. It's new. Just take it, if you like it.' 'What's the catch?' I says. 'My husband he gassed isself in that there car,' she says, 'and I don't want to see it no more. You just take it away.' Talk about luck! Pretty good, wasn't it? What do you think of it?"

We didn't think too much, and soon made an excuse to continue our journey by foot. Of course, in a story, the whole thing could have been a vision, and he the gassed husband. . . .

We sketched the donkey sleds at Clovelly, and etched the harbour view; and at Boscastle we drew in an old inn with a ceiling made from a century of uncleared cobwebs, a huge grey cushion above one. We climbed down in the twilight to the entrance to this natural harbour, a cleft between the cliffs, where the huge waves sucked and dashed at the rocks; from Tintagel we visited King Arthur's Castle. One misty rainy night we set out for Land's End, and were only stopped from eventually walking on and over the cliffs in the blackness by the sudden opening of a door unexpectedly in the fog. The emerging figure was eagerly accosted as he stood framed in the yellow square, like someone in a Stanhope Forbes Newlyn canvas. We were taken to a cottage and were shortly enjoying supper in a Victorian parlour; the next day, with the weather clear, we inspected the rocks and lighthouse at leisure, being however much bothered by a little old whiskered fisherman in cap and jersey, who would keep following us and telling us about the stones—"They call that one the old woman; and that over yonder—" We finally convinced him we had to return to the village. "*Thank* you sir," he said. And waited. Thank *you*, we said. "*Thank* you sir." Still no result. He stumped off, with the final remark—"Well, I wouldn't *go* on holiday if I hadn't got no money."

Back at the art school for the summer term, we were all encouraged to sketch out of doors on the beach. I developed a scheme of criss-crossing the sky in a pen and watercolour sketch—I had given up the rough Whatman blocks—to give the vibration of glittering sunlight to the scene of pier struts and paddlers against light-reflecting sea and sand, and I began to paint pochards in oil on small wood panels, mainly from the backs of old pictures, the frames of which were available in their dozens for sixpence a time in any junk shop. I used bright and primary tints for these direct effects.

In August 1948 G. and I set off for Paris by the simple expedient of taking a bus to Newhaven and boarding the eleven thirty-five steamboat. The first matter of interest in those days of real steam were the engines; and one could go down and walk on a catwalk to look at the great plunging pistons that drove the ship along. Then, up on deck, to see the water glittering bluer even than it appeared from Brighton beach, while a trio of dolphins, green on the back, white below, gleaming and shining, leapt back and forth across the bows as we steamed along, as if specially employed not only as Brighton symbol, but as a travel poster in three dimensions full of exhilarating enthusiasm.

I had been reading Wilenski's *Modern French Painters*—a remarkable book for the student—which had made not only the Impressionists and their successors come alive, but also the historical periods in themselves; and this, coupled with *The Meaning of Modern Art* and *The Meaning of Modern Sculpture*, by the same author, had given me a fund of artistic awareness to draw upon.

We came into Dieppe—the dwellers in the caves in the cliffs waving—and got to Paris by 6 p.m. The Gare St. Lazare seemed unchanged since Monet; and the Boulevard Montmartre was as Pissarro had left it. We settled into the Y.M.C.A. in the Rue de Trevise (after an initial first night in a more expensive hotel) and set off to find a restaurant. "Vill you '*am?*" said the waiter at last, to my indecision in ordering, due to difficulties of translation of the *jambon.*

In the Luxembourg Gardens I took out my pen, ink, and watercolours (we carried little other baggage) and all at once the whole approach and technique I had been waiting to acquire seemed clear before me—clear and simple. I knew how to do it. Just write it down, that's all—jot it all down, as if describing the scene to a friend. Describe it to yourself—there's a statue—like *that*—the head tilted *so*—here's a child looking up at it—here's the bit of flowerbed—wriggle, scratch, zig-zig-zag, comma, note. . . .

I had this style organised in five minutes, and have used it ever since. After a while one had no need to consciously consider proportion, and scale—it evolves with the describing and notating. It must be correct—you wouldn't have put it down if it wasn't. There was no stopping now. The method was turned on to scene after scene—view from the windows of the Rue de Trevise, with the archway at the end; down below in the street, an old man walking along with a loaf. He has long hair and is wearing a tall conical artist's hat with a wide brim, c. 1840—possibly the last one left—I've not seen one before or since. Who even knows of them, now? They don't even symbolise the artist any more; and haven't for a hundred years, in any case. One forgets that the basis for the Romantic Movement in the first place was a Mediaeval revival in clothes and hair and beards as opposed to the Eighteenth Century Classical mode; and that far from looking like denizens of Montmartre as we think of them (á la Lautrec) the artists of the mid-Nineteenth century wanted to look like something out of Durer.

We discovered the Musée d'Art Moderne—this was at a time when no one we knew had been to France, except as a soldier—and admired Modigliani, Maillol, Kisling, and all the artists of (in fact) the Twenties and the early Thirties. We admired the work of the artists we had seen in reproduction, not what was actually being painted by artists at that moment—to that extent we were already out of date. But then England's concept of French art was out of date—Picasso and Matisse (after the V. & A. show) were the Moderns to England, whereas in France they were elderly men of the older generation whether still working or not. British artists of the contemporary generation were in fact far more accepted and known in their country than their equivalent age group were in France. In addition, we had artists truly remarkable; though at this time there was still the notion about that nothing English in art was really to be compared with anything French—an interesting example of the way the Fry–Clive Bell propagation of French art and Cezanne had demolished a regard for all English art as a corollary to demolishing the school of Sargent in the first place. It was known as French flu, when a student turned to Cezanne's style as a great discovery; and woe was he, for he seldom gave it up, and the tipped forward table and blue lines round the over purpled green apples still survives here and there today, and still, even merits a minute degree of respect, as "being on the right lines." Fashion is indeed as incomprehensible as its own inversions. . . .

Apparently, if you had frequented the Lapin Àgile, you were a great modern master—possibly there was some degree of truth in this. But in England we had Sutherland, Moore, Nash, Piper, Burra, Bacon, Spencer (mind you, artists hated *his* work for its thin paint and subject that *meant* something) but none of these were considered equal to a doodle from the School of Paris—or even Paul Klee, the respect for whose work knew no bounds. Well, we enjoyed all these modern paintings ourselves, and found much to admire. We discovered the galleries more or less by accident, or by talking to people in bookshops who recommended them. We went to the Jeu de Paume, where the revelation was Manet's *Olympia*. What a lesson for painting in that butterfly wing modelling of her right breast! Peinture Claire—all the essence of tone in art was there. The painting students in the Art School would work away on their life-studies: umber and blue-grey would disfigure the flesh—flesh which is luminous, like flower petals, and should be regarded as such, otherwise why paint it? If you are after form, use a dustbin. (A useful place to put your failures, too). Fantin Latour's portrait groups were an additional impact—the breadth of monochrome modelling and the directness of the head of Rimbaud. And Lautrec's great canvas panels for La Goulue's sideshow, flowing house-paint-brush on old sackcloth, showed (as Sir Joshua Reynolds had once demonstrated, with a finger dipped in ink on a scrubbed kitchen table—I wonder if he caught it, from the cook) what could be done, by an artist, with the coarsest of materials.

The small Degas head of a girl—already somewhat of an icon for us (in reproduction) as an example of unkilled paint in portraiture—was here. We went out, and roamed over Paris with our pen and wash. We went to Versailles, and saw the Petit Trianon in actuality; we came upon the Rodin museum, and apart from the inspiration of his own pencil and wash nudes, of everlasting freshness, were introduced to the amazing out-of-focus portraits in grey and umber by Carrière, whom I have always regarded as a main mentor since. We sketched in and from restaurants and cafés, and went to the Folies Bergères and drew Lautrecian scenes.

We had taken packets of coffee with us to Paris to exchange for bottles of brandy—this had been a useful exercise, as all the French had was acorn or nut coffee. In every street, people approached you—had you any watches to sell—? Did you want to buy anything—a woman—Luger pistol—I supply . . . anything, you ask—There was a kind of wide-open cowboy-town atmosphere. Up on the Boulevard Rochechouart of an evening it was even more so—every café and bar a seething mass of light and music and uproar—plenty of soldiers of all kinds on the spree—fights in the street, people being bodily thrown out of bars into the gutter—a feast for the artist as regards material. Back at the Y.M.C.A., after supper of a bowl of soup in a great shabby hall on old tables—the whole scene exactly like Mr. Bumbles's establishment—I made drawings of Paris by night, or rowdy scenes in old Montmartre.

We left Paris, and returned to sketch further in Dieppe, where we missed the last boat. The customs officials kindly lent us the custom house for the night—it was the old orange painted shack that had been their since time immemorial—apologising for locking us in as they had to leave it closed. They returned for the early morning boat, just as I had put on a coat and peaked cap, and was giving what I felt to be a lively impression of a French Custom officer from behind the barrier. I looked round to follow G.'s pointing finger to see the laughing faces of the real officials all in the window behind me outside.

On a more sombre note, we met later a father and son, waiting also for the channel boat. "We've been up to Dunkirk. It's a ghost town. Makes you think, don't it? All them streets, running with blood." It was indeed, despite all our fun and enjoyment, not so long since all had been very different here.

Back home in peaceful-seeming Brighton, the Art School seemed a little tame. Inspired by what we had seen, we set up a studio in a room over the main road, and found models by simply going down into the street and asking any passing girls if they would come up and sit for a portrait. In this manner we painted all day until the autumn term commenced, when we spent every night in the life class, experimenting with different techniques, from Rodin and Lautrec to Pascin and Modigliani. The painting students were working at a mural in the room by day, and their scaffolding gave a high view of the model and students below. We took to sitting on this eminence and drawing the models from another angle. The teacher in charge had no objection; and the models themselves frequently wished to buy—and did—the pastel and wash drawings I made of them. I also began a series of elaborate pen and watercolour café scenes, in which I placed members of our circle—we had by now formed a small group of artists, students and other non-art-school friends of literary tastes—and members of the Impressionists. White-bearded and black eye-browed Pissarro sat at a table with G., and bowler-hatted, checked-trousered Lautrec chatted to me. Scruffy Van Gogh glowered as Gauguin, in beret (we too had arrived back from Paris with berets) and striped shirt, bewitched some of our own art School models. The older members of this profession, who had been interesting anatomically, but hardly aesthetically, had now been replaced by a new group of younger women whose appearance when portrayed had some semblance of style and beauty, of which we made the most artistically.

My café drawings were unfortunately bought from me almost as soon as finished; and I have known someone rent a room in Brighton years later and tell me that one of them hung on the wall. Of course, these had been sold for minute prices, as I did not regard myself as a professional mature painter in business, but more as somebody just discovering it all—which was certainly the correct approach.

In the evenings, after the life class, we would visit a fish and chip shop and return to the studio; where we would set up still life groups of fish, or prawns and a pipe, or a bunch of flowers in an empty milk bottle, and paint them by the light of an oil lamp, which gave a striking contrast—even if the yellows were

subsequently over-toned by daylight. The gramophone played *Leave the Dishes in the sink, Ma,* or *My Mama's in Town,* from the bands of Spike Jones or Ted Lewis, and the hours went by. Next morning we were at Art School by nine-thirty as usual, after a walk along the seafront, or perhaps a swim in the King Alfred baths. We painted mainly over the Victorian canvases that were on sale so cheaply, repainting the elaborate gold baroque of the huge frames with white or grey or suitably tinted undercoat; providing immediately upon completion of a picture a setting in which it could be at once hung on the wall. In this way the two rooms of the studio became like the Jeu de Paume in no time at all, to the amazement of the little old man who lived on the floor below—a Boer War veteran who would come up and sing and dance to us if not circumvented.

Victorian art was its lowest apogee; and I have seen the porters of Museums round in the back yards breaking up Victorian frames and ripping canvases to pieces, just to get the cellars free of all the rotting rubbish. " 'im upstairs says they ain't no use no more—help yourself—" but I didn't want to get involved. Years later I commented to a London dealer who was exhibiting some Victorian masterpieces (by now re-evaluated) that some of the pictures in this loan exhibition were in remarkably good condition. "Those are the ones that have been in private collections," he said. "The ones from museums were left in cellars and next to radiators in the Thirties and Forties, presumably in the hope they would disintegrate, and they usually did. Makes plenty of work and a lot of difficulty for the restorers these days."

Early the next year our group put on an exhibition, and were interested to read the comments from the local press. I had now moved into using a palette-knife only. A local firm had developed a range of "Decorator's Colours," in huge tubes, very cheaply, and one could spread this like butter with remarkable effect. I painted a good many pictures, but have none left so cannot say how the paint has fared with the years. After the manner of one's early works and possessions, they have all disappeared—jettisoned as not good enough, abandoned in old studios, given away, one or two sold—but in general now non-existent. One cannot keep with you forever all the articles and pictures and studio equipment one collects. It is carried from place to place on barrows, with the help of friends, when one is young. Later, one can have no option but to leave whole sections of your life's work to be collected by the dustman, or taken to the tip. I have had many studios, and have left the whole contents at times in a building which was to be demolished, including frames, Victorian furniture, and collections of books and ephemera. I have left work too long deposited in the houses of others which have also, in turn, been demolished. An artist needs a permanent warehouse. The exhibition was reviewed by the young critic of the local daily paper—then Derek Granger—who commented that there was much evidence of palette-knife and brush handle in my work, but did not seem otherwise to totally dismiss it.

I had seen an exhibition of American Art at the Tate a year or so earlier, and the paintings of John Sloan, Edward Hopper and the Ashcan school had been an inspiration. The atmospheric city etchings of Martin Lewis had also added to my vision. The late-night loneliness of an unpicturesque city has a great deal of strange attraction—somewhat of the atmosphere of the Edward G. Robinson Fritz Lang classic *The Woman in the Window*. The young relate to the late night, as they are seldom tired. We also admired, in the Illustration group, the collection of Ben Shahn's paintings that came to Brighton—they had formed one of the excellent series of Penguin Modern Painter monograms that had brought Piper, Pasmore, Paul Nash, Spencer, Burra, Bawden and others to a wider consciousness in the public of British contemporary painting. The Ben Shahns exemplified Leslie Cole's dictum of shape and texture, plus presenting a message both social and acidic. The stark detachment from sentiment, despite the inherent sympathy, was appealing, and I was soon to commence a sideline of such pictures, as it were, that employed such stark social images and a formalised style of approach. These were to be quite separate to and different from my work made from life; and I have always continued to make them from images that had struck me forcibly—basically, as an enjoyment.

In this student period one liked to try everything; and an exhibition at the Art School of facsimile reproductions from Seurat's chalk drawings sent us into imitations of his cloudy blurred manner that yet made the form even more solid: his famous dots would seem to have been suggested by the surface effect of the chalk on the heavily grained paper. I had sold several of my etchings at our exhibition, but was about to give up this interest totally for some years. I had taken my National Diploma in Illustration, and now left the Art School, without taking the final teaching practice year, in order to commence (as I had always intended) my profession as a free-lance artist—very possibly the most difficult and potentially disappointing career (though it is really a dedication) that one can follow. My final work on copper was a series of drypoint studies of a frog from the art school pond, whom I brought into the etching room and placed in a dish of water. I was now painting with one of our circle—she had been a student in the wood-carving class I had attended—in her attic studio in a high Victorian house, the lower floors almost all occupied by very old ladies, each in separate rented rooms. The ground floor resident wore her hair in a sort of netted beehive—she had enormous slippers, and usually carried a great brown cat. Whenever any of us mounted the staircase—which was pretty continuously—she would appear at the end of the passage, muttering "Up and Down, Up and Down!" There was a cheerful arthritic who could only move upstairs on all fours, and would take half-an hour getting her slop-pails up to the bath-room on the next floor to empty them in the convenience there; placing the pail on the step ahead, then pulling herself up, then advancing the pail, and so on. Her room was large and dark, and hung with her own paintings, made as a student in the Edwardian era. One day a black and white kitten attached itself to us on the sea-front, and followed us back. It stayed from then on, and appeared in many paintings, including a portrait study which was later reproduced in the *Studio* magazine.

It is interesting that young artists so often find themselves in such close contact with the aged poor, who have not succeeded in life, for one reason or other—not necessarily due to their own faults, but life is not a kind affair. Young artists and these aged poor are the two facets of existence to whom cheap rents are the essential. I recall an old man, always in an ancient mackintosh and cloth cap; his room uncarpeted—kitchen table—colourless wallpaper— dangling light-flex, glaring bulb, no shade. All the romance of Pinter—the evening paper with the racing results, and a large Alsatian dog. Rembrandtian subjects everywhere. In some ways, it is an advantage for the artist to remain unsuccessful himself for as long as possible. It is the only period in his life when he has time to look, and is surrounded with inspiration. He is not obliged perpetually to satisfy an increasing demand, which only increases even more when he raises his prices to lessen it.

I was given a commission to illustrate, with some sixty tailpieces and vignettes, *A Dorset Anthology*; and this kind of applied work was something I had been trained to accomplish; otherwise I roamed the South Coast and the countryside making pen and watercolour drawings, with an increasing freedom, from Worthing to Rottingdean. I drew in the beaches among the sunbathers, adding chalks and coloured inks to attain the strongest effects. I drew under the piers—the struts under the minarets above—and sketched the arrival of the steamer through the rain from the end of the pier as she approached. I drew furiously as the ship drove against the ironwork, seemingly holding herself there unwillingly, before rushing off again, paddles trundling, like a fractious beast. I sold most of these efforts, regrettably enough, instead of keeping them not only as valuable studies for later reference, but as fragments of a past time to be preserved for the future when their subjects should be no more. But I needed money for my work to continue, and I was pleased at the time that people wanted my pictures.

The pictures that I did not sell—no one would have wanted them—were the stark formal paintings that I worked on in the studio. I began with a canvas of the old woman I had seen in Switzerland in 1947, turning her into fierce shapes, her hands a frustrated cat's-cradle. She was set in the bare boards of her home, with a window showing dismal dark mountains—more tantalising to the one who cannot escape, even though the doors are open, because age and incapacity prohibits it, and the cage has become home. A cheap religious card—consolation tacked on the wall—the only approach to decoration. I went on to paint other Swiss subjects—a family at supper—gathered dispassionately around a long table; the old lady preoccupied with the cat—the father engrossed with a newspaper—the young man brooding, his back to the wide

open mountainscape seen through the window; and, leaning on the sill, a girl lost in dreams as she contemplates the distance and again ponders Escape. Brooding and melancholic, obsessed with her seething imaginative yearnings (although outwardly thoughtlessly mild and merely pretty) she appeared in several subsequent pictures. Later, I was to discover her in real life. These black-clad people, bound by custom into the circumscribed regularity of their existences, re-enacting their Mediaeval forbears over and over, were stared at and contemplated for many hours, and often destroyed as having missed the evanescent point of their creation, or even overstated it. I painted the street below the studio, the black trees, the old ladies and cats who were such a feature of it; I painted various small canvases of old ladies' heads—from memory, from careful observation of the subject. This observation could, however, be made in a moment. With practice, the eye once inspired takes in at snapshot speed all that it requires; and as the brush is taken up all comes out like a positive print.

In other Swiss subjects black-garbed women worked in the fields as I had seen them, their skirts black and grey striped, Breughellian, as no one will ever see them again. I worked on canvas sanded smooth, or hand-applied and built-up gesso on panel. Sometimes I drew in first with pen and ink, then adding oil paint with white undercoat as the medium and thinner. I had been interested in the great exhibition held of the Munich Collection; and Cranach's nude with violin suggested a line to follow; though the picture I made was a self-portrait with a cat, tall and thin, in which I wear the Tobacco Tie—a batique creation I had bought in the Rue de Rivoli, and which included pipes

and cigars in a pleasing colour scheme of yellows, greys and browns—colours I too tended to employ for these works, leaving the vivid primaries for pictures made direct from the bright spectrum of Brighton beach, or Sussex sunset light on cattle—which demands an intense palette.

In order to make money, we painted Watteau-like vignettes of flowers and ribbons and country implements on imitation antiques for a local dealer; we painted Dutch flower pieces on old canvases, and toned and varnished them; and at times the studio was filled with bright new children's wardrobes and chests-of-drawers, on which—for a local store—we painted Mickey Mouse and Donald Duck motifs. All this sadly took away from art; but I sold some watercolours—mainly, my earlier Paris ones—and set off, in 1950, once more for that engrossing city.

Chapter 5

I found that Paris had changed a good deal, simmered down; and a relaxed atmosphere had taken the place of the bartering desperation of but two years earlier. I took a room at a pension near the Place d'Alésia. It was a kind of flat-iron building, on a sharp corner, with a small triangular enclosed garden at the front, with trees and old railings. The dining room led through French windows into this garden—a fine subject for Bonnard or the tasteful Vuillard, and was floored with black and white tiles on which were placed marble-topped iron tables. In the rooms upstairs were huge wardrobes and gigantic double beds with a single cement-hard bolster. With tall shuttered long windows, and a small balcony, one could scarcely have created a better setting for a film set of the life of an artist in Paris. From here, when not sketching from the window, I made my daily sorties, walking from dawn endlessly around Paris; stopping to make watercolour drawings wherever I might find myself, with no one to please but myself. Consequently, I made each day like a week, as I never rested. I studied art in all the museums, and particularly liked both Picasso's early umber cubism, and a flowing grey black and yellow decorative subject of interconnecting loops, in the Museé d'Art Moderne. *Guernica* was for some reason on exhibition, and I thought it a wonderful disposition of shapes; though it didn't occur to me what the subject meant; I found it far from savage, but aesthetically gentle and pleasing. I assumed it was an arrangement—as meaningless subjectwise as modern art had taught us to expect of its productions. As Picasso's domestic subjects also employed the same technique of jagged broken shapes and flowing lines, it did not occur to me that this was a savage indictment of violence anymore than was the *Night fishing at Antibes*; which I suppose was a curious lack of receptivity perhaps on my part. I saw an exhibition of abstract sculpture—painted scaffolding poles prefiguring perhaps the Pompidou Centre of a later decade, and I wandered about the vastness of Les Halles in the early morning. In those days, we in England knew little of the Social Realists who were working at their best at this point, but whose fame was to fade almost as soon as recognised with the advent of the new large American abstract vogue; a replacement not unconnected with the political situation. But although I had read in the *Studio* magazine's excellent and informative pages (I had taken it since 1945) which included a letter from Paris, fate did not take me near any works on display by Rebeyrolle, Lorjou, Simone Dat or even Bernard Buffet. Les Hommes Témoin were not witnessed by me, unfortunately; I was still learning from what *had* been painted, annotated, and museumed. Young artists tend to find what they need—they come across, apparently by chance, what they are looking for, and I spent many hours in the Louvre, looking at Gericault—not far off the Social Realist scene himself. I liked his fascination for the macabre—the still-life studies of guillotined heads, the portraits of madmen in the asylum: they were at least not simpering and ingratiating best frock portrait commissions. There were certain portraits, nonetheless—by no means bizarre—that yet stood for me as examples to see and see again: Raphael's *Castiglione*; the three wonderful Ingres portraits of the Rivière family, and his M. Bertin; David's Madame Sérizat . . . these were the acme of the genre. In the Jeu de Paume once more, I looked at Boudin and the early Monet. I looked up at Rodin's great Balzac as I toured the streets, and went again to see the collection in his studio, and admire the different versions, nude and draped, of the Balzac figure as it progressed toward the great swooping upwards final state. As an admirer of sculpture, I was an early viewer of Epstein's Smuts when it was set on its plinth in Parliament Square—the letters to the Times doubtful of its ever being accepted as were the other statues; but now it is difficult to see it as differing particularly from its neighbours.

I admired the Delaunay Eiffel Tower paintings, and went at once to immortalise it myself in pen and coloured inks—observing that it does indeed appear—if you draw it from beneath—to bend, because you have to alter your angle of vision to see the top, and so get a different centre point of perspective.

My paintings of stylised figures had all been of what are called cabinet dimensions; approx. 24×20″ was my favourite size canvas. My last work become coming to Paris had been a grey *Industrial Crucifixion* with the cross being made of iron girders. This was inevitably an imaginative concept, but in general I liked to work from an image seen rather than imagined . . . something that prodded itself on the retina of the inner eye. I would recognise a kind of

michael Blaha
Seine - Tour Eiffel - et quinze état
Paris 50 une moderne

99

super-perception, a timeless moment that in fact only lasted for a second. Advancing down an avenue of pavement trees from the Lion de Belfort was a figure on crutches, hopping slowly, feet missing, ankles bound with rags—a gay striped shirt on his back in jazzy opposition to his truly terrible situation . . .

As I emerge from a second-hand book shop, a person goes by whom I recognise in some ways as the sister of the old Poschiavina, except that her profile is made of rubbery curves rather than sliced slabs. The black headscarf, the hump, the yellow ivory of the aged skin—"she who was once the helmet-maker's beautiful wife"—the large slippers with huge round grey pom-poms; the long loaf clutched under her arm—fresh bread that would be stale and hard by tomorrow, like a speeded-up symbol, as significant of transience as herself. . . .

For a while a ceaseless downpour prevented all expeditions. I had already bought a stock of paint and canvas; using one of the chairs as an easel in my satisfactorily typical and impersonal room, I began to pin down some of these images that were so anxious to get themselves recreated in pictorial form. The rain curtained the street from me—the tall window with its iron balcony, the huge old pieces of furniture, were no interruption to my preoccupied hours of work. . . .

When the rain stopped and the sun came out again I went to the Jeu de Paume, where Renoir, Van Gogh and Monet shimmered like old friends trying to catch one's eye. I hesitated for a while at the Douanier Rousseau—his patterning, his almost Flemish approach had an appeal; but his basic incapacity, despite the tremendous lack of uncertainty, seemed a dangerous element to absorb into one's style. I liked Monet's figures on the crests of hills, fuzzy close-ups in the palest of lilac tints—I enjoyed the easy pleasures of Renoir's *Moulin de la Galette*. But I left these artists at last for yet another drink at the Louvre. . . .

One morning I found myself outside the Grande Chaumière art school and in curiosity went in. One studio had a model sitting whose interest went beyond that of a mere plaster cast capable of movement. He was a dark, skinny little old man, with an immense black beard and wild hair. I had no need to stay longer. Abandoning my watercolours for the day, I went back to the pension and painted him from memory, against a black background, like a captured biological specimen. I had been drawing near Sacré Coeur, covering all the traditional settings as well as my own discoveries, when I felt a chill come upon me as if by bewitchment. With head spinning, I groped my way into the back of a café and ordered four pots of tea, which I sipped one after the other until I fell into a terrible sweat. When the haze settled down again and I could see the tables and drinkers clearly once more, I went out, quite cured. As I passed the entrance to Sacre Coeur a cadaverous priest passed me, his mouth open, his eyes turned upwards . . . I painted him as I saw him, contrasted with two more jovial clerics, their skirts creating volutes beneath which their black boots skimmed happily. I have made several subsequent versions of this subject, over long periods of time; and should still like to paint it the size of life.

When I eventually left Paris to return to Brighton my load of art works was a heavy one. I had about seventy watercolours, and a bundle of canvases kept apart by wooden discs with a nail protruding from each side. I left all this below, and went up on deck. It was exceedingly rough, and the returning holidaymakers who had been happily guzzling in the saloon while we were at Dieppe were now in a sorry state. I seemed to float up and down the steps and companionways while keeping a hand on the stair-rail, such was the extent of the rolling. Passengers were turning a peculiar green, a real painter's green; some sprawling about deck in the water pouring in and out of the scuppers seemed unconscious, and were being slowly collected up by stewards from the alternating slopes of planking, and hauled below. Eventually, I seemed to be the only one on the deck, hanging on to a great iron ring. The ship gave a mighty leap, and I was at once in the air, coat flapping, new hat whirled away, but still I may say holding the ring. At this I went below at the next interval between the waves. At Newhaven, passengers were being taken ashore on stretchers.

. . . . .

When I returned to Brighton the setting of my home town seemed less inspiring than I had supposed. I felt the need of being alone to think and write, and moved into a room in a picturesque old mews. The first night in this room I was lying in my bed beneath the window, with the rain rattling against it. I heard the sound of the sash slowly pulled down—was it some burglar? Half asleep, I sat up—immediately a heavy weight, evidently alive, crashed on me. It was a cat—who had habitually returned this way from nocturnal adventures while the room had been vacant. The second disturbance was a mouse in the basin used for washing. The mouse had fallen in the bowl, and was racing round and round endlessly, like a wall of death rider, apparently in the hope of creating sufficient impetus to rise to the top.

Once, walking home to my studio in the mews, I was accosted by an elderly lady, who asked me to climb her fire-escape and open the kitchen door at the top, as she had mislaid the front door key. Thoughtlessly obliging, I climbed up the rusty old iron spiral. At the top I paused—stepped on the final platform, and then for some happy reason stepped quickly back to the top step. At the same moment, like the drop of a gallows, the whole grating—rusted through at the ends of the bars—fell straight down six stories into the yard. I climbed over the void, opened the door as requested, and went down to let the old lady in at the front door. One wonders how many long unused fire-escapes await only to precipitate fleeing would-be survivors more swiftly to the ground than they might expect.

On my return from Paris I had gone down to Swanage for a week or so and made watercolour drawings of Studland, Paul Nash's Ballard Point, and the donkeys on the sand. Together with some rather bolder studies of the downs, these provided the basis for some new experiments in painting from drawings—using them in fact as studies. However, this approach seemed basically false to me at the time, and insufficiently vital for what I considered to be of most value—absolute intensity in the formation of the image; and I scrapped them all, and began to move into a cubist-futurist manner of sharp movement and semi abstract paintings and sculptures.

I had spent a considerable amount of time prior to my Paris expedition in going round the galleries of the London dealers. The Gimpel Gallery (then in South Molton Street) had shown several works by members of our circle the previous year, subsequent to our exhibition. I suppose perhaps twenty-two is a somewhat youthful age—Charles Gimpel said to me that, "in Paris, an artist is regarded as young until he is forty, and is not expected to have formed a mature style until then." He had in fact encouraged me in going to Paris, suggesting that I might learn something about art there. On my return I took to show him a semi-cubist picture I was rather pleased with, ignoring the fact that—like most people—what he had liked and shown were my pen and watercolour pictures. The cubist canvas was of a card party, with all the players split into transparent facets so that all the forms of people and table and cards were also visible as a surface pattern. It was extremely intricate.

"Wyndham Lewis would have liked that, "Charles Gimpel remarked; adding inconsequentially—"he was in here five minutes ago. You only just missed him."

To have missed Wyndham Lewis has always been one of my great tragedies of absence of experience—so to speak. I once missed a drawing of his, as well, to add yet another grain of salt to the wound. It was a beautiful pencil portrait, female, marked ten and sixpence among a box of reproductions marked down in a second-hand book shop. I could scarcely believe my good luck. It was too much. I hesitated, took a slight walk around for five minutes—and it was gone.

. . . . .

I took my Paris drawings to G. S. Whittet of the *Studio* Magazine. He was always encouraging and sympathetic, and had reproduced pictures by members of our group that I had taken to him after our show. Now he reproduced my watercolour drawing of the back of the Musée d'Art Moderne in full colour—an exciting experience for me. I took work to show Oliver Brown at the Leicester Galleries—one of the most interesting places in London. I nearly bought a Whistler etching of la Mère Gerard there for four pounds, framed; but then for four pounds you could spend a week in Paris. I exhibited in the well-regarded Artists of Fame and Promise summer shows at this gallery, where you could see works by the leading British artists, including William Scott, whose kitchen table images of saucepans and frying pans were highly admired by the cognoscenti. . . The Redfern also took some work—café subjecs that included cloth and silver paper collage. Based on actual places, one was the *Chien qui Fume*, with the sign of the dog smoking a pipe. Charles Gimpel sent me down to the newly opened Marlborough Gallery—they were looking for artists at this point, and Harry Fischer asked me to paint some London oils for a show they were soon to have. But by a twist of fate I thought they would look better under glass; and this coming into contact with the still wet paint in the carrier's van, they were ruined and so not included, and the association lapsed.

The founder and director of Goya Perfumes, D. R. Collins, saw some of my watercolours, bought them, and subsequently selected a whole series of my Brighton and Paris watercolour drawings. He also introduced me to the celebrated Jack Beddington (then of Coleman, Prentis and Varley) who had been instrumental in commissioning, in the Nineteen-Thirties, the young and advanced artists of the time to create posters for Shell-Mex. He had produced M.O.I. films during the war years—films that set a standard unusually high for that period. Jack Beddington bought one of my Paris watercolours—of the Arc de Triomphe—an interior of the old church at Shoreham, that I had done there while sheltering from the rain while out sketching; and later on a study of the Élite Café. "I'll look at your pictures," he said, taking the portfolio; "and you look at mine." There was a select exhibition of his collection around the walls of his office—small pictures, in wide frames that had been coloured to suit the subjects and treatment. There was a Sam Rabin, and a Mary Kessel, I recollect. "I see you're looking at my newest acquisition," he said: "I was very pleased to get that." It was a fine James Pryde, typical, and not too large. At the sale after his death I saw one of my watercolours auctioned with the rest at Christie's. Many of the artists he had bought from were in the sales room, looking on.

I showed my work to Dr. Roland and to Delbanco, who laughed at my café scenes and said, "I find them very funny; but I could not sell them." However, he showed me the upper room where the richer patrons were introduced to the jewels of the collection, sat me in the grand chair before a kind of stage set, and then placed a luxuriously framed Boudin or something of that quality on the small easel, and directed the spotlights upon it. *"That's* how we do it," he said.

Only one gallery in London appeared to be representing the new French Realists, and that was the Adams Gallery, where one could see marvellous works by Minaux, one of the very finest of them. There was one huge canvas of a dead stag hanging in a butcher's shop—they favoured such subjects, as being both Real and also—if one looked at things that way—in some way symbolic of an existentialist acceptance of the state of nothingness; the concept that we are perhaps spinning through dead space in a totally void universe. This idea to me seemed on the whole more comforting (being true) than the miasma of literary and religious spiritual pseudo-comfort and would-be psychic dogma, ceremony and belief that has enslaved the minds of the world since the Attic gods, but many people found it depressing and unfaceable. The dealer at Adams said no one seemed to like the French Realists at all. They just didn't catch on. Their landscapes were black and rainy; it was always half-winter, without even the picturesqueness of a snowfall; Rebeyrolle, with his *Trout*, came the nearest to being liked, and then for the wrong reasons—their works were not meant to be sporting pictures. Eventually these artists grew sweet, perhaps in desperation, and it all vanished. But I have always admired them at their best—de Gallard, Simone Dat, and the others.

But in England it was Festival of Britain time, and not the moment to be gloomily philosophic! Everything was Blake and Palmer romanticism—Sutherland was in the ascendant; and delicate architectural fantasies—half-sculpture, half-engineering, that bordered on whimsy and were not that far away from Emett's trains (also included), were the art of the day.

An exhibition of Bernard Buffet—extraordinary and powerful images that appeared to be black ink on greaseproof paper stuck to cardboard, attacked with a vigour and enthusiasm alien to an English artist, was almost laughed out of the country. Critics and public likened him to Ronald Searle, without the jokes. It was all rather sad, particularly as Buffet's spidery crucifixions and still life groups with a bottle and an automatic pistol did in a sense wryly satirise even themselves.

It is curious that years later, when his series of deserted Paris streets and townscapes—obvious satire again, as they took the most obvious of postcard views (rather like his master Utrillo) to gloomify—were themselves published as postcard views, they were immensely popular with English visitors. But you must not take liberties with the human image, in England—it is the centre of the universe, and we take it personally.

A notable character in Hove in those days was one Hugh Willoughby, an elderly but lively collector of Picasso paintings and drawings. He had built up this treasure-cave in the Thirties; had gone to Paris as a youth, become a bootblack, he told me, a newsboy; he had gradually worked himself up the business scale, buying and selling works by the modern masters. He came to our exhibition, and made me look at a huge volume of all Picasso's Blue Period, which he claimed were the only real School of art for a painter—forget the Art Colleges, he advised. I had reservations about this, considering the standard of Picasso's albeit much publicised draughtmanship, but recollecting Canova's observation that the English see with their ears, was careful not to be too influenced by my new acquaintance. However, I passed many enjoyable hours talking with him about these pictures hung round the walls of his flat; and when he died it was strange to see the pictures first in Sotheby's, and then to come across them in various dealers' galleries, awaiting the next collection to which they would be added—the very works beneath which one had sat, glass in hand, discoursing upon the artist's intentions and philosophy. Pictures are always turning up in odd places to give you time-jolts like that—even, much later on, a Klimt in an exhibition in Vienna, that one had supposed was safe in the National Gallery at Trafalgar Square, and not fleeing back to its homeland.

I had painted in many styles during my experimental year in the room in the mews—it had a picturesque effect like a stage-set, with a wooden staircase up to a wooden gallery that ran around the side of a triangle of old stables. The rooms, wood-boarded, had been stable-lofts; below, there were now garages. When it rained the roof would leak in several places, and one's security was at an end, with pails and saucepans placed everywhere. I had gone through modernism now, and was finally up to Social Realism. I spent whole nights painting, unhurried by anyone, the world black and quiet outside, and time pacing itself for me as I chose. I painted a dead hare—fish—subjects I had tried before, but with the aesthetic of Chardin.

Now, I preferred to give my subjects a more solemn treatment, and to see them symbolically.

Of course, if one wished to see it, the beach around the corner was full of summer bathers, in travel-poster cheerfulness of hue. The Realist concept had really nothing to do with Reality. All comes alive in sunshine, and all is drab in rain. One is taken in charge by the aesthetic you select, apparently as a free agent, but in fact a cultural slave.

In July '51 Foyles Art Gallery in Charing Cross Road gave me an exhibition of paintings, drawings, watercolours and sculpture—a résumé of my work of the past two years since leaving art school. At that time the gallery covered the whole top floor of the building. The press and art magazines were cautious,

mixing admiration with admonition. "Not one artist but a dozen," complained (with cause) the *Art News and Review*—this was the art newspaper that really held the art world together in those days. I would have done a great deal better to have narrowed down my exhibits to a few in one style, and aimed at building a reputation for one manner at a time. But to the artist in his early twenties time seems short, paradoxically enough. He wants to show what he has done, and be off to new discoveries. I sold a number of pictures—the exhibition was opened in a grand manner by the celebrated actress Margaret Leighton, and various theatrical personages were also present.

Derek Granger came up to review the exhibition for the Brighton press. I had included a painting of a bird show in the Hove Town Hall that had included (by virtue of the wings) a fruit bat, or flying fox, that rather enjoyed, upside down, to be tickled under the chin—from above. I had put this engaging creature into my semi-abstract. My severe critic felt that this was carried out with "great resource"; although in my *Lady with a Poodle* the "intended effect— presumably one of dramatic grotesquerie—slips unwittingly into caricature." However, the *Arts News and Review* critic found this "although intensely mannered, well-designed and individual." I was flattered to be the recipient of these varying opinions, but felt it was time I lived in London in order to be more continuously close to what a capital city can offer, both in experience and opportunity. Shortly before I left, the young man whose small garage business was beneath my studio was killed by a car-jack—a shaky affair I had often contemplated dubiously—sliding down the slope leaving the wheel-less car to drop down upon him. I came into the mews just in time to see him being carried away on a stretcher, blue and still, like a dead crusader on a tomb. It was a dismal ending to my stay there. I sold my dinghy, and with the small sum it fetched, set off for London. I took with me the painter and sculptress with whom I had worked and exhibited for the past two years or so, and a banjo, which I felt might perhaps save us if pressed to the point of total poverty. I had begun to learn chords (although I tuned it to a guitar and played those formations) and the jazz revival had already commenced in Brighton with a jazz club, to which we often went, and with various concerts in the Hove Town Hall and elsewhere.

Although Brighton had by now recovered its pre-war appearance and to all intents and purposes even the utility period we were still actually in appeared never to have happened, with flags flying and bunting on the pleasure boats vying for custom with the familiar chant of "Moderboadgoing," London (once you were off the main streets) was a very different matter. It was even more run down than the streets below Brighton Station which were the happy haunts of the seeker after junk-shops. One was in the drab greyness of existence in London—still in the Nineteenth Century, in fact. Yet, the bed and breakfast houses also gave one the Nineteenth Century treatment. We might still be in the jug and bowl and pail era with a washstand in the bedroom (that had been my facility in the mews also), and it was a good idea always to look in the jug and see that it wasn't growing mould due to a week or so of not being changed—but you also got a Nineteenth Century breakfast. Kippers, cornflakes, tea, as much toast and marmalade as you wanted . . . and all for a few shillings. We lived in these establishments for as long as possible—Sickert interiors every one, with views from attic windows straight out of the *Death of Chatterton*. I delighted to wake in London and lean from such a window, watching the smoke from the roofscape chimneys—so erratic in their construction, so irreplaceable once demolished. London meant slate roofs, from the moment the train approached Victoria, with the sun glinting golden—blindingly, if there had been recent rain—and then the dark wet effect drying out to variations of deep green to palest lilac. This phenomenon was a visual treat in Brighton also, weather-wise; from the eminence above the railway the sun reflecting on the west-facing wet slate roofs after rain would provide a kind of vast mirror of blinding gold—like a glorious omnipotent manifestation informing the world that the storm was over. With the advent of tower blocks and tiles, this effect was abandoned by the obliging aesthetic elements.

By day, in London, we looked at galleries, and sought for part-time work—the eternal pre-requisite of the young artist—so that we could rent a studio, and paint for the rest of the day. We did not wish to be sucked into some occupation that would dominate our time and slowly mould us into something else. But nothing turned up, and we began to conserve funds; gave up the comfortable living, and spent the nights in the Lyons Corner House in the Strand that stayed open all night. The smokey room was emptied every three hours and the great crowd of seemingly homeless characters would all drift in a group (in order to keep warm) up the Mall and down again to return for the next session and another cup of coffee. The restaurant was a recognised meeting place for various groups of friends, and a warm camaraderie was established, in spite of the waiters pointedly waking anyone who fell asleep across the table. Occasionally somebody would set off a firework that mingled with the clouds of tobacco exhalation, and caused general alarm and amusement. In the Mall, in those chill hours between 2 and 4 a.m. of a November night, one could meet the four greatcoated soldiers, with heavy bearskins, an officer and a lantern, making their regular duty pilgrimage from the Palace, on foot, to the City and back in obedience to a custom of some centuries standing—as they explained when we accosted them. Sometimes we went to Victoria Station, where, if you presented yourselves just before the gates were drawn across and locked, the gateman would let you sleep (or doze away) the hours between 1 and 5 a.m. in the waiting room; where, comforting oneself with the glow of sunshine depicted in a poster of a Cross-Channel steamer sailing to France upon a summer sea, one was at least in the dry, in the company of various other tramps and vagabonds and sometimes the occasional genuine traveller who had missed the last train. These amateurs endured the night sitting stiffly upright, looking woefully miserable, while the others sprawled and snored in indifferent abandonment to their circumstances, their chests padded with old newspapers under their coats.

The longest time of the day was in the early morning; when the long grey-yellow light of a dawn that seemed so long in arriving made one shiver in the damp, standing at Piccadilly Circus watching the glittering reflections of the lights in the puddles go out one by one. Both Lyons and the waiting rooms finally ejected you at dawn, and there was a dismal interval before the Lyons opened at Marble Arch and you could go there for a grilled mackerel or herring with mustard sauce—an economic meal advertised as the cheapest breakfast in London. Then, a wash and brush-up; if you hadn't been able to afford any breakfast you could go down to the Tate when it opened and use the newly restored facilities there—probably the cleanest in London.

Eventually, an idea struck us, and we applied to the British Museum Reading Room to see if they would employ us. I was interviewed by somebody I think in retrospect must have been Angus Wilson; he said I was over-qualified for the job of a Reading-Room clerk, and with my artistic experience I would never stand it; but he was amused, and let us try. We were employed as Temporary Civil Service Clerks Grade III. The day's work would be over at 3.30 in the afternoon, and we would receive three pounds, fifteen shillings and two pounds seventeen and sixpence a week respectively, less tax. I found myself seated at a desk all day in company with a room full of similar clerks. We all read books from the shelves most of the time; and waited for a sufficient number of requests to fall into the tray from the tube on our right to make it worthwhile journeying to look for them. When these had mounted into a respectable sheaf, we took a trolley, if necessary, and wheeled it out of the yard and descended to the cavernous vaulted cellars, where bundles of magazines and journals sat, still awaiting classification and filing. We were issued with torches, but no one had provided a battery. Old leather was considered hard wear for clothes—"don't dress in anything good," an old clerk advised me—"the Eighteenth Century bindings are fatal."

Lying along the cellar corridor, dusty and neglected, was the enormous North American Toten Pole that now fills the well of the North staircase, cleaned of stubbed out cigarette ends and grandly resurrected. Hoa-Haka-Nana-La (now deprived of his name) no longer broods over the entrance hall at the foot of the main staircase as he used; he is now an inmate of the Museum of Mankind behind the Royal Academy; but every morning on arrival at the British Museum, I would enjoy greeting this giant Easter Island statue, with a friendly nod. These perennial sculptures, that outlast all lifetimes ("thine also mighty Nineveh?" to quote the Rossetti poem on the theme—an interesting reflection) are a permanently comforting image, in some ways. Two bronze life-size dogs sit at the entrance to St. George's, Hanover Square—for forty years I have given them a pat while passing.

Having found the books, we would load our trolleys, return to the surface, and wheel the books across to the main building, dodging the rain. The waiting readers were always complaining, particularly at the fact of having to come back in a week's time for their required volumes; but it often took some hours to find what was wanted, and all the books between O and P had been blown away by a bomb that had hit the Dome at one point. Between the curved ceiling of the Reading Room and the outside skin were the bulk of the books—tier upon tier, miles of shelving. One got to them by a series of iron stairs and corridors called the Catwalks. Looking up or down you could see through the bars and struts other clerks four or five tiers above or below. It was rather like the Brighton piers.

I spent a good deal of time on the "Tube." One sat in the booth in the centre, took requests and inserted them in a metal canister that at the touch of a lever was sent under air pressure through to the waiting (or reading) clerks, in the same way as the change went to the cashier in old draperies of the period which often still used this method, or that of a capsule flying on a wheel on wires above the customers' heads. Some of the staff of the museum had been employed for a surprising number of years. The old doorman had sat here since before the Boer war, quietly, while history went on outside the gates—"1895, I came here, as a boy . . ." he said, sipping his tea. We lived for a while in a suspicious establishment in Coram Street, full of threadbare once flashy red carpets, where the overnight inmates changed rapidly and couples entered all day and night . . . leaving this somewhat unrespectable house I discovered, after much tramping the streets, a two roomed flat in Notting Hill, for three pounds fifteen shillings per week. It was expensive but excellent. A little Parisian balcony gave a romantic quality to the tall window, and one could crawl out onto the roof leads through panels in the sloping walls and see the classic dome of the cinema behind the chimney-scape. On Sunday mornings I would paint studies of the red sun hanging in the mist, or versions from memory of the Reading Room with its varied patrons. Sunday afternoons we spent at the Tate, studying the English School: Paul Nash, Spencer, Wyndham Lewis; Augustus John's marvellous great mural study of Galway peasants— and, of course, the Pre-Raphaelites. As the day darkened, it was interesting to see the tones of the paintings alter and stand out with greater or lesser effect before the lights were switched on. The prevalence in many galleries in later days for exhibiting paintings under a static lighting system certainly deprives one of this pleasure of enjoying one's favourite pictures under different circumstances.

One night at Pembridge Gardens we were awakened by the sound of engines and water. We crawled through the skylight out onto the parapet above the front of the house. A room on the first floor of a hotel opposite was a mass of flames—fire-engines were pouring water into it with little effect. One by one, the lights in the houses of the curving street went on, as person after person awoke to the unfamiliar sounds. A necklace of lights—progression like the pyres that warned of the Armada; heads peered from windows, sashes rattled up. The overnight tenant who had fallen asleep smoking did not survive, although the fire was eventually successfully confined to his room.

The landlady was a pleasant lady, alone in the world as a result of some tragedy. Her son had died young, and at Xmas she made a display of his toys on the hall table, on a cottonwool base to simulate snow. The panorama of toy soldiers and farm animals greeted you on entry. She invited us in for a seasonal drink, and the atmosphere of the house was individual and comfortable, more so than that of an earlier one where we had lived, in which the residents seemed long-staying but poverty-stricken. One of them was an old foreign gentleman whom we used to see also at the British Museum. "My friends say I must have been a bookworm in an earlier life," he said—"I spend so much of my time there."

Whenever, in these later days, I order a book from under the same soaring dome of the same Reading room, or stand perusing the same old pasted-in catalogues, I have the sense of detachment from the world outside as one felt then. It was easy and pleasant work; but one day at the corner of Bond Street we saw a card in a window advertising a cellar for rent, at eight pounds a week. It was carpeted, impressive, newly decorated—it would have made an excellent little gallery. We thought about it for a fatal hour, but returned to find it taken. Fired with the idea we went across directly to White, Druce and Brown in Hanover Square opposite. We warmed ourselves before the open fire in the Georgian fireplace of these offices—fine buildings now demolished—explained our requirements and after some thought a drawer was opened, and a large key produced. A Victorian clerk appeared and we were taken over to nearby Avery Row, just behind New Bond Street and shown two rooms on the first floor front, that we could have for £2. 5s. a week. The ceiling had collapsed at one end, and I was obliged to pull down the laths and replaster this, which was simple enough. We painted the walls blue, the woodwork white, blue-distempered the hall and passageway of the ancient building, painted a sign for our gallery and hung it at the street door; polished all the brasswork, inserted a gas radiator (Nineteenth Century) by fastening the rubber tube over the gas tap in the hearth, cleaned the windows and found a large old carpet to cover most of the floor.

Having given notice at the British Museum, we also gave up the Notting Hill flat, deciding to camp in the gallery at night. What was a bit of discomfort? It was all part of the campaign. In any case, one often painted all night; and if the gallery was to be open to the public all day, it would be the only time left in which to work. The building was an easy-going establishment full of tailors' sittings. They too worked all hours, day and night, Mediaeval fashion.

I was painting in a broader, freer manner now, with thick paint put on with a brush instead of a palette knife, building it up as I worked. I used motifs from round about—the Avery Row cat, a tabby who sat in the window of the Sickertian public house almost next door (a place of secluded Victorian panelled nooks) became a sombre striped monster; studies of turkeys hanging in Leadenhall Market were more symbolic of French Realism than Caldecott Christmastime; and weighty studies of blue-green turnips with a black bottle seemed to have a more than merely objective implication in their threatening presences. Our first exhibition, however, had to be of something saleable—or so we thought, though in retrospect it might have been better to risk all and load the walls with great potential masterpieces of the future (though mere millstones at that moment) and trust in genius being recognised. However, in the event—possibly sensibly—we bought old frames from junk shops, painted them, cut new mounts and inserted drawings and watercolours—some of Brighton and some of London—and hung a rather restrained but somewhat presentable show. I designed and had printed a folding catalogue-card which we sent out extensively; and we were rewarded with success. We advertised in the leading newspapers, and announced our appearance in the *Arts News and Review*. The critics came to inspect our premises and exhibits, and inserted reviews. "A line from me is worth fifty pounds to you," the critic of one celebrated newspaper told me, and he was right. Our courage and enterprise in opening a gallery at all was much commented on, and everyone liked the fresh effect of the blue walls and the patterned Victorian carpet. The pictures looked well, and sold well, although the prices were not exaggerated, and I had made a point in my article in the invitation card (somewhat of a mini-manifesto) that young artists could only succeed by selling at a reasonable price. Certainly it was essential at the time, though I think now one should keep one's prices high, even as a young artist.

Other dealers called round to see how we were progressing—Charles Gimpel from up the road; and Jack Beddington's brother, Colonel Fred Beddington, of Wildenstein's called round and viewed our efforts with amused indulgence. He had never minded my overstaying a visit to his gallery, and talking endlessly about art as young enthusiasts will, and had obligingly looked up the biographies of Italian artists in his encyclopaedias to whom I claimed to have some kind of kinship: a kind and enthusiastic personality.

The opening times of our gallery, once advertised, were strictly adhered to. There was nothing Bohemian about the establishment. I thought it important to be professional, not like students having a lark, despite one being only twenty-three. One gallery offered to lend us some Picasso etchings in order to create an ambience of the expensive and impressive art world, from which highly priced items we could then sell our less eminent works at a lower, but only relatively lower price—more than we were asking at that present moment. It would have been perhaps sensible dealing, but I did not feel I could be responsible for such articles, which again may have been a mistake. We had opened, however, with the laudable intention of helping young and unknown painters, and soon they began to appear and show us their work. We were now in the different and difficult position of being their arbiter; and disappointed those whose works had too many personalities present, none being their own; or who just weren't good enough, or who were consistent, but a total—though probably unknowing—copy of someone else. However, some we took, and we ran three week shows, with a week between for hanging.

We met other, established artists, who called in to chat, or encourage, or see what we were showing. William Scott, whose work all young artists highly respected, came in and talked all through one afternoon; and celebrities as varied as Roland Penrose of the I.C.A., Wilfred Hyde-White the actor and Peter Pears came in to talk and browse. We observed how many of those celebrated in one art had a deep, near-professional interest in the others. Maurice Collis, the controversial biographer of Stanley Spencer, offered help; also R. O. Dunlop, who said he had tried something of the sort himself once. All this attention was encouraging, but mainly for the fact that the gallery seemed accepted as being on the right professional lines. Of course, the young artist, when older people applaud him, may feel it is his talents they admire; but it may be merely his youthful optimism and enthusiasm—tedious in an older man, but forgiven—even refreshing—in one who was but yesterday a schoolboy.

. . . . .

One of the regular visitors to our gallery was a Mayfair hairdresser with a taste for art. He asked to borrow a picture—hung it in his booth, above the mirror, and sold it within the day. A succession of paintings were sold in this manner by our amiable friend. His own patrons included a number of film-stars, gods at the time to a world starved of personal romanticism, and these idols would be directed by him to call at our establishment, which orders they summarily obeyed, to our great interest. An elderly gentleman who lived nearby bought a drawing from me from time to time. Eventually, he purchased a more expensive picture, a small portrait of an old lady. He told me subsequently that his wife had found it so hideous, however, that he was obliged to hang it in a cupboard, and only look at it at intervals, or for long as he could stand it. My pictures of this kind were certainly not intended to be attractive at this period; I meant them as statements, almost sermons, of stern import. My patron preferred basically the sketches of the old masters, which, having bought at auction, he would bring in for a pleasant morning's discussion. He said he would like to possess the work of any painter of distinction, except perhaps Gauguin. Considering the nature of Gauguin's life—and death—he said he would no more want a canvas of Gauguin's in the house than he would want a pair of his trousers . . . .

One never knew whom the opening door would next present: an ex-crocodile hunter from Australia—young artists with work to show, going the rounds of the dealers . . . . D. R. Collins called in from his Bond Street offices, pointed to an old room over a stable in Brooks Mews as we looked from the window, and said: "I started over there, with my first workshop." Looking at my paintings of portentous Realism, he confessed he preferred my gentle scenes of Brighton or Paris; but life in London seemed, to me, removed from that aesthetic. I had decided, in any case, to paint in the future only if a subject gave itself to me with overwhelming force. Practice was not essential—only importance of statement. I considered that the line, the pattern, was of great significance; and that the sharper and fiercer the drawing the greater the impact upon the memory of the observer. Having developed, by visits to the Tate, an enthusiasm for English cubism, I now progressed to the early Italians. Crivelli was a logical move. He was, in fact, the only painter in the National Gallery whose work could have been linked with early 20th. century art. The Gothic spikiness, the absence of facial expression, the hardness of the jewelled surface, the cut-out-of-tin aspect. . . . He even possessed a link with Tenniel, who had always been a constant influence on me for his sharply defined blocked-out shapes in *Punch*.

From all these influences I felt my style forming into a manner more emphasised and better to fit my new subjects. Part of every day I spent in museums and in the dealers constantly looking and evaluating, as one can in London, with such a wealth of art continually passing through the galleries and auction houses. One young painter told me Sotheby's was the best school of art in which to study in London, and he was right. I had begun to draw satirical studies of diners in cafeterias—lonely, isolated eaters, turning up their eyes suspiciously as they shovelled in baked beans. My pen and watercolour work had become less lyrical: drawings of people standing round a coffee-stall late at night; we would wander all over London in the small hours looking at damaged buildings by lamp-light, the shattered holes in the ground that had been Georgian or Regency palaces. Grosvenor Square nearby had great chunks out of it at the corners, and down at the end of New Bond Street the foundations for the Time-Life building were just being laid, to the sound of pneumatic drills day and night. I used to go out and draw in the wastelands round St. Paul's, that had once been narrow lanes between high buildings, and were now like gardens, festooned with rose-bay willow herb. Office workers would sit on the grassy slopes and hillocks, from which picturesque rocks of brick and masonry protruded at intervals as convenient seats, and the vista—apparently not to be rebuilt for some time—had an atmosphere of ancient Greece, the attic slopes of some golden age; so quickly does nature cover over destruction and tragedy. The desolate bombed alleys had become country lanes. There was inspiration everywhere, however. The railway delivery wagons, with fat Dickensian carter driving, and great shire-horse pulling, would turn into Avery Row and park beneath the gallery windows, the driver sipping a cup of tea from Otti's café, the horse's head sunk in its bag of oats. A little sweeper with the look of an ex-jockey would feed the horse with apples, and help with the nosebag. I drew such motifs as this—a sudden, extra-illuminated piece of life that demanded pictorial expression. I followed tramps about to study and draw them. There was one intriguing little figure around the West End at this time, an archaic creation, wrapped in a grey-black ankle-length coat. The distinguishing element of this tramp was his choice of hat—that of an Edwardian lady. It was a huge broadbrimmed affair, festooned with deep blue-green ostrich feathers that had somehow preserved their colour and luminosity. Where did he get it—to whom had that luxurious hat belonged to, now out of time so miserably? His immense black beard and long hair had an oddity all the greater in a period when people did not favour extravagance in personal appearance. The age of austerity in all things was with us yet, and apparently forever. This tramp would occupy his time sitting on benches in Hanover or Berkeley Square, sewing stitches into a shapeless piece of cloth. Another tramp, a long thin dismal person with a bowler hat, walked the streets on the kerb edge, as if on a tight-rope, up and down Avery Row all day. A female tramp, with voluminous layers of dresses giving the appearance of a vast untidy crinoline, and a broad-brimmed hat tied on with a veil, hurried nervously from one end of Oxford Street to the other, continuously . . . the fat, bearded billboard man would give a yellow-toothed grin, a wolfish, mindless gape, as she drifted by, his curly-brimmed bowler hat repeating in its circular shapes the wide circles of his eyes. I drew and painted all these images.

Once, finding a corpse-like figure flat on its back in an alley, I went to the police station nearby to suggest they helped her. My concern was a mistake, however, it seemed—she was merely asleep on the warm grating above a restaurant kitchen. All the tramps knew the best gratings over which to spend a winter night. Claridge's Hotel backed into the mews opposite the gallery windows, and on a Sunday morning one vagrant employed a regular way of raising funds. He had discovered that if one sung against a certain part of the wall, the voice was amplified by the brickwork and air currents to give it an incredible booming, loudspeaker vibrancy. This unbearable sound brought everyone at Claridge's to their windows. After a while, as the terrible voice showed no sign of weakening, knotted handkerchiefs containing money would begin to flutter down to him; and after a final warning note, to remind them as it were of his re-appearance next week-end, the blackmailer would depart with his booty.

As eating was a not very frequent occurrence, one's state of mind came to be one of extra-perception, with long periods, however, of non-receptivity; which meant that when one did notice something, it came slowly to the conscious mind, as if one had dreamt about it previously; and it was all the more important for that. Normal nourishment when we had any consisted of bread, spaghetti, oxo cubes, coffee, and our cheese ration, two pounds of it, as we were vegetarians, and fried cheese sandwiches were a staple food. We sat of an evening watching the mice climb out of the chimney to search for pieces of uncooked spaghetti. I remember one mouse picking up a piece about six inches long, and trying it this way and that against the bars until he last thought of poking it *between* and going round the other side to pull it through. The old building was full of rats, that fought and squeeled under the floorboards, thumping their tails. A large one, about the size of a rabbit (it seemed at the time, although professional rat-catchers are contemptuous of such superlative reports) once leapt from the fireplace and ran round and round the gallery until it found the fireplace in the back room, up which it scrambled to disappear into the mysterious corridors behind the grate. The fireplace has a romantic aura that central heating has dispelled. Once, this outlet from every room had a mystery, a fantastic quality about it. What lay beyond, what went on behind it? *Through the Looking Glass*; Tom's adventures in the *Water Babies*—fairy tales are full of images of things leaping from the chimney, or up it, or behind it, never to be seen again. A room without a fireplace is devoid of mystery, with no way out for the mind; a room without a soul. A classic conception of a prison cell is a room with but a small window, and no mantelpiece, no *hearth* or perhaps heart. It can be terrifying if a bird falls down and flies blindly out of the fireplace into the room. As disconcerting to others as to itself; the hysteria of the sootblackened winged creature gives it the image of a demon out of hell.

Life in the gallery slowly became a somewhat narrowed-down, limited existence. It didn't seem so at first, but by degrees we became more confined; by day, we were in the centre of a busy metropolis; by night, in the dead heart of a deserted blackness of empty shops and deserted offices. In the establishments of our tailor co-tenants at Avery Row each room included six or more sittings; if one fell vacant it was advertised as "Sitting Vacant" on a card at the newsagents' at the end of the Row. The tailors were strange characters, living in an outmoded manner in a modern city. They worked cross-legged, each carrying about with him a white-shaded light bulb on the end of a plugged-in flex. The use of the great iron was, it seemed communal. We would hear it all night thumping overhead with a regularity echoed by the thumps of the rats beneath our feet.

The tailors removed their coats, collars and ties to work, but not their waistcoats and bowler hats. Late in the evening, most of them drifted away into London; choosing, it seemed, the alleys and courts rather than the main streets. An elderly, small, Kaiser-moustached figure was the grand old man of the house. Known as "Brighton Jack" Boxall, this tailor remembered his home town mainly for the day in '97 when Queen Victoria paid her state visit. He was in the crowd and watched her received by the mayor (who happened by chance to be my great-uncle John). It was my name, of course, that prompted "Brighton Jack's" recollection of this incident. Apparently he hadn't visited the town for some fifty years. Each morning he took the huge communal teapot over to the cafe opposite to be filled. The motif of bowler hat, upturned moustaches and teapot was one I was inspired by and eventually painted. "Brighton Jack" had two apprentices of long standing, being nearly as old as himself, whom he called his "lads." One of them at last absconded, never returning from an expedition for his master's weekly pension money he had been sent to collect. "On drugs, 'e was," one of the tailors told me. Another of the tailors—"Welsh Charlie" lived permanently in the top room he rented, into which he had moved an old brass bedstead. Once, when the police knocked thunderously at the door in the early hours because a ground floor premises light had been left on, Charlie descended and begged us not to answer it. The landlords seemed to have no objection to the round-the-clock tenancy, although the house was not residential as such. However, we worked all night, and the tailors worked all night to finish garments; but Welsh Charlie, seemed to favour a complete anonymity of existence. He was slowly going mad with loneliness, and would sometimes slam the door of his room incessantly and rhythmically for half an hour at a time, accompanying this with an endless stream of curses, as if exorcising a deadly self-hatred.

The house itself was 17th. century, with old winding staircases, the doors and rooms becoming progressively smaller as one approached the roof. Once, Tyburn Brook had flowed before the building, at the end of their now-vanished front gardens; one can trace these little rivers, now driven underground, all through the West End—they follow the small streets and alleys; or, rather, the streets and alleys, being there before the main thorough-fares of a later date, followed the brooks and presumably used them as drains and sewers. If one looks at an old engraving of Burlington House before it was the Royal Academy, over in the distant countryside to the north-west, where Bond Street now lies, Avery Row can be seen as a lone terrace. Our building was used as an isolation hospital in the Great Plague, being well away in the distant lanes. I often looked at the door and our first floor windows, and tried to remove, mentally, the nearby city, Bond Street, and the back of Claridges; and visualise the clear view across the countryside to what was to become like Hyde Park.

In the hot dusty summer, when the deserted West End of a July evening was too much to endure, one could walk up to Regent's Park, no great distance, and row a boat about, if one had the money for such a luxury. In the winter, apart from painting, there was nothing to do—no radio, television, or even armchairs. But sitting on the floor by the incredibly economic single gas jet in the cast-iron radiator we read most of Dickens aloud, in good Victorian-fashion, which occupied the evenings of many months. By day, I roamed about (when not taking my turn of looking after the gallery) sketching the dead animals in butchers' shop windows, or studying the orators at Marble Arch. At this period, when inspired to paint, I produced enigmatic symbols—dead rabbits, calve's heads and tall black bottles in the French mode, the idiom of the new masters across the Channel. As yet, the British kitchen-sink school had not yet arisen, with its rather more romantic outlook, treating these subjects less as experiences of intellectual philosophy, and more of a further aspect of old-fashioned picturesque Bohemia.

One tall panel that I painted was of a dead hare with its head hidden in the cup into which its blood collects. The butcher's shop images were haunting to me, particularly around Christmas, when one wandered through the Leadenhall Market, hung with geese and turkeys. I identifed these rows of hanging corpses as unfortunate individuals, symbols of the eternal movement towards impersonality, against which all poets fight—so dangerous a step for the individual, so essential for the progress demanded by the Arch-terrorist, Nature. The idea stayed with me—I looked at the pale heads of the dead calves; possible versions of a Slaughter of the Innocents occurred to me—one always comes back to the Bible for the best subjects. Eventually, after many trial sketches, some paintings and drawings, I decided on the motif of an actual butcher's shop, with the butcher surrounded by symbols of birth and death, as the two major realities (in that they are both so close to total darkness). I employed a Futurist device for his head, giving him that of a bull, many-faceted, as it spins in a confusion of ideas that he cannot resolve in his mind, while at the same time remaining sufficiently detached to continue his usual work. He has, of course, a universal application.

Over the head of the butcher hangs a dead pig, and nearby a pair of dead rabbits, their bellies meeting in a tender hopelessness, their heads locked in the iron masks of the tin buckets, the handles tucked round their ears; graphic symbols of non-communication. In one hand the butcher holds the head of the dead chicken on the slab before him; in the other an egg. This eternal sequence of events, comic in a universal sense, tragic to every individual, is the subject of the painting. I exhibited it in the gallery, but it did not seem to please anybody; painters in this period were interested only in what they termed the painterly qualities of paint. Stanley Spencer was universally despised by other artists because of his so-called dry paint. In an austere era, the almost eatable effect of thick, luscious, dripping paint was considered more aesthetically interesting. I certainly favoured it myself in my earlier work. Even the French Realists used great slabs of paint laid on with a trowel. But true intellectuality, in the literary sense, was about to depart from art; and the vacuity of the American abstract painting was now on the horizon.

My next painting, and the one I considered the most important of all those I produced in London, was the *Crucifixion of Indifference*. The central figure was that of an orator I had studied on his soapbox at Marble Arch, arms outstretched in Messiah-like supplication. He had seemed to be a particularly inadequate Christ; his audience were detached, uninterested. This, in fact, was the only element that gave to him a certain nobility of pathos. In those days, fortunately, madmen were not followed eagerly, but were left to themselves, and consequently awarded a kind of respectful pity, as one gives to those dedicated to a life of certain failure. He had not even the satisfaction of being mocked, let alone the exultation of getting himself crucified. To become a saint, one must be of a *successful* nature. But indifference has greeted my orator, rather than eager partisanship, for and against, seething round his platform. On one side of him I placed the little tramp with the Edwardian lady's hat, clutching three fishes and a loaf of bread, indifferent to all but these symbolic essentials. Balancing this figure, the impersonal motif of a passerby looking at a watch, concerned only with the passing of time (and that only in a cursory manner) oblivious to that eternal symbol of terror, the clockface, perhaps the greatest memento mori we have, more devastating even than the cross.

Across the canvas, my old Parisienne leans over to pat the head of a tabbycat. In her other hand she holds the famous dead hare of the Social Realists—she is indifferent to the anomaly of caressing one furry creature while intending to devour another (a somewhat marked feature of the French markets, when one considered the live rabbits sitting on the counter together with the vegetables that would be served with them). Behind the orator, paths swing towards the city in the distance, and a pair of lovers suggest the only hope, because they alone have a tomorrow; their dream-world is constructive; they do not belong to the picture. The others are obsessive, habitual, locked into their nightmare of isolation, like all outcasts who have not the strength to bring the rest of the world into it and thereby get free.

My final picture on the theme of London Life as I found it was a frieze of the street musicians and other odd characters who would stand at the corners, just one degree above the complete vagrant, actually offering something in return for a sixpence. I called it *A Difference of Philosophies*; and included the driver of the railway wagon, and the little sweeper, as types of more stable and successful vocations, by comparison. The old poem-seller, Smith of Oxford Street, his wooden leg fastened to his hip with an array of braces and straps; his poems (that we used to buy each month—semi-illiterate satires, in fact) printed on coloured card with an old Adana hand-press. I included the tramp with the feathered hat, this time routing in a dustbin, and looking with disdain at the *Financial Times*; and finally an itinerant street piano-player and his wife, as I had sketched them in Marylebone Lane under the lamplight, with an old lady as poor as themselves stretching wide her purse to peer within it.

A street-musician outside the National Gallery possessed a novel instrument—a wire stretched between two nails on a plank. He knelt in the gutter (not much room there today) running his finger up and down the wire, and vibrating it at one end with a glass bottle, in place of a bow. At a glance, in a moment, like a revelation, I suddenly understood the value of *tones*; in painting, in music, in everything—their simplicity, and their closeness. It was a lesson I never forgot, that made the world suddenly clear. One could see at once how to play a one-stringed fiddle, or a violin, to paint a figure in monochrome . . . tones are tones, whatever the medium.

The great Smog of '52 that descended over London was so thick that an outstretched hand did in fact disappear at times. Eventually, a severe cold like influenza inevitably developed from breathing in all this smoky water vapour. The yellow fog was so intense that the building seemed to be floating in outer space. For several days the far end of our little gallery was lost in mist, and it was certainly difficult to breathe. Outside, it was practically impossible to find

one's way. Suddenly, you would become aware it was the middle of the road under your feet, not the pavement. Four artists who were holding an exhibition nearby took advantage of the obscurity to drive their old London taxi about the streets posting up bills advertising their show. When the fog cleared, these were seen to be all over the West End. I actually came upon them in the fog in Grosvenor Square as they were engaged upon this enterprise. These old taxis had recently been sold off for £25 each, and were in very good condition, with plenty of space for carrying pictures—consequently they were bought up most generally by artists.

. . . . . .

One day an artist entered the gallery—evidently a very poor artist, in worldly goods. His clothes were in a disintegrating condition, but his work was very strong. Large pastel portraits of animals—giraffes, leopards. But the work we were showing at the time was in the post-cubist, lyrical Palmer amalgam that was typical of the times, and his work didn't fit in at all. However, we listened to his story—he had taken a place as an assistant keeper at the Zoo; where at least he was near his subjects. As he had nowhere to go home to at night, his superior had allowed him to sleep in the straw in the elephant house.

Some months later, he again appeared, this time dressed impeccably—a black coat with fur collar—hair sleek—glasses gold-rimmed. He had been selling well—a successful exhibition—commissions. Such ups and downs are as much a part of an artist's life as an actor's. Either you are at the top, or you sit eating chips in Charing Cross gardens, with the other vagrants, wondering where all the sunshine in life has got to, and if you will ever see it again.

Nearby, in a street off Oxford Street, I came upon a gallery run by the son of Alfred Wolmark. Here were collected masterpieces by not only Wolmark, but Epstein, Gaudier-Brzeska and the others of their circle. The book of Gaudier's marvellous drawings, published while I was a student and then remaindered, had consequently become available to a generation of students who could buy it for sixpence and become deeply influenced both by his aesthetic and the flowing freedom of the drawings. Wolmark, whom I met once in the street, was a diminutive elderly black-bereted figure yet with all that eternal youthfulness of the true creator, octogenarian or no. He admitted wryly that his prices had fallen to an unprecedented low at that time, and that he did not terribly admire Henry Moore. It was unfair to compare Wolmark, in his old age, to Gaudier's colossal flamboyant portrait bust of him in youth. His day was of course to come again, but he was not to see it.

As an interesting example of the same object changing in value across time, I bought in 1951 a copy of Patric Dickinson's anthology of War Poems, with lithographs by William Scott. These were piled on a table outside their publisher's office, at a shilling a copy. The last time I saw one of these—how many have survived?—it was ninety pounds.

Eric Wolmark also owned one of the old London taxis; like the others, a marvellous creation of glittering brass and polished woodwork. I remember him driving it down to the Tate with the Gaudier portrait bust of Alfred Wolmark carefully propped on the back seat. The Tate—at that time acquiring works of art on funds that seem incredibly small compared to those of later years—had wished to consider the purchase, but couldn't make up their mind. So back the bust came. One hopes that this remarkable work, so dynamic a creation, so interesting regarding both artist and sitter has now been cast in bronze to ensure its permanence. It did eventually stand in a Gaudier room at the Tate, a fitting little memorial chapel for that shortlived but energetic sculptor.

. . . . . .

Whatever happens, one wonders, to those artist couples that live so penuriously in London. They would have been at art school together, no doubt; and by some malevolent stroke of fate, been persuaded into an attachment, married; and produced the inevitable children. Both artists, or at least both claiming to be, they would make one of the corners of the room they rented into a kind of studio—another corner would be the nursery—another the living-room. Time would go by—the ubiquitous baby would cease to fill the room with his noise and hygienic appurtenances—he would become a destructive toddler—later, a school-child eager for a yard or a garden in which to play. At this point, the father would give up the few spare days a week his part-time job gave him, and which he pretended to use for the practice of *Art*, and take a full-time teaching position (if lucky enough to find it) and a mortgage on some dull little semi-detached that had everything except the romantic aura—for an artist—of an old Victorian house with huge rooms, in the centre of London. And so the family, added to at intervals, would eventually settle into the conventional pattern ordained by life and custom for 99% of would-be painters. For myself, the situation appealed not at all; from children to tired wife, to half-hearted painting and hated teaching seemed a split existence of a hypocrisy unbearable. Visiting the rooms of these artist couples in their early days one was always surprised at their courage and ambition, and their curious faith that things would be satisfactory in the end—success was but round the corner . . . pathetic, sad—what a waste of time! What misguided effort. I didn't even admire them. They wanted to have everything. For the artist to succeed, he can not permit himself the luxury of attachments. And by success one means a successful self-comprehension and realisation of his style. He must jettison all that wastes his time and causes him to work at occupations that stultify the mind and kill sensitivity. For how soon those eager couples, setting out to conquer London, become but jaded grandparents, and of no interest at all as persons of achievement, either to others or, in fact, themselves.

. . . . . .

A curious occurrence, perhaps due to an excess of sensitivity engendered by little food and over-concentration, at this period, is memorable to me. One morning we were each looking down, from separate gallery windows, at the crowds of passers-by in the street beneath. We were quite close to the tops of their heads—shoppers, tramps, idlers, tailors, well-dressed successful men in a hurry—failures walking up and down the street all day, eyes downcast—nowhere to go, why hurry?—night will soon be here. . . . All at once, I noticed a shortish man—dressed in dull black and grey—not old or young—round face, black hair—walking through the crowd at a smart pace. Nothing unusual about him at all. I trembled, my flesh felt cold; I felt extraordinary and irrational terror. He went by. I leant back from the window, exhausted with the tremor I had felt. I looked at my companion.

"Did you feel *that*?" I said.

"Did *you* feel it?" was the reply.

What was it—who was it—how did we both receive this aura from him? Was he the Devil on a visit—or a murderer whose premeditations we had latched on to? Or, perhaps, a potential murderer, with proclivities unknown even to himself? We were used to seeing life in terms of symbols—we were very intense about everything—we were neurotically over-conscious that a dead chicken was a pale pink corpse into which diners sank their fangs; poultry did not suggest Dickensian festivities, but barbarism . . . we were geared to receiving impulses that we translated into pictures of powerful symbolism. The sensation of that person passing, however, stays with one.

. . . . . .

One exhibition we staged was of the work of American etcher Sam Kaner, who had persuaded Picasso's printer, Lacourière, to take him into the atelier. Kaner according to Buckland-Wright, was the innovator responsible for developing the relief-etching technique of William Blake into the deep bite and relief two-inking process—an approach that was to become universal in the following decades. It is interesting that our one-man show of some sixty of Sam Kaner's etchings was probably the first one-man show of modern etchings of this kind to be presented.

At this point we had still been bringing out our card-catalogues with an introduction; and this had progressed to a monthly Gallery Bulletin—a give-away sheet with articles, news and information about our artists. As it was somewhat expensive to have printed, however, and the sales of a gallery are always better when it is a newly-opened novelty, I decided to in future handset and print our catalogues myself. I bought an Adana printing press, and set it up in our back room. Here, through the nights, I laboured away, learning how to set the type, lock it into the form and print, with an occasional half-tone block borrowed from the *Studio* magazine. This procedure, which resulted in eight page booklets printed both sides, evolved towards the publication of a monthly art periodical: the *Art Gazette*, containing articles, illustrations, reviews—This was printed professionally, however, and after we had written all the copy I typed it out at night in the editorial back kitchen, and designed the lay-out for the printer. I also designed a variant of Playbill type for the headings and titlings which I named Blackberry Gothic, as it has a blackberry decoration on the letters, picked out in a somewhat Beardsley-like manner. I also included a series of episodes describing the thoughts of and influences upon an imaginary young painter of the day: "William Bloodstock." I wrote the first episode one morning at about five o'clock, when at first light I was staring at the grey sky of yet another wintry day; suddenly, I found the theme in my mind, and began to write; the grey day at once becoming a romantic surrounding to the life of poverty-stricken Bohemia that is the right of every young artist, and the shame of every old, as Marcel observes so rightly in the Murger masterpiece.

In my capacity as editor and art critic, I was invited with a crowd of other journalists to the opening of the new Time-Life building in Bond Street. This was one of the first luxurious modern offices to rise like palaces from the drab bomb-site landscape of the times. We of the Press admired the stone facings of the ground floor, and the contemporary works of art by fashionable and decorative artists of the era—advanced and up-to-the minute in '52. In fact it seemed certain to go out of date quite soon, so perfectly did it mirror current taste. . . .

I had observed, one grey morning when I had been roaming around Bond Street at about 6 a.m., the huge Henry Moore pieces arriving up from the country in a lorry, packed with straw. They do, in fact, swivel on a central axis in their places, and the intention was to create an ever-changing facade to the building.

"And now we will take you upstairs, where we will enjoy drinks and a sumptuous lunch," said the elegant lady representative showing us around. "You will be surprised at this lift—we shall go up the full complement of floors at super-speed—."

The journalists, eyes lighting up with the prospect of food, let alone drink, began to cram into the first lift that opened its fully automatic doors. I stood back with natural politeness, diffidence or caution.

"I'm afraid they seem to fill that one," said the lady to me. "You and I," she went on, "will take the next one—ah, here it is—."

She was right—it was fast. In a moment, we were at the top floor. We looked about for our party—nobody was in evidence. We pressed button and switches without success. After some ten minutes, however, we succeeded in landing the original lift, catching it before it again sped from our hands. The doors opened—twenty journalists fell out, red-faced and panting, ties and collars ripped off. . . .

"We couldn't control it!" "We didn't know what to do—" "Talk about the black hole—"

Cool and calm, the lady attendant and I led them to the lunch, where the ruffled tempers were soothed a little by the unusually luxurious refreshments in that age of austerity and ration books.

We were invited to the private view of the retrospective of the Scottish painter J. D. Fergusson. I was interested to meet this celebrated figure, and getting into conversation, we were soon involved in one of those artists' talks that seem to exclude everyone else. We were eventually separated by his dancing-impresario wife, somewhat to his displeasure, I thought. I met an abstract painter at this occasion, and we talked about Nicholas de Stael, the French abstractionist who had recently taken London by storm—and created a pervasive influence of his manner among other artists—with a show at the Matthiesen Gallery in Bond Street. I had described this impact on my character Bloodstock in the *Art Gazette*. The abstract painter was a friend of that artist and said he was off to Paris that very night and was taking a copy of the magazine to show to De Stael. I often wondered what his host had made of the episode, which described how the cool yellow and grey television screen shapes had so affected the aesthetic vision of my imaginary painter—as they had indeed that of so many who were real. Later, however, De Stael committed suicide by leaping, tragically, from a window.

. . . . . .

Late in 1952, we decided upon a new scheme to unite all the capable young artists we met or who came to the gallery with complaints of insufficient opportunity for showing their larger works. This, the perennial problem of painters, caused—as it has always caused—many of the potentially best artists to disappear into obscurity as if they had been guillotined. Which, in a sense, they were. They may have continued to exist, corporeally; one meets them later in life—tired, lost, with all the old fire out for good, vainly devoting their last energies to some irrelevant hobby—making furniture, perhaps, with all the skill of a professional, but in fact merely finding subconscious excuses for not taking up their palette and brushes. Their original artistic self, that entity with a genuine thought, an original idea, a potential, is lost in the past; an irretrievable bit of history that didn't even get written. I recall one artist, Michael Toothill—he made huge triptychs and polyptychs with perhaps a dozen separate canvases joined together to present a symbolic religious theme—the figures all strange, monumental, Blake-ish creatures . . . what happened to him? Did he merely lose heart one day? I remember him as a tall, fair, modest youth full of enthusiasm.

At first, I contemplated renting the nearby R.W.S. Galleries in nearby Conduit Street, headquarters of the Royal Watercolour Society and the Royal Society of Painter-Etchers and Engravers. I went over to discuss the fee with Harry Philp, the then Secretary. Hanging at one end of the main hall was a huge Cuneo of a civic occasion. This official sphere of art, of course, still existed side by side with both the new abstraction, the lingering Euston Road manner, and the advancing Social Realism, but it was in another context to the younger artists of the time. The R.W.S. galleries, however, were too small for what I had in mind, and the number of artists necessary to pay for the proposed show, so we went to the R.B.A. Galleries in Suffolk Street, a large complex of rooms with a long history of exhibiting societies that had inhabited them. The exhibition was to be called "Artists Under Thirty" and we conducted an elaborate survey to find exhibitors of a sufficiently high standard of work to warrant invitation.

We visited art college exhibitions looking for the promising leading students—we studied the reviews in magazines in order to invite all those who had begun to make their mark. Many of these were to achieve positions of respect and celebrity, either then or later—Eric Atkinson, David Gentleman, Claude Harrison, Bryan Kneale, William Thomson . . . others fell by the wayside; no one can tell who will survive from that excess of talent of those in their twenties.

The artists were totally mixed, stylistically. How they worked was up to them. We invited over a hundred artists, all under thirty, to show; they paid £5 and selected their own works to fill a specified area of wall space. It was self-supporting and non-profit making.

We hired Bourlet's, the famous old-established framers and exhibition organisers, whose premises in Wigmore Street still possessed, unaltered, the very same Georgian atmosphere and skylighted appearance that they must have presented to Reynolds and Morland. On the appointed day along came the men with hooks and plates and screws. The expected pictures—already annotated and catalogued—also began to arrive. Some were of immense size. We published a small booklet to accompany the exhibition—some thirty reproductions; the cover yellow, as were the posters, with the Blackberry Gothic lettering that I had designed and had made into blocks for the printer. Each exhibitor had been invited to provide a photograph of a painting for inclusion in the book, at no extra fee.

There were memorable images—a huge orange composition by Peter Foldes—a great black and umber picture by Roland Jarvis. These were figurative but formalised paintings. Our own work was included, and I showed my *Crucifixion of Indifference* Orator painting, and my portrait of the ninety-seven year old Miss Mary May. Through an introduction, we had come to know a well-known illustrator-designer and his wife. The streets of London were full of his posters in that Festival of Britain period. The liveliness of this era somehow came to an end the next year with the death of the King, when barriers were erected cutting off various streets so as to direct the crowds and the procession more easily. (This was to coincide with our eventual withdrawal from the metropolis, as the Festival had coinicided with our arrival.) A visit to our new friends for supper, however, made an oasis of comfort and pleasure for us—a flat hung with pictures and drawings; books on art everywhere—the very supper tables topped with plate glass beneath which were more conversation-inspiring reproductions. As one came out of the grey cold evening, the welcome was full of warmth, light and colour. We would walk there and back; past the old Craven A Egyptian Temple, with its giant seated cats, and cat-faces as metopes along the frieze. As we returned to Bond Street, we would pass by the morbid purple lights of the shop windows, and might see Brighton Jack, a tiny Bowler-hatted figure drifting through the shadows past Haunch of Venison yard. . . .

. . . . . .

Our friends had suggested that I should sketch in a home for elderly people in Hampstead. It was a place for those who had been in service in the Victorian era, and who were now without friends or relations. To sit with them in the large refectory was a strange experience—all of them seventy or over, the sound of conversation whispering, thin and dry, like autumn leaves. Their meals were small—their appetite seemed sparse. Afterwards I saw the bed-sitting room that Miss Mary May shared with another elderly lady. Miss May was ninety-seven— the other, at eighty-five, seemed almost over-youthful. Miss May, in black, with ebony beads and a silver brooch given to her by her employer, Lady Napier, of Park Lane, was neat and precise, with a small ivory face, enormous glasses, and grey hair pulled back in combs—a wonderful subject. While I was drawing her, she told me of her life and experiences. She had gone into service at fourteen, as a housemaid with the Napiers. She spoke of running everywhere with coal and water jugs. On the evenings when the family gave a ball, the young maids would lean from the upper windows to watch the lights of the carriages approaching down below in Park Lane. By degrees, Miss May evolved to the place of housekeeper. A great occasion was when Austen Chamberlain was present at a party. He came below stairs to join in a dance the servants were having—and insisted on partnering Miss May.

One of the other ladies mentioned Bernard Shaw, who had just died. His nonogenarianism presumably put them all into more or less the same club. "Silly old fool," said one. "Tried to climb his apple-tree. At his age." Shaw had apparently succumbed in his own garden.

I had my pictures well-framed by one of the best framers of that time. He called round for his bill to be settled, but said, as he sipped a cup of tea, that my relatively small amount was of little importance. One gallery he said, "owes me hundreds, and I don't know when I'll get that. You can't object, because the big galleries go on employing you." His words were a prophecy. In all these picture-selling occupations, that so often turn upon the luck of sales and chance buyers, the spectre of the cash-lag is always present—particularly if you are one of those daring entrepreneurs who go into this field without the backing of a couple or so Boudins in hand carefully laid by to mature.

When our exhibition opened it caused a deal of interest, particularly as all the artists were under thirty. The then Minister of Education bought a number of works to hang in the offices of the Ministry; Lennox-Boyd, Minister of Transport, also came in, as did many other celebrities of the day, including the leading critics (many of them now forgotten)—Neville Wallis, Alan Clutton-

Brock, Eric Newton—curious how influential were their writings at the time. Sir John Rothenstein, Director of the Tate Gallery, came and selected a number of artists to be invited to paint large pictures for a show at the Tate of massive masterpieces. Largest of all in the subsequent exhibition was to be Michael Toothill's great panel of a marching crowd with a banner—called, I think, *The Witch-hunt*. This seemed to me to presage great things; but this was the point from which that artist seemed to disappear. I watched Sir John Rothenstein and his companion hesitate before my *Crucifixion of Indifference*. The friend lingered, but Sir John pulled him away. True to his real-life inspiration, the orator was again ignored, his message shrugged off. I was not asked to be one of those invited to participate in the Tate show.

The exhibition sold a number of pictures to private buyers, all of which proceeds of course went to the artists. We, as organisers, kept the gate-money only as payment for our time and trouble. It seemed to work well, and I intended to repeat the success the following year; but this was not to occur. The *Art Gazette* was now taking up most of my time; we had put it out in all the West End bookstalls and newsagents, and the obliging proprietor of the New Bond Street Kiosk next to Sotheby's had created a decorative effect with the first issue, and framed the whole of his booth with copies. The Tate, after an initial refusal, agreed to take it after I had appealed to Sir John Rothenstein, and it was subsequently displayed across the book and postcard stall in the Foyer, and did well. We sent out a large number of leaflets, but received insufficient subscriptions and advertising to warrant continuing the periodical after its fourth issue. To a certain extent all these activities were beginning to be over-exhausting, and running us into too many expenses. The organisation's funds could not carry us for long enough for the period necessary for the schemes to succeed. We began to fall back on to selling odd possessions for immediate money—the commencement of the fatal slide; the appearance of the dreaded Cash Lag. Soon, our various valuables began increasingly all to go the same way: to the pawnbroker. We favoured a large one in Holborn, where a tactful alley at the side, and two small doors, beckoned you into a stall (either ladies or gentlemen) that still protected your anonymity. Few of the pawned articles were ever redeemed. Any sentiment regarding valued items had to be suppressed; we began, however, to evolve perhaps too sensitive an outlook to criticism. Once, when an art magazine derided an exhibition we staged, I went down to the offices and demanded the editor.

"He's out," said the secretary; but I could see his shoes beneath a curtain over an alcove, and eyed it pointedly until he emerged.

"Why didn't you just write an angry reply?" he said, quite unembarrassed. "We could have got up a controversy. *I* don't mind what they write. They're only graduates down from Oxford who want to try their hand for experience. I give them the chance. Of course I don't pay them."

This all seemed so comical that I laughed, and we parted on friendly terms. Curiously, at this point, the exhibitions at the gallery were of an increasingly impressive standard. We had come to keep a permanent selection of pictures on show, changing them at intervals, and eschewing the expense and exhaustion of regular three-week affairs. The public seemed to enjoy calling in to see what was new on the walls, and we should have perhaps commenced in this way. A William Thomson roofscape I recall, and some still-life—an interesting early Brian Kneale, of a formalised dwarf in a landscape . . . but our exhibits were no longer expensive; and I tended to rely on my watercolour portfolio to keep us in food and drink—up to a point.

At times, before being saved by some providential sale organised by the guardian angels who hovered above (inconstant, but quite good at emergencies) we didn't eat sometimes for days. Ten days was the longest, and it was hard going. One's feet seemed like millstones, and double the size. All one's thoughts were disconnected; very odd. Then, a picture sold—all we could think of were luxuries like ice cream and chocolate and a visit to the cinema. At one point, I thought, now where, *where*, would one expect to actually *find* coins? Where would people habitually *lose* their money? Like a voice from heaven, a voice seemed to say—look underneath all the park benches. I went out, scraped the gravel from below all the seats in Grosvenor Square—and returned with a treasure of green sixpences and corroded shillings. Of course such decisions as suffering for no reason but devotion to an impractical way of life are rightly attended with inconvenience.

I remember one odd unconnected experience while walking about London. I met an old friend not seen for years. In the course of talking, he lit a cigarette, waving his hand airily as he talked. A lady emerged from a shop, closing her handbag. At that moment, my friend's cigarette somehow flew in the air, dropped neatly in the handbag, and snap! was enclosed. The passing lady was at once all but lost in the stream of Oxford Street. My friend set off in pursuit, pushing the crowds aside. Catching her at last, he had to convince her of the unlikely existence of a lighted cigarette in her handbag. There were denials, protestations; eventually prevailed upon to look, she discovered the smouldering article, none the worse. Taking it back with as much savoir-faire as he could muster, my friend rejoined me to continue our conversation, and to continue smoking, as well, the adventurous cigarette.

At this period, Leonardo's little portrait of Ginevra di Benci was on loan at the National Gallery from the Liechenstein collection, and almost every day I went to look at it. His work has, in general, an abundance of easy, lyrical, almost lazy rhythms; gestures almost of sensual disdain, dispassionate only because too idle to take the active course. But the Ginevra portrait is quite different. She is taut, intense—the mark of the true sensualist. It is invariably suggested that Rubens and those who follow him are sensual painters. These are painters of but self-conscious abandon. The real sensualist is one whose mouth is dry, who is poised in the form of a neurotic spear. He never shows his desire; he is burnt up from within with it. The would-be Bohemians, a fat wench in either hand, are but happy vulgarians. Lautrec's acid line is nearer the mark. His reserved, ironic, Degas-like astringency denotes a sensual vigour before which a Rubens or Courbet would retire from the field exhausted, early in the day.

This little Leonardo, balancing on the razor's edge of all emotions, and falling into none, was an all-weather Mecca to my developing aesthetic sense, and I recognise her faint echo in many later works of mine.

It is curious how one can tread the places where one will one day be, in a different time, and not know it. On one of my long walks round London I went up Grove End Road to St. John's Wood—an area so far unknown to me. I found a small park, quite near to where I would one day live, and but a few yards from a church in which I would one day be married. In the same way, one can tread the places where one *has* been. Sometimes, thirty or more years afterwards, I go through the open door in Avery Row—alone of all the establishments in the street apparently totally unchanged—though where now is Brighton Jack?—and walk up the same stairs to the Gallery, and wonder why it is *now*, and not *then*. The bumps in the doorpost where I filled in the holes after I took down the hooks for the sign can still be felt under the paint. All is unchanged: except that when I last passed at the door of the Gallery an uproar of barking arose from within, as if a devil of hell was on the other side. It could have been the echo of one's own desperation so long ago. Or, at least, that the sagacious canine within was perfectly cognisant of my musings. . . .

.   .   .   .   .   .

It is certainly curious how inanimate, unchanging places can flit in and out of the time-era of one's life, with but little difference to their own. While in London, I often walked to Kew or Richmond and back, as long walks in cities had a romantic appeal to me. I recall going up Richmond Hill and looking at the bow windows of a little shop and imagining that I either lived there or knew somebody who lived there. Twenty years afterwards, the shop was converted to a house subsequently owned by some intimate friends. I often stayed there and when walking up to the unaltered shop-front facade I sometimes crossed to the opposite side of the road, tried to put myself back in time, and imagine I was back in that grey utility era. The contrast, as one then stopped forward, opened the door, and was greeted with warmth, cups of tea and demands from the children to paint them yet another portrait of a toy horse for their room was like being in a dream of the future. . . .

The final show that the Gallery staged was in fact of my own large canvases, and smaller related ones, that I had painted in the gallery in the nights and evenings. The great Orator was there, and the *Revelation in a Butcher's shop*. *Miss May*, also, and a stark picture of the old lady of Hove with the bee-hive of hair and the brown cat, who I had recently resurrected from my memory. There was also yet another version of the old Parisienne with the pom-pom slippers, and a head of a coalman like a mediaeval archer in his leather hood; the black bottle and turnips, and a stylised portrait of my grandmother. I was planning a new subject—the bill-board man of Oxford Street and the thin-faced lady tramp were to figure prominently; but time in London was running out, and my aesthetics were already leaving the field of stark design and social realism. I had come under that most sinister and potentially damaging of all influences—that of the old masters. To realise their incredible standard, and to wish to emulate it is absurd; but it is perhaps a valuable phase through which to go, if it does not demolish you altogether.

I had been looking round that fine establishment no longer existing—"Better Books," in Charing Cross Road—a shop that took all the small press publications and individual poetry, literature and art magazines. They had stocked the *Art Gazette*, of course . . . I was walking past Zwemmer's, when I noticed the painting reproduced on the front of a Skira publication. It was Caravaggio's *Conversion of St. Paul*—the horse pawing the ground, St. Paul flat on his back beneath, hands outstretched. This was the first time a painter of the later Renaissance had the kind of effect on me that is like recognising a real friend. To achieve something of that quality and ability seemed worthwhile. This kind of work, that depended on the accurate drawing of an image only by an acutely aware mind, seemed to me basically more profound than even the reality of the contemporary realists of France (that I albeit admired) with their heavy impasto and continued reliance on those heavy outlines taken from Van Gogh and Gauguin. Once converted away from the kind of painting done by the artists of my own time and age, and I was fully lost to all but the past. The Pre-Raphaelites were still so out-of-fashion at that time that it was quite difficult for even devoted followers to admire them with complete sincerity— one felt it such a perverse denial of accepted public standards. I remembered once again the impact made upon me by the Rivière family, the glittering trio by Ingres in the Louvre. I remembered the great portrait of Castiglione by Raphael . . . the portraits of Holbein . . . of Roger Van der Weyden. Clear, sharp colours; defined shapes, precise finish, the complete illusion. These artists could complete a painting without making it appear tired; without losing the flourish of the sketch, or the immediacy of effect; it was if the figure had been peeled from a transfer. No artist of our time had the ability to paint so convincingly, yet with such apparent ease. Slowly, painting was becoming more important to me than the gallery. It seemed the only occupation that did not stagnate into repetition. All the varied ideas and activities, all the meetings with differing people of those London years seemed to crystallise, Stendhal-like, one's way of thinking. My conclusions were that it was necessary to leave them, to be on one's own—in order to cement one's essential detachment, without which there is no perception: Fabrizio del Dongo was the only one on the field of Waterloo who could actually *see* it, because he was uninvolved.

It had been an important part of my development, and the living of a life of such Spartan hardship had led to a confidence of thought and style in my work, certainly. But, like all artists who have tried to run their own gallery or exhibitions, we found that it took too much time and dedicated effort—there was no freedom; that essential freedom merely to wander about, years at a time if one wished, even half-asleep perhaps, but still absorbing and considering all the while, until the vital moment occurs, the convulsive jerkings of the new style, the next step, evolution—the new sequence of images that can portend perhaps five or six satisfactory years of artistic activity. There seemed but one solution—to return to Brighton, to forget the exigencies of life in London as a gallery-owner. The paintings that had been on show went back to the artists; and despite many sincere cries of disappointment from friends and contemporaries and suggestions that the Gallery must be kept on somehow, a van was ordered for possessions and canvases, the key was sent back to Mr. Bracket, the agent's clerk, and we took a taxi to Victoria Station as a last lordly gesture of life in the capital.

Back in Brighton, I decided I needed to enter a more solitary period of introspection, and to write, paint and consider what it was I was after in the arts. I had spent too much time in group activities and the organisation of exhibitions and activities with other artists. I was heartily tired of exhibiting and wished to paint on my own for as long as possible, and forget for a while about showing the results to the public.

I went out day after day with pack and materials, walking mile after mile, finding my subjects as they occurred, in country villages, on the Newhaven docks, on the beach at Brighton, or twenty miles to the north round Horsham.

Paradoxically, having left London as a resident, I still continually went there for the day; continuing to spend much time in the museums and galleries, which is the only way to learn. I had begun, when I first lived in London, by admiring the early cubist work of Picasso, pictures in grey and ochre of great originality and subtlety; but by now I was taking the great Italians as my exemplars.

I was at one of the first *Young Contemporaries* Exhibitions—an early and inspired attempt to give students a change to exhibit. Sir Kenneth Clark opened the show, and eventually climbed onto a table in order to address himself clearly to the crowds, who clustered informally around his eminence. He said that a student should take an artist he admired as a model—say, Degas—and paint as far as possible in that manner for a year. There were murmurs of dissent from those who were fiercely individual—or would-be individual, for in fact, that is the course the most enthusiastic and art-struck students do tend to follow. One must imitate to produce anything of quality, one would think; otherwise your work has the look of an amateur, who has looked only at nature—albeit extremely honestly—but has not taken the trouble to first swamp himself in the museums, in order to acquire eyes with which to see.

Once, at an exhibition of Gaudier-Brzeska drawings and sculpture off Bruton Street, I found a small man, in a neat black suit and heavy moustache, sitting beneath Gaudier's drawing of himself—Horace Brodsky—as a powerful young man forty years earlier. I had always been interested in both artist and sitter.

The sitter, to an admirer of the artist, had for long taken on the image of an icon. They both belonged to that infinitely attractive era of Wolmark and Fergusson, Wyndham Lewis, Katherine Mansfield . . . a lost era of creative thought. I encouraged him to talk about his friend—"Shot between the eyes," said Brodksy, tapping his own forehead—"right here."

The interest of London to a young man, the famed and celebrated mingling with the less individualised or less fortunate, in a striving of achievement and failure, was a continual fascination. With a kind of bemused dreaminess, one wandered about, looking, thinking; wondering what caused old Feathers to sit in Hanover Square sewing his bit of cloth. Once I came upon Lord Beaverbrook standing on the corner of Bruton Street (looking exactly like his recent portrait by Sutherland) while the gallery he had just visited buzzed and trembled with excitement.

Curiously, at this point, the British social realists, who had been presumably working away quietly all this time, now burst forth into exhibitions at the Beaux Arts Gallery, and the Kitchen Sink school was born, and had a brief flowering, its title disliked by, apparently, the artists so designated. In a sense, it should have happened before. It portrayed, and was distilled from, the utility years; but these years were now almost over; rationing itself was about to be ended. British Social Realism, with its drab ochres and greys taken from the French influence, was still, in many ways sweet, even romantic, compared with the French counterpart. It wasn't intellectual; it was about painting, and rather like the contemporary novels of those years. They were apparently not connected—didn't know each other—but the zeitgeist was present in both . . . and neither of them in fact are that far away from Dickens. One extra touch of human sympathy— or more fatal still—comedy, and existentialism collapses into Coronation Street, the music hall, and the lower classes treated by *"Punch"* as a good subject. The British never really got hold of what the French were after with social realism. It's not the character of the nation. The British do not like detachment and sadness unless it's cosy—sunsets and Samuel Palmer. There is no one better at sunset sentiment than Samuel Palmer, because he really *feels*. But you can't be a social realist and a lyricist at one and the same time.

Chapter 6

I continued to write, and read a great deal of Sinclair Lewis, Theodore Dreiser, and other regional devotees of the American scene. Their interest in portraying their surroundings, the atmosphere of their own times, was what I had been doing with Bloodstock; Waugh and Huxley still interested me, but their brittle intellectual approach seemed now a selfconstructed barrier against excess enthusiasm that prevented their works having the grand, unashamed involvement of Zola and Balzac. I became interested in the other French masters—Daudet, Flaubert, Stendhal, and began a series of short novels featuring imaginary writers and artists. My interest in the Pre-Raphaelites increased, and I devoted two years to study and research in the reference libraries and museums in order to write an account, for my own interest, of Victorian Painting.

In my own painting I was still a confirmed follower of the artists of the Renaissance. I painted a small subject picture of a grandmother and child, using my grandmother and a child cousin as the models. The old woman looks at the child with a kind of sorrow that its superficial lightheartedness will so soon be affected by the cares of maturity. Both figures are dressed in black, and the little girl holds a posy of white flowers. The canvas represents the theme of transience and replacement—very Victorian.

By chance, my old friend A. appeared again that year, and we fell into our old ways of long country walks—cooking meals over fires on lonely beaches—wading round Worthing Pier at low tide late one summer night. One blue winter's night, by contrast, we were walking along a deserted lane at about one a.m., the frost white all round us. We heard a strange noise, like a mechanical mower, that seemed to be following our steps. At last we discovered the cause. Slowly keeping pace with us in the field to the left was a great white horse, cropping the frozen grass as he padded along.

A. and I visited London—walked round the streets looking at the great houses of the successful Victorian painters—Holman Hunt's now flats; Leighton House we could of course visit and enjoy the archaic atmosphere, the strong pictures—some small oil sketches in elaborate gold frames—and the fountain in the arab hall. This led us to make a pilgrimage to the Watts Gallery at Compton—surely one of the strangest manifestations of selfconscious Messiahism in art history.

We commenced by taking a green bus from Pool Valley to Guildford, and climbed the hill to inspect the cathedral. To enjoy the gaunt immensity of that hilltop building one has to go back in time—it is out of date, in a sense, but pleasingly so, as presumably such a building has to wait for time to look back at it in any case to be appreciated at all. The niches, Gothic-like, await their sculptures. Some were occupied with Gill or Gill-like works already—the inside was dusty and incomplete. We paid for a brick in order to move the effect even nearer towards the eventual point when it should mirror the suave watercolour visualisation of its architect, Edward Maufe—a future that would eventually have the new Coventry Cathedral to contend with as an example of art and design; not to mention Liverpool.

Leaving the attic heights, we came down the stark steps, redolent of an era—and descended through lyrical lanes, close-hung with summer fruit and flower-bearing hedges, deep down into Pre-Raphaelite Compton, where among the cottages and gardens in the hot enclosed valley lies the weird low red-brick Watts Gallery. Inside, one could be in a deserted room at the Tate, slightly forgotten and scheduled for renovation. The period atmosphere is remarkable. I have been there many times since, and always one leaves real life and is transmuted into the studio at Holland House—pulled down aeons ago—where Watts would sit with the sermons of his genius bearing down upon him. It would be difficult to write much about Watts after having read Chesterton's remarkable book on him; but there is always one's personal view, after all. A cupboard below a case had its door open. There, through the gap, sitting upon a pile of old paint cans and rags, was the plaster death-mask of the Master, apparently undervalued, even jettisoned. Later, however, on subsequent visits, one found that this sinister trophy had been resurrected and placed with sepulchral reverence on display in a glass case. Jonah gesticulates, and the huge symbolic females swim in a haze of thick grey and pale yellow paint, laid on with a trowel. Paola and Francesco, cement statues, are borne aloft into never-never land. The sense of his conception that he was the Master of Masters seems to emanate from all about. Well, who are we to judge? Perhaps he was.

. . . . . .

For a short while in 1954 I worked in a studio opposite the Hove Town Hall, a fine structure in red brick by Waterhouse, regrettably destroyed by fire some years later. The room was rented from a strange old woman who repaired umbrellas; and the great clockface of the town hall filled the view from the studio window in an eerie and enigmatic manner. I was still looking for subjects from the world of the outsider, and found, as I sketched on Brighton Race course, an archaic world of tipsters, bookmakers and jockeys of eccentric individualism. I made a huge painting, six by eight feet, from my drawings, and sent it to the Royal Academy. It would certainly have made an impact; but unfortunately it was returned to me, rejected outright, like everything else I submitted in those years. The Royal Academy did not seem to favour enigmatic symbolism, and I, not very sensibly, disdained to send a small watercolour and pen sketch such as I brought back from country walks. At night, I often wandered home across the Downs, guided by the Pole star until I could see the orange glow of the lights of Brighton. On such occasions one would be sometimes brought up sharp in the dark by walking into a barbed wire fence. Sketching on a lonely twilit hill, with dusk descending, and a herd of cattle encircling one in a strange dance, head down, slowly advancing, is an uncomfortable experience. They are, of course only bullocks; curious in that insanely persistent way they have. Even so, with their ever-closer progress, they disconcerted one. Would the watercolour wash of the sky never dry? By this time, the horns of the cattle would be actually prodding, the lowered heads snuffling in my pockets—cloven hoofs in the palette. Packing in feverish haste, shouting wildly, leaping to my feet as they backed, I broke through the ranks and took to my heels into the night. Sometimes a tribe of cattle, interested in the watercolourist as he sits imperturbably ignoring them, will actually charge in a line, only swerving at the last moment, as if intent upon trying every trick to gain notice—rather like children, who are in some ways a worse ordeal to the outdoor artist, because he has to be kind to them; and then they are all round you, the youngest playing with the brushes, the oldest telling you his life story (of the past week). Not to mention that vast number of able but insolvent passers-by, young and strong enough (one would have thought) who squat by one's side, pass a few complimentary remarks, and then demand money in a familiar, yet menacing, manner. Others, in a group, more disconcerting still, will gather round, kick over your paintwater, try to disturb you, again like animals seeking attention. The only way to disarm them is by talking while you are working as if you have always known them—to some extent true—and asking how good they were at art at school. Often, it seems, they were very distinguished; and they begin to talk about themselves, swelling with pride at the recollections of their genius. Soon, they are on your side, and can be relied upon—in fact, delighted to be asked—to chase away others like themselves who would bother you—" 'e's *workin'*, *see?*" and defending you whom half an hour before you heard them discussing—"Shall we go over an' take the mickey, 'en?"

Working from nature anywhere is beset with difficulties. Some tourists will stand round you in a complete circle, blocking every view; or the lone chatterbox will stay the whole afternoon, telling of that universal aunt who paints so well, interrupting his flow with: "Not *worryin'* you, am I? *Good!*"

But despite all this, I continued to work constantly from nature, walking end to end of the promenades with my gear . . . at Worthing among the boats, or to Shoreham, cutting through the maze of dock and jetties along the side of Aldrington Basin behind the Lady Bee boatbuilders—all Goff country for etching. Amberley, near Arundel, was an artist's village where I found, as had many others, subjects all about. Stott (not of Oldham) had been the great figure here, and had put the village on the map as an artist's venue. His portrait bust tops his tomb in the churchyard, set in a broken pediment—a cheerful informal piece of sculpture by his friend and neighbour, the sculptor Derwent Wood. The eyes still twinkle, and the tie is careless and flowing, despite the years of rain that have dripped in summer and winter from the tree branches close above. Derwent Wood himself lies close by under a self-designed and made memorial. Robert Goff, whom I mentioned a moment ago, was an ex-army officer who became a distinguished R.E. In Holland Road, Hove where I spent my childhood, there was an odd little house with seemingly space for only one room. Looking at a folder of Goff's work in the Print Room of the British Museum, I came upon a plate of the house, with an etched inscription—"The Artist's Studio." Goff's etchings of Brighton—there is a wonderful etching of the promenade, with a sunset effect over the pier—of Shoreham, give one the sensation I have always received myself from these subjects. My master the watercolourist C. A. Morris made splendid watercolours of Shoreham all his life in a style that paid a respectful tribute to Wilson Steer. He told us once of old Hartrick (whose memoirs are highly readable): "Do you know there's an old artist of ninety living at Shoreham who was actually a friend of Van Gogh?" Each town has its resident master, of course, who has almost invented the views round about, so that you cannot see them except through his eyes. Charles Knight, R.W.S., was of course the Ditchling immortaliser as C. A. Morris was of Shoreham.

I had met a group of artists—like myself in their mid- or late twenties—mostly one-time students of St. Martin's in Charing Cross Road, who had come to Brighton to live and work in, and find jobs teaching art in various schools and art colleges locally. We shared the expenses of models, and painted and drew portraits of each other. This practice in the sphere of objectivity took me from my symbolic and literary pictures, although I exhibited the *Crucifixion of Indifference* and other canvases in the exhibitions at the Brighton Art Gallery. Also, I made a good many pen and ink drawings (of an etching-like detailedness) from friends or models posing. This seemed to lead back towards etching itself, so I began to attend once more the Friday sessions at the Art School (now College) and so had, by degrees, been slowly returned to the aura of what had always been my favourite medium.

Etching is an elaborate process; it is also expensive, primitive, hard work, and dangerous. Fire, nitric acid, heavy rollers, all add to the hazards. It is not surprising that if many take it up for a while, few keep at the craft. They try a few plates, and then abandon the whole difficult business. If you are not at an art college, of course, you need a press; and if you are after a genuine Victorian model, you may search for years. . . .

I worked still on the expensive copper plates—seldom over five inches by seven. I spent long days on the sea-front, working directly on the spot with the grounded plate, and made a Brighton set; not quite as Meryon made his Paris set, for he set it back in history, with his passion to emulate Zeeman. I wanted Brighton as it was at that moment, which was still in general as it has always appeared—except that most of my plates showed the off-season face; very different to when the promenade is swarming with people. But in that case, not only would it have been difficult to concentrate with such intensity as I needed in these plates—and they are very detailed and precise, with windows, railings and spaces all correctly counted, a difficult job on so small a scale—but in the heat of summer the beeswax ground would melt unless you were well in the shade; and even then the atmospheric heat could reduce the ground suddenly to a lard-like consistency. This was still the era—the very last moment of it—of steam-trains, capstans, fishing boats and paddle-steamers—all the panoply of

Brighton long familiar to me, but always worth sketching. I was fortunate to have the time to record so much. I also painted a number of landscape oils, and a series of fish still-life canvases, using the palette-knife freely in their case. Eventually, I thought it would be best to attend the Art College full time, and have access to classes all the week particularly as it was autumn and quite soon out-of-door work would come to an end—except as regarded snow. I always made pen and watercolour scenes out-of-doors in the snow, shivering under a promenade shelter as the blizzards swept around me. I have known a watercolour wash freeze hard rather than dry, and then crack off the paper. I needed the year's fees, however, as a paying adult student, and had not sufficient to spare. However. . . .

I was standing somewhat aimlessly at a corner, in Kemp Town, Brighton, considering these matters; I decided to invoke the shades of my ancestors, those eminently successful Edwardians. "Show me the way!" I cried, calling out the Blaker names. A face looked down from the scaffolding above my head. It was that of an old art school acquaintance. "I'm building a new front on my house," he said. 'The old one fell out. I've got a load of bricks, new window frames, everything. Do you want a job for a few weeks?"

I worked with him until we had replaced the whole front of the house, and could at last take down the tarpaulin that had protected the exposed rooms from the southwest gales. In one of these gales we had carried a sheet of plateglass along the planks and scaffolding, and fastened it into the top floor window frame. The glass sung in a sinister manner as the wind hit it. Working up the building, we concluded by hanging new slates on the roof. Then, with my wages, I went round to the art college and put the amount on a year at the college, as if it were a really promising horse.

I was quite pleased no longer to have to climb the scaffolding of a morning. It was only the first climb of the day that worried one; after that I swarmed about like an ape. Curiously, at the very moment in the late Fifties that I re-entered art school life in Brighton once again (after eight years) the world all at once lifted itself from the utility ration-book drabness that had coloured—or discoloured—it for the past seventeen or eighteen years. The post-war era had been distinguished for shortages, depression, and a general absence of any sort of visual beauty, particularly as regards clothes and personal appearance. Now, colourful and interesting dresses began to appear—commencing in the art colleges, where everything of any aesthetic value always shows itself first.

The girls arriving for the new season were, compared to their predecessors, quite different; they had beauty, because they were relaxed, assured, undeprived. The young men equally were another breed. To the worried, uneasy, complex-full characters of the austerity world, these new people were free and confident, guitar-playing, influenced by Lonnie Donegan's Skiffle Group and a host of other entertainers, from Rock and Roll to New Orleans Jazz. In 1957 two incidents had memorable import. One of my old painter friends arrived at the studio one day with the news: "John Minton is dead."

This to the art world of the time (although apparently a suicide) equalled in shock quality the later Kennedy demise. It was indeed the end of a certain era, but Minton's brilliant romantic-cubist style had itself been moving recently towards a would-be academicism.

His portrait of the celebrated critic Neville Wallis, Apostle of the Return to Realism, had been bought by Brighton Art Gallery—a strange picture, in the mode of Whistler's Carlyle. Minton at that time had been making a number of repaints of masterpieces. His version of Maclise's *Death of Nelson* mural in the Houses of Parliament had been hung at the R.A. I saw Minton once at the Lefevre Gallery—tall, olive-skinned, youthful, but with strikingly bright disturbed eyes, and an air about him of genius and authority, coupled with diffidence and indifferent self-sufficiency. (It was at this Gallery that I saw Dali hanging the exhibition of his great flying crucifixion and the large Madonna of his wife, Gala. He was quiet and efficient with the hangers, and seemed like a modest bank manager in dress and appearance; quite unbizarre—not even really noticeable). An elderly artist told me some years later that after a typically enjoyable evening at the Chelsea Arts Club, they had left Minton alone there, as he seemed to want to go to sleep on the sofa. "We none of us thought there was anything wrong, that he was planning anything. He had these pills, it seems. Next morning, there he was. Dead on the sofa. They thought he was asleep."

The other event, significant of the beginning of a new era rather the close of an old, was the advent of the film *Rock around the Clock*, with Bill Haley's Comets. A girl who came to model for us appeared in a state of excitement. "Have you heard this new music—Rock and Roll? It's going to change everything—" it was, and did. Elvis Presley had of course been around for a while, but the sleepy old-world popular music, that had become increasingly relaxed—Bing Crosby still at it, Frank Sinatra with a tremendous following, but not precisely aimed for the youth market—now stayed where it was for an older generation. Bill Haley (oddly, his band were not particularly young either) now seemed to symbolise the new image of the seventeen-year old. In my own day no one had thought of creating any such music particularly directed at us, and we had no fashion-uniform. At this moment also, the blue-jean era became generally accepted. Youth became recognisable and different; the girls were no longer absurd selfconscious imitations of the sophistication of their mother's fashions. The vulgarity of bright red lipstick (that perennial and repulsive ego-boost of the previous age-group with their desire to look like a film-star) and orange-pink face make-up (that had made professional portrait painting a dreary penance and finally a dead art over the past three decades) was relegated to the elderly and the middle-aged, who continued to bedeck themselves like circus clowns, while young girls took on the aura of the Impressionist era or the Renaissance. Renoir, Lippi and Botticelli were everywhere; the gentle beauty of the international Gothic style, combined with a sad Victorian pathos that we catch in 19th. century photographs. At the Art College great hooped skirts and lace petticoats appeared, the hair grown long, with pony-tails and braids. All these elements seemed to form a new atmosphere about the teen-age world that filled the etching-room and studios. A new world was here with subjects abounding. Suddenly, call-up ceased, and the depressive threat of an unknown period of military service—anything from eighteen months to two and a half years—was removed from the young man's horizons. Some twelve or thirteen years after the war, we were about back to peace-time.

Beauty, in life and art, had been something of which to be ashamed in the military atmosphere of 1945. The girl had been liberated, called-up; was equal to the man. A buxom, balloony pin-up was the man's dream-ideal, far removed from reality; Betty Grable the fantasy figure-head. Now, in '57, the feminine element returned; the new students that year were beautiful as the old film-stars never were. Their hair styles were masterpieces of careful arrangement, their dresses objects of restrained subtlety. The older girl students, with their corduroy trousers and headscarves, were aghast; deciding that the new generation were frivolous, interested only in ephemera, not the business of training for a career. This was in fact possibly true. Their diversions were considerable. The young men played guitars, were actually playing them, and singing—in earlier times, nobody could really play anything, even when they took lessons with the ponderous seriousness that had marked every activity in the immediate post-war times. But now, skiffle groups were arising everywhere; they made the music for their own dances—dances every week, in place of the old once-a-year select concourse of waltzes and fox-trots that nobody could do properly anyway.

In jazz clubs all over the country young people were jiving. In the antique room at the art school in the lunch-hour, a few students with banjo, clarinet, guitar—all playing expertly, varying a chord sequence, not playing from music—would create a jazz session. Everywhere these was dancing—expert, informal jiving, at incredibly high speed, full of interesting and personal variations, yet all carried on with the most precise timing, with the absolute essential of dancing accurately on the off-beat. This way of dancing on the beat that was *about* to happen—rather than on the one that *was* happening, gave one a timeless, tireless ability to dance all day and all night. You only got tired when you stopped and relaxed back into the present. You could hardly tire yourself by dancing in the future, after all. It created a kind of philosophy of life, that of being just ahead, always ahead . . . an awake kind of state of mind. You can't exactly learn to jive—it is more like remembering how to—which is, of course, what real ability in painting and drawing is, after all.

In art, in my own work, a more consciously Zen approach affected my procedure. To become the eye, the ear, the very person you are drawing, as a cat becomes a mouse to catch it, as the archer becomes the arrow and is also the target and the bull's eye, and therefore cannot miss even if he shoots with his head turned away . . . no error is admitted, because no error can exist. With the same approach, you can play any instrument that depends on a sequence of individual notes, provided you do not think about them when you are doing it. Of course, for chord sequences an analytical period of learning is necessary; but mouth-organs, one-string fiddles, slide-whistles, can all be played in the Zen manner, provided you detach your mind completely. Nobody ever thinks what they are doing when they whistle a tune while working, but the tune is there. Transpose this detached whistling into your finger on the string of the fiddle, and you can play it—perhaps. At least, it's a theory.

There were a new breed of students in the etching room, also, although things had not got to the strange point of about ten years afterwards when I came upon a young student from the Art College scraping his newly polished steel etching plate up and down against the rough surface of the Palace Pier sea wall. He told me he had been sent down to the sea-front by the current instructor to study surfaces and find some new kind of texture that had the quality of Brighton beach about it. I left him still vandalising his plate, with rapt attention; he was oblivious to sea, sky, boats, the design and construction and history of the piers and what remained of the capstans; he was eager to get on, though, he said, eager to get his diploma, and this was the way to get it. . . .

But we were still ten years or so from the Cultural Revolution, and even a break-away from the copper plate seemed a daring step. Students were now appearing from other colleges, to take their final year of teacher training at a now fully developed department in the College. "What's all this old-fashioned rubbish you do?" one kept taunting me, as he placed his plate on the floor, and ignoring the dustbox, spattered the resin for the aquatint haphazard across plate and floor. We had been used to whirl the fan in the dustbox, and then place a plate within so that a gentle snowstorm of resin might descend consistently like dust on a neglected piano.

I realised that I had concluded at last my tributes to the past, and I put away my copper plates and took up an old zinc litho plate. I polished the back, and etched directly and freely on it, getting the nearest student to sit for the portrait, and working with the needle as with a freeflowing pen, following on the biting—as free and direct—with a loose aquatint series of tonings.

I took to this new approach with enthusiasm—even creating a kind of Mezzotint by scraping the surface with a brick and sand, and then scraping out the high-light—perhaps I was not so far away from my cultural descendant-to-be by the breakwater. I had recommenced etching where I had left off in 1949, with a Whistlerian scale and vision, carefully biting my plates with timed accuracy. I stepped over a barrier, as it were, and found myself. The subject I wanted was at hand, everywhere—the delicate balance of sensuality, refinement and even pathos of the young girl; her natural development affecting—disguising, for a brief period—the actual character of the matured individual, which would be set within a few years. But for this interim period provided by nature in all species as a delusive (but no less real) visual inspiration, the artist is presented with subjects that make all others—the middle-aged nude model, the still-life skull and bottles, or lobster and grapes, the pictorial composition of trees—racehorses, interiors, abstract shapes, surrealism and so on—seem contrived and repetitive. The young girl, like the young dog or cat, is never the same two days at a time. You may take one of them, and paint her each day of the week. Each day you will find that her mood, her appearance, alters by the hour. Her clothes, her hair, her very actions, denote her soul state, her subservience to creative nature. . . .

I bought large sheets of zinc from the metal suppliers, laid acid-resistant grounds upon them, and began a series of studies direct on the plate, as usual without preliminary drawings. The students were happy to sit for me as required, and eagerly collected the results. It seemed odd to me that other students did not appreciate the opportunity of so marvellous a sequence of potential masterpieces in these subjects close to hand; but I recollected that in my own more formative period I had found the curious character-become-caricature of the aged an inspiration above all others, rather than the appearance of my own contemporaries.

My friends among the students also sat for oil portraits; and here I referred not, as yet, to freedom of approach, but to the portraits of Ingres as example and high-water mark of excellence in this field. I do not think one can do better, in every sense, I looked continually at books of reproductions of these unforgettable works (we have few of the originals in Britain) and The Comtesse d'Haussonville, Madame Devauçay and the others—as live as characters out of Balzac—encouraged me to try yet again and again to portray factually my own contemporaries. It had taken me ten years of study, thought, observation, and reading to learn to perceive the kind of quality in the evanescent features around me that had been perceived by Raphael, by Holbein and Ingres, by Botticelli and Filippo Lippi. It is not *prettiness* that one is after—it is the understatement that yet rings out, shot-like; it is beauty that one does not suspect or at first, perhaps, even realise is beauty. Most of the students, as I had been myself at that age, were primarily concerned more with technique than subject; with style and approach. They pursued for the most part a kind of academic Impressionism which created great problems; they altered, they worked over their pictures—endlessly. In the graphic arts, a more direct medium, they were more personal in approach and much more successful; particularly in lithography, in the spirit of French tastefulness or German Expressionism. With my own painting, I was keeping to a limited colour scheme of greys and umbers, of drab greens and purples. I pursued a restrained and linear technique, low and sombre in style. I did not believe in altering, or roughing-in. Each stroke, each line, is put down in harmony with the last. If you go back and alter the first, what possible harmonic sequence can your brushstrokes have, what possibly valid statement can your picture make, save that of muddled thinking and indecision—of the removal of corner-stones and key-blocks?

One student whom I particularly liked to paint was a complete work of art already; black hair and ivory white complexion, and great brown eyes. What more had one to do but pray she would keep still, and that no interruption would lay a conscious thought upon those delicately abstracted features. There are certain people who stand out recognisably from the crowd, even at one glance; who, from every viewpoint, in every gesture, are a gift to the artist, a constant prompting to pictorial creation. I painted *Pensive Girl, Girl in a Dufflecoat, Girl with Auburn hair,* and a series of nudes. I tried to keep an Ingres-like simplicity of line and pose, and to give the figure something of that placid immobility Raphael gives his portraits—the restraint and balance of the Castiglione, for instance; where the eternal and the momentary are played against each other so happily. The matter of sympathy is essential with a model, although you need not be in complete rapport—your detachment is an essential—yet you must not be completely outside her psyche. You have to hold your breath, as you hold it when drawing a cat or dog. The tones of skin are luminous as flowers, and present the same problems. A tone a point or so out, and the petal (or the skin) is dead. My portraits suggested to me a new large picture; and I took up the semi-religious subject matter of my earlier work in London. I worked here from drawings, the students posing for the preliminary studies of hands, feet, drapery, faces and details. I painted a large Pieta, taking not the Christ-image surrounded by figures of legendary celebrity, but one of the Thieves, forgotten and unhonoured except for the solitary and inevitable girl (there always is one) brooding alone above his thrown-down corpse. Her head upon her hands, elbows on knees, her eyes gloomily upon the observer of the picture, she seems perhaps to suggest the Inevitability of Conclusion.

· · · · · ·

My next large work was a 6×5′ canvas—*Angels on a Roof*. One angel floats between the chimneys in a fairly happy mood—in contrast to most of the figures in my paintings, whose mood is generally one of philosophic resignation, if not actual disquiet. The other two angels, sitting on the slates, perhaps make up for her airborne content. One impassionately contemplates a child—the other, with empty hands, her eyes upon her inmost thoughts, could seem to be previsaging the tortured moments of her own future. My third large work of this time was a larger version of *One of the Thieves*, including not only the mourning girl—the type of the Magdalene, empty hands held outwards—but a passing Roman, a clerk of little authority, pausing to glance indifferently over his shoulder at the supreme tragedy for another individual.

It is odd that pictures should come to one, evolve in the artist's mind—slowly he gathers together drawings and preparatory sketches. Why does he work from this model or that? Is it mere accident, or is he led to a certain individual, a particular person, because there is that in them that suggests and sums up the conception of his theme? Does he select his theme in the subconscious as a deliberate symbol of his mental state, much as the subconscious selects the tune you thoughtlessly whistle, because its title has some bearing upon the matters of the passing moment? (This is an experiment you can try with yourself and others.)

When not etching, I was on the beach near the fish market and the boats; a place conducive to reflection and constructive thought. With the sun making Seurat-twinkles in the blue-green seas, the clear sky beating down, Balzac, Stendhal, bread and cheese and cherries, and my watercolours and etching plates, I was set up for ten hours or more—from the faint sunny mists dispersing at ten a.m. to the long clear evening, the fishing boats trawling for mackerel—whose excited spurts and jumps gave the water the effect of torrential rain on the suface. Brighton, of course, is the land of the lotus-eater.

A notable local character who lived on the beach was one "Sunshine Joe" a tramp, who produced, with chalk and pastels, odd drawings of faces and animals on the inside panels of dismembered cornflake boxes. He offered these for sale on the lower promenade. With a knitted cap and an old yellow raincoat even in summer, black beard and unwashed appearance—no beach tramp ever deigned to actually bathe in the sea—he was unmistakeable. I was once standing behind him in a queue at Joe Lyons'. "Fourpence for a meat pie?" he was muttering—"Could have bought a pig for that in 'Thirty-six."

I had become interested in the art of the film, which was in the fashionable ascendant intellectually at this period. Belonging to a film club, which showed a selection of masterpieces with a once a week meeting, I attended a special showing to select the year's programme. We commenced at nine-thirty one Sunday morning, and watched some twenty films, until one o'clock the next morning. Curiously, none of us could recall even the titles of any but the last three, and fell back on our notes made at the time for any decisions regarding them.

Brighton was the home of cheap eating-houses, with plank floors, old unpainted tables and chairs, and catering to early morning workers or vehicle drivers. Divall's had two establishments, one in Middle Street, one next to the station. The meals were excellent, but there were no visual luxuries, except to the eager eye of the artist. The places were full of character—and characters. A delicacy was the Tidioggie, which for threepence or so gave you a meal in itself—a kind of meat and potato pasty. No one could eat more than one Tidioggie at a sitting—or standing; or a walking munch. There is an etching by Whistler (in the Thames set) that gives the impression of a Divall's type of eating-house precisely.

As I wished to practise etching as a main interest and profession I decided to apply for membership of the Royal Society of Painter-Etchers and Engravers. I had shown my watercolours for some years at Aldridge's gallery at nearby Worthing, and they kept a regular stock of my work on hand. Mr. Aldridge, the elderly proprietor, would always buy anything I took in—albeit at very advantageous prices to himself—and would set me to spending whole days drawing at Worthing subjects: I would then take them back to the gallery before he closed, and receive my pay for them. He kindly framed six of my best etchings, placing them in impressive handtooled mounts and oak frames— "leave it to me," he said. The resulting images looked (presentation-wise) like loan exhibits from the British Museum, and I was elected an Associate. So commenced the friendly and constructive connection with other etchers and engravers so essential to the pursuance of the craft—a freemasonry indeed, and as difficult to be accepted into unless of the right spirit. The President, Malcolm Osborne, said again and again to me—"always remember, this is first and foremost a *friendly* society—." I attended the meetings, private views, and the highly interesting Print Collectors' Club evenings when a lantern-lecture and talk might be given by some expert, curator, or artist. Apart from my activities on the one hand as a second-time round art student, and my inevitable participation into a younger social life, I was able as well to meet the best and leading etchers and engravers at the same time. I went on to exhibit at the R.E. my new large aquatints—I had been elected on the small, earlier copperplate work—and these boldly patterned portrait prints stood out and gave me some notoriety—it was a day when etchings were still in the traditional mode for scale and technique, and only the large woodcuts gave the walls huge colour images.

One of my portraits of girls—*Girl in Black*—was selected a P.C.C. print of the year; and A. S. H. Mills, the then secretary—a tireless and generous worker for the Society—came down to Brighton with the edition for me to sign. Not having a press of my own, they had been printed for the Society elsewhere. My thin zinc plates had at first seemed to pose something of a problem. W. P. Robins, a great expert and pundit, viewed them with disgust as an intrusive innovation, and voiced his opinion that it would be impossible for anyone to get a print from them: "Too thin; impossible to print." However, it was achieved. I sold my new work very well from the R.E. exhibitions, and James Laver of

the Victoria and Albert Museum came over at the Private View to tell me that
he liked my textural effects, and to ask how they were achieved. I was also
asked to write for the *Artist Magazine*—a connection and an interest that has
lasted for thirty years. I felt that I was succeeding a little. As Marcel says in
Murger's *Vie de Bohéme*: "Art is looking up; we're earning almost as much as
errand-boys."

In addition to my etching, I revived my earlier interest in Natural History.
Curiously, Mr. Mills, on catching sight of some stuffed voles and mice in my
studio, had commented that his hobby also was the study of small mammals.
My new art student circle now took an interest in my taxidermy and dissection
and gave it a fresh impetus. Soon, students began to bring me dead birds and
animals they had found. I skinned, preserved and mounted a seagull, a pigeon
and other birds, and hung them in the etching-room, from which students
would borrow them as subjects to paint or draw. One cold winter evening,
walking back from the art college in the side streets, eating chips from one of
those friendly and romantic establishments that warmed the chill lanes at
intervals, I came upon a dead tabby cat, only recently knocked down, without a
mark on him. The tabby seemed a fortunate find. It was now after twelve, and
the street lights were off as was then the custom. Picking up the cat by the tail, I
continued my way through the gloom. A shaft of light fell on me; there were
hurried footsteps, and large helmets.

"What's this? What have you there?"—I recalled suddenly a constant journalistic item in the newspapers (revived whenever news was scarce) relating to furriers descending to cat-poaching. . . .

"It's a specimen."

"*Is* it, and what do you propose to do with it, *Sir?*"

"Paint it, to begin with; then preserve it."

"*Paint* it?" Nonplussed! I explained that I was an *artist.*

"*Oh!*" That explained it; I was suffered to continue. "That's all right, Sir. Didn't realise you were an *artist.*"

Next day I made a careful still-life study of the animal; I then skinned it, and preserved and cleaned the skull. The skin I gave to a fellow-student, who used it to protect the outside of his painting-satchel.

In a jazz club, while talking of this, a student from a nearby art college along the coast asked me if I wanted a fine preserved badger, stuffed by his grandfather. It cluttered up the house, his mother said. He promised to leave it for me in the locker room of the Art College the next afternoon. At five o'clock I went to the College, and walking up the steps was stopped by a bearded young man who had approached from the opposite direction.

"I'm a Technical College student. Do you know where the locker room is?" he said.

"I'm going there myself. I'll show you."

"I've come to collect a badger," he went on. "It's been left there for me by a chap I met. I'm interested in taxidermy and natural history."

I paused. "So am I. And I'm sorry, but it's been left for *me*, I believe."

He objected. At last we agreed to go and see if it had been left anyway. There on the table in the empty locker room stood the stuffed badger on its stand, and next to it a sack containing a freshly dead badger, evidently killed (as they so often are) by a car on the roads at night. Our surprise at this coincidence was considerable. Why should two taxidermists be left badgers by chance acquaintances at exactly the same moment, and meet at the same time to collect them? There probably never had been a badger, either stuffed or dead, in that locker-room before. We parted firm friends, but I never saw him again, nor heard from anybody that they knew him. Oddly, too, nobody else had been either on the art college steps or in the building near us during the whole incident. It rather reminded me of an incident following the demise of my paternal relation some years previously, when I was alone in the house, and in a low state of spirits. A little old gentleman called, very lively, who announced he had been my father's school master—I tried to make instant mental calculations regarding age; but he interrupted me with a flow of anecdotes for a full hour. He was small, brisk and sharp, wore a very loud check suit, and was unknown to anyone to whom I mentioned the incident subsequently. . . .

As at school, when I used to mount fox-tails and the like for sixth-formers who owned guns legitimately, I was soon set up at the art college as a kind of resident natural history lost property officer. Once you have a reputation for taxidermy, specimens will appear about you miraculously. I was sent a kingfisher by a friend who went away to teach in the fen country, and also a kestrel. I dissected this latter, and made an inventory of its stomach. The main contents consisted, eerily, of about a dozen little *hands*—the feet of mice, that had resisted the dissolving fluids to which the bones and fur had succumbed. It appears, consequently, that the feet of mice are particularly resistant to acid, and probably any other corrosive agent. The skins of rats, kittens, rabbits, and weasels now began to appear on the walls of the etching room, in some profusion. At the end of the Xmas term at the art college I was obliged to borrow a barrow from the nearby fruit market to remove all my specimens and mounted birds to my studio. The collection now included starlings, thrushes and so on, often mounted flat on boards as if in flight. A police constable soon stopped me (of course) accused me of stealing the barrow, and kept me waiting outside a police box, in a heavy shower (that ruined all the specimens pretty well) until he had contacted all the people I could think of as likely to testify to my integrity including (happily) the owner of the barrow.

As I always enjoyed swimming in the rough seas, I (with my friends) were apt to ignore the danger signals set up on Brighton Beach for the benefit of weak swimmers. One afternoon when it was fairly rough—a south-west wind blowing—myself and one or two companions were the only people on the beach. My friends were sitting against the wall, out of sight of the promenade. I was lying in the surf, allowing the waves to pick me up, throw me on the beach, and then scoop me back into the breakers. After a while, I came out of this dream-world activity to observe an evidently large crowd on the promenade. Without my glasses, I could see only a blurred group. Somebody, however, now detached himself from this crowd and came striding down the beach. I had just been thrown up on the pebbles with some impetus, and was collecting my breath, when this person suddenly pounced, pulled me out of reach of the waves, and commenced pressing my back in the approved resuscitation manner. I hardly knew what to do, being so surprised. It seemed that the crowd had been watching what they supposed to be an unconscious body being tossed in the surf, and eventually washed up. One of my friends on the beach now got up and came down to us.

"They think you're a corpse, Mike," he said. "Actually, this is a friend of mine," he told the rescuer. My rescuer looked up astounded. I took the opportunity to slide away very hastily into the foam, where I swam under water until I was safely out of the situation. From the waves, I could see my rescuer walking away with my friend, expostulating; while the crowd, evidently disappointed at the non-tragic end of the incident, dispersed in disgust. In fact, the really rough sea can be incredibly dangerous, even to the swimmer who feels he is confident of handling it, like a trainer with a tiger. It is the giant breakers that are the danger, and which have the strength. You can get through them by standing upright, hands pointing above your head, leaning forward a little. The eight-foot wave rears above you—crash—you are through and swimming out to sea. To return to shore, you have to come up with a breaker, swimming on the top of it, to be thrown up on the beach—and you must at once scrabble furiously to elude being drawn back into the underflow and smashed down by the whole weight of the next wave, which could be very dangerous indeed on a shelving sloping beach.

I have once ill judged a return, and got caught by the breaker behind me. I was picked up, as if by a great hand, and thrust down and down—as if indeed a huge hand was pressing between my shoulder-blades. Pebbles and stones rattled madly about me, banging at head and body, cutting my chest, my face pressed ever more heavily into the whirling maelstrom. The important point in this more than surprising experience was not to forget to hold your breath—if you panicked, and opened your mouth (a great temptation instinctively) you would be finished. I had to wait—eternally, it seemed—for the breaker to retreat, its power momentarily spent. It did, at last, and I scrabbled with full panic at this point, directly I got some air. No more jokes with the sea on that occasion.

Recalling experiences at Brighton brings to mind a time in my earlier period at Art School, when myself and several others accepted the offer of a touring company presenting Shaw's *Devil's Disciple* to join the production for the week as soldiers. The play was being put on at the equally ancient old theatre that stood next door to the famed Theatre Royal, in New Road. These archaic Sickertian gilt-laden survivals, full of resident ghosts and age-old memories, were marvellous structures. Everywhere was a mass of tunnels, minute changing rooms under the orchestra pits, passages leading no doubt to the other secret tunnels that run reputedly everywhere under Brighton. From above the stage of the *Dolphin* theatre, in that vast area of ropes and pulleys up in the roof, I could crawl across the platforms and planks to the area above the stage of the *Royal* next door, and look down at the performance on *that* stage. Then (still in the uniform of a redcoat of the 18th Century) climb down to be in time to come on stage in our own theatre. The *Dolphin* later became the *Paris* cinema, where we enjoyed many historic film masterpieces. Eventually it was demolished for the inevitable anonymous offices; hygienic, sensible, constructive perhaps; but devoid of ghosts and romanticism.

Our parts as soldiers necessitated our being drilled in a conveniently empty bar, by the actor impersonating our sergeant. In fact, he broke a mirror with his musket in his demonstration of efficiency as he flung the gun to his shoulder. The actors, nerve-laden young men playing officers, were hysterically ill-at-ease and dissatisfied for the first two performances; after which they recovered their confidence, and with now nonchalant sauvity, passed their evenings up to seconds of their cue drinking in the bar next to the stage door, in full dress uniform. As actors, the students were more than efficient. We dragged the irate Dick Dudgeon off to prison in realistic style, with strangleholds on him as he struggled.

"Not so tight, you fools!" he was hissing, red and stifled, and furious with us once we got backstage. It was interesting, that once in the uniform of ordinary soldiers, everyone treated us as if we were Eighteenth Century jail scrapings, rather than near graduate students; while the actors playing young officers became supercilious to the last degree. Such is the power of dressing-up; and the effect of *costume*.

. . . . . .

The summers of this period in the late Fifties were very warm, and as usual I found long night walks a pleasant way of employing them. To walk the country roads, slowly entering a town in a hot July night, shortly before dawn, is like landing on an uninhabited planet. For these few hours, even the traffic was in abeyance, in those days. A hot, still quietness had taken over, and the buildings, gaunt and deep-shadowed in the street lighting, seemingly lonely for people, had a set-piece theatrical look. If you are tired at such a time, you sit on the nearest wall and rest, roll a cigarette or two. You don't hurry—you wander—and get there faster, because you don't care if it's today or tomorrow. In the open country, the sides of the road were lit with glow-worms—strange green lights in the tufts of grass. Curious, almost unbelieving, you bend down, and discover the amount of light you might expect from a cigarette-end—only green—emanating from a little grub half an inch long. A few in a glass jar will give a kind of illumination, as in the fairytale illustrations; but it would seem a kindness to replace them in the hedge subsequently. And then, of course, at night there are the hedgehogs. A rustle nearby—you pause, wait, reach into the roadside undergrowth, and sometimes pull one out before it curls up. If you rock it slightly, it will uncurl. Stroke him under the chin—he will bring his visor down, his nose tilting backwards into the wrinkles of his forehead. But keep rocking, and he will get quite tame and not mind you. One evening I was carrying a specimen along a lane, and deciding to conclude my walk on that occasion, called at the nearest house to ask my way to the railway station. The householder, not caring for my then Bohemian appearance, called his sons, and a solid phalanx refused my questions at the door until I went away. They then evidently phoned the police, for I was quite soon apprehended. It was a very dark part of the lane. The car stopped, figures leapt out, surrounding me. A voice read off what was evidently a description: "Beard, glasses, long hair—they didn't mention a *hedgehog*, though, did they Bert?"

A few words of conversation of course put matters right, and I was given a lift to the railway station after all: "They didn't realise you were an *artist*, Sir."

"Do you mind the hedgehog?" I said, as I was getting into the car.

"You'd better bring it along, Sir, if you want to," said the constable wearily. While waiting for the infrequent train to Brighton, the porter and I bewhiled the night hours by letting the hedgehog run up and down the length of the platform to each other like a large clockwork mouse, which it seemed perfectly happy to do. It subsequently lived happily in a friend's garden.

A dead hedgehog is difficult to skin satisfactorily, but has an interesting skull. The teeth are very varied. For primitive creatures, reputed to have been contemporary with the dinosaurs, they have lasted well—particularly when so many are run over every night on the roads, although there now seems to be a theory they have at last learnt not to curl up on the highway. Another animal often seen about at night was, of course, the fox. I have come across them padding about the suburban streets, among the mock-tudor residences. The most beautiful image of a fox I ever observed was when I surprised one at the edge of a spring cornfield one sunny morning, and he sprang through it, leaping over the blue grass corn while it bent and flowed like the waves of the sea; his chestnut colour contrasting, with marvellous visual effect.

One of the pleasures of being awake at night, and out and about, is perhaps the sensation, be it illusory or not, that one has more space in which to *think*. All about, mankind are no longer working, talking, quarrelling, driving madly about—they are reduced to mere pairs of bellows, slowly breathing—their personalities dissolved—quieted as if dead. The night is far from lonely, for the one left awake—it is free, empty, ready to expand into. Sometimes, if too tired to continue walking it was possible to spend the night outdoors in repose; but you will be incredibly cold once you go to sleep, even in a heatwave, without covering. Passing a hayfield one starry two a.m. it occurred to me to make an igloo, or nest, of hay, and doze peacefully looking up at the Milky Way. Nearby, the steam trains roared down the line, with screams and roars; a flaring cloud of smoke, illuminated orange by its own fire, over hanging the engine like a demon. But I was glad when the sun rose, and I could become warm again. You need a sleeping bag out of doors to be completely comfortable, with a groundsheet above and below, as there is always a heavy dew—unless of course you sleep by a large fire, when you need no cover, and there is no dew. The romance of sleeping under hedges just as you please is a romantic myth. But with proper equipment, provided you do not care about rustling insects and small rodents, you can be perfectly comfortable; and to wake out of doors, in the morning air, is a pleasure equalled by few. Nonetheless, to overlook minor discomfort is necessary for a roving life. I had endured over the years the ability to sleep anywhere—night or day—merely curling up under my donkey jacket, like a dog on a mat.

The first band in which I played was located in Burgess Hill. I had been standing in the crowd watching the procession on the occasion of nearby Ditchling's Carnival Day. A group of skifflers passed by, guitars and clarionet—and one, whom I knew slightly, called out "Got your mouth-organ with you?" I always carried this instrument. I had found it on the beach, after throwing pebbles at it idly for some time on the assumption it was an old sardine tin. On going home to clean the rust off, I discovered that I could play it, provided I thought about something else at the time. My grandmother subsequently informed me that my grandfather would play the mouth-organ for their dances when they were all young immigrants in the Nineties, so perhaps it came through. I stepped off the kerb and joined the procession, and so began my interest in playing jazz. The village was full of sideshows and booths that day, and mummers performing St. George and the Dragon—an old world atmosphere prevailed. I had recently been elected to the Handworkers' Guild, and showed my prints at this annual exhibition of arts and crafts held in the Village Hall. One of the members was a typical elderly lady artist—there were many in this village of the arts, living quietly in their cottages up the lanes, tending their flowers, wearing huge straw hats. Mrs. Webb painted somewhat in the style of Helen Allingham, and her watercolours stood out for their high standard of technique and drawing—attributes that have been slowly diminishing since less importance has been given to that aspect. Mrs. Webb had been the daughter of J. C. Dollman, a celebrated Victorian painter; and her house was reputed to be a Tate Gallery of R.A. gold-framed masterpieces. I never saw it, regrettably; but Mrs. Webb would tell me of her early life as a girl in the village, and how she and her father would climb to Ditchling Beacon, and look down on the serenity of Edwardian summers as they worked at their watercolour sketches.

It was in the autumn of '57 that we formed at the art college the famed "Eminent Victorians" spasm Band. The skiffle and jazz revival was at its height. Once a week every village and town had its jazz club, and there was always a dance somewhere on a Saturday. The bands were local, dedicated, and idealistically uncommercial, which was why they were so good. In fact, to go commercial was to commit an act of betrayal to the religion of true jazz. One would play for drinks and refreshments, or for a pound or so each if it was a dance; but, mainly, the point was to *play*. These were essentially *dancing* clubs. What counted was the atmosphere. If it was right, the music was remarkable, having a quality that can seldom occur in a recording session. The bands were known in their locality to their fans, who journeyed to other villages to dance to them when they played away, as it were. There was a constant link between the small towns of Sussex and of course, in all the counties, the same situation existed. The number of good bands was surprising. All were devoted wholeheartedly to playing in the way their favourite early jazz bands had played and thought. There was a modesty about the whole activity that belied the extravagant claims one made for one's band and musicians, introducing oneself and them as champions, and prizewinners of musical competitions that had never existed; but this was all part of the fun, of not taking anything so seriously as to let it worry you. Nothing was worth worrying about—except keeping the beat, once the leader had "stomped off," being sharp and clearcut when the breaks came, and ending all together: suddenly stopping, all at once, a number played incredibly fast. The real, honest, good, unpretentious jazz of the Twenties, the precise subtleties of King Oliver and his world, of Bessie Smith, of the musicians who played in almost every great group of the time, Kid Ory, Johnny Dodds and all the rest, was something one worked towards—not to imitate them, but to achieve their same kind of airborne detachment, when the jazz seemed to be playing itself, invoked as something arising from the band, the dancers, the whole evening's session of vitality unique to that precise moment. It was an aesthetic very allied to one's preoccupations in painting, and writing; and if the session was good, it had the same sense of inevitability that only the best and simplest has in art, the sensation that the artist is always still painting that picture, still with it, *in* it; or, if a jazz recording of the Twenties, that the band is actually playing here and now. Good art does not date, it drags you into its own period. Our bands imitated that earlier period only in a spirit of the truest reverence, such as the Downtown Syncopators, who played, in their own way, in the style of the Original Dixieland Jazz Band c. 1918—dressing in the same formal manner, and employing the same staccato rhythms.

For myself, I liked the piano playing of Lil Hardin, immensely powerful yet immensely relaxed and understated: the strength behind King Oliver, and Louis Armstrong's Hot Five and Seven; her beautifully precise introductions and lead-ins cool and indifferent, but suggesting a passionate electricity that was never allowed too near the surface. The whole point of art is summed up in that attitude: to possess an omnipotent force, but never show it. With jazz in particular, this is the important factor. Sometimes, every player is harmonising around a theme which *nobody* is actually *playing*—a line played as it were by a ghost, silently. This is where you find the power; because you may, when dancing, be dancing to an invisible beat—filling in the beat yourself, because all the players are on the off-beat to this beat. To devotees of the jazz world, the clubs were places where you met your friends and acquaintances, and often friends and dancing partners whom you only met at these clubs, whom you expected to meet. It was—before the commercial musical scene took it up briefly, brought in everybody who merely wanted to follow fashion, and then left the clubs empty and dying, having driven away the original fans—a small community yet one closed to nobody. The followers of popular music, of the recording stars with big names of the Rock era, were not interested in jazz. The jazz groups had a local flavour—you knew the musicians because you went to their clubs and dances; you didn't read about them in magazines; they weren't in the image of god; you didn't scream and faint in their presence—you were often one of them, in fact.

The Eminent Victorians were not a jazz band in the purest sense; we were part jazz, part blues blowers, part spasm, playing the kind of music we wanted to play, in our own way, on any instruments we fancied or happened to learn, from cornets to kazoos. Firstly, we had a very definite beat, as we were all devoted jivers. Our conclusions were remarkably neat, the contrasting sounds all culminating in one mighty bang. The rhythm section of backing instruments playing on and around the chord sequence was composed of piano, drums, woodblocks, tuba, banjo, with a front line led by paraffin-funnel and trumpet mouthpiece, the traditional blues-blower, where all depends on a sense of tone and expert lipping. I played a mouth-organ occasionally, although mainly Swanee slide whistle. With trombone, kazoo, banjo, blues-blower, piano, guitar, tuba, drums, and a girl as blues singer, this was our line-up.

We commenced almost by accident, when R. and myself bought secondhand frock-coats for the annual carnival day of the student "Rag," a major event in those days. In this period Victorian clothes were easily come by, and not yet avidly collected. We decided to busk around the town with banjo and mouth-organ. Our particular group of associates joined us, the band was formed by lunchtime, and the day ended with us performing at the evening Rag Dance in the Technical College. (Curiously enough, we had been joined momentarily during the day by the actor John Slater, who asked if he could join in on tuba). From now on, we were in demand, photographed by the press, written up by the local newspapers . . . we played at dances, during intervals at

jazz clubs (which was pleasant, because we could then enjoy the evening's dancing as well). Wherever we were, our impeccable formal clothes (contrasting so forcibly with the usual jeans and art school dress worn when working) caused us to receive special and preferential treatment. Also, the fact that we were a closed society of the most influential students at the college, yet welcomed anyone else (of any year) to activities we organised—not of course as members of the band, but as fans and followers—gave the art college a social coherence, between students of all ages and years, that it had not possessed before. We appeared as cabaret turns as required. There always seemed to be somebody wanting us to do something. . . .

We collected Victorian waistcoats, high collars, ties, pince-nez; we wore our hair long, grew beards and moustaches to suit our new characters. The girls who were in our particular group of friends made long hooped Victorian dresses to wear. We possessed a Victorian book on etiquette, which we used as a kind of

157

official bible, addressing each other with great formality. This coming to the notice of the then Independent Television, we were approached to appear in a T.V. film about the new cult of the Victorian Revival. Certain scenes of this required filming in a house in London. I was staying a few days with friends in the country—I received a telegram from R. to meet him at Victoria Station, at once. There was no time to lose—the scene was to be shot that very evening. I put on my frockcoat and top-hat, walked up the lanes to the station, arrived in London, met R., found the television director, was wafted to a house that had retained its Victorian characteristics unchanged and waited for the cameramen to arrange the lighting satisfactorily. Having at last a moment to relax, I looked around—the walls were hung with original cartoons from the early days of *Punch*—Charles Keene, Phil May, Linley Sambourne . . . Linley Sambourne in particular. . . . Our director was talking to an attractive lady over by the fireplace. I approached them: "Excuse me, but did this house belong to Linley Sambourne?"

The lady turned to me eagerly. "Indeed, yes, have you heard of him?"

Certainly I had, the illustrator of the *Water Babies*, and all those strangely personal political cartoons in the 19th. Century *Punch* editions.

"Nobody else here seems to know much about him," said my informant. "It's so nice to find somebody who does—I'll show you some more." Eagerly we discussed the drawings on the walls while the film crew waited impatiently. Her enthusiasm was so great I asked if she were a descendant. She was; his grand-daughter in fact, a driving force of the Victorian Society, and the Countess of Rosse. The house had been preserved as Linley Sambourne had left it. It was here, I was told, that the artist had entertained the political celebrities of his day, and planned the weekly cartoon. I was now obliged to recount, however, a humorous anecdote concerning the band; but something went wrong with the filming, and the sequence eventually was never used; so the whole expedition, the cameras, lighting, the girls (from an agency) in Victorian clothes (not at all convincing—they might have asked for our own girls) were all a waste of time. However, R. and myself were taken down to the Victorian dining-room, a splendid survival from its period, and entertained to luxurious delicacies by the Earl of Rosse who obligingly helped us to all the drinks we required, but demurred at Victorians accepting such un-Victorian refreshments as Dry Martini and gin and ice. But we explained that one of the main points about the Victorians was (as Chesterton observed) that they always surprised you when you least expected it, and he agreed that this was possibly very true.

On Queen Victorian's birthday, we formed a small procession, a miniature marching band in full regalia, and marched round Brighton playing, to conclude at the famous statue of Queen Victoria put up by my great-uncle John in '97, (with Brighton Jack Boxall in the crowd looking on). Here we laid a bouquet. The police were a little annoyed, as we had neglected to inform them of the occasion; but the local press arrived in time to photograph us toasting her. For the purposes of the photograph some wine-glasses and a pot of cold tea had to be fetched from the art school café, to simulate wine. Somewhat pointlessly, the feature was then titled "Queen toasted in cold tea."

We were treated to a more proper respect by the civic authorities a little later on, the grand occasion of the Pig's Funeral. The pig itself, by name Grover, had been a favourite animal belonging to a local farmer at nearby Saltdean. The story was that it escaped one night, broke into a shed where a number of vats of home-made wine were in process of fomenting, drunk them all, and in an intoxicated state staggered around the farmyard until it fell into the well and was drowned. This story, syndicated world-wide, eventually reached Texas, where a town went to the trouble of having a tombstone carved in stone, inscribed to the memory of "Grover, the swine who died of wine." They then shipped it to the Brighton Town Council. They at a loss to know what to do (the pig himself having been long since removed from the well and disposed of) the local Students Association was approached for suggestions. It was accordingly decided to have a full-scale funeral procession through the town to the site of the well, and set up the stone beside it. The idea somehow snowballed, and the actual event achieved an unprecedented importance, once the newspapers and television took up the story. On the appointed day, all traffic was diverted from the main streets of Brighton, huge crowds lined the streets, and the cortége set off to a slow march pace. It was headed (apart from the T.V. news coverage and cine-cameras mounted on trucks that moved slowly before us) by the Eminent Victorians Marching Band. The blues-blower, my mouth-organ, and the trombone slowly moaned out the doleful sounds of *Didn't he ramble*, and other classic New Orleans sepulchral numbers. Behind us followed the rest of the band, and a great old motor hearse (owned by one of the architectural students, who collected such items), festooned with flowers on top and inside. Through the long glass side-panels could be seen a silver dish holding a pig's head (from the butcher) the whole being set upon daffodils. Behind this came hundreds of students from the art and technical colleges, dressed in black top-hats and frockcoats, with the girls under black veils, and all giving a steady mournful lowing wail that flowed and died away with an incredibly eerie effect. R., unable to participate, as he was sitting his final examinations, could hear us approach and pass the Art College. . . . The effect was macabre, impressive, surrealist in the extreme, and carried out with deadly seriousness and a fitting sobriety. Not a smile was on any face as the police stood by the silent crowds. A service was held at the Aquarium, and a fleet of motorcoaches then conveyed the mourners to Saltdean, where the procession reformed to set up the stone by the well, where a salvo of rifle-shots was fired. The story went the round of the world's newspapers, and pictures of the Victorians, hearse, and the procession appeared in various foreign newspapers, captioned in a variety of interesting ways. We also appeared in the *Illustrated London News* and the *Sketch*.

At Xmas, a Victorian music hall was organised at Ditchling. The music hall gave us a fitting opportunity to fall into our places as Victorians. Our tuba player had adopted the guise and dress of a vicar, when a parcel of Victorian clothes donated to us when we formed the group had been found to contain this uniform. It suited him so well that our audiences were always convinced of his authenticity. However, his sidewhiskers and Victorian sporting parson appearance, with clerical collar and low widebrimmed hat, contrasted on occasions with the pint of bitter in his hand, and we would wait each evening for the slightly disapproving and worried looks from the more orthodox members of our village audiences. However, this was always cleared up sooner or later when they got into conversation with him, and usually ended with further refreshment being ordered all round.

The music-hall ran for the greater part of a week; we played our jazz numbers; one of the band did an inspired improvisation as a comedian; R. and I, in military uniform, sung *Comrades* . . . it was all a great success, as usual. A magazine now included us in one of their comic strip features, and I had the unusual experience (having been interviewed and lent photographs to the editor) of seeing myself portrayed as a character in a black and white cartoon adventure with balloons of words issuing from my mouth. Another of our activities was to form a Victorian football team, to play other student teams. The girls made us long striped long trousers; we wore black waistcoats, and collars and ties; but although we practised in the park a good deal, we never won a match. We once played a team of commonwealth students, and were overwhelmed by their enthusiasm (and superior ability).

The frockcoat that we affected was of course an *afternoon* dress to the Victorian gentleman, and in summer worn with light trousers. When we played all night at a party, we carried our day time dress with us in Gladstone bags, hiring one of the students as valet to help us dress, buy us drinks and introduce us to young ladies with whom we wished to dance. This was an idea of R's; he would indicate the prospective partner to his valet, and wait until she was brought over to him, when he would rise and bow and lead her into a sparkling jive. . . .

. . . . .

We were hired to play for an all-night party and dance in a country house in one of the nearby villages; the dance was held in a barn; we played our last number just before dawn, and in the grey early light walked into the village to find a cigarette machine—the ghost-like effect of six or seven tall top-hatted wraiths surprised a milkman and an early morning police officer, but there were so many of us, and all so cheerful, that we seemed to make friends everywhere. Back at the party, we changed into day dress, and had the occasion immortalised by the official photographer we carried with us—this was de rigeur, in our Society, as the Victorians themselves always looked forward to posterity. We then set off to the next village, where, as the Victorian's Stoolball team, we had entered the county Stoolball Tournament. This activity flourished at the time all over Sussex, the teams visiting each other's villages. We lost, of course; none of us had played before, except one, who was something of a local champion on his own ground; but not even his despairing expertise could carry us towards the cup.

In some ways, it was extraordinary how much energy everybody seemed to possess, in these years. I myself was, of course, some years senior to the group with which I moved—they were teen-age and early twenties—but the impetus of always having every moment filled swept us all along. There was the long working-day at the college—nine to nine, more or less; the week-end dances and parties and jazz clubs, the trips about the countryside during vacations—and always, wherever one was, sketching; or finding people to sit for etched portraits. Any spare time was devoted to continual band practices necessary to extend the repertoire and improve our ease and confidence. Any room that contained a piano was eagerly begged, borrowed or rented for an hour or two—it was not at all easy to find places to practice with a full band; the date to be made, and the members of the band informed of the time and place. All this required a deal of organisation; and art students can bear any hardship, but they won't endure being organised. However, the Victorians seemed to organise themselves. Determinedly, we refused to admit of anybody being titular head or president. We were essentially democratic. If anybody wished to

Michael Blaker

be leader, he might. We all politely agreed, provided he did not claim the post too often.

Not everybody owned tape-recorders in those days, but we borrowed one for a session on a single occasion, and so have a tape of some half-dozen numbers; and this oddly concrete survival of a past now but a misty dream curiously evokes not the era in which it was made, but appears (like all the best art) to exist on a weirdly timeless plane. Of course, the Victorians were also hardworking students taking their examinations for diplomas in the fine arts, and this period was to represent but a part of their early days—in a sense, not really themselves at all, but themselves in a formative period, in a united phase to which all contributed.

Each year in nearby Haywards Heath the Dolphin Fair was held. A selection from the Eminent Victorians decided to visit the Fair, competing in the various competitions. Our trombonist won the competition for smoking a cigarette in the shortest possible time, and beat the others by several minutes by taking it all in one non-stop drag. He was awarded with a credit-slip for five pounds at the town grocery, which gave us supplies for the day. R., observing a long line of pipesmokers being judged for the "Most Original and Curious Pipe," pulled his hat over his eyes and joined the end of the line, his old commonplace briar between his teeth. Like every other non-winner, he was given a tin of tobacco as a consolation prize. With food and tobacco, we enjoyed our picnic, watching the sheep escape from the sheepdog trials and disappear over the hill, to the surprise of dogs and shepherds, and to the amusement of the crowd. Huge rockets were sent up at dusk—one of the descending sticks, a six-foot spear, thudded point-first into the ground ten feet away from me as I walked across to the sideshows . . . later, at the evening dance in the Heywood Hotel we offered our services as a novelty group (we had brought a selection of our instruments, and the piano was at hand). We were a great success, and pints of refreshing bitter were lined up for us, while dancing partners clamoured for our expert accompaniment.

It was at this fair that I came upon a student from the Art College whose grandfather had been a notable patron of etchers in the period of 1890 to 1930—the greatest era in which to have collected—but whose acquisitions at this moment in time were at their lowest ebb in history, sales-room wise. This does not matter to a dealer, who merely keeps them by until the market shall rise, or even buys more in with discrimination. As one dealer said in my hearing: "You can always make money in the arts—but there is just one point—you must always buy the *best*."

I went to see the collection, which was staggering. Not an inch of wall was free of yet another thin black frame and monochrome masterpiece within. The family were about to dispose of this potential fortune, having found it too much to dedicate their lives endlessly to preserving intact—I was glad, by their kindness, to have been able to spend a day studying these masterworks.

At the Art College, I printed some of my etched portraits on panels of cotton, which were sewn into a dress by some of the girls who formed their subjects. This made a costume for our blues-singer to wear. R. at this time painted a gigantic picture of the base of the Cross, with soldiers gambling, and somewhat surrealist additions such as members of the Victorians with bicycles. This was spirited away from the painting studio by some of the girls, and hidden in their cloakroom, while the artist stormed about the college wondering how a painting twelve feet by four could have disappeared so utterly. However, it was later set into the panelling of the wall in one of the architectural rooms, by a far-seeing professor who discovered it abandoned by the artist during the vacation.

In June, 1958, the students at the Art College conceived the idea of "Jazz in June" a huge jazz festival dance to be held at the Corn Exchange—the largest possible venue available—in which a dozen or so bands would take part for a prize. This prize in itself was relatively unimportant, as no bands cared about that kind of prestige, unless it was a crate of beer. And everybody—in the tradition of jazz—claimed they were the uncrowned kings of everything they did, anyway—they would have played in any case. However, the beer was indeed always acceptable, and the main requirement for a jazzman playing all evening. The ball was to be in aid of charity, and the tickets were printed, and the hall booked. The students, abandoning their studies, roamed the town, in and out of shops and offices selling the tickets for the grand occasion. By lunchtime of the Day only half the tickets had gone—by six p.m. it was a sell-out. The event was a tremendous success and was repeated on successive years. All the Art College staff attended, and all the most admired bands. The Eminent Victorians scored a great success with our unique and individual sounds. Also, we were enabled to jive all evening when not playing; and this huge train-shed of a hall, that was more accustomed to flower shows and military selections of operetta than the strains of New Orleans, presented an amazing vista from the balcony, as the couples whirled and skipped to the timeless music.

Many of our interests were connected with Ditchling in those days, and I passed a good deal of time there in these years of the late Fifties. The summer of '58 was very warm, and for a while I gave up my series of watercolours of Brighton Beach (a steady source of income for me) during these years to sleep in my tent in the field next to a cottage occupied by some ex-students who liked to have the art school characters about them whenever possible. Here we lived an idyllic existence, painting, shooting rifles, making a collection of skins of specimens, reading, talking art and philosophy, playing jazz, painting. . . .

An inconvenient way of being awoken in a tent is by the buzzing of a wasp hovering before one's eyes (in perfect focus: my eyes without glasses only seeing clearly for two or three inches). The great demoniac yellow and black banded monster is a real peril at such a moment. . . . At intervals, a large bull would escape, to be discovered sometimes in the lane at twilight. If one took a single step into the field he shared with his adoring and attentive harem, the bull would advance with the speed of a motor bicycle, and gallop back and forth by the hedge looking for you, his angry breath hanging in clouds in the evening air. We found a wounded hawk, and tried to restore it to life, but it lasted only a few days. I dissected the eyes, and extracted the extraordinary lenses, with which the hawk perceives the movements of field voles far below in the fields. These lenses would enlarge small type, like a minute magnifying glass, if placed over a newspaper. I set boxtraps, and caught fieldmice, which I kept in a large cage. A shrew caught in the trap evinced so much character, biting and growling at the bars, that it was released as a general tribute to its courage, as opposed to the docile hopeless attitude of the trapped field mice and voles. Once, straying with a shot-gun rather a long way from the cottage, I shot a partridge, that glided down into a field of cabbages. As I went to retrieve it, a personage with gun, gamebag, breeches and full sporting equipment suddenly came up from the greenery like a surfacing diver, and announced he was the owner of all the land and consequently the partridges thereabouts, and was taking me in charge. But the conversation somehow got on to ferrets, and then the fact that I was an etcher. We searched for the partridge but never found it, as I had taken my eye off the point where it had disappeared. (The next time I met my new acquaintance was when he allowed the Victorians to change in his barn, at some village function.) In the evenings, in the country we would drive to village pubs, and sometimes entertain them with the piano and guitars, singing the skiffle numbers that were popular at that time. Sometimes, weekends involved the most varied of expeditions, one following on the other with no time for rest or even sleep. . . .

One long weeked commenced on the Saturday with a friend and myself hiring horses in Southwick from one of the art-students whose interest was in breeding them in an old dairy behind his house, and spending his summer taking them on the sands to give rides to children. In this profession he soon had a considerable success. We walked the horses through the streets, admiring our centaur reflections in the shop windows, cantered on to the downs, and ended by galloping. I had not been on a horse before, and was interested to find that years of concentration on Westerns in Brighton cinemas had not been entirely a waste of time. Returning from our ride, we drove with friends to Newhaven and visited an acquaintance who was repairing an old sailing barge. A new mast was being put in by the two piratical members of the crew. We cooked newly caught plaice in their galley, and then drove on to Bexhill. Here we attended a birthday party of one of the students, together with most of the Art College. The party was at a hotel with a built-in dance floor. The dancing continued until seven a.m., when we left and walked seven miles in dream-like early morning sunlight along the sand to Hastings. Here we visited friends with a house on the clifftop. The rent was exceedingly low, as the cottages were almost due to be condemned, the cliff crumbling away beneath their foundations. Looking from a bedroom window down to rocks and swirling waters far below was sufficient to make the head spin. Eventually, late that Sunday evening, we found ourselves walking down a country lane in what we hoped was the right direction for Brighton. Entering a village we looked up at the night sky, found the Pole star, turned ourselves in the right direction, and boarded a last bus that fortuitously appeared. This kind of continual walking-about-adventure at weekends was a constant feature of the summer. In the late Fifties, there seemed a soporific dream atmosphere to the scene in general. It was still a matter of wonder to the world that we had finally emerged from the wartime period; and colour, freedom, and music, were sufficient to intoxicate on their own. We seldom touched alcohol. No one could afford it.

I continued riding whenever possible. I was thrown from a large white horse while riding bareback—all at once there was a curved, white moving wave beneath me, where had been a docile creature a moment before. I was flying high, with the ground coming up slowly, vertically, from the left, connecting like a door slammed into one, as it were. Fortunately, I wasn't injured. Another time, I took a short cut across the swampy floor of a valley. My horse sunk in the swamp up to the belly. The hoofs were reaching down to nothing, and the animal, usually so firm, tilted this way and that as if we were riding on a cloud. I got down, not sinking in so far as my unfortunate horse—or somebody else's horse, in fact, which made it even more distressing. Visions came to me of returning with only the story of a horse swallowed up by the marshes. . . . I pulled and pushed and encouraged him, until he abruptly made a great effort and lurched somehow onto firmer marsh, and came up (from being semisubmerged) with a sort of impatient lunge. Later, walking him home to the stables, a low flying plane suddenly roared across the hedge in front of us. My horse gave a great start, and broke into a frantic gallop. Not liking to pull him up or even try, while the hooves were striking sparks from the metalled road—or felt as if they were—I encouraged the wild flight by slightly standing in the stirrups, the sensation being rather like riding on a giant rockinghorse. We cambered round the corners of the lane like a motorbike—luckily meeting no advancing car; and once in sight of his home gate, the annoying animal slowed back into his usual shambling movements.

One afternoon, out painting N. and I were invited in and taken over the house where Eric Gill and his family had once lived. We were shown the upper part of the artist's studio-type living quarters where the tin bath had been. Gill, it seemed, had not permitted bread other than home-baked to be eaten; all vegetables were to be grown in the garden; and even the dresses the women wore were, ideally, to be of homespun material. We progressed through to the long low shed building that had once been a little theatre for the home-constructed puppet shows of Pepler, Gill's partner in the original setting-up of the Guild of St. Dominic's nearby. . . .

. . . . . .

As always, I went out sketching whenever the weather was fine. Discovering an old steamroller in a Brighton street, I made some elaborate drawings of it, and fell into conversation with the driver. Where was it kept?

"Oh, it stays here all the time—on the job," he said. "No one can damage a steamroller! In fact, you'll notice that it's the very place all the tramps come to sleep by of a winter night. You see, she stays warm for hours after we leave her. Oh, she's cheaper to run than a diesel roller. But she'll be scrapped next year. The snag is that a steam roller takes half the day to get up steam; so a diesel roller, though more expensive to operate, gives us more *time* . . ."

I thought this sufficiently interesting to annote as an appendage to the drawing.

One evening in Brighton, on an autumn evening, when we were sitting round the fire in one of our studios, a student who had been silently brooding for some while suddenly leapt to his feet, took up a pack, and announced he was off.

"Where?" we asked.

"Germany," he cried, and plunged out into the midnight snow. Nothing was heard of the adventurer for some months, then he re-appeared. Gone was the wild student look, the pack. He was neat and elegant, carried a suitcase and a large imposing box.

"I started off," he said "—got across the channel—hitched a lift. The chap was going home to a town in Bavaria. We got talking—after a while he offered me a job—I've been living there ever since, going round Germany as a commercial traveller. I've come back now to try and establish a market for us in Britain."

We couldn't believe it. What was in the impressive box, however? He opened it, and took out two impeccably made mechanical figures, Bavarian peasants, which he wound up. The contrast to the adventurer and his return had a fantastic quality about it . . . however, upon reflection he decided to take up the interrupted degree course and forget about his other profession. But there were the materials of a novel somewhere in the episode.

One cold morning in December, when staying with friends in their cottage at Ditchling Common, I awoke to find the countryside covered with snow, sparkling in the early morning sunshine like artificial frost on Christmas decorations. I spent the day painting watercolours out in these Arctic conditions; later, at dusk, we took the shotguns out to try for a duck, as they regularly circled the great pond on the common at sunset. It was a fine clear sky of bright orange-yellow—the duck were precisely on time—I fired my .410 directly above me. A duck fell, thudding into the reeds. We couldn't see clearly where it had landed, and the light was fading more each moment. My companion waded in and poked about for a while, but it was no use. Later, back at the cottage, I sat by the old-fashioned fireside stove with a deal of restlessness, thinking of the lost supper. At last, with determined foolhardiness, I took a large electric torch, and walked back to the pond. The snow was freezing hard now, crunching like spilt sugar on a kitchen floor.

Arriving, I removed my boots and trousers and waded in, breaking the ice ahead of me with the torch. After some ten minutes of unsuccessful searching, directing the beam among the reeds with no success, I realised that I could no longer feel the mud and stone of the pond floor with my feet. My legs had lost all sensation up to the thighs. With some difficulty I got to the shore. It was impossible to draw on socks, shoes or trousers over the immensely heavy—apparently wooden—limbs, somehow no longer a part of me. I took up my clothes, and ran for shelter, taking the wrong path, finding it again, going through brambles and over stones unfeelingly, as if on wool, with a floating sensation. Finding myself on the road I ran as fast as possible, feeling no sensation of contact with the asphalt at all, and falling over at intervals. Eventually, arriving at the cottage of people I knew well, I plunged into their peaceful evening's reading-aloud, demanding warm water. After some hours of them bathing and rubbing my legs, the life came back to my unfortunate limbs.

· · · · · ·

I had stayed over in Mid-Sussex after a party. It had not been a very late affair, and waking at five o'clock after two or three hours of sleep, I decided to walk back to Brighton, a day of evidently bright sunshine before me. I walked for some while through open country, and then descended into a small town. Ambling past the still closed shopfronts, I sensed I was being followed, and looked back. In the deserted high street, a cow was following me, patiently; keeping a steady twenty paces behind. When I stopped, she stopped; when I walked, she walked—when I ran (I tried this) she ran. We continued in this manner for some while—through the village, up the hill, and into an area of rather larger and more expensive Victorian villas, with carriage drives of gravel, neat front gardens and high red brick walls. Eventually, tired of the cow, I slowly let her catch up with me, and then spun around, clapped my hands and shouted; in the hope that this bovine doppelganger would be sufficiently affronted to turn and flee. The cow, however, leapt nervously in the air, turned away and cantered up the nearest drive. Feeling in some way responsible, I followed, calling her back in vain. The cow was discovered standing on the front lawn, on the billiard table turf, sniffing at the roses in the centre plot. Whispering urgently, I tried to beckon her to follow me back to the road. It was useless; the cow began to eat the roses, which vanished at great speed. With desperate courage, I approached and grasped the animal firmly by the horn, as being the nearest thing to a handle of sorts by which to drag her away. At this the cow became completely hysterical, broke from me, and plunged round and round the garden, in and out of flowerbeds, trampling the rosebushes, smashing all the carefully tethered delphiniums, tearing down trellises, stamping the valuable blooms into the soft earth, scarring the lawn to bits with her cloven hooves. . . .

In dismay, I leant back against a wall contemplating the awful damage. There was no way to stop her—the more caught up she became, the more she plunged and trampled. Mayhem and chaos—the cow paused, panting. A French window opened, and two elderly ladies appeared, dressing-gowned, grey hair uncombed, wild-eyed, hands clasped in supplication as they viewed the tableau—the pensive artist, the ruined garden, the four-legged author of its destruction—the rising sun gilding all and throwing long over-dramatic shadows. . . .

"Please, do, *please*, take your cow away," they cried—.

"It's not my cow," I tried to explain.

"Just take it *away*—take it *away*—."

"But it's nothing to do with *me*—you see—."

At this point there appeared a sturdy countryman and a boy. Presumably they had trailed their charge. They entered the garden, slipped a rope around the cow, and led her off without a word. These guardian angels, these dei ex machina having departed I turned to the ladies. . . .

"And as for *you!*" They began hysterically, advancing with rising notes of rage—but visions of arrest and prison cells sent me quickly back to the deserted early morning road, and I continued on my way, keeping well in the shadows.

At Whitsun, an advance guard from the Art College went out to the Downs near Lewes, and discovered an old abandoned chalk pit set in picturesque woodlands. Telephoning a key-figure among the students we told her to contact the others, and they soon began to appear, with supplies. Meanwhile, we had commenced the building of igloos of chalk rocks, making three-foot high walls, fastening branches shorn of leaves into these walls, tying them at the top like wigwams, and thatching the huts with large flat leaves from plants near the brook. With branches of fir we carpeted the floors, and dug firepits before the doors. By evening, there was a considerable community. Refreshments were brought up by motorbicycle from the village inn. We called the place Chalk City. Cooking meals, playing guitars, building huts—the inhabitants soon created a kind of primeval atmosphere in the valley. At night, climbing to the downs above the chalkpit, where the early downs dwellers had traditionally hidden from invaders in the folds of the hills, the huts, each with a twinkling campfire before it, looked equally pre-history.

By day, we amused ourselves sketching, looking for fossils in the cliff, chipping flint arrowheads and making arrows with feathered flights, and bows with which to shoot them. We discovered that to chip a flint axe it is necessary to strike one flint with another so that a kind of electric shock shivers off the piece you require. If you strike in the wrong place, the shock goes into your hand and numbs it instead. I made a number of watercolour drawings from life of our "primeval village" before we all walked back home to Brighton.

CHAPTER 7

Towards the end of the summer term at the Art College, a student who owned a collie that had died asked me to stuff it and set it up in a lifelike pose. I agreed, provided the cause of its death had not made it impossible to preserve successfully. She promised to send it to the etching room, but neglected to notify me she had done so, and several days later I was asked if a large hamper in the corner belonged to *me*. It was the last day of term; I opened the hamper; there, of course, was the dog; not in a very good state of preservation; but still just possible to skin, as the fur didn't come out in handfuls when gently tugged. As it happened, the matter could not be attended to that day, as the band was booked to play at a party. The College, however, was to be vacated of all students' possessions at once. What to do with the dog? The only solution was to take it with us to the party. With everything else to carry, we were overloaded. However, R. took one handle of the basket, I the other, and we arrived carrying the hamper as if contained tasty contributions to the festivities.

"What's in there? Something good?" said our hostess.

"You'll see later on, perhaps—a surprise for after midnight."

"Great! You'd better put it out of the way then—under my bed—nobody will find it there."

We knew that by midnight the hamper would have been forgotten. The party continued—jazz and dancing all night—watching the dawn come up as we drank coffee in the garden in those rare mid-summer early hours that are still as warm as the evening before, with none of the usual dawn chill about them. The party continued all next day. At evening, we all departed to yet another gathering. At dawn the following morning, I suddenly remembered the dead dog.

"We'd best go back for it." said R. We retraced our steps to the site of Party One.

"Your hamper? What a shame! We never opened it! Oh, it's still under my bed, I expect. I haven't looked—"

We took the hamper and carried it back to Party Two. But this had dwindled away during our absence. There seemed nothing now to prevent us getting the corpse to some convenient place where I might set to work upon it, little as I now fancied the task. But, finally, the questionable freshness of the specimen had departed. It was too large to bury anywhere—we weren't in the country, and to take the hamper and a spade on a bus would seem to be courting trouble. It appeared to be the only solution to consign her, Viking-like, her to the purifying waves. At midnight, we carried the hamper to the end of a breakwater that ran far out to sea, and with fitting solemnity lowered her into the still and moonlit waters.

The next day, being somehow impelled, as in all classic examples, to re-visit the scene of the act, I walked along the promenade to the beach by the long breakwater. All the beaches were full of holiday-makers. Scintillating sea, sunbathers, children, sand, happiness all about, the full panoply of summer in England. But in the centre of the beach a wide space was not occupied. In the midst of lyrical paradise lay a memento mori, with nobody within a radius of fifteen feet in either direction. The dead collie had been washed up, and lay on its back, four stiff feet directed to the sky. Hastily, I walked away. I felt I could do no more.

It seemed to me, at this period, that I was immersed in a confusion, a pleasing dream of ceaseless activity; dances, jazz-band practices and performances, elegant subjects for my etchings—outings and expeditions of all kinds. The large figure composition oils I produced in this period, however, suggest an artist participating, but looking, nevertheless, blackly ahead, observing that every party, every outing, is sounding its own deathnote and bringing the dancers closer to the time when all such levity shall have ended: "that day when all days are one day to you," as Rossetti says. But it does not bother one at the time. One doesn't even know one is thinking such thoughts. Only the picture you are working on knows. You can hide nothing from your own work. It is necessary to realise the importance of the psychological depths artists draw upon, when creating a painting. Unconscious, in the preoccupation with the technical department of their work, of the extreme intensity of their message . . . Munch, Van Gogh—silent scream or cypresses swaying tormented— paradoxically, the creation of such works was the only comfort of the artists.

. . . . .

In August '59, R. and I equipped ourselves with packs, groundsheets and sleeping bags, and set off on a pilgrimage to Rome in the traditional manner, except that we hoped to assist our walk with hitch-hiked lifts, not considering it possible to walk the whole way.

We boarded the channel steamer at an early hour, settled ourselves comfortably, and awaited the full complement of passengers. The customs officials had been polite, but a little personal.

"No question about *your* identity, eh, Mr. Blaker?"—looking at my Eminent Victorian Piccadilly Weepers in the passport photograph and comparing them with the originals before them. At Dieppe we shopped for supplies. R. was a part-time territorial soldier and was constantly calling attention to the necessity of regimental neatness. Whereas the accoutrements of my companion became daily more compact and orderly, my own seemed possessed of a character of their own. When R.'s pack was standing at attention against a wall, mine was sprawling untidily on its back . . . "You must *cherish* your pack, all the time," R. proclaimed, incessantly pulling little straps and fastening buttons whenever he stopped for a moment.

With wine and cheese, sausage and bread, we walked up and away from the coast, on the road to Rouen, with occasional appeals to passing motorists. There is little to recommend hitch-hiking, unless it be useful as an accessory to the study of human nature. Fate follows closely the hitch-hiker. He is not permitted luxury; but having reached a point of fatigue when he really no longer cares about anything, he is then sometimes permitted a lift on the way; and one of the endless stream of cars kindly stops, and is found to contain a human soul. The traveller is lifted from his location in a second, and all fatigue vanishes.

It is a great mistake, however, to sit by the roadside hoping for free travel. It also seems to me unethical and degrading. No; one must be a traveller, walking, enjoying the places one comes to—and then, if at a certain moment, one feels like suggesting to a more mobile traveller that *you* would like a lift if *he* would care for company, then the bargain is struck to the benefit of all parties. However, this had happened but once in the three hours since leaving Dieppe, and it was now seven o'clock. Summer evenings are long, though, and we were equipped for all conditions, and in no hurry . . . at this point we paused in our march, for a sip of wine; and as my eye turned to the vista of our way, a long straight road, it met the moving image, a hundred yards further on, of an ancient autocyclist. At the moment of my eye lighting on it, the autocycle seemed to fold up and crumple itself on the road. We ran to it as quickly as possible.

The autocyclist had risen shakily to his feet when we came up; he was a very small elderly man, with beret, grey moustache, and lined brown face. He was holding one arm stiffly, and looking very blank. He straightened his crooked glasses, and thoughtfully clenched and unclenched the fingers of the injured arm. A sack of potatoes on the back carrier told an obvious story of overloading.

We set the machine up at the roadside and stood about somewhat vacantly, wondering what to do with our new acquaintance. Naturally, we could speak French no better than any other Englishmen. We tried to stop a passing car, but not even to help the unfortunate would they cease their headlong pace. At last becoming reckless with impatience, we walked into the road and stood bodily in front of the first approaching vehicle, which was obliged to stop. The driver was furious, redfaced, immobile, like a carved wooden totem. The moment we came round to talk to him he started the car, all but sending us into the ditch.

A decrepit van, driven by a bereted, blackjowled, but by comparison almost genial French farmer, now paused; and after lengthy negotiations directed us to lift the autobike into the back. We followed it in, as the driver suggested, and all entered Rouen as a grey rainy twilight began to fall. The van was directed up hills and through neat little suburbs. We stopped at last; down the long garden path came a stream of aunts, sisters, sons, children, old lady . . . lamenting, explaining, gesticulating, they conveyed the autobicycle, the old gentleman, the potatoes, us and our packs, and the protesting vandriver, into the house. Handshakes, chairs offered, the wine uncorked—R., the driver and I the heroes of the hour. But after a while, and a deal of talk, the driver caught our eye, raised his glass, barely touched our glasses, emptied his own, and so suggested it was time to go. Accompanied to the van by a grateful family, with more handshakes, and we were driven down into Rouen. We visited the cathedral, were reprimanded by the police for walking across the road against the traffic lights, said we were English, and were answered by a kind of hopeless and despairing shrug; and began to climb the long steep hill out of Rouen towards Paris.

It seemed a long hill, and we were now somewhat tired. All the gates and doors we passed were locked and barred, the windows shuttered. It appeared that night-time here was not considered a very safe period to be out and about . . . no lights gleamed from windows; only the savage barking of dogs broke the silence. We came to a fenced-off agricultural countryside. The ditches by the roadside were wide and commodious, gentle depressions four feet wide and packed with hay; a sort of endless bed. Unpacking our sleeping-bags we lay down to sleep, while long car-carrying trailers thundered by at our ears. At about two a.m. a light rain commenced; I pulled my upper groundsheet well over my sleeping-bag and was sufficiently protected.

At dawn we arose and set off once more. We were in a flat, pleasant country-side—we observed an immense badger-skin tacked on the door of a farm-house. Stopping at a wayside cafe-bar for black coffee, we continued along the lonely road, being overtaken by two policemen on motorscooters, who examined our passports and departed with amiable explosions from their machines. The morning traffic commenced, passing by cheerfully, waving at us with genial good nature. At last, after walking all day, a very old lorry bears down upon us. It carries four English hitch-hikers with packs, who prevail upon the ancient driver to halt. He is carrying in this lorry a crumbling cement mixer, and is taking it to Paris. The cement mixer has been painted (evidently the night before, in an attempt to disguise the rust) a brilliant yellow; and as the lorry slides about considerably, and there is very little to hold on to, we are soon patched all over with jaundiced stains like our fellow travellers. But, however; by four o'clock we are deposited on the outskirts of Paris, trying to hold a conversation with an old gentleman who lived for twenty years in Liverpool but has forgotten all his English. We now have to find a place to stay; I recollect the Y.M.C.A. in the Rue de Trevise, and cubicles are secured. The next morning we saunter through the streets, buying summer t-shirts on the way, to the Louvre; and I gaze once more at Ingres; that is to say, at his Grande Odalisque, who turns and gazes back in a detached manner, as if willing to be awoken from her lassitude yet not really caring very much about it, either way. Next, to resume acquaintance with the family of M. Rivière—this permanently urbane, attractive, successful young man, with his lyrical wife swathed in loops of white, her black hair singing against it. Their daughter, the third picture in this superb group, is the tragedy, of course, in that she died (still a child) the year after being painted; so we have here the Rivière family at their high-water mark of happiness. To take Ingres as one's standard means, of course, that you will never be able to stop painting, because you are never likely to approach one who is always so superior to you. After lunch, we stroll to the Museum of Modern Art, and its display of engaging and decorative colour explosions, which the memory of the Odalisque yet puts in their proper place aesthetically with a vengeance. An idle around Paris, and then a train to Dijon. Why did we not walk? Alas, we possessed money, and were a little tired of the open road, for the moment. . . .

The air of Dijon was hot, and strange to us. The town was aglow with lights—a band played in a café window—every shop open—the town alive; yet midnight was approaching. We bought a loaf of bread and some cheese, and set off towards Switzerland, some uncountable number of kilometres to the east. The streets beyond the main thoroughfare were high and dark, cobbled and empty, save for an unseen piano heard from a high window above—a square of yellow light. We stood in the dark below for some time, pondering upon the atmosphere created . . . as we turned towards the open country, we were still followed by Chopin; but this slowly metamorphosised eventually into the sound of millions of grasshoppers and crickets . . .

A cup of coffee at a roadside café—the television was describing a tour of Paris; we felt curiously nostalgic for the place already, as if we were looking at pictures of home. But we wandered out to the fields, and made camp. R. emphasised that a good soldier always looks for cover. He himself put his sleeping-bag in the dry ditch, while I had selected a site in the open stubble, on an old overgrown path. To placate him, I changed my position. I had no sooner done this, when a motorbike rushed unlit, unexplained, at top speed, down the path I had been lying across.

Morning was fantastically lilac and yellow, a living breathing Van Gogh . . . also, it was Sunday, when, it seems everyone in France goes fishing. We picked up a keep-net that fell from one of the rod-laden automobiles. I also found a sable, knocked down by a passing car; a watershrew, and a black rat; each of which highly unusual specimens would have been most interesting to have skinned and preserved; but unfortunately, I had brought no taxidermy equipment. There were many dead hedgehogs on the road; and, an elderly farmer giving us a lift, I enquired the French for "Hedgehog," simply for the interest of it. He was puzzled.

"Un animal avec—epingles?" I hazarded.

He was uncomprehending. I became more explicit.

"Un animal," I said, "mort sur la route—"

He braked suddenly, screeching the car to a halt.

"Mort sur la route?" he cried, peering from the window, thinking he had unwittingly perhaps passed by an accident casualty.

"It's all right," I tried to pacify him in English, realising I had no grasp of his language at all—"only a hedgehog." But he continued to be disturbed until we left him.

Some hours later—although it was by now still only around nine a.m.—a little tired, we were sitting by the roadside. The Sunday fishing traffic was dwindling—the early morning anglers were all at their posts.

"What about lunch in Switzerland?" said R. But Switzerland was many miles away.

A small car, one of the odd-looking tinny Citroens, stopped. A young man leant out.

"Going anywhere near Geneva?" we enquired. Apparently he was heading in that direction. We climbed in. It seemed he had left Lille, far in the North, at one a.m.; and was intending to arrive at Nice by midnight, so completing a twenty-four hour traversal of the country. We would be happy, we said, to stay with him; Nice was vaguely on the way to Rome and we were in no hurry. We stopped for lunch in Switzerland after all, in very fact; the flat fields slowly evolving into a landscape firred and mountainous. The scenery became grand and dramatic—we crossed the frontier; Jacques (our benefactor) becoming highly nervous and cigarette-consuming on account of not possessing a passport; but by slowly creeping behind a large car ahead, and rushing across the border in its shadow, we succeeded in entering the country. Jacques then fell asleep in a restaurant, while R. and I bought cheese and milk from a surgically clean dairy, and picknicked surrounded by a flock of children, on a green in the centre of the tiny village in which we had stopped; the mountains around us, and far down on the plain below Lake Geneva mirror-like in the sunshine.

The inexorable Jacques now awoke, summoning us to the car, and away we went over the Alps, climbing higher every moment, the sunshine fierce as we drove round the picturesque shores of Annecy . . . Jacques was now stripped to the waist, chain-smoking, indignantly refusing the offer of a spare sunhat. His hands—he held them out to show me—were raw and bleeding from holding the wheel for so long. He had not expected blisters to form, then break; but there was nothing that could be done about it. As evening approached, great plateaux upon plateaux were achieved—distant views of a frightening immensity included the motifs of whole villages sitting on ledges below mountains; and below them, yet more churches and towns. The road spun in and out of tunnels, round precipitous cliff edges, and we became sleepy. Twice I dozed over on to the driver and was roughly pushed aside. It was now dark, and we were going full speed; I fell asleep every minute and then awoke; like a long sustained blinking of the eyelids, with a new sense of consciousness every time. Once Jacques himself fell asleep as we entered a tunnel; a white wall between two exits looked for a moment like a broad highway. He woke just as he was driving straight for it, but swerved to the right in time, giving me a woeful grin. The speed, the endless swinging turns as we descended in loops and curves had become the normal—we had been driving now for twenty hours. Below us lay vistas of sparkling lights—towns and cities . . . once we paused at a village for brandy and coffee, going through the bead curtain into the brightness of a bar . . . suddenly, however, we were down on a flat road—we had crossed the Alps. Jacques was saying: "Nice is quite soon; you had better camp here."

I woke R. We walked across the road into a field of vegetables. I unrolled my sleeping-bag between two rows of crops and fell asleep. The last sound I heard were three gunshots in the far distance.

The next moment, it seemed, I awoke to brilliant sunshine. I raised my head slightly above the leaves. Some six rows away was a farm worker in jeans and straw hat, hoeing. R. was nowhere to be seen, having carefully camped in the shadow of a nearby shed. Another worker, with bare feet, cycled by, whistling. Waiting until the hoer had progressed to the other side of the field, I got up, and joined R. by the roadside. We set off for the coast, past palm trees and strange vegetation. A dead bat in the gutter was a mass of ants . . . suddenly, round a corner, down a lane—there was the Mediterranean, sparkling in the morning light. We ran forward over small round flat blue pebbles like pirate gold, put on swimming costumes, and plunged into the water. An elderly beachcomber, very like Picasso in appearance, looked on dispassionately. Around the bay were the white houses of the Nice promenade. Behind, blue hills, and overhead the great roaring airliners. I brought out my watercolours and made a Victorian sketch in the true Nineteenth Century Grand Tour manner.

At mid-day we inspected the town, having deposited our packs at the railway station. We lunched at a large cafeteria, which seemed to represent an attempt to impose the quicklunch principle upon an easygoing and café-haunting community. It was not highly successful. The cheerful manager greeted my long-haired and bearded appearance gaily as "Davy Crockette," and continually exhorted the diners to pass along quickly; but as many of the dishes required cooking to order, a number of waitresses were employed to take them to the tables. Confusion reigned; R. having spaghetti brought to him twice in place of veal. While waiting we drank our wine, and some more wine. By the time our meal arrived the wine had affected our near starving condition considerably. We talked and laughed animatedly . . . all at once we noticed we were both being covered with little drops of mustard. Where was it coming from? "It's extraordinary," said R.—"I can't make it out." We looked all about us—the mustard continued to fly over us . . . "Why, it's you!" R. cried . . . it was indeed me, thoughtlessly stirring the pot too vigorously. . .

The manager was at our elbow. "You 'ave finish. Will you leave?" He was pleading. Somehow, we made our exit, despite all the chairs and diners that seemed to make a point of looming up in our path to trip us. As we reached the other side of the street after a lorry had done its best to knock us down we all at once came to ourselves and realised the potency of this Southern alcohol.

That afternoon the sky clouded and torrential rain fell, drying rapidly after each shower. Meeting a small Frenchman (from Paris) standing at a bus-stop, we fell into conversation. He was travelling from one Youth Hostel to another, by bus and train. "But once," he said, his eyes glowing with the potential romance of it, "I should like to sleep under the *sky*."

"*We* should like," said the unromantic R., "to sleep under a ceiling, just for a change."

We were joined by another young Frenchman, and two German girls; the rain continuing, we all took a bus to the Youth Hostel, and passed the afternoon making tea and toast and reading comic books; trying to translate the balloon words into each other's languages—being unable to communicate otherwise, in these Mediaeval times in which we live, when people living but a few hundred miles away from each other speak a different tongue. . . .

At nightfall R. and I returned to the beach, having collected our packs from the station, and slept by the calm Mediterranean. For some days we swam and idled about, diving down among the rocks and silver fish in the clear water, sunbathing and making watercolour drawings; until, feeling refreshed and ready to travel, we took the train to Pisa. It appeared to be the hottest day in the recollection of all those on board. The line continually entered and emerged from numerous short tunnels in the mountainous backdrop to the coast along which we were travelling, and an aging lady in our carriage possessed that widespread complaint, fear of dust and cinders, and was continually ordering R. to either open or close the window for her. He was thus constantly leaping up and down, becoming warmer and warmer as he became more obliging. The frequency of tunnels, and the pantomimic gestures of hopelessness from R. soon reduced everyone in the carriage to helpless merriment.

"Good for his muscles," said the lady, wiping her eyes. Eventually, the tunnels ceased, and two more elderly ladies entered, one with a husband. The three woman struck up a conversation. It commenced with the weather, of course, continued with R.'s muscles, progressed towards the ladies' grandchildren, and culminated with husbands. Photographs were brought out, followed by lugubrious descriptions of how the gentlemen had met their ends. "One day—big strong!—Next day—*pouf!*"—sad gestures, head-shakings, tears imminent. Great misery all round. The potential diseases of husbands thoroughly gone into. During this part of the discussion the one surviving husband remaining became increasingly more melancholy and uncomfortable. He tried looking out of the window, reading a magazine, but it was no use. He was drawn irresistibly by the magnetic attraction of what might happen to *him*.

At last, with a sigh, and a shrug, the window-closing lady threw off the misery atmosphere, as if it was beginning to bore her, and gave a flashing smile. The three ladies were now comrades. They knew each others' histories; they could relax. With more cheerful conversation they beguiled the hours. During the course of the journey R. was continually calling my attention to the lizards he observed from the window, but I never seemed quick enough to see them. A trio of peasant girls on a mountain path, each carrying earthenware pots on their heads, in true archaic fashion, was some compensation, however.

In the calm of the evening we arrived at Pisa. The inhabitants were ambling about, or sitting on bridges, immobile in the listless warmth. Through them strode R.'s British Army boots, like the herald to a procession. Heads turned as we marched to the Tower, which seemed like a piece of sea-smoothed skeleton, very beautiful, with children playing on the grass around. A large and poetic watercolour drawing; a Ruskin coloured by Whistler (paradoxically enough). But a storm was coming up; the lightning began to fly about the sky, lighting up the scene with magician's blue and green fire, like Victorian theatricals. As yet there was no rain, but fantastic noise from the thunder, and balls of crackling luminosity rocketted about the clouds. We took a train to Ponte Ginori, where some friends had given us an address where we might meet them. We never found it, of course. The town was small, with everyone wandering about looking at the storm, even though it was by now past one in the morning. Finding a bar, we persuaded the owner to telephone to our elusive address, but without success. A small crowd of youths having collected to see what we would do next refused to leave when the bartender suggested closing. In despair, he went up to bed, whereupon his customers invaded the bar, telephoning again, ostensibly on our account, but giving us messages such as "He's on his way here," "He doesn't live here," and the like. It became more boisterous and we sensed practical jokes; we got up from our table at the end of the bar and defiantly marched through them. They followed us, shouting happily, for a short distance, but soon returned to the bar. Out of town the road ran between deep woods. It was now raining fitfully, between the illuminations and the sulky roars from the clouds. As I laid down beneath the trees in my sleeping bag I looked up. Above my head a great telegraph pole ran up to the stars. What a lightning conductor! I thought, and fell asleep on the instant.

At ten o'clock the next morning I crawled out into quite an English morning. Damp, sullen, pessimistic. I went down to the road. R. was still in his bag, half-covered with dead leaves. The road was wet and deserted and led towards some unknown range of hills, light brown and dotted with little trees, a background from an Italian primitive. R. came out and joined me. We stood irresolute. Where were we? Where was Rome? A large motor-coach now appeared, splashing through the puddles. At least we can catch this bus, we thought! I stood directly in its path with upraised hand, being determined not to let our only chance go by. It stopped, a door opened, a head looked out. Shaking the rain from our own heads, we climbed in, selected seats, stowed our wet packs away, and cleaned the steam from the window as the motor-coach started up. The passengers looked curiously at us. R. had sunk back into sleep, but I felt a growing unease. The passengers all appeared to be fairheaded young men of Nordic aspect, wearing leather shorts and large boots. . . .

"Excuse me," I said, to the nearest, "but this *is* a public motor bus, I hope?"

"No," he said politely. "This is a German Cultural Tour. We save all year for the trip."

I thought about this in silence.

"Today," he went on, "we visit the historic hill towns of Tuscany—Volterra, San Gemignano, Siena."

"Would it be possible for *us* to come along," I said—"as we seem to be here anyway? We don't mind contributing, if necessary—"

The young man pondered. His brow cleared. "I shall have to ask our Leader!" He marched up the length of the coach, returning after a long and serious discussion with a slightly older man with the look of authority. Returning, he announced:

"It is All Right. Our leader says you may stay."

I nodded my thanks to the Leader, who smiled back. We were accepted. We got into conversation, and I brought out my collection of watercolour drawings, refusing several offers to purchase them. The coach took us up winding roads to towered hilltowns of Mediaeval aspect. At Volterra we stopped in the main square.

"We stay here one hour. You are to return, you understand, at eleven o'clock exact!"

With the feeling that fate was out of our hands, we left them and went to explore, looking at churches, carvings, frescoes; walking down narrow archaic alleys, and taking a stroll along an elevated path that proved to be a prison wall; we were directed to get down by an armed guard on one of the towers above us, who waved a rifle threateningly. It was satisfyingly Mediaeval.

Looking for a shop in which to buy a nut and bolt to mend my mouth-organ, (which was falling to pieces) I was taken for a Frenchman, and asked to help a French child make its purchases by translating into Italian; which as I couldn't speak either language gave me a good deal of confidence for future attempts, as the transaction was successful. At eleven o'clock we were back at the coach, and talked with yet more of the German tourists, not all of whom proved to be young and athletic. An interesting exposition of national character—or, to be fair, perhaps, personal temperament—now occurred. The roof of the coach was of glass; and over the upper part of the window by each traveller was a blind, protecting each person from the sun. This had now fortuitously appeared and the day was warm and holiday-like. We were passing, at this point, an imposing scene that required, for visual appreciation the upper blinds of each window being let up. The leader gave an order to this effect, and snapped up his blind with military vigour. The person sitting behind him leapt to attention, as it were, and snapped up his blind also. The next followed, and the next. Snap, snap, snap, down the coach. A pause, R., with a look of detachment, ignores the drill. A moment's hesitation, then the snaps proceeded, like an electric current having jumped a gap, leaving the lone shaded Englishman. But unfortunate little International incidents of this sort served in no way to prejudice our popularity. In San Gemignano we were befriended by yet more of the party, and eventually photographed with everybody. At Siena we left them, deciding to stay on, but we had no sooner found a room and changed into our more formal Victorian stiff collars and ties than we came upon them in the cathedral. We all welcomed each other as old friends.

At Siena we found a monastery style hostel, with white-washed rooms overlooking a garden court. Next door a large church was undergoing repairs, a surprising combination of massive altars, dust, cement and parked motor-scooters. Siena being a fortress city of the Renaissance (and presumably earlier) people and cars made their way with difficulty through the narrow streets encircling the main square. The beautiful cathedral, with its interior of black and white stone arranged in a stripe pattern in banded layers, was to me an aesthetic revelation. Black-shawled old ladies shuffled by to pray. I made a watercolour drawing of a priest sitting between two striped pilasters outside. Siena was not a place one wanted to leave; also, to sleep in a bed was a welcome relaxation. One morning as we came into the square, we found that wooden tiers of seating were being erected over the fronts of shops. The sunlight was intensely bright; in the centre of the great open space a long thick line of people were clustered into the shadow of the great tower. The shadow moved fairly quickly, so that the line of people ticked slowly across the square like the marker of a gigantic sundial. We joined them, to see what was happening. Between us and the seating was a fenced-off track of sand; all at once, from the door of the town hall came six or seven riders, bareback, at the gallop. Flying round the track, slashing at each other with their whips, it was not surprising that a rider should be thrown into the fence, his horse caught in the railings. He was carried away, limp, recumbent . . . it was all part of the Palio festivities, which we had unwittingly come upon. But we had given up our room, and were not able to re-rent it. We decided to walk on to Rome, with the chance of a lift on the way. Leaving Siena by the southern gateway, we strolled along, stopping to draw at intervals. By and by we came to a lonely building with a bar. We had previously bought, for lunch, some bread and sausage. Leaving these supplies for a moment on my pack while I bought a drink, I turned to find they had disappeared. While sitting at our table lamenting this, we were joined by a young Englishman also travelling about Italy. Curiously, a week after I had returned to England later on, I met this very person coming down the steps of the Tate Gallery. We greeted each other as if it was natural we should run into each other once back in our home country. Only afterwards did it occur to me that the coincidence was odd, to say the least.

A mile or so down the road we met two young Chinese students. We imagined them, as they approached, footsore from their long overland trip from the east; they were bound, like us, for Rome; but were returning to Siena to take a train, the chances of lifts being infinitesimal, the Italians not trusting hitch-hikers. We decided to follow their example. "Where do you hail from?" R. asked them. "Wolverhampton," was the unexpected reply.

It was a long evening's train ride, and we stood all the way, very nearly. The passengers were for the most part a detachment of Alpine soldiers, with picturesque hats, and a sergeant in charge, about thirty years their senior. He left the carriage, and I took his seat for a moment, standing when he returned to give it back. But his politeness matched my own, and he refused to resume his position. An American student took the trouble to come and tell me that we should change at Chiusi—and at midnight we were at Rome, at long last, the Hub of the Ancient World. . . . Having nowhere to go, we looked around the great clean modern station. Our American friend suggested the waiting room, where there were many other travellers in various stages of repose. R. fell asleep, but leaving my pack, I wandered out, very thirsty, into the city and bought a bottle of Chianti. Some time later I returned. The waiting room was closed, deserted. A mournful voice nearby disclosed R., sitting on some machinery with the packs. The earlier room had been closed, and we were all to go to another. In the centre was a sort of raised marble block. I lay full-length on this, and fell asleep. The police arrived at some point, waking people by beating their feet, and looking at passports, apparently; but they were so amused at my recumbent effigy image that they forebore to wake me. I was the subject of many jokes "a dead Victorian" but slumbered on—being told all this when I awoke next morning.

Next morning we shouldered our packs and entered the city. I shouldered mine a little too enthusiastically, in fact, and the bottle of Chianti, being rather loosely tucked in, flew out like a bomb, rose high in the air, over a parapet, and exploded at the feet of a cleaner in the subway below. His despairing expression necessitated my going down to apologise and help, but he politely implied it was of no importance. At the Colosseum we came upon one of the Chinese from Wolverhampton. We told him of our night in the waiting-room. He clasped his hands, and his eyes glowed. We seemed fated to meet romantics at every turn. "To spend but one night in a *waiting-room!*" he cried. "*I* wish to *rough* it, yes; but my parents they say: *No*. Here is money. Why torture yourself?"

"Certainly," we agreed.

"But I spend all the money on portable radio, cinecamera"—he tapped all the equipment hung about him—"yet *still* they give me enough for hotel. Is it fair?"

We agreed he could come to the Vatican with us next day. He seemed overjoyed. Perhaps he thought the expedition might be coloured by our evident propensity for "roughing it."

In the evening of our first day we journeyed to a distant Youth Hostel somewhere out of town. A great crowd of mixed nationalities were waiting for the one or two places available. We took a bus back to the centre of the city. Near the station terminus, however, we saw the red neon-lit sign of the Y.M.C.A., and within moments had secured a luxurious room with nearby shower, towels, a cool stone floor and real beds. We stood under the showers, singing Gilbert and Sullivan. We then put on our white shirts and high Victorian collars, and went down to the restaurant for a somewhat luxurious meal. After dinner we found a library with television and watched a Donizetti opera.

In Rome we went to restaurants, lived well, as a change from our travels. Backwoodsmen in town, as R. said. All around were beautiful young Madonna faces, with fine gentle features. But I thought those of Siena had been the most inspiring. Every passing girl's face a subject to enthuse upon, to inspire the artist with regret that he was not sitting drawing these Fifteenth century faces from Perugino and the early Raphael, from Botticelli, and (particularly) Filippo Lippi, who seemed to be everywhere. In Rome, the faces had more character, possibly less abstract simplicity than those of Siena—more of an ivory effect than a warm bronze; but it was enough to look at such people, let alone the paintings. This kind of experience is the kind that returns again and again to one's work in after years—a sufficiently vital visual revelation will set up a train of aesthetic thought that works away subconsciously, coming to the surface perhaps a decade later, matured and vintaged; with the irrelevancies smoothed away together with the excess sentiment that the immediacy of novelty always produces in the artist, making him forget his usual critical selectivity in an orgy of that greatest of the artistic vices, *enthusiasm.*

St. Peter's, as it had been for so many others, was a beacon for our travels. Unfortunately, it was closed for some special occasion, so we could not see it for some days. However, there were plenty of other places to visit and sketch. We discovered the Bernini fountains, where I painted an evening watercolour, laying wash upon blue wash as the clear tones deepened. Rome, to a great extent, *was* Bernini, one of my subjects of admiration for the past few years. To study sculpture, particularly sculptural portraits such as his, is perhaps better for the etcher than the study of paintings and drawings. In my studio I prefer not to hang reproductions of the work of other artists, not even the favoured Ingres, Raphael or Holbein, or any other severe and lineal painter whose influence might be thought never to be pernicious; but I hang photographs of sculpture, which serve to remind one that three-dimensional form is the real lesson to remember. In Rome, I drew the Forum, and sketched the horsedrawn carriages that stood everywhere ready for hire, giving a particularly Nineteenth

Century atmosphere. Having come in the character and with the romantic predilection of a Victorian I for one felt no disappointment with the hub of the universe. A favourite sketching ground of mine was a pit of stray cats in the ruins: innumerable bandit cats, of all colours and conditions; cats with limping, dragging limbs, with knocked about features, with an air of blatant savagery, lounging in the sunshine like a tribe of miniature lions, and fed at intervals by philanthropic (and evidently universal) old ladies.

At dinner we were accosted by two Americans at the next table, who came over to join us.

"I can see," said one, "that you are limeys on account of the way you handle the cutlery."

In Rome we seemed to make many acquaintances. One afternoon I was drawing an interesting fountain, in the form of a triumphal arch—part of the arch was covered with posters advertising tobacco, and the interior was tenanted with a window and a balcony from which a man was leaning in vest and jeans. A small crowd gathered to watch me. An American, of about sixty, bent down to look more closely—I always sit on the ground to work, on a small sketching cushion—"Hey," he said, "that's pretty good. Say, what do they call this technique?"

I told him.

"Hey, you speak English pretty good!"

His enthusiasm was slightly damped by the information that I *was* English, but unquenchably rekindled itself as another thought struck him:

"Hey, could you draw *me*, you think?"

"If you like."

"The fellers at Coney Island, they charge a dollar—no, I guess that wouldn't be enough—you being a *real* artist—well, you tell me what it'll cost me—English, hey? We're going to look in on your country on the way home; I guess I must look up our i-tin-erary. Going to see those two college towns—Oxford, and—what do you call it?"

"Cambridge?"

"That's it, young feller, Cambridge! Hey, how long you been at this painting game? Guess you're pretty good, huh?"

"I'm thirty-one."

"Hey, you don't look old as that. You ain't wrinkled. Why, fellers back home all burnt out at thirty. Quest of the elusive and almighty dollar. Guess money don't interest you much, hey? Well, you draw me—I'll pay whatever you say—"

He took up a heroic poise, removing his hat, arms folded, head high, one foot forward. Good for him, I thought. Most people pose in a contemptuously self-deprecating manner, indicative (presumably?) of their true estimate of themselves. The crowd grew larger as I began the portrait. An English voice could be heard at the back, in an anxious voice—"I *say*, how much does he *charge?*"

Three policemen appeared on the other side of the road, watching the crowds swell. I had already been told twice not to sit on a grass verge to sketch the Victor Emmanuel monument. . . .

"Hope this isn't going to cost me too much, young feller?"

"Do you want it coloured? That will be five thousand lira extra."

"Anything *you* say."

The police had decided to move over and break up the crowd. As they advanced I signed the portrait and thrust it into the American's hand, as he poured coins and notes into my own, and we made a speedy move from the scene in opposite directions.

When I returned to the Y.M.C.A., where R. had spent the afternoon washing his shirts and sleeping, he said: "Did you meet the American?"

"What American?" I asked. It seemed he had dreamt I was out painting and had met a wealthy American who had ordered sixty pounds' worth of watercolours from me. The actual profits from my millionaire were not quite that, but at least sufficient for another few luxurious dinners, at all events. Sixty pounds, of course, was quite a large sum at the time. Later on that evening we visited the Villa d'Este with our two other American friends, to see the gardens and fountains by night. Floodlit fountains, a fantasy illustration drawn by Aubrey Beardsley—a dream-like expedition, with strange carvings, and signs every few steps to warn one against actually drinking the ubiquitous flowing water. In spite of this, we found a whole family with a tin cup sampling the streams from the fountain as if they were some sort of magic potion, while others looked on with horror.

The next morning, at long last, we were admitted to St. Peter's, that great construction appearing almost to enclose all outdoors. The Bernini carving of Constantine on horseback, a great stone curtain billowed above as if caught by a tumult capable of moving rocks—the figure of Death with an hourglass, grinning down from the marble drapes of a monument—all this marvellous Bernini movement made the temple sparkle with immediacy . . . the chair of St. Peter, borne aloft (a little ridiculously, it must be admitted) on solid gilded clouds. . . . Later, to the Vatican galleries, to see more sculpture; the Laocoon, the unforgettable Belvedere torso, and the Raphael frescoes. The Sistine chapel, was the final aesthetic experience, with the works of the Fifteenth Century artists of Florence forming a frieze above which the Michelangelo figures writhed and struggled, or despaired in the fabulous Last Judgement on the end wall. And yet, despite their transports (and even considering that the artist had torn down a pair of Peruginos to create his visions of hell) the Michelangelos never ruffled the superior calm of those greatest mural painters of all time—Ghirlandajo, Botticelli, Signorelli, Pinturicchio and the others. One must worship, of course, that amazing, seething Last Judgement at the end of the chapel, yet it was these earlier artists who inspired me most, who made me wish to paint, from whom I could learn. Yet Michelangelo was the one whose *spirit* dominated. One felt his quick little personality at one's side, pointing out details, his eyes darting everywhere—sort of celestial custodian. It seemed incredible he had actually painted here, treated this place like a glorified studio, for so long. One could see the other artists, too—coming down from their platforms and ladders, looking up with their heads on one side, saying to their friends: "*I* don't know. What do *you* think of that arm?"

We noticed a large, beautiful, dark girl lying flat on her back on a stone bench to view the ceiling—with her curves and glowing colour, she was like a Michelangelo in the colours of life—we felt the artist at our side again: "Don't bother with my frescoes! That's work past and gone! Look at *her*. That's what *I* was after—vigour, life—ah, for a drawing book—"

As we left the galleries, we passed a small shop full of second-hand musical instruments. Naturally we entered, attracted by two interesting tenor horns with spring valves that operated with an unusual movement. R., being a capable performer, blew a note or two, and asked the price. It was highly expensive. We offered about three pounds. The two proprietors collapsed with incredulous laughter, falling into each others' arms with gestures of contempt. Feeling a little put out, we left, their laughter in our ears. . . . Anyway, we thought, we didn't really want it. We should have had to carry it around, after all. We had turned the corner and were well away from the shop when we heard shouting. A passerby tapped our shoulder and directed us to somebody running up the street, pushing people out of the way and calling to us. In one hand he waved the tenor horn high in the air. He was the smaller and more athletic of the two shopkeepers. . . . "O.K.? O.K.? you got the money?"

We continued on our way a little poorer, but the richer by a new asset to the Eminent Victorians Spasm Band.

. . . . . .

Leaving Rome at last we travelled by train to Florence, staying at the Youth Hostel, a large ancient building with a central court; here we met two art students from the Slade, displaying their sketch books; but as all the sketches were abstract designs in coloured chalks it was difficult to see (from a Victorian point of view) how they could have benefited by their travels. To enter into the atmosphere of a place, to draw topographically, to learn to see a new city, particularly those so ancient as those in Tuscany—so essential to our whole cultural tradition, even our way of thinking—should be one's reason for coming here. To impose the universal fashionable style of the day on one's mind, to blank out receptivity to the past, and all that one can learn from it is perhaps a sacrilege of the worst kind. In my dissatisfaction at their work I climbed to the roof and made a Ruskin watercolour.

In the Uffizi we made for the *"Birth of Venus."* R. declared it was basically his sole and only reason for coming here; in fact for coming to Italy at all, in a sense; his striped-t-shirted figure disappeared in the crowds to be discovered later in the Botticelli room, arms folded, immobile before the definitive nude.

These Fifteenth Century painters, we perceived, had all the Italian light and clear warmth, that kind of special afterglow one perceived each evening, in their work. The afterglow, in very fact, seemed a kind of philosophic attitude in the paintings. The sadness, the still, eternal atmosphere in Lippi, Botticelli— the avoidance of stress, or action at all, if remotely possible—above all, the perception of beauty as an aesthetic first and foremost—seemed to stem from the weather effects.

On the train from Florence to Paris on our homeward journey, the line took us round the coast once again to Genoa. As the evening drew on, I studied the faces of the young Italian couple sitting opposite. They were of the sallow type of complexion, and as the evening descended and the afterglow filled the air with gold, their faces became Leonardo paintings. They were in fact living illustrations to the artist's dictum: "Study the faces of people at twilight."

As the train climbed into the mountains we also became aware of our companions as people. One of them was a little Genoese girl, with a wide smile, and another a middle-aged elfish man. There was also a dark curly-haired young fellow with a black moustache, whom I obliged by drawing for him his portrait in pen and watercolour, making a second study of him for my own record of the pilgrimage. We talked until three a.m., with an interval for refreshments sharing our mutual supplies. This was followed by a concert given by R. and myself, on tenor horn and mouth-organ, which was received with great applause. I had at last repaired my mouth-organ (the nut and bolt being of little use) with a bent nail. This formed, however, a kind of projecting hook. I kept the instrument in my hip pocket, and curious incidents kept resulting. A man in Rome came up to me in the street one day, unhooked the mouth-organ from his coat and said, "I should imagine this is *yours*." A lady getting off a bus in front of me turned and politely handed it back—the hook was continually attaching itself to any one sufficiently close. Eventually I lost the instrument, finally, in the underground at Willesden Green. I had never bothered to replace the nail with the correct nut and bolt; one imagines it constantly travelling, passed on from person to person.

By four a.m. our friends had all disembarked, and we were alone in an empty carriage. We slept in our sleeping bags, and woke at Paris, where we returned to the Y.M.C.A. for another stay, visiting the galleries. Leaving Paris, we stopped for a while too at Dieppe; the heat-wave weather gave a South of France atmosphere; we walked across the square, the statue of Duquesne black against the shimmering light reflecting from the cobbles, and quickly changed some of our money at the bank for a set of tubes of mint-new franc pieces, to use in the future as poker chips. Leaving France at last, we came into Newhaven to be greeted by the Customs. "Nothing to declare," I said cheerfully, swinging my pack onto the counter. Unfortunately it contained yet another omnipresent wine bottle; the cork was of course loose, came out, and wine splashed plentifully over the officer.

"I like wine," he said in surly tones; "but not that much."

"Nothing to declare," said R., to change the subject.

"Nothing to declare?" said the Customs Officer, drying himself with a towel—"why, what do you call *that*, then?"—pointing to the tenor horn.

"Oh, that's for our band," said R., dismissing it.

"I can't help that. You're importing musical instruments."

Naturally, this made us burst out laughing.

"Is it an antique?" said the officer, busy with papers and forms.

Was it good or bad to be an antique, we wondered?

"Doubtful," we said at last—"difficult to say . . ."

"Because, if it is, it's not subject to duty."

"Oh, it's tremendously old!" we cried—"look at the spring valves—"

"Over a hundred years old?"

"Good Lord, Yes! Centuries!"

With a groan, the Customs left us to enter the country freely. . . .

. . . . . .

Having returned from this Continental venture with my mind full of Fifteenth Century images, the walls of cathedrals covered with carefully painted and beautifully conceived groups of figures, I wished to continue working in a similar idiom. I had in my mind Leonardo's *St. Jerome*, his great cartoons, his strange half-finished paintings. I recollected Lippi's Virgins, and the Botticellis—and the beautiful originals we had seen in the streets of Siena and Rome, the faces that surprise one so completely by their very perfection of line and tone; that restore all the faith one didn't know one had lost. It is visiting Italy that makes the Italian rooms at the National Gallery ever more vauable to one. You haunt them, to experience an echo of all that they represent. It is Italian painting that, basically, is what painting is, what all painting has departed from. . . .

However, there was of course something of the Renaissance approach to art and art craftsmanship centred at nearby Ditchling. Here was an Inn-sign painter, with a vast studio Mediaevally hung with great heavy metal squares and rectangles, taken down from their sites and awaiting renovation or new designs. An assistant was required, mainly to paint a large many-figured sign for the Railway Hotel at Bognor. I took this job at once on returning from Italy. The house, of which the studio formed a large section, had previously belonged to Sir Frank Brangwyn, that prolific decorator and etcher, of whom odd little ghosts still appeared here and there. On screens in the studio one came upon minute pencil sketches of figures in action—a scribble for some great potential composition. Brangwyn's chair still stood in the dining-room—his immense dramatic etchings around the walls. The three as yet unmarried daughters of the house, one of whom had been at the art college the past two years with me, filled it with life and amusement and the local young men. Here Brangwyn had lived into his nineties, an almost forgotten recluse, never leaving the house and grounds.

Working at the Railway Hotel sign and others I had the opportunity to learn about glazing, gilding with gold leaf, and working in the traditional method of underpainting in umber and white. The composition, squared up from the sketch, was in all particulars painted as a Fifteenth or Sixteenth Century Florentine would approached the task. The laying of successive transparent coats of paint, to give a glowing luminosity and lightness of atmosphere, is a particularly pleasing method to employ; later, I was to use it for my own paintings. It is only, of course, with longtried subjects that one can retain a balance, a restraint with which to confine oneself to experiments with technique only. The favourite model one has painted a score of times—that familiar view of the beach. With these one is not subject to the over-enthusiasm and possibly complete illusion that a new and inspiring person or scene creates. Holiday paintings are seldom successful. The artist chooses all the most familiar views in the place, thinking he has been the first to select them, and subsequently finds each subject for sale as picture postcards, taken from the identical place; and not two paces away from his own selected view-point in any direction, so that it appears he has simply copied the first handful of cards he came upon, and indeed, might as well have done so. Renoir's surprise that Gauguin needed to travel to the South Seas to find a subject—Degas' expressed fear of stepping away from his humble dancers in their tawdry little school—one should remember these examples as warnings.

. . . . . .

While working as an Inn-sign painter, my friends at the Guild of St. Joseph and St. Dominic up on the Common, two miles north of Ditchling, had suggested I live in a gypsy caravan that stood empty near the workshops. The Guild, founded by Eric Gill, lived and existed in the shadow of his ghost, so to speak; but rather than being a ghost of artistic remains (not that they were absent) this was a ghost of living tradition, and a way of life. The caravan had been built by the painter and illustrator E. A. Cox, the father of Mrs. Anne Pruden, who allowed me to use it. Dunstan Pruden, the celebrated silversmith, lived and worked at the Guild; I had been taught silversmithing by him when I was in my teens at the art college in what now seemed an earlier incarnation some fifteen years before.

Living in a caravan is of course, the ideal situation for an artist—*in the summer*. It is compact, and as economical of space as the ship's cabin it so much resembles. Of course, I mean a real caravan—a gypsy caravan. One soon learns to live with a kind of doll's-house precision, storing possessions away carefully, or just getting rid of them (like Thoreau at his pond) so that they no longer give you orders and command your existence. The smallest cooking utensils are to be preferred, and in summer you build a fire outside the van, extending your living space into the open air as far as you wish. The fire is easily kindled because the ashes remain warm, and you have built a pit with bricks and a grid of old iron railings from the hedge or the nearest rubbish tip.

The stew is kept simmering all day, ready for your lunch or supper—if raining, you cook on a paraffin burner in the van. At night, with the miniature curtains drawn across the doll's-house windows, you lie in your sleeping-bag on the bunk, with one elbow almost out of the window, and one foot all but through the door, feeling like Alice when she grew too large. Beneath my head, deep in the old padding of the bunk, a family of mice lived, and I could hear them all night beneath my pillow, squeaking happily. By lifting all the bedding out, they could be discovered, but as they did no harm, I didn't bother them. In the stormier nights, with the rain dashing down, the caravan swayed and rocked on its springs and the branches of the oak trees above creaked and groaned, while trains shrieked past on the line nearby.

I commenced a new series of paintings, which I worked at in the summer evenings after I had cycled back from Ditchling. These, in contrast to the cramped confines of my living quarters, became increasingly more vast and broad. Being painted out of doors to a great extent, the five by four foot hardboard sheets I employed seemed smaller than they would have done in a studio. There were always people about to sit for me—friends, fellow-artists, students—a constant series of visitors from the art college or the jazz club in nearby Burgess Hill. I often painted the nine year old little red-haired girl who lived in the picturesque wooden shack nearby. Across the yard Joseph Cribb, the sculptor, worked at his Stations of the Cross, or his large lifesize group of a Bishop on a horse. His work was invariably commissioned for Catholic churches, and all day one could hear the chip-chip of the hammer and stone-chisels. The weaving workshop had been Eric Gill's studio, and when Gill decided to found a new Guild in the mountains of Wales he wished to take his followers with him, but their wives rebelled. "*You* can all go with him," Mrs. Cribb told me they informed him; "but *we* are staying!" Consequently, it was Gill alone who moved on to found new communities; but it was only this, his first attempt at communal workshop life, that had continued to survive and flourish.

The members of the Guild and their families lived like Gothic craftsmen, with a frugal simplicity, united in their disavowal of Twentieth Century mechanisation. The chapel was decorated with Gill and Gill-tradition works of art—the atmosphere of the quadrangle with its surrounding workshops was one of unhurried calm, where there was always time to think, to talk; to sit in the early morning sunshine on the old church pew facing the orchard, discussing great artists and writers, religion, philosophy, Gill. . . . Visitors from the Brighton Art College would come over for the day and leave feeling relaxed yet inspired. . . .

My paintings included scenes of Mrs. Anne Pruden reading to her small daughter before bedtime—or by the white and gold Madonna lillies that grew like weeds before the cabin door—or perhaps on the steps of the caravan, with the cat Ebenezer . . . these great boards, painted each one at a sitting, were stacked in a corner of the barn like a giant's sketch-book.

As in most country districts, apparently so depopulated and lonely, any local news travelled about quickly—the egg woman, the man who drove a truck full of paraffin and glass chimneys for lamps. It was surprising how much went on—how many perhaps expected and predictable but nonetheless engrossing events occurred to interest one. I remained in the caravan for nearly a year. In the winter, with the snow, it was very cold; I kept warm by the dangerous expedient of surrounding myself in my bunk with large beer bottles filled with hot water.

E. A. Cox, who had died as a very old artist the year before I arrived, commenced as a painter of large murals in the traditional Brangwyn style. He had, in fact, once worked for Brangwyn as an assistant. In an unpublished manuscript in the possession of his daughter, E. A. Cox had written some notes of his life, as a short autobiography. He described how, in the early Nineteen-Hundreds, he was successful in being chosen as one of the leading young artists of the era to decorate the Royal Exchange with great panels illustrating British trade and industry. He described how he went out and ordered materials, arranged for models to sit, and rented a large studio—"I had my first commission—I was a real artist at last," he commented. The war interrupted his career, and the old style of painting fell from favour, so this auspicious start had eventually a different result. After his military service—he was never sent abroad, but each subsequent commanding officer, finding he was an expert portrait painter, kept him in the barracks to be handed on to immortalise the next C.O.—E. A. Cox became a celebrated poster designer and illustrator. Whenever I look at his painting in the Royal Exchange, I can see in the little red-haired girls in the picture (taken from his daughter, Mrs. Anne Pruden, when she was a child) the resemblance to my young sitter as she was in '59. As had the Pre-Raphaelites I too appreciated the marvellously paintable quality of that red chestnut hair that sadly changes to pale auburn and then to grey so soon and so regrettably.

E. A. Cox related how he saw one day in a butcher's window in London a great dead swan being used as a centrepiece. He bought it at once and carried it to Brangwyn's studio, crying; "Here's a subject for you!" Brangwyn, as inspired as Cox, set the swan up and painted it immediately, completing the background with some of his usual fruit and floral still-life material. But the swan stands out with the touches of a real master. The picture is in the Tate Gallery collection, and is perhaps as fine a piece of still-life work as Brangwyn ever achieved.

Joseph Cribb, the sculptor, was an interesting artist, a real craftsman in the Mediaeval tradition, the kind who had created the cathedrals of the Twelfth Century, uninterested in individual fame or the concept of the artist as an extra-personalised individual. To Joseph Cribb, the workmanship, and the fact that one kept on working, was the important part of the vocation. His hobby was the collecting of insects, of which he had cases full of specimens. Sometimes I visited his house of an evening and listened to his reminiscences. He had been wounded in the 14–18 war, and left for dead in a shell-hole; escaping being buried alive by a rescue party because a sergeant saw a faint movement. . . . When Epstein carved the Wilde Memorial for the Pere Lachaise graveyard in Paris, Joseph Cribb went across with him to cut the lettering on the stone. Much of the carving about Brighton was from his hand—from the great pylons, as you enter Brighton on the main road from London, to the small carvings above the porch of the new church at Rottingdean, that I found him putting the finishing touches to one sunny morning when I was out painting.

Spending an evening with Joseph Cribb I asked about David Jones and his participation at the Guild. "David—why, David carved those door latches!" I looked at these interesting items—polished versions of garden-gate latches in place of door-handles. I said tht I hadn't associated the artist with sculpture. "David! He was always carving! He'd carry a bit of wood in his pocket, and take it out and carve at it with a penknife all the time, wherever he was. Then he'd polish away at it—never liked to waste a moment. When he'd finished it—wherever he was; might be in a pub, or something—he'd hold it up and say 'Who'll give me five bob for this?' Then he'd take out another piece of wood and start another one right away."

David Jones while at the Guild, had painted a mural, in a primitive and formalised manner, in a bedroom of a nearby house where he had been staying. Although this was fortunately photographed (and reproduced in the Penguin *Modern Painters* Series) a subsequent tenant of the house incurred great displeasure locally by her painting-out of this work, it being of course an immoveable part of the house upon purchase. The great crucifix relief from the

(railway) spoil bank near by the Guild, carved from a plank by Gill, lay for a long while, rotted and weathered—taken down, its work done—on the woodpile; and was eventually burned. Seemingly Gill would have approved its end, not feeling that works created for a specific purpose should be artificially restored and cherished for their own sake separately, after their time had been and gone.

One morning early a herd of bullocks from the common invaded the quadrangle. Driving them out with sticks and shouts Mrs. Pruden and I—nobody else being about at that early hour—encouraged them up the road, into a farm yard and barn. Following the animals in, I was all at once pinned against the woodwork and beams of the stalls by horns and hoofs. Clambering with difficulty out of reach, it occurred to me that but five minutes before I had been sleeping peacefully—however, when they quietened I was able to escape.

Once, Ditchling was electrified with interest at the arrival of a newcomer—a poet, reputed to be rich. He had rented a fine house and studio, and proposed to the local printers that they should be his partners for a new venture, the publishing of his own poems and those of others, together with illustrations by local artists. A new practitioner in the arts was always a source of intense interest to the village—he could be a great asset to the local art exhibition societies or the drama group. The new poet, a cadaverous man in his early fifties, was very persuasive. He had soon organised the setting up of his publications, and several artists were already at work for him on the drawings. One day he called at the Guild; somebody had suggested me as an addition to his fold. We discussed details, but whenever I mentioned payment, there was a pause and change of subject. Eventually, he declared it was surely honour enough for me that I should have the opportunity to illustrate his works. I pointed out that this would not do. At the art college small publishers and agents were often requesting the students to work at pictures for proposed children's books, and then vanishing with the drawings, never to be seen again. Eventually, the poet and I reached a point where nothing more was to be said. My commercial attitude did not please my friends and associates, and my conduct was considered cruel. However, some days later, the police went to his house and carried him away. It appeared he was that classic but unbelievable character, the escaped lunatic; and he had practiced this same deception in other places on previous occasions. Naturally, none of the artists nor the printers were reimbursed for what work they had so far accomplished.

Nearby, lonely in the fields, was a cheaply constructed house built all of wood. This was inhabited by the two Misses Lucas and their brother, a retired army officer—somewhat senile but pleasant enough—who spent his time wandering up and down the road, dangerously oblivious to the traffic. The Luci, as they were known, had lived there for nearly fifty years. The Misses Luci were two little thin brown women, rather in the Virginia Woolf image—typical artistic ladies gone countrified. Originally Royal Academy art students, they had chosen for their 1914 war work to go down to Sussex and work on the land. A farmer gave them the wooden house at a nominal rent, and there they had stayed ever since. For a while, their student and artist friends and teachers had visited and stayed with them for painting holidays—drawings by Sickert and Nina Hamnett still hung on the walls—but by and by these contemporaries had faded away, become history; and the two sophisticated London girls had evolved into archetypal members of the local art society, exhibiting at the yearly shows in the village hall, and regularly taking their paintings to the R.A. and other shows, though rarely being hung. As painters they became worse, the more experienced and the older they became, which is the mark of the provincial artist who has cut himself off from the capital and the regular society, not necessarily only of other artists, but of great works of art. It is important to look at the old masters once a month at least, to remind yourself that they are still just ahead of you. You will go back to your studio inspired and ready once again to compete with them—as Reynolds, in fact, remarks in his sixth discourse.

I first met the elder Miss Lucas when I was taking a circus poster off a telegraph pole (after the performance) for my collection. I intended it should decorate the caravan, which was already full of stuffed animals and kitten-skins and the like. These colourful old-fashioned lithographs had been left stapled to trees and poles all round the district after the circus had passed on. Miss Lucas got off her bicycle, and stumbled across the ditch, hurling imprecations upon me.

"I little thought that *you*, of all people, Mr. Blaker—an *artist*—would support such a wicked abuse of poor animals as to be putting up circus posters—"

I explained that I wasn't putting it up, I was taking it down. It took some time to explain, but ever after she regarded me with deep suspicion.

The Luci were famous in the district for the Affair of the Bear. It appeared that some years previously they had visited the Brighton Aquarium, which at that time included a small zoo. In this collection, their attention had been caught by an unhappy-looking bear disconsolate in a corner of its cage. They asked what was the matter with it?

"Oh, I'm selling it off to a travelling sideshow," said the proprietor. "He'll get pretty rough treatment; I expect that's what's worrying him."

The Luci were aghast at this, being vegetarian, anti-blood sports and circuses, and particularly opposed to cruelty to all animals. They asked what the bear would be sold for.

"Fifty pounds—but if you ladies want to save him, I'll keep him a couple of weeks for you to raise the money."

One feels they had fallen into the hands of an unscrupulous character of the kind only too easily and too often found in Brighton—however, they went away and organised raffles, bazaars—a "Save the Bear" fund; they made flags, and sold them on a special Ditchling Bear Flag day. They made cakes—auctioned pictures—eventually, somehow, they succeeded, by adding to the fund a great deal of their own savings, in raising the £50, a considerable sum in those days, which they were able to send to the zoo-keeper. They had *saved* the bear, and triumphantly announced the fact. What they didn't realise, however, was that they had by so doing *bought* it, as well. A few days later, a large crate with an extremely angry bear was deposited in their garden. It was impossible to get near the crate for the teeth and claws visible through the slats. The terrified ladies, afraid even to sleep lest it escape, and unable to approach near enough even to feed it, were obliged to persuade another zoo to come and take the creature away. They were, of course, responsible for carriage. Philanthropy is an expensive business.

Eventually, one of the Miss Luci died, suddenly; the other, and the elderly brother were considered by the authorities to be incapable of looking after themselves (which may have been true) and were one day descended upon, to their great surprise, dismay and indignation, by a benevolent social service, and taken off forcibly to some distant Home. They were never seen again, and the wooden house fell into disrepair. Eventually, the ruins were demolished, and a modern house built on the site. Probably the Luci had neglected to buy their shack all those years, with what little income they presumably possessed; but when one considers their arrival as lively art students, owning the earth, as art students do—and then their way of their going. . . . It is a strange little parable of different times.

One day that summer, the circus having moved to Brighton, I went down and asked for permission to draw the elephants. I was leaning against one of the supports in the long narrow elephant tent, drawing the great creatures as they munched hay and swayed back and forth rhythmically . . . all at once, the other onlookers began to run for the exit behind me, and at the same moment a zebra, with pink feathered head-dress, sprang into the tent from the opposite end. It had evidently broken free and escaped on the way to the ring for the afternoon performance. It quietened for a moment, then trotted towards me, ears back, eyes rolling. The elephants ignored everything. I put my hand out—the truant moved closer; but at this point four circus attendants ran upon the zebra from the opposing ends of the marquee, and the animal went wild with panic, with me in the centre of it all. Leaping in the air like an enormous rabbit, he exploded hooves in all directions. I had a kind of instant tableau impression, like a sculpture in colour—the black and white banded body, with leaping and dodging figures—one man down with a kick in the head, another groaning—I shrank back against the elephants—the zebra eluded those he hadn't dealt with, ran up and down once more and eventually disappeared through a flap in the canvas, with those still able to run pursuing him. . . .

. . . . . .

Christmas at Ditchling meant a midnight service at the village church—for the Protestants. The Catholics at the Guild of course had their own midnight mass. The Ditchling church was Dickensian—candle-lit, with apples, holly, leaves and flowers decorating the aisles and pews in profusion, giving an immense romanticism of atmosphere. Next door to the church, at a lower level, was the yard of an old cowshed next to the great barn (later removed, though not, happily, demolished). Here was set up a living representation of the nativity by the daughters of my employer the Inn-sign painter. With living angels, sheep, donkey, Madonna and Child, the whole lit by lanterns, this was an incredible vision to come upon as we filed out of church after midnight. I had helped by making a halo or two. The event concluded with hot mulled punch for Madonna, Angels, and friends.

At Christmas, also, the annual Arts Ball was held at the Brighton Aquarium. This was, in fact, nothing to do with the Art College, but a commercial enterprise. However, the management presented a block of tickets to the students, provided we built floats for the carnival procession round the ball-room, a highlight of the evening, when the rougher element was permitted to tear them apart. However, we thought we might as well make the floats, and a group went along. The first year we made a fullscale coach and horses of board and papier-mache—the second year the Victorians had evolved, and we built a Mississippi steamboat.

196

Artists, inevitably, are always in demand for carnivals and theatricals. At Ditchling I was asked to paint a backdrop. It was needed urgently. Could I paint it that very afternoon, in time for the final rehearsal? I went down to the empty village hall—all I had been told was that it should represent a garden. I found the paint cans, and commenced work, becoming inspired by the vast space to cover, and using larger and larger brushes, brighter and brighter colours. Having been painting large garden pictures in any case, I was accustomed to plants; I filled the backdrop with great sunflowers, a blue sky, the wall of a cottage—hollyhocks—roses . . . eventually, it was a Van Gogh such as Van Gogh never dreamt of, that carried his themes, his ideas and technique to the ultimate. It was the kind of picture Van Gogh might have been expected to paint had he accompanied Gauguin to the South Seas; I went back to the caravan very pleased with myself. The next morning the producer arrived, furious. The play was due to commence that very evening—and the cast had been obliged to act the final rehearsal before my unfortunate *joke*!

What was wrong with it? I was told. The play was *The Chalk Garden*, in which the very barrenness of the garden, wherein nothing grew, formed the substance of the symbolism. . . . I had been misinformed by the person who had passed on the directions. Overlooking the fury directed against me, the fiery apoplexy of panic, I picked up my brushes, and led the way back to the village hall. In an hour, I had covered my masterpiece with a simple, empty panorama—a lonely plain of white with a few scattered rocks like the surface of the moon. With the exuberance of the sunflowers hidden away, the first night was a relative success; although from my seat in the stalls (which I had been obliged to pay for!) I felt a certain resentment more against the playwright rather than the management.

One lunchtime, as I was sitting enjoying a plate of stew on the steps of the caravan, I received a cryptic telegram: "Leave at once." This had caused some consternation in the community, as it seemed to presage a family tragedy at the least. However, I recognised the style. It was from my friend B., the architect, who had studied at Brighton Art College, and was now living and working in London, where he had rented a mews flat. From this point I commenced living a concurrent and separate life in London, in addition to the life at the Guild in the caravan, so that my Ditchling paintings, and my new series of London etched portraits, became two spheres in my work that I was able to jump to and from at will—leaving London whenever I felt like it, perhaps even in the middle of the night, and returning to Ditchling; or vice-versa.

In London, I made a kind of miniature flat on a shelf overhanging the upper staircase, in a space about six feet by two; here I placed my sleeping-bag. I decorated the wall by the shelf with reproductions and small paintings in order to create a sensation of space. With the other architects who shared the flat, and their circle of friends—including four girls who shared a flat in the same mews—I had plenty of sitters for my etchings; and of course, new patrons.

In London, I spent most of my time once more in the museums, looking, pondering, contemplating—with particular attention given, as always, to the masters of the 15th and 16th Centuries, the Italians and the Flemish; Botticelli, Pollaiuolo, Memlinc and Van der Weyden. A study of these absolutely thorough artists is all you need to make you into an artist, whether you want to paint pub-signs or Resurrections. Their knowledge pervades their pictures, from aesthetics to technique. If you stand before them long enough, they will tell all they know. You could gain no more by speaking with them, for what they have to say is said there in the panels.

I drew the Elgin marbles in the British Museum—sketched in St. Paul's, and the Natural History Museum—painted watercolours—went to the dances in the Royal College of Art and jived to the Temperance Seven, or perhaps The Happy Wanderers, that interesting street band that could be seen any day on its regular beat from Oxford Street to Charing Cross Road. Once I bought an L.P. of them and then watched them actually in performance through the window of the bus on the way home. The resonance of the two banjos, the drum and the brass section, playing either jazz or regimental numbers, was as familiar a sound in the London Streets of that time as was the famous harp and violin in Brighton of Tony and Alexander as you walked in the sparkling morning sunshine of East Street.

On a foggy November day, B. decided that he wanted the flat decorated with large mural panels. We bought a quantity of board, battened it with wood so that the murals could be removed when necessary, and set to work. R. was summoned from Brighton, and arrived with two of the girls from the Art College in the costumes they had worn on our Riverboat float as saloon girls. With these models and each other, ourselves and our patron, we produced giant paintings—R.'s represented, surrealistically, girls and musicians on the turn table of a massive record-player; in mine they sat on a roof in a December fog, with cats and chimneypots. The chimneyscape as a motif, and in fact a place to be, was a favourite setting of ours. When B. lived in Brighton, we climbed from his attic window one night and onto the narrow ledge that formed the apex of the roof. This was two feet wide, and the intervening chimneystacks were pierced so that one could climb through and continue walking. It was a clear moonlit night, and we walked the length of the street, chatting and discussing the stars. At one point a head twisted up at us from an attic window below and asked what was happening. "It's all right," said B. reassuringly—"We're just taking an evening stroll."

Painting my mural, I first met B.'s future wife. I turned from my ladder, saw her standing at the door, framed in the darkness beyond, cried: "Don't move," and painted her into the picture, on a second's acquaintance, as it were. The mural now hangs in their house above the piano, and when playing it one looks up at these perennial people on their fogbound roof, caught in time, locked into the late Fifties. . . .

After completing our decorations, R. and I set out to hitch-hike back to Brighton, where we had a band date. As usual, we enjoyed little luck with lifts, and eventually found ourselves on a lonely strip of road, with no sympathy at all from passing motorists, until we thought of the idea of posing as master and servant. I put on my frockcoat and tophat, which were with our other costumes in R.'s Gladstone bag. I sat on a log grandly and impassively, while R., dressed as a Victorian manservant, stopped the first car, with a commanding gesture. It was a very large Rolls-Royce, sumptuously appointed, and the owner drove us in state to the coast, listening to our Eminent Victorian anecdotes with keen enjoyment—or, at least, humorous indulgence.

At one point, a mass scooter race was held (for charity) between various colleges, each college providing a motor coach and a child's scooter. On this we took turns, each riding for some hundred yards or so through the wet November afternoon and evening, on the main London–Brighton Road, then handing it to the next rider and being picked up by the following coach. The event was covered by the film and television news. Being in a cinema a week or so later, I looked more closely at the screen at the conclusion of the Gaumont-British news (I was buying an ice at the time in front of the stalls) to see a giant-scale image of myself flying along the road on a child's scooter—a gaunt, thin, bearded, black silhouette. The audience cheered, while I crept back to my seat feeling diminished and embarrassed by this immense pictorial doppelganger up there.

Brighton at this time was busy demolishing the picturesque streets on the hills behind the Art College and elsewhere. Someone discovered that an old public house, recently closed, was to be the next building on the list. It was decided to have a grand party there the night before. Candles in bottles were brought along, a barrel of beer, and the bar was re-opened. The old piano had been left behind, so the Victorians were able to provide the music. At the end of the party most of the guests took home a chair or stool with them from the "Fitter's Arms" collection. Much of this furniture was used in a studio some of us later shared for a while, but which had to be vacated because of a difficult tenant below in the basement. At the least sound, as of an easil shifted, or a person stepping across the floor, an outraged cry would issue from below: "Hey, *Guv'nor!*" We would drop a sheet of paper sometimes, and wait for the explosive epithets; or at least, that was what we claimed. . . .

Some weeks later, I was sitting in a train bound for Worthing—it was about one o'clock in the morning, and the last train that night. I was staying on the Lancing coast for a while, painting a series of seascape oils and watercolours for an exhibition I was to have in Aldridge's Gallery, Worthing, sharing it with the Academician, the late R. O. Dunlop. Although it was about 2 a.m. the carriage was full. I saw the young man seated opposite eyeing me as if doubtful whether to speak. At last he leaned forward in an authoritative manner. I assumed he wanted the window closed (which I had just had the temerity to open) but he said:

"Are you Blaker?"

I nodded.

"We've not met, but you've been described to me—and I've seen your chimneyscape mural—would you paint a large sign—a seven foot figure of 'Justice' on the outside of a restaurant I've just designed?"

We talked—the next week I went to the London offices of his firm of architects and met his partner; curiously, I never met *him* again, but I agreed to paint the figure—in Essex Street off the Strand. (The building has since been demolished). While working, I ate my meals in the restaurant, which was an enjoyable bonus. Up on my ladder, high above the jostling crowds, I employed myself at this age-old craft putting all my recent experience to good use. I had made a careful drawing, posing a girl from our circle in a classical toga, with hair bound up in Greek style. I felt the ladder tapped, and looked down to find a wizened little old man peering up.

"Speaking as an old pencil-man myself," he said, "that's not a bad piece of figure-work."

I felt cheered and encouraged by this remark, coming from a member of the craft, whose grudging admiration is worth all the compliments of the uninformed. One always respects the opinion of the practitioner, even when it would appear that a life-time's efforts have only left him a little poorer in worldly goods. But in the final estimate, it is not wealth we admire, but expertise. The old craftsman who can make a wagon, join the wheel, shrink the tyre on—is a god among lesser men.

One evening that summer one of the other architects and I went down to the Palace—it was during the official visit of General de Gaulle, and as we walked through Pall Mall, every building had its gas flares in the railings alight, great flames leaping and waving five feet high. I had always assumed these iron torches to be but part of the rails, not realising they could be turned on. The streets from the Athenaeum to St. James's (with the perspective as one looked back making the flames merge into a wall of fire) were intensely hot, and the evening was warm and summery in any case. Outside the Palace a crowd had amassed—it seemed composed of Londoners; the commuters had all gone home by now. Vociferously, the crowd cheered every manifestation on the balcony, which usually seemed to be a man with a broom, who looked embarrassed. Eventually, the Royal Family appeared, and then the General, looking immensely tall in the centre. Holding his arms wide apart in a welcome gesture, he was received with silence, until my architect friend, carried away with enthusiasm, cheered as if a devoted admirer. The crowds followed his example, and De Gaulle waved in response. The first fireworks went off in the set pieces, the crowd turned its back upon the Palace, leaving the celebrities in the Royal circle, as it were, and we watched the portraits of those behind us carried out on a gigantic scale in the pyrotechnic medium. It was all very like a kind of Ditchling village occasion magnified. Afterwards we glimpsed the Royals driving past us, sparkling tiaras on their heads, as we all walked home.

In the mews, one could look from the first-floor window—once a stable-loft, and still possessing half-doors, and hear Big Ben chiming if you leant far out and listened. A new tenant moved in across the way, and from outside we could see him moving about in his empty house, painting the walls . . . hallo! It was H., one of our architects! It was H., in there, painting the wall. With his extreme kindness, he must have offered to help.

"Don't work too hard!" we cried from the window, all gathering together to lean out in an intimidating group.

"If you *want* to work, come and paint the kitchen in here!"

"I say, where did you get all the sudden energy?"

"Careful, now, don't kick the paint over—" the gems floated through one open window to the other. At this point we saw somebody walking up the mews. He paused at our door, unlocked it and came up the stairs. It was H. The tenant across the way bore an unusual but superficial resemblance to him. . . . Somehow, we never became friendly after that day, although invariably the mews dwellers formed a kind of intimate community. . . .

In B.'s room hung a portrait I had made of him, in a frock-coat; various other works of mine decorated the house. At this point another resident joined me on the shelf. B. had come across an unfortunate girl with nowhere to live; her husband had died in an accident and she had nothing but a six month old baby, a lorry-load of furniture and her husbands paintings (which were not very capable anyway). We laid planks across the well of the stairs, at the end of my shelf, and in this area, five foot square, she established herself in a kind of nest, baby cradle and all, regardless of the precipitous drop.

The possibility of falling over this edge seemed not to worry her; she seldom spoke, and merely descended from her lair at intervals to the kitchen and bathroom. Eventually, she wandered away, never calling back for her effects, which filled the garage, and had to be disposed of piece by piece. The unfortunate husband's paintings were eventually all painted over with new pictures, of course—the inevitable end for the works of the undiscovered genius.

The Victorians, although now appearing less often in public than in their great days, were, nevertheless, still in demand. We played for a Roman Orgy fancy dress party in a hotel in Surrey, and also belonged to our own Dining Club, financed by our playing. This was inspired by a phrase in our bible of Etiquette: "Savages eat; *Gentlemen* dine."

As time went by, however, and many of the Victorians became more preoccupied with examinations than they had been as first-year students, rumours began to evolve that the Eminent Victorians were a manifestation not only of the far-off but of the recent past also. A leading Brighton newspaper printed in large black letters: "Death of the Victorians," and commented: "A prominent feature in Brighton two years ago was the Victorian Jazz band, but this once famous band has disappeared from the limelight. What has happened to the group of art students who used to entertain the crowds with their outlandish dress? . . . their 'Victorian' Jazz soon caught on. They took their collection of improvised instruments, including a Swanee Whistle, a blues-blower—that is, a paraffin funnel with a trumpet mouth-piece . . . to Ditchling. There they scored a top hit with a show called 'Granpa's Night Out'. "In 1959 the Victorians appeared in a show on I.T.V., which furthered their already spreading fame. People were soon coming to Brighton to see the Royal Pavilion, the Palace Pier and the Victorians. People were soon swaying to 'When you wore a tulip', 'Golden Slippers' . . .

"Victorian dress was acquired from local second-hand shops, and Brightonians grew used to the sight of top-hats and tails. A teenager magazine featured the Victorians in one of its strip cartoon stories. The peak of the band's career came when it achieved fame during the funeral of the local pig that drank too much and fell down a well.

"But following the successes, one by one the members of the band left the Art College until its numbers dwindled to half the original strength. And now it is unlikely that Brightonians will ever see the top-hat-and-tailed band parading on the prom again."

This brought forth an indignant letter from R., who was now an art teacher, having left the district. His letter appeared in the Brighton Herald under the heading: "Victorians not dead after all." He wrote:

"Let this certify that the eminent Victorians are still in existence. Their apparent 'death' is due to a strategic withdrawal to gather forces. Since my hasty exit from the Brighton scene some five months ago, I have not been lying idle. Indeed, I have been searching throughout Lincolnshire for 'new' old sounds, the course of which has led me to join several fine and distinguished brass bands, gathering information and tunes such as 'Murmuring Breezes', 'Soldier's Tale' and 'The Stilt Walker', to name but a few from a vast and truly magnificent repertoire! At this moment my capable colleague and good friend Michael Blaker, Gent., is transcribing and, indeed, composing melodies of such great magnanimity as will shake the very foundations of the known world.

"Never, no never, will we pass away pianissimo, but rather fortissimo grandioso. 'Like a lion did we come, like a lion shall we go!' "

But not even the hyperboles of the redoubtable R., and his Stiltwalker—let alone my (purely imaginary) masterly compositions—could stay the end, and the Victorians eventually disbanded; to become members, in many cases, of other, subsequently formed, jazz bands.

. . . . . .

One warm evening our trombonist and I were wandering around London, and happened to be in Regent's Park at twilight. Trying to take a short cut out before the gates were closed, we came through the trees on to a gentle slope under a tree, upon which sat half a dozen winged fairies in grey gossamer skirts. As we stopped short, in a kind of gratified surprise that all adult disbeliefs were in future to be considered as erroneous, I glanced across the shadows and saw the audience. It was an open-air production of *A Mid-Summer Night's Dream* that we had stumbled into. We hurriedly disappeared back into the natural scenery.

. . . . . .

A little before this time, on the August Bank holiday of '60, the trombonist and I set out to walk to Rye, two days' march from Brighton. Some of our friends from the Art College were living in a cottage for the summer in the near isolated village of Stone-in-Oxney, some five miles from Rye. It was heatwave weather—that atmosphere without a breath of wind, that so very occasionally descends upon an unbelieving world. We walked through Lewes—past Chalk City, or the site of it—under the overhanging trees at Firle—on to Polegate and Pevensey, the sheep grazing quietly in the castle grounds. As we marched in to Bexhill, a deep summer night had come on. At about two a.m. we came upon a workmens' hut, a temporary shed near a road-up sign. The door was open—we slept on a pile of sacks full of sand and cement, covering ourselves with an array of jackets that had been left hanging on pegs. We were somewhat worried that we would oversleep, and be discovered by vengeful workmen under their clothes; but by 6.30 a.m. we were again on the road.

At Hastings, where a fishing boat (with deckhouse and square stern—so different from the Brighton fishing boats but a few miles down the coast) bobbed in the calm blue sea of dawn, we bought coffee at a beachside cafe; surrounded by shivering, grey-faced young men who had spent the night trying to sleep out on the beach. Pebbles are the coldest bed of all.

By lunchtime we were almost in Rye, coming out of Winchelsea, where Millais painted *The Blind Girl,* and in whose church he worked on the background for *The Random Shot.* Below us, on the plain, was Camber Castle, and—further across the reclaimed land—our destination. It was late afternoon as we trod the marsh road by the military canal, dug to stop Napoleon as a last-ditch stand . . . suddenly, from the blue sky of a moment before, a rainstorm blew up and fell upon us. We arrived wet and cold, soaked through, and were obliged to dry all our clothes by our friends' fireside, unexpected as we might be; but that was art school custom in those days—endless hospitality.

The trombonist, dried out, left the next day to walk on—striding out across the marshes, pack on his back, until his tall figure was lost to sight. I remained to assimilate myself into the life of Stone-in-Oxney. We sketched in the fields and from the hill of the church. We spent our time fishing in the river by the old Inn, frying our catch for supper, playing guitar and mouth-organ to entertain the public house regulars, and to earn our pints of bitter. Kent was a famed place for brass-rubbing expeditions, so we read in a Victorian book on the craft that we had discovered. In Rye, we bought lining-paper and heel-ball, and went up to the church; where, according to our instructional volume, "the best brasses are to be found *behind* the altar." We sought out the vicar, and asked if we might take some rubbings.

"Dear, dear, there's been so much of this," he complained, rather testily. "It's wearing away the church fabric—which did you wish to take?" *"The ones behind the altar,"* we said, impressively.

His eyes opened—his frown vanished—a look of deep respect replaced it. "I didn't realise you were *professionals*—of course, of course . . ."

We discovered another old church where the leads on the bell-tower roof were inscribed with outlines of Queen Anne period shoes, scored round the originals with a knife point, and the owner's name and the date scratched within the boundaries. These were shown us by the vicar, an interesting personality who combined his clerical vocation with that of an art-dealer. We cycled, on borrowed machines, up and down the narrow lanes—there was always something to do. In the evenings we sat in armchairs reading endlessly as we ate our spaghetti or stew supper, cooked by one of us each day in rotation. At a nearby ruined barn, I looked at a wide crack in the rotten wood, and thought "Just the place for a bat to be," prised it open, and took out a struggling little pipistrelle. Intending to return it in due course, I carried it back to the cottage in a handkerchief and showed it to one of us, who happened to be unwell and in bed. The bat ran up the bedclothes, took to the air, and hung fluttering as if on a hook or invisible wire. Having listened to all the vibrations in the room, he then sidestepped from his position and in one moment flashed through a door but two inches open, and in the same long sideways flight went straight through the narrow space open at the top of the bathroom window.

Curiously, a little later on, I found another bat (or the same one?) in the same place in the same barn. This time, however, I took it out in the field to let it fly, hoping to see it in the air with more clarity than at dusk. The bat fluttered upwards for a moment—then, as if by prearranged signal, from an apparently empty blue sky, the air was suddenly full of swallows, swooping, diving in a frenzy of hate and fear. The bat, dodging, ducking, and swerving, eventually got away into the bushes. So strong and instinctive, evidently, is the hatred of those of the day for those of the night; instinctive and implacable. I would not have released the bat had I known this unfortunate fact.

I returned with the Rye group to Brighton at the end of the summer, and rented a studio with them in one of the ancient and still picturesque sectors: Little George Street, Kemp Town. There was still sufficient summer left to enjoy some of the famous Brighton beach life. From the studio the beach was but a few minutes' walk. We would go swimming, come out, build a small fire at the waters edge, and fry sausages and bacon in a pan, to the envy of those with uninspiring sandwiches. The studio itself had originally been an old scene-painting loft. A removable floor plank the width of the room gave scope for a backdrop to be painted on rollers fitted above and below the floor. Previous to that vocation, the studio had been a simple stable with a hayloft, and the stable remained below us on ground level. An exterior ladder of wide steps provided access to the loft: now the large painting-room with a small room adjoining. From the studio window we looked into the courtyard of ancient almshouses built round a central quadrangle. Aged pensioners sat before their doors or hobbled lamely about, seldom going out through the great gateway into the street; where, within a minute's distance from each other, were fish and chips, pubs, restaurant, second-hand and antique shops, picture framer, grocer . . . in fact, the complete artist's village. I began to paint 24×26 inch impressionist views, oil on board, of the courtyard and the chimneypot landscape, taking the same subject by day or night. Sometimes, carrying an easel out onto the pavement on a dull and rainy evening in October, I painted a view of wet road, hurrying people, and reflections of lights and cars in the mirroring puddles. In December and January dusks, with a raging sea beating the Palace Pier, we took out paints and board and sat on the pebbles, close to the immense waves, finishing our pictures on the spot (with no re-touching allowed) in the best traditions of outdoor work. Once back in the studio where we could warm ourselves by the stove, glass of bitter from the pub, and rolling liquorice-paper cigarettes, the paintings were seen to possess all the atmosphere of a stormy evening in Brighton in the late 'Fifties. This, as Ruskin would agree, was genuine Historical Painting.

By day—or night, as the case might be—we found them interchangeable—I continued my series of large free-style portraits, ordering quantities of 5′×4′ sheets of hardboard to be delivered. I painted directly on the surface, without priming, enjoying the effect of the bold brushstrokes on the already mid-toned surface. Our circle of friends were as usual employed as subjects for these paintings, and for etchings. Locally we enjoyed a large acquaintance from the Art and the Technical Colleges, and also from the Ballad Tree. This was a coffee bar in a sidestreet off the town centre, the first Folk centre in Brighton, where strolling musicians were always weclome, and could sing and hold informal sessions. In those times uncommercialised Folk guitarists played to a limited and select few of admirers, making the world seem small . . . in a new town, one could find people one knew, by going to the local unofficial Folk centre—usually the back room of a coffee bar—not the large successful coffee bar, but the small, practically non-profit-making one, of which the proprietor was a musician himself.

After storms, we combed the beaches for quantities of driftwood to burn in the round stove we had taken from a rubbish dump and set up, complete with long twisting chimneypipe that wound round the studio to escape through a hole made in the roof. We did not at first realise that the far end of the chimneypipe would become intensely hot—consequently it set the roof rafters on fire. However, we dealt with this and remedied the fault.

Gradually, we accumulated a number of twelve foot planks, carried from the beach after storms. We laid these across the roof rafters and created an upper storey where one could place a sleeping bag and relax comfortably above the draughts, if one disregarded the possibility of rolling off the edge. . . .

One morning, as we were returning from George's Cafe after lunch, we found two girls, in the current universal uniform of scruffy black sweaters and jeans, and uncombed long hair—an effect creating a deliberate affront to any other contemporary mode—and one which I often painted—waiting by the studio door. With them was a sack of hay and a donkey. They told us the story—the donkey had a propensity for escaping from a field near the London Road; they had found it, taken it back, and been told to keep it by the owner, the animal being more trouble than it was worth. Hearing from the Ballad Tree about our stable, here they all were. The donkey, they pointed out, was a cross-donkey, with the traditional mark on its back where Christ sat on the entry into Jerusalem; not that this in any way affected its reception.

The stable now occupied, with the donkey happily munching hay, was too good a subject to ignore—we brought board and easels down from the studio, and painted by lamplight—we had either that, or gas-mantles—while the donkey stood patiently immobile. While it was interesting and amusing to possess this new model, the time came when we too had no more time available for him; and a field was found, where he had the company of ponies, and, by mischance, a highly ill-tempered horse. A year or so later, apparently, the donkey, having been persecuted by this horse, received a kick so severe that gangrene set in. By this time the leading spirit of our group, J., was living in another part of the town. Hearing about the donkey's condition, he took it to live in the backyard of the house where he rented a room, and where all the

family were devoted to animals. In fact, they possessed a boxer dog of so fierce a disposition that it attacked all strangers on sight, and on one occasion sealed off the entrance to the street (a cul-de-sac) and prevented any resident entering. When I first met this monster it had recently given birth to five puppies, and if anyone so much as glanced in the cupboard where they dwelt, she pounced furiously on the intruder. Not realising the nature of the animal, I arrived, bent down and pulled her ears when she entered the room, patted her, opened the cupboard looked at the puppies, pulled her ears again familiarly, and walked out, while the boxer stood amazed and aghast at such liberties; or that there existed somebody who did not fear her reputation. The next time I called, however, I was timid and cautious, having been apprised of her true nature. She scented my fear at once, and I only escaped by leaving by the window and closing it down behind me.

The donkey lingered only a few days, and then died—in the kitchen, where J. had led its last steps in the hope that the warmth might help. Faced with a dead donkey in the house, that had died in his arms, and now seemed a good deal larger and more unwieldy than in life, J. was obliged to visit the local slaughter-house and explain why the huge corpse was preventing the family cooking any meals. It subsequently cost five pounds for a van and crew to remove the ill-fated creature.

. . . . . .

At the Art College at this time was a student who lived in a neighbouring small town from which he travelled in to Brighton each day. In his room at home he had a vast number of road signs, shop signs—any kind of notice board or official sign was his obsession—bought, begged, borrowed and purloined. One evening, he was dragging home a large "Road Up" notice when he perceived two police officers behind him. He got the sign indoors and up to his room as quickly as he could, but not quickly enough. There was a knock, and the police were into his bedroom.

"And what," they said, "do you think you're about with that notice, eh?—"

They looked about them as they talked—slowly, their gaze faltered, they gaped. All round were scintillating notices—diversion, road up, pull cord to stop train—others more obscure and diverse—one's receptivity ran out half-way. . . .

The police turned back to the student with a different attitude, one of humble respect.

"I'm sorry, Sir," said the senior constable, "but we didn't realise you were a *collector*. . . ."

At about this time I caught my hair alight in the studio gas-mantle. Stooping down to peer at a carving I lifted my head suddenly and broke the fragile object. The flaring gas ignited my long frizzy hair, which blazed up. At the same moment as I felt the scorching go down to my scalp, J. leapt upon me with a blanket and extinguished the flames, but the hair never grew again properly. Another near accident occurred when I jumped over a hedge at Ditchling and on landing found that I couldn't move away. On bending down I found I had landed on an old plank with a four inch nail projecting upwards. The nail had driven straight through the sole and out of the top of my boot, between the side of *my* sole and the inside of the boot, fastening me securely, but not in fact even breaking the skin.

One Xmas Eve, an elaborate and festive occasion in Brighton, R. and I concluded the celebrations by going over to Ditchling as usual and eventually escorting one of the girls on a long walk back through the country lanes to her parents' home near Burgess Hill. It was a cold night, and had been snowing, and it was freezing hard. The cold moonlight seemed attractive—we had decided to hitch-hike back to Brighton, as all the last buses and trains had ceased. On arriving at her home, it proved impossible to wake her family. Not liking to abandon our unfortunate friend, we discovered the garden shed, with deckchairs. In these gaily-striped summery seats we spent an endless night, slowly freezing, and talking philosophically of detachment, as we rolled the last of our tobacco. The next morning, with powerful colds already developed, we at last gained access and after a drink of tea set off to Brighton. It was my coldest experience since wading the Ditchling pond after my duck.

Chapter 8

In the late summer of '61 I moved to a studio on a hill on the outskirts of the town. I continued to stay at Ditchling intermittently, and added to the store of my studies there; a stack which reached such proportions that I had to organise a large van to bring them to my new studio for safer storage. The portraits at the old Brighton studio I removed by hand, renting a barrow and stacking the great sheets of board and canvas on it to form a load five foot wide, and incredibly heavy. This immense weight ran away with the barrow as I turned to go down the hill of crowded traffic—St. James's Street. I was carried away, the handles of the barrow lifting me off the ground as I tried to hold it back. Fortunately a friend on the pavement came to my assistance, and somehow we stopped the runaway. It then took some six hours to drag and push the load up the long hill to their new place of storage.

I was walking through the Brighton Streets about this time, in my comfortable old shoes, when the rain commenced. Before long, the shoes were soaked through. A little more walking, and the tops began to detach themselves from the soles. A few moments more and the soles had come away completely; I was now walking in my socks on the wet pavement, with the tops still tied on with the laces, flapping. This seeming worse than useless, I took them off and threw them away. The socks were now wet through so they followed the remains of the shoes, and I perforce continued barefoot. The next step was of course to find a shoe shop and buy some more shoes; but first of all a pair of socks was required for the trying on . . . it was all getting very tedious; however, the socks were bought in a store—the shoe shop presented a slightly more difficult problem. However, entering in an anonymous manner I found a quiet corner, dried my feet on the carpet, put on the new socks, and requested to be shown a pair of new shoes, hoping they would not notice I had no shoes actually on my feet.

"How do they feel?" the assistant asked when I had put them on . . .

"Not too bad," I said, "I might well take these . . ."

"It doesn't seem to *me*," he said, "that you have much choice. I take it you won't want them *wrapped*?"

At this period I was playing with the Union Place Revivalists, a jazz band based at Worthing. They were students at the Worthing Art College, and I had met them one Rag Day. I now played rhythm section piano and occasional slide whistle solos—it was interesting to stand on the stage of a vast hall with the dancers below all jiving to the sound of the whistling pipe until the band took up the theme again, and I returned to the piano.

We played for club dances—anything—and for long sessions. Dances began at eight and went on sometimes to twelve or one. Eventually, I left this band, as I was also a member of the Spasmodic Seven, a spasm band of Brighton students. This had commenced as the Magnificent Seven minus Five, consisting of myself and S., a leading light of Brighton jazz student circles and a professional chef, whose occasional banquets were enviable sessions to attend, and for which I designed and etched the elaborate menus. These would be followed by a musical entertainment in which the diners participated. The Eminent Victorians had finally ceased to function. Some of the members, such as R., joined the Spasmodics; others joined the Wolverines, who played at art college dances. As the Spasmodic Seven, we featured banjo, piano, drums, trombone, slide whistle, phonograph fiddle, occasional cornet, and vocals by our girl singer. We played as cabaret at dinners, intervals in jazz clubs, college dances and so on—for fees, drinks or the fun of it, whichever was offered; besides the weekly practices, so essential to any band for improvement.

We practiced in a room lent to us by the Brighton Boys Club; and to pay for this concession were required to perform before the governors and Trustees, and the Mayor, at the yearly concert. We included as an innovation in this a blank cartridge revolver, which was fired by our girl singer to neatly fit into the alternate breaks of *Muskrat Ramble*—which, with *Mississippi Mud*, formed one of our most successful numbers of the repertoire.

I first met S. when he was judging a beauty competition, in full legal regalia, at the Grand Hotel on the sea front—later, on the way home, I came upon him in the early hours in East Street, the lights throwing dramatic shadows of his long cloak and flat-topped bowler hat across the deserted pavements. . . . S. commissioned a series of giant portraits of himself from me, on the heroic scale, and hung them around the walls of his Brighton flat.

Together, we wrote songs and music—S. the lyrics and I the melody and chords. When performing, I played piano while S. sung through a megaphone. We participated—as the Magnificent Seven minus Five—in concerts such as the annual staff entertainment of the Brompton Road Hospital in Fulham, rewriting the words of such of our numbers as "You Sadist You" to fit the idioms of the medical profession. For these appearances, as with the Spasmodics, we dressed in a medley of the Victorian and military costumes from our now extensive sartorial collections. With constant parties, dances, practices and band dates, every evening of this period was a considerable social occasion. By day I painted, either from a sitter or out in the landscape. Financially, jazz band playing was useful, but as with painting, the greatest sin was to try and please some real or imaginary public. The great thing was to do what seemed essential, and let results evolve as they might. I painted numerous portraits of people I knew, either for interest or on commission, painting for whatever prices they could afford.

In the winter of '60–'61 I was out painting on the long beaches of Lancing (a favourite scene for subjects) when I came upon a large dead turtle floating in the placid misty water about four feet out. I waded in, and dragged the specimen to the shore. The shell was over a yard long. The animal had been dead some time, so I removed the head and buried it near the beach huts, for future resurrection and cleaning, and wedged the body into the breakwater, in the hope that the action of the sea might eventually clean the shell for me. However, the rough south-west gales soon swept it off.

Some months later, I was walking the beaches at low tide about a mile away. At one point, for no particular reason, I went down to the exposed sand at low tide, and crossed it diagonally. A clear patch of sand attracted me—in the centre was a small ridge of bone three inches long projecting from the sand. I paused, looked, recognised it—with a piece of driftwood I dug out the buried turtle shell, now beautifully cleaned and empty, and recognisable by the three bullet holes in the top, which had presumably caused its death in the first place. They were of different sizes, as if it had been fired upon while diving deeper to escape.

In the late summer of 1961 I met Tony Mandeville, writer and poet, and together we formed a small organisation to make our own films, which we showed at the monthly Film Society sessions. This medium became of obsessive interest to our group, and we passed most of our time in cinemas studying the works of those film-makers we most admired, from Griffiths to Bergman, whose *The Seventh Seal* had been a great inspiration to the Film Society and the art students in general. With the early masters of the camera to emulate, and the new Continental directors to discuss and admire—at a time when they had not yet become great successes, adulated by all—film became

the world, as it were. Fellini, Antonioni, Visconti, Truffaut, and all the rest
. . . we kept to black and white, like the film-makers who meant most to
us. . . .

Some of the smaller Brighton cinemas could be surprisingy informal. We
were watching a film in one small establishment, when it jammed, or the
sprockets leapt, or perhaps the switch to the next reel was faulty. The film
jarred and bounced for about five minutes. There seemed no staff about—it was
mid-afternoon. I went up to the projection room—it was empty. I happened
to know that the projectionist lived in a small terrace house a few doors
down the street. His wife showed me in to the kitchen. There he was,
drinking tea. "Film's on the Blink." "All right, I'll come along. Keep the tea
warm, May."

With ourselves, members of the bands, Brighton characters and acquaintances, and any costumes, horses, weapons and so on that we could borrow, we
went out film-making by day and sat up all night writing scripts of a symbolic
and philosophical nature. We made Westerns, also, as a tribute to that idiom,
for which we had a great liking; we did not disdain genuine popular traditions,
but only bad art. My particular interest in making films was in the creation of a
mood combining the supernatural and the lyrical, by using the people I had
about me who interested me visually. In effect, making a film was rather like
painting a subject like my *One of the Thieves* or *Angels on a Roof*. One of our
films, *Angelic Behaviour*, required a small angel to sit brooding on a Victorian
tombstone. We selected one of the prettiest and most photogenic of the girls
about, dressed her in a Victorian nightshirt, and drove to the old Brighton
graveyard on the hill on the downs, where some of the more elaborate and
decorative Victorian tombs moulder away in idyllic peace. On her back I
fastened a pair of barn-owl wings from one of my specimens. While the other
actors needed were still being prepared behind the trees, I placed the angel on
the stone, head in hands, brooding, and went to see how the team was
progressing. At this point I glimpsed, glancing through the leaves, a little old
couple plodding up the path—up to the tomb they came, stopped, gazed at the
angel. The angel, not liking to move, gazed back soulfully. The old couple,
after a long, long while, looked at each other, and continued walking. I often
wonder what revelation they felt had been vouchsafed them, and if they ever
mentioned it to anyone else—or even to each other.

For other films I used the Brighton Tip—a marvellous place of desolation—
the ground a black slowly-burning swamp that scorched the shoe-soles if one
walked across too slowly. Here I made a First World War miniature epic. One
film I made was of a snowstorm among the old tombs in Brompton
cemetery—the supernatural can figure successfully in the film medium, as all
know. When we borrowed horses for our Westerns from diminutive little girl
riders of apparently seven or eight years of age only, it was amusing to see our
actors falling off the horses at the least movement of their mounts, despite all
their hats and boots and cartridge belts and revolvers—while the tiny

jodhpur-clad owners of the steeds attempted to put them to rights, flourishing their little whips impatiently.

Aces Alive was a slightly different kind of Western. We were all influenced at this point by the film made out-of-doors at low—or non-existent—budget, using only a few actors and the happy accidents of what one found about one. We went out with the actors and the camera, and created the film, as we did by coming upon an old sofa in a dump and using it as a fulcrum to the conception. You could, of course, increase your actors by including yourself and making one of the others act as cameraman. We eventually decided that each member of the group should take a turn at being director, when his decision was law. If everyone's ideas were included—however constructive—nothing ever got accomplished without endless discussions; and, as always, the essential light began to go.

A film we made—*Day of Omen*—that featured items of the past not always to remain commenced on a small steam train from Brighton to Bramber. By placing the actors further up the train, and telling them to lean out at salient points of the landscape, I could film them by myself leaning out of the end carriage and catching them in the view-finder as we lurched round a bend. The film continued in the Potter Museum, and is perhaps one of the few records of the interior of that immortal establishment.

Brighton in this period was somewhat like New Orleans might have been in its Jazz heyday—or, at least, we did all we could to create such an atmosphere. I was of course still playing piano with the Spasmodic Seven. Apart from cabaret, at dinners and such functions, we busked on street corners on the famous Rag Days, held in October, when processions of floats created by the students followed a route all throught the centre of Brighton and Hove, and all turned out to watch. As the Eminent Victorians, we had created a Victorian gin-palace with dancers in red plumes, black stockings and lace; as the Spasmodics, we loaded a piano on to a lorry, and played from it as we drove along, as we had carried a harmonium on and off the stage for Art College dances.

The processions were invariably led by Ted Owen's Excelsior Jazz Band, to which he added an immense line-up, for the occasion, of brass players; so that the sound was both incredible and exciting. Ted Owen had been a student of silversmithing at the College, and all day one could hear from the workshop the sound of the clarionet as he practiced it. I made several etchings of him with or without the clarionet and had been a regular fan at the Burgess Hill Jazz Club Tuesday evenings when he played there regularly. His idol was George Lewis, yet when that elderly jazzman came to Brighton Dome for a concert, having been rediscovered in the light of the revival, and set on the road again for a second career, some people were disappointed, feeling that the performance was not equal to the early recordings. Another excellent group was the Croydon-centred Original Downtown Syncopators, who wore evening dress, and were a pleasure to dance to, with their very neat and sharp rhythm. The banjo player was an architecture student at Brighton, and they often performed at the Saturday night dances in the old church hall next to the Art College that had been converted for such use, and included a stage—it was strange to dance in this one-time setting for Victorian hymns and sermons, with the high Gothic windows and vaulted roof above.

My own preferred favourite of the Twenties bands were King Oliver, Jelly-Roll Morton's Red Peppers and his Rhythm Kings, and of course Bix Beiderbecke. The less streamlined the better, was our liking. Jug bands, simple blues instruments; anything but the awfulness of a band gone mainstream and smooth. Johnny Dodds and Omer Simeon on the clarionet, Kid Ory's trombone—Johnny St. Cyr on banjo—these were the gods. I actually attended a concert at the Dome when Kid Ory's band arrived in person—a little nut-brown old gentleman by now, yet a legendary myth, there before one—incredible.

The most admired and respected band of this era was Ken Colyer's. I had discovered his club a few years before, while roaming round London. Set in a cellar off Leicester Square, it was a small crowded place full of tremendous impact—the light and music rushing up to meet you. He had the real quality of the Twenties bands; he wasn't just a revivalist. He was totally dedicated to this religion. I went to a concert at the Dome where he was sharing the programme with the Temperance Seven. During the interval, we strolled out into the Dome Gardens, and found Ken Colyer alone on one of the benches. We went up to tell him we had enjoyed his recent playing—he said he preferred not to play at a concert; it was too cold an audience, however enthusiastic; the concert hall didn't suit jazz; you needed an informal atmosphere where you could play yourself in, and really get somewhere with the sound.

We were all regulars at the so-called Chinese Jazz club in the Brighton Aquarium dance-hall of a Friday evening. This popular venue had succeeded the Coney Hill jazz band in Montepelier Road, a favourite place of the mid-Fifties. Humphrey Lyttleton often played at the Chinese, and Chris Barber and Ottilie Patterson, whose *Nobody knows you when you're Down and Out* was a classic favourite. Her relaxed authentic style showed a deep study of the real Bessie Smith quality of the blues singers of that immortal era.

The proprietor of the Chinese Jazz Club was an unforgettable character called Bonnie Manzi, and always referred to himself in the third person when taling, as "your Uncal Bonnie." The handouts advertised Crocodile sandwiches and Fried Lice, and he often announced from the stage that they were available; though asking for them was like applying for your Artistic Licence the first day at Art College. The Chinese was a mecca and a meeting place for jazz enthusiasts; although eventually it had to bow somewhat to fashion. Jazz went into the Charts, became a temporary craze for all, in place of a smaller, dedicated following, and then went out of fashion leaving successful only a few bands who had followed the Pop approach. The result was a falling off in attendance at Jazz clubs and eventually the whole scene fell away to wait for a new revival some twenty years later; though this seemed to exist, when it evolved, more in playing as a pub group than for dances; whereas the Fifties and Sixties bands more usually played facing a hall of jivers. Nevertheless, some very interesting bands came to the Chinese from the Rhythm and Blues scene. Manfred Mann featured an incredible and energetic young singer, Paul Jones, later a great success in musicals. I have seen him continually running up and down the stage, singing, microphone in hand from eight to eleven-thirty, with only a short break between. Alan Price, Georgie Fame—these were other stars, though in a quite different style to the jazz scene.

We spent Saturday nights, if not playing personally, at a dance in perhaps the Hove Town Hall, the Technical College, or the new University; although this eventually went in for famous bands, and a dance became a crowded Pop event, and so lost its local character. Also, the tickets, that had at first been available to all members of the Brighton Students Union, were then barred to them. It had been at first supposed that the University would happily become a part of the B.S.A.; but over-large numbers presumably precluded this.

Eventually the members of the Spasmodics went their separate ways, and half of the group joined a new band, the Portobello Jazzmen. We played two or three times weekly as the resident band at the Ship—a large old pub on the Lewes Road, not far from where I had rented my first studio. The Ship had originally been an army pub—the old barracks were still opposite—and had a stage, space for an audience line-up of chairs, and plenty of room for bar, billiards and general activity. The evenings when we didn't play, the grand piano on the stage was taken over by the resident solo piano player, Ron the Stick, whose badge on the poster advertising him outside was his permanent walking-cane. As piano-player myself in the band, I was always eager to see what instrument on a gig lay in wait for me. Sometimes this brooding monster was an impressive affair; at other times a knocked out old upright; although only once or twice have I found one so below pitch that it was impossible for the other instruments to tune to it. The band at the Ship was a real pleasure to me. It had sufficient power and full quality for the drummer and I to keep up a semi-telepathic conversation rhythm-wise during the numbers. Of course, this is what happens all the time anyway in a jazz band, and is the main purpose in playing, when towards the end of the session everyone is blowing with so much sense of union, with imperceptibly subtle questions and answers and echoes between them, that real creativity is occurring—even, or perhaps particularly so, with the well-tried numbers like Tiger Rag, Royal Garden Blues, Sister Kate, and the Original Dixieland One-step. These and a host of others are the hymns of the religion; they are not jazzed up songs—they are jazz numbers, and expressed by jazz best.

As we played, fans at the bar would pay for drinks to be sent up to their favourite players, enquiring from the barman what were their preferences. I have looked up and seen six pints of bitter arranged along the top of the piano, seemingly having appeared from nowhere; and on looking round at the audience recognised by instinct the character at the bar who has recently sent

Come & Hear & Dance to..

TED OWEN'S

FABULOUS, RAVIN

EXCELSIOR
NEW ORLEANS

JAZZMEN

GRAND OPENING SESSION AT NEW PREMISES

The Richmond Hotel
(Licensed premises)
Opp. ST. PETER'S CHURCH

GRAND PARADE, BRIGHTON

24th MAY, 7.30 - 10.30

Free Membership

ADMISSION 2/-

A JAZZ DANCE
BY
THE WOLVERINE JAZZMEN
AT
BRIGHTON ART COLLEGE HALL
(Entrance in Carlton Hill)

ADMISSION 2 6d

8—11.30 p.m.

The
Union Place Revivalists
FOR PARTIES AND FUNERALS
PHONE

Bolden's Basement
Club
GRAND PARADE :: BRIGHTON
Member

B.S.A. SOCIAL COMMITTEE
PORTOBELLO JAZZMEN
Jiving to this popular band
at THE TECHNICAL COLLEGE
Saturday 2nd. June 7.30 - 11.30
Tickets 2/- 2/6 at Door

Michael Blaker

JAZZ SHOWCASE OF THE SOUTH

Brighton Chinese Jazz Club ★★★★★★

EVERY FRIDAY at the FLORIDA ROOM (Adjoining BRIGHTON AQUARIUM)

Uncal Bonny has pleasure in presenting its forthcoming programme . . .

November 15th   The Pearly Kings of London
THE LONDON CITY STOMPERS

November 22nd   Without doubt the King of Jazz
● ● ● KEN COLYER JAZZ BAND

November 29th   BY DEMAND!
Winners of the M.M. Poll and the All England Jazz Band Championship
ALEXANDERS Jazz Band

December 6th — RHYTHM and BLUES with
➜ THE ROAD RUNNERS featuring **Ken Barton** ⬅

December 13th **MONTY SUNSHINE'S SHOWCASE JAZZ BAND**
featuring **THE DICKIE BISHOP FOLK GROUP** and vocalist **Valery Wiseman**

December 20th   _Chop Chop - Extra News Flash_
The Club's Xmas Party
ALEXANDERS JAZZ BAND
★ **Xmas Tree Presents** ★ **Surprizes** ★ **Balloons, Etc.** ★

December 27th **CHARLIE GALBRAITH'S ALL STARS**

NURSES HALF PRICE   —   STUDENTS ADMITTED ON STUDENTS CARDS
Please help me to help you by passing on this pamphlet to a friend or putting it up in your favourite Police Station or at Work or College.

Licensed Bars ★ **Crocodile Sandwiches** ★ **Foo Youg Ny** ★ ★

Chop! Chop! Uncal Bonny would like to take this opportunity to wish all his members **A Velly Chop Chop Xmas and Happy New Year,** and to thank you all for your support, I only hope that I have added a little pleasure to your year!

Chop! Chop! Velly Good! **UNCAL BONNY**

up this refreshment. One acknowledges with a nod, and his eyes accept your appreciation of his gesture. You look up again after a while, and find all the tankards are empty—sip by sip between numbers you have drained them all. After the sessions, we stayed on for a while, playing bar billiards to all hours, eating pickled mussels and the like with our last pints—on the house. Being up half the night, one slept to lunchtime next day, drifting to a cinema for the afternoon, and in the evening beginning the round of pubs and jazz clubs if not actually playing. Between all this there was of course the film-making; and the varied settings in which one found oneself provided inspiration and impetus, and a permanent range, also, of willing models for etchings and paintings. The band, with full line-up, played not only at dances and Youth Clubs, but also gave jazz demonstrations at schools. At times, at the rougher Youth Clubs, we were given a degree of trouble. I have had the piano pulled half off the stage while I was actually playing it, and we had bottle-tops hurled at us on the same occasion. At this point we in fact decided against the further helping of these institutions as they regarded any visiting entertainer as merely an opportunity to further break up the place; apparently from no motive whatsoever—exactly as a certain type of person will wish to interrupt an artist painting.

On one occasion we made a film during the course of a dance at the Hove Town Hall—our actors had to chase each other through the jivers, while I filmed them from above, and down the corridor lined with Canova nudes—these statues were saved from the fire that destroyed the building some years later. We also filmed in snack bars and Divall's type eating-houses—our actor, impersonating a rough intruder, elbowing his way through the indignant bus-drivers, while we filmed from the table where we had earlier taken our places to drink cups of coffee and buns. I made a similar film entitled *Lonely Girl in London* in which I filmed the heroine in the rainy evening streets, in buses and the Underground; concluding with morning in a deserted Trafalgar Square when she finds company with the pigeons, who whirl around her in a kind of ballet, while the camera dances with them and her, at all angles.

Officer Material was a Kafka-esque satire, with a robed martyr, S.S. men, Victorians, and the like. We made a long epic, *Some Rise by Sin*, incorporating as actors art students, members of various bands, and other characters. We had already made a short comedy, *Man on the Roof* in which a burglar is apparently thrown off the edge of a four-storied building to be spread-eagled on the pavement below—after which, Buster Keaton-like, he gets up. Scrambling around on the rooftop among the chimney-pots caused passers-by to look up askance; but we had become used to the public staring. Our Epic production required many different settings, as the Wanderer hero penetrated various time and space levels, climbing up a flat pavement vertically by using as the rungs of a ladder the legs of people waiting at bus-stops . . . and going from indoor to outdoor settings through huge screens of newspaper appearing in a wintry park. The film, made and directed by Tony Mandeville, was a film accompaniment to a long epic poem he had written. Various picturesque girls acted parts that were supposed to be in summer weather, although by now it was chill January—crouching by fires as peasants, or wandering by lyric brooks as fates or presentiments. The final version lasted over forty-five minutes, and was shown to an audience at Brighton Art College, although few seemed to understand it. However, it is the case with such symbolic pieces that concentration and a further viewing are essential for comprehension. One does not look at great paintings once and once only.

At the conclusion of a day's filming our regular haunt was the Long Bar at the Pavilion Hotel at Castle Square, known colloquially as the Pav, and full of people (on a Saturday night particularly) hoping to hear of a party to go to—friends one only seemed to know from such occasions would pass you a match box or back of a cigarette packet with an address on it. When you got there, and had driven through the black countryside to find it, one would generally find everyone you knew there, and the organiser had meant to ask you anyway—so village-like was Brighton in those times.

The Pav was an essential prelude to all evening entertainment. Here were a collection of characters to be found as varied as any author or artist inclined to social depiction—or even caricature—could wish for; a strata cutting across age and class, and all looking for an hour or so away from being themselves. Salesman, lonely old schoolmasters, layabouts, summer-workers on the piers looking after the gambling machines and the sideshows, with three-foot pockets sewed into their trousers in order to filch half the takings daily; rugger types; a few beatniks with long hair and beards reminiscent of the Middle Ages still sufficiently unusual in a crowd as they devotedly paid homage to Kerouac; picaresque and therefore predictable, and perhaps only diverting visually—but what more is an artist after? Rembrandt tramps are not really philosophers, just poor old men who haven't made it. Masses of girls abounded, often the most interesting as personalities; and, of course, useful sitters.

However, there came a point when it seemed that this life of exotic Bohemia was beginning to claim one as a participant more than an observer. I decided to withdraw from the spectacle and the carnival; I had finally left the band, together with some of the others, as the front line wished to move from New Orleans on to Bop; and providing a backing for mere extended riffs was not my aesthetic ideal. I had a crowded canvas of themes to portray and write about. Various friends were marrying and settling, the jazz scene was fading away—local bands were losing appeal as the Pop scene developed into the archetypal image of the Sixties. The electric guitar and amplifier were in, a newer generation was calling the tune, and even my younger student friends, now qualified and out in the world, found themselves outmoded by a newer youth. I had made many huge five foot by four portraits of the characters of the Brighton scene . . . now I began to move away from these giant pochades, portraits of immediacy. The momentary effect still interested me, but I came to use this manner only for landscape, while returning to a more studied and composed form of studio painting, working carefully and at leisure upon toned canvas, rather than sheets of board. I had moved, also, from cine to still photography; and inspired by a new wave of interest in Mrs. Cameron and the other Victorian photographers, took many 35 mm. pictures, which I enlarged myself in the usual impractical and improvised dark-room. I bleached the prints, and retoned them sepia with the relevant chemical. At Brighton Art College a new photography department had been set up, and during my return period there I had taken a course in it, which included printing and developing using plate camera and glass plates. I had taken my etching sitters up to the photo studios, where models stood upon huge sheets of paper posed with fashion consciousness.

"An artist should have no difficulty," the teacher told me. "All these commercial art chaps know the technique, but they can't visualise. That's where you have the edge on them."

Paintings, etchings, watercolours—I sold all these here and there, but also took up any other odd job that came along. One such was to repaint some armorial bearings and coats of arms that formed a stucco relief around the frieze of a large panelled room in a Sussex mansion. By day I worked on my ladder, being careful not to drop a paint-can on one of the suits of armour that stood at their places below, like mediaeval sentries. At lunchtime, the butler appeared among them with a large tray and summoned me down, and I ate in solitary state at the long table, while the hollow men looked on—hungrily, I fancied. . . .

. . . . . .

An inconvenience that had affected my mobility a short while earlier had been the wrecking of my motor-scooter. This had been of great use (when I was still in the band) for late-night sessions and dances. I was setting off for a practice, with someone's trombone held across my back on a strap—I jumped on my bike, and headed full speed down the steep hill. All at once the brakes ceased to function and at the same moment the accelerator jammed full on. We were going faster and faster—impossible to use the gears. I spread out my arms and legs and jumped off backwards, just before I lost control—landing on the road on my back at the same speed, so that one shoe was torn off and the sole ripped from the other. Apart from holes in clothes and cut and grazed skin I was unhurt, as I was wearing a heavy sheepskin coat, although no helmet. The trombone had flown wide as I jumped; the scooter continued down the hill, hit a garden wall, somersaulted and burst into flames and was of no more use subsequently.

It was some time before I found another vehicle; but eventually an old 1954 175 cc. Bantam-Super turned up. It was just the right size for a mobile easel, as it were. The panniers loaded with paints and supplies, the boards strapped to my back, I would set out for the countryside. Up Snaky, as George VI Avenue was known in its country-lane days before the modernisation widening at the time of the Coronation—it has always seemed overnew to the local residents—

and onto the very Downs themselves. Walking by the side of the motorbike, hand on the throttle, one could let it negotiate steep slopes, carrying all the equipment with no difficulty. The painting site once selected, the board or canvas could be propped on the handlebars support, while the petrol tank supported the palette, and the seat—was a seat.

I spent more long days on the beaches painting, my oils and boards about my chosen spot, together with my favourite writers, Balzac, Stendhal and Dreiser. I was writing, also, a series of novels on artist life, and based my style on Lucien de Rubempré's manner as quoted in *A Distinguished Provincial in Paris*, that marvellous evocation of life among artists and journalists—the parallel between the ideal and the corrupt, between the Rue des Quatre Vents, and the editorial offices of Finot. My first Bloodstock series had evolved into this would-be panorama of such characters, although—unlike Balzac—I did not cross-cut them from book to book.

I had ridden to London; and my motor-bike having broken down, and the rain descending at the same moment, I decided to enjoy the luxury of a rail journey, for both myself and the useless machinery, back to Brighton. I bought tickets and with two minutes to spare pushed the bike on to the platform. The guard was looking out from his van.

"*That* got to go on, has it?" he said. "Well, let's see how we can *get* it on."

But the bike was heavy, and the ramp was steep. A porter passed us, slamming the doors of each compartment.

"Here, give the gentleman a hand here," said the guard.

"*Me?*" said the porter. "That's not *my* job. Nor yours neither."

"Don't *you* cheek *me*," cried the guard.

They began to argue, almost coming to blows—the passengers craned from the windows. Meanwhile I had succeeded in getting the bike in a position half-in and half-out of the guard's van. At this point, a station official appeared, with a large watch.

"What's all this about?" he demanded. "We're a minute late already! We can't have this, you know—"

The guard and the porter began to complain bitterly of each other.

"Never *mind!*" cried the official, mustering them. Together we all pushed and pulled at the bike.

"Just a minute, though," said the official, "Have you emptied the petrol from the tank?"

"No, I just had it filled," I said.

"Half-a-pint, you're allowed—that's regulations. We'd better empty it."

"You can't empty it in here," said the guard, thinking of his train. "It's highly inflammable!"

"If we had a can, or something," said the porter, looking around helplessly—"or a syphon—"

Another official came up. People were getting out of the train and coming over.

"We must get *off!*" cried everybody, officials and passengers.

"I've paid for two tickets," I reminded them, "but if you'll refund them I'll take the bike outside and try to start it instead—it will be less trouble."

After some while, my tickets covered with pencil authorisations, I was back at the booking office. Re-pocketing my money, I took the bike out to the road, where it fired at the first kick. The rain had now stopped, and I set off to Brighton comfortably after all. . . .

My motorbike, being somewhat ancient, seemed to excite a great deal of interest from officers of the law. I had but to glance at one of them while riding it to be beckoned over.

"And just what," said one constable, "do you mean by having a licence not *one* but three years old?"

"Three?" I said.

"Three years out of date. The buff colour was in use three years ago."

"Yes," I said, "but it's also in use this year again. I bought this a week ago."

"Oh! Well in that case," magnanimously, "you can ride on!"

Not a word of apology—but I suppose it wouldn't do. . . .

. . . . . .

In '64 I again visited Italy, but this time by air, seeming to see far below the roads we had originally walked on my earlier trip. Mont Blanc, a great tooth, seemed be rising towards the floor of the aircraft, like a kind of potential tin-opener; but we floated gently down to Pisa in the gentle warmth of spring. Looking again at the great paintings and sculpture—particularly that of Bernini, I wrote in my diary: "It would seem that the cosy commonplaceness of Impressionism—that rid the world of the imaginative element—must give way to a *new* imaginative art. The classic subjects of the old masters gave artists the opportunity of producing epics like film-makers."

I was beginning to think once again not in terms of direct painting from people or landscapes, but of painting great themes of a tragic or portentous nature—the great and only Wattsian realities of Love and Death; with all the pathos inherent in life, in that it does not last for ever, despite the immense and tremendous emotions of individuals, who might as well save their breath. The artists of the Renaissance, so addicted to such themes, were once again an inspiration; and not only for their poetry, but their technique.

Donatello's Magdalene; Lippi's Madonnas, live creatures in the warm Italian twilight, like the real ones all about. At the tomb of St. Anthony, hung with photos of those whose patron saint he was, with wristwatches, jewels, gifts . . . hysterical pilgrims were on their knees before the effigy, flat on the floor, weeping and moaning—while English tourists politely and apologetically stepped over and between them. I found marvellous Altichieri frescoes, like Giotto but more elaborate, yet divinely simple in the true sense.

I made myself a little unpopular in Ravenna by saying that Michel Angelo was a decadent, and that the mosaics were pure because they are like comic-strips. It appeared I had denigrated both styles in the one remark—perhaps something of an accomplishment.

At Assissi seven young tonsured monks, teenagers of the Middle Ages, roll up the great carpet to the altar and carry it out on their shoulders. Out of doors, on the rough turf, they pull it back and forth to clean it, the patterns dazzling red in the sunshine. Background of tower on little hill. Giotto at my side says: "Hey, don't bother with all those frescoes of mine inside, they're not good enough really, but look at *that!*" Cimabue, Lorenzo di Credi, me, we all drop our brushes and dash out, leaving the plaster wet. The monks roll the carpet and bring it back. What material for a film!

At the Tivoli Gardens once more . . . the Beardsley walks, the extravagant tastelessness that is Baroque, Art Nouveau and nonsense all combined to make something extraordinary and unique.

On the return flight the pilot announced we should fasten our safety belts as he had insufficient fuel to continue avoiding thunderclouds, and was obliged to enter the next one. We flew towards what looked like a grey cliff. Once in, a sound like a wave full of pebbles crashed and rattled on the roof. The aircraft descended like a lift, and rain beat at the windows with, artistically, a great overplay of dramatic effect. The passengers went from a pale to a green silence. "Pretty unusual weather," I observed afterwards to a stewardess.

"But bumpy," she replied, absently.

Once again, Italy suggested new lines of painting, giving fresh inspiration and ideas for the future. Artists over the years have resisted this dominance, accusing the pull of the Renaissance of convention, banality, predictability—but it is always there, and always will be, as an impossible standard ever to achieve again. But Bernini is the keynote in Rome, as he is to the Baroque in toto; and his portrait busts, with their extraordinary realism, were another incentive towards the careful delineation of character in one's own portraits on canvas. Lively of eye, natural of gesture, as if they have only paused for a moment in their work while a painter-photographer snapped them, these popes and cardinals seem all too lively for their plinths.

Of course, although one paints and draws endlessly, the great difficulty in art is the waiting—waiting until you are old enough to be worth taking notice of by the world. It is important just to keep on your course, laying up treasures in heaven, as it were; the meanwhile making five-year plans that you must try to keep to. The world will of course try to circumvent all this, and philanthropists will sacrifice their friends on the altar of their own kindness to others; but you must not get involved in all their schemes, or all is lost—for time is not only money, it is life. Your time, which appears to be your own to direct where you wish, must not be lost in the miasma of others' dilatoriness.

I made a short trip to Holland, and sketched the strange views of the tulip fields, from which I afterwards made a series of highly formalised paintings—long vistas empty except for the acute triangle of a field of red flowers, like a streak of pain. The Rembrandt quality did not manifest itself to me at all in Holland. There was too much colour, too much neatness. I could not see the images of his untidy grey and sepia world—they seemed to belong to a different Holland—inevitably, *his*.

      . . . . . .

About this time I stayed for a few weeks at Pigott's, near High Wycombe; the last of Eric Gill's workshop guilds, where craftsmen lived and worked in a communal setting. Gill himself was interred nearby, in the graveyard of a small village church. We went to visit the place. It seemed extraordinary to consider that he was down there, this artist with so many ideas, with the strange originality that can take something from the past and make people see it afresh as a contemporary activity. On my way to Piggott's I had been given a lift by one of Gill's daughters, who kindly stopped her car to offer me this. She was anxious to return home quickly in order to listen to a radio programme on the life of her father. We arrived in time to switch on the set, and the first words I heard were of the recorded voice of the lady who had a few minutes before picked me up.

It was considerably interesting for me to be able to talk to his family. I lived during my stay at Gill's old sculpture workshop, where my friends had set up their silversmithing activities. It was strange to crawl into my sleeping-bag, alone in the great workshop among the benches and chisels, which looked as if the Master had only just put them down a few minutes before. Above me rose a huge stone crucifixion, fiercely formalised and angular—not at all typical of the flowing line and almost playful affection of Gill's nudes and Madonnas. I tried my hand at carving a head during my stay, using some of the tools and a piece of stone from a pile of jettisoned material outside the workshop. Delving into this, I found, deep down, a small fragment of worn and lichened relief work that just showed the faint traces of the heads of two figures who had perhaps stood by a crucifixion. I was allowed to keep this souvenir, and have always valued it as a memorial of that great artist. To come upon it, as a host of small children gathered to watch, was rather like being an archaeologist who comes upon the essence of some forgotten culture; but in this case, of much greater import—for myself.

About this time also I was given a commission, by a lady who owned a restaurant in Brighton, to paint her black and white pekinese. I worked away, producing an Expressionist flurry of piebald dashes of piant. The picture completed, she looked at it, and said: "Where's the dog?" She then went to fetch an earlier portrait of the peke—a small profile image sitting on a cushion. It was clear of what her view of art and dogs consisted. My painting presupposed one had absorbed the Impressionists and Bonnard, at least. However, she generously provided the requisite meals of the contract, and hung the canvas in the restaurant, though as she said: "I shall never see a dog there, though I look forever."

However, I continued to paint dogs, for pleasure or profit. I worked very directly, on board, with a free and speedy technique, as they move every two seconds, particularly if one works carefully. A series of low whistles will make them keep awake, once a position they like is finally established. In fact, their difficulty as models lies in the fact that they are either over-active, or disappear altogether into somnolent hearth rugs. I painted a Great Dane as a commission through a friend for the owner of a stately home; and have had the interesting experience of subsequently buying a ticket to be shown around by the custodian, and hearing the somewhat huge picture pointed out for the attention of the group of visitors; the subject of the picture meanwhile lolling happily, tongue out, in the grounds beyond, visible through the window.

By the mid-Sixties, in a large basement studio, I had commenced on a series of lyrical panels, deliberately echoing, in archaic form and technique, the paintings of the 15th. century Italians, Botticelli, Lippi, Ghirlandajo and the others. In addition to the larger subjects, I painted a series of small portrait panels, using my etchings as preliminary studies, of which I had a large number. I worked in the traditional style of underpainting and glazes, and spent much of my time in the National Gallery and the Victoria and Albert, immersing myself in the period. I then wrote a novel on the life of Botticelli; and further novels concerning painters and actors and life in London in the Sixties. I also painted a large composition (repeated several times) of Charon ferrying his boat across the Styx, a Paola and Francesca, and other typical subjects employed by the early Italians and/or the Victorians. It was a valuable and interesting course of study. I made careful preliminary drawings from life of faces, hands, feet and drapery, in the traditional manner. I also worked on a series of canvas hangings, rather like tapestries in effect, taking the canvas off the stretcher on completion and fastening a length of dowel round-section batten to either horizontal side, so that they might be rolled up or let down as instant murals. I painted thinly with turpentine in emulation of the size paintings, matt and chalky, of Dirck Bouts and others. The National Gallery has one, and it is possible that their relative fragility has ensured that few have survived. The quality of the canvas is retained in this style, and the portability and ease of storage is advantageous, like the Japanese Kakemono. When one considers the giant frames of traditional painting, which have illogically stemmed from the architectural mouldings around murals in great schemes of palace decoration, and were not meant to be transported from exhibition to exhibition at all, it reminds one again that this kind of evolution does not rely at all upon a design being created for a purpose. A picture frame sent around the country should ideally be light in weight and not covered with plaster volutes, and should be designed with *no* regard for the inconveniences consequent upon convention. It is rather like the engine in a car being for so many years placed at the *front*, because the *horse* had to be.

I continued to exhibit etchings, printing them on the old 13″ wide bed visiting-card Kimber press I had acquired, but my new paintings remained in the world of my own studio. At the Royal Academy I sold numerous prints from the plates, often to doctors and to Americans. My friend B., during a visit to the States, was introduced to a new acquaintance whose father possessed a proof of the same print as the one B. had taken over with him. When B. returned I went to stay at his new flat. A mouse had been troubling them they said, but no one could catch it. At dinner I spied the mouse in a corner, and with one movement fell from my chair across the floor and caught it by the tail. Such disturbance at table was scarcely worth the notoriety I achieved among the guests. However, I took the mouse down to the garden to let it go, rather than let anybody kill it; doubtless it returned the next day.

I painted a picture subsequently of a section of floor and wall, with a blur in the centre, where a moment before had been an image. I called this "Absence of Mouse"; so fast do they go, leaving your eye upon where their image still lingers. One has to jump to where they will be; just as when your hat is blown off by the wind you must grab not at your head, where it *was*; but further back, where it will *be*.

. . . .

Once, at the R.A. with my aunt, we found the rooms strangely empty. Next, a deputation of small Orientals asked us politely if we would very much mind looking at a different painting to the one engrossing us. "*We* didn't mind," we said, there were plenty more around, "but what was so special about this one?" "It's his own portrait and the photographers want to take him with it," we were informed. It appeared that the Crown Prince of Siam was visiting the exhibition. We stood back while he and his pretty wife, or queen, were photographed. They thanked us, and we went back to the painting. Later, as we stepped out from the gallery, down the steps, we were greeted with cheers from flagwaving crowds, which ceased when our identity was perceived—or lack of it, from the point of view of the crowd.

Another day at the R.A. I realised that the lady looking at a painting on the opposite wall was a member of the Royal Family incognito. With a natural interest, I walked across the gallery to have a better picture, so to speak. Those elevated to a god-like position must expect their subjects to find *them* an engrossing subject. Halfway over I was bumped into by a large passerby in a grey suit as he walked through me, as it were. Recovering from this accident, I tried once more, coming round in a circle from the other side. Bump! Again I was winded by yet another careless gallery-goer. At the third forcible encounter I had to applaud, silently, the subtle machinery by which Royalty remains undisturbed and free to venture where they will among the populace.

. . . . .

My basement studio was comfortable and friendly in that passersby could be seen as they wandered by, and the scraps of conversation as they paused to chat, or even sit on my low wall, gave a pleasing contact with everyday life. The roses in the back gardens of the Victorian houses grew along the high walls and fought the cats for space along the narrow tops. This was a subject in itself, to which I applied brush and board. The great wheels of the red doubledecker buses were company, also, as these last of the stagecoaches thundered by, making the house rock; until a J.C.B. excavator tore up the old Nineteenth Century woodblocks, and a new road surface was laid down that absorbed sound—it would have saved much straw outside Victorian houses of sickness. The house itself was early Victorian, built 1866 from a pattern dating from the Eighteen-Thirties, a kind of semi-Regency. The fireplaces in the basement were complete, with decorative iron fender, black-leaded; low cupboards in side niches; a red-brick floor in the corridor; and the original glass and wood over-mantles. With a good carpet on the plank floor, it was a studio to work in with a sense of complete comfort, a fortress against the world if one chose—an easy place of access for one's friends when invited round. To an artist, the casual visitor is anathema, taking always the best light from your painting hours and proving the old saying that when a visitor calls it is to waste your time, not his own. The artist, most gregarious of creatures, has nevertheless to be quite selfish in this matter, and one cannot paint chatting over your shoulder. It is for this reason one has to give up sharing studios, at last. One must work alone to achieve anything of profundity.

I painted every morning, keeping to this work-time, and outdoor-sketching or painting in the afternoon. Evenings, I wrote, or printed etchings. Outdoor painting is a mere relaxation. In the studio, one must be a god, or the devil will move in and ruin all your pictures; but outside the artist can permit himself the easy detachment, the cool pace, of the Chinese artist. Crosslegged on a cushion, your paints about you—four or five hours will go by in a moment, as you ceaselessly match your tones to those in the scene before you, touch by touch, never altering or going back on your work. . . .

I was painting in a wood on the side of a hill; having nearly finished the picture, I yawned, stood up, and walked up the path a short distance, to stretch my legs. From behind me I heard a crashing as if somebody was following. Returning to investigate, I found the path blocked with leaves and branches. A tree had fallen across my cushion, paints and picture. Never sit and paint on a hillside facing north where the ground is damp and the roots of trees rotten, and barely fastened in the soft soil—at least, that would seem the lesson to be learnt.

With my motorbike, in twenty minutes I could be in the depths of the country, or alone on the downs, the view of Sussex laid out before me. A minute or so down the road and I was at the beach, waiting patiently for the moment I wanted to paint, when the sun should have moved above the pier to dazzle the water with golden reflections, against which the black cast-iron of the Victorians sang their contrasting chords.

In the studio, on wintry days during the long period of work time from January to April, before all the important exhibitions of the year commence, and for which one must have work ready, I painted my large subjects—images of a lyrical semi-religious nature—sad girls and madonnas sitting in endless evenings full of wildflowers and moths. The people seemed basically pagan. Perhaps I had picked up the original classical revival inspiration of the Florentines. One visitor to my studio observed that my girls were all without hope—they are not naïve, they possess experience (she said), yet they await, hopelessly, a fulfilment they will never enjoy. This interesting critique was from a girl, a student who called unexpectedly. I had last seen her when I drew her when she was four years old. The echoes still remained in my work also of those artists whose work I liked, whose personalities continued to interest me, to whose pictures I turned for aesthetic enjoyment—Holman Hunt, Millais, Rossetti and Burne-Jones and their marvellous dream-world.

I painted more scrolls depicting flowers, angels, nudes, children—the world of the mille-fleur tapestry, where people live in a weightless universe, unworried, and concerned only with being perennially decorative. Writing, I found, belongs to the night. If you write by day, you lose that part of the day. You cannot note, feel or see anything physical or visual when you are writing, other than what your pen, that mystic instrument, the magic wand, conductor's baton, symbol of authority, extension of the personality (as Kipling says) evokes. The artist and the writer little know what powers they wield, and *might*;

what magic they are capable of pulling out, summoning up from the concentration of thought, the crystallisation of energies. Not for nothing were the earliest wizards and magicians the artists of their communities—the alchemists were artists—the early priests were painters—the architects of the Gothic cathedrals were monks. . . .

Again, mummifying. The preservation of the dead (the art of the taxidermist in fact), the process of embalming, was the sphere of the priest-artist. Who else could direct the building of the temples, the carving of representations of the gods? Who else would know, with the superb detachment the practice of his art gives him, all that can be observed and felt about a person, a community, a landscape, even the shade of atmosphere in a room? As a ghost-hunter or a psychiatrist, the artist is pre-eminent, because he works by instincts, not precepts. The artist knows everything, because he sees without looking too hard. And when he paints from his mind, when he creates images and themes and shades of thought; when the scenes and the people he paints seem to arrive on the canvas of their own volition, and all but paint themselves, what has he done? What shades has he invoked? What powers has he in fact let loose? In fact, these images of the world we are impelled to paint on board or canvas, these worlds in miniature, so convincing, that break the flatness of the support and take us at once into the realm of the fourth dimension—by what magic can we do this? We have but to believe in the scene we are creating for it to exist—and to exist for generations ahead, with greater and greater reality; until it becomes the only reality, the only visual existence we possess of a period that is past. And yet, at the time, it was only someone's dream.

It is through their art that we see Fifteenth Century Florence, or Seventeenth Century Holland. The late Eighteenth Century we see via Gainsborough and Reynolds. And yet, our view of the past may be entirely incorrect. The art we see it through is only the personalised vision of a handful—and they all artists! With an artists' imaginative recreation of what is before him, and further coloured by the conventions of seeing possessed by his period. No; it is the photograph that gives the sordid, honest, hopeless reality of a period, that gives it away, so that it always looks, basically, out of date; that mirrors it entirely; that damns it forever. Not the photography of the great masters, of course, *they* are artists too—Julia Cameron, Hill and Adamson, Nadar and the rest; but the ordinary amateur anonymous photograph, the actual, thoughtless inartistic image of somebody's limited day. It is this, unaffected by Romanticism or art: absurd, commonplace, the true banality of our doomed selves, that sees clearly. Which is why, of course, we must have Romanticism; whether the romanticism of religion or the romanticism of art, to save ourselves, to delude us with poetry and ideas; to detach us at all costs from the human condition.

With such musings I continued my paintings—picturing a philosophy of despair, of flower-haunted pathos, whispers of melancholy colouring the lyricism of the summer evening—or *taking* the colour from it, perhaps.

I showed one of these paintings at the R.A. It was hung on the line, but as the adjacent picture was of a white windmill against a black sky, the girl in her delicate twilight world was outfaced altogether, and faded modestly away. From this period of increasing isolation and de-communication I was saved by S., who was now chef to a Summer School for American students in the nearby countryside, in a setting of idyllic rural calm. He summoned me over to stay the weekend; and, as his tame artist, to paint an equestrian portrait of himself. It was to be some time before I returned to my ivory basement, and then with a different set of themes for my painting. In a space of hours I had become the artist of a country house party; painting views of the house and gardens and portraits of the students and learning something of the making of fantastic works of culinary art as a bonus. No expense was spared to give the students some conception of the finer points of eating and drinking. It was a non-stop Victorian dining club. I was asked to give lectures on etching; and then to teach watercolour drawing and oil painting. I developed the conservatory into an arts and crafts centre, with metal-work, and casting lead in plaster from clay models. Besides the equestrian picture I painted a giant "Bishop" of S. as a Roman, in true classical manner, leaning pensively on an urn, with the implements of his profession at the foot of the pedestal. One evening S. produced a Mediaeval banquet . . . the diners ate with their hands, washing them at intervals in a large bowl. A boned and glazed boar's head, Castles of Tours, Fowles of the Indies pies, mead to drink, the floor covered with straw from the stables, and coats of arms and tapestry decorations that I produced as required.

By eating Victoria plums between each course, an effect of negativing the effects of each delicacy enabled one to recommence eating. With six courses or more, it was an endless gourmet extravagance.

Leaving the summer school, I wandered in France during late August and September of '71. Unhurried, taking a train or bus from one city to another—a room over a bar anywhere, and you are a resident . . . when tired, move on. . . . To study the stained glass of Notre Dame and Chartres is in some ways all the lessons an artist needs; the main points are there so strongly: extreme brilliance combined, incredibly, with such subtlety—effects that read at a distance; and, most essential of all, the shapes, the people depicted, the sparkling patterns, are all as interesting, as attractive to the eye as a sparkling pen and ink drawing. The long thin sculptured figures at Chartres have the same inner life, that bursting yet controlled vigour of the Gothic spirit. To see these, after the Eric Gill tradition in Sussex, was to see what he meant by his enthusiasm for simplicity and emotion. Such sculpture, in its quaint, unextinguishable working capacity, has the boisterous mushroom-moving-a paving-stone quality of life itself.

Albi, with its cathedral of small bricks, like a fortress, possessed a Doom of a Spencer-like vision—the dead souls waiting for judgement having little open black-edged books hung round their necks—the history of their days—a fine idea exploited happily by the fresco painter in his patterning. With no fixed

purpose, one came upon Béziers, and the Feria—a festival of bull-fights, bulls let loose in the streets, flowing wine for all, intense hot evenings, dancing to open-air jazz bands through the night in the long treelined central walk of the town. An absorbing place with few tourists, a bus ride to the coast where wide sands and warm sea awaited—Béziers is set on a hill, with the cathedral protecting the town like a mother hen, looking warily to the west from its cliff vantage, like Albi.

To see the bull-fighting in the great arena at Béziers was to become a Roman at the Colosseum. The black bulls skipping, weightless, like enormous beetles—the cheering crowds, clapping their hands *above* their heads—the awful precision of the perfect kill—the dead bull half the size of his recently alive self—the conductor of the band matching his music to the action like a pianist of the early cinema, referring to the mirror before him as he faced the band with the arena behind him—the romance and reality of the Death motif about it all.

Even in the square in the town a small corral was built in which the local boys might test their courage against young bulls, the horns tipped with blunting silver spheres to prevent a *sharp* injury. The game was to run across in front of the bull without getting butted—the aim to insult *his* manhood, and emphasise your own. Your friends could taunt him to take his mind off you. In essence, a mini-bear-baiting, in a still mediaeval era.

I caught a morning train along the coast towards Nice, and enjoyed the panorama of the whole range of the south. The sun glittered on the foliage precisely as Van Gogh had painted it, taking the paint so far as to become in its thickness seemingly the very glowing vegetation itself, writhing and moving in the haze as did the view from the train window. I had tried a painting myself in Albi, but left it by the ticket office at Beziers while buying my ticket. However, it was far below the works of the masters that I *saw* as we progressed along the line. Near Aix the sea had the quality of a vertical slate-blue upright wall, as Cezanne had stated so often, and which one had never quite believed. The white-cube barns on the hills round Aix were again straight out of Cezanne, and the colours exactly as he recorded them. I seemed to see Cezanne and Zola as boys, dreaming romantically, among these woods, of their future poetic eminence; or playing in the town band, Zola on cornet, Cezanne on clarionet. . . .

I intended to get out at Eze-sur-Mer. It was extremely warm. Half asleep, drowsy in the late night warmth, I looked up to see I had arrived and leapt from the train as it paused a moment. All was dark. Midnight, and not a light, not a café open. . . I saw a sign, "to the village"—a path wound up the black cliff-like heights that towered above. In the dark, I could see neither my way, the surroundings, nor anything but shadows and trees. Up and up went the path. Occasionally I paused to sit on a rock; sometimes large insects and creatures brushed my face; something large and fluttery bit my arm somewhat painfully. Once I fell, heavily, and rolled to an edge. Eventually I seemed to

have come to the end of the increasingly steeper path. Far down below the sea appeared to be faintly visible in the faint moonlight. I decided to retrace my steps to the road before I became quite lost; I was half-asleep with tiredness, and beginning to forget what I was doing. With no companion, and no daylight knowledge of the surroundings, there was a blind, dream-like unreality about everything. Halfway down I reached for my small grey bag, in which I kept two bottles—one of wine, and one of aqua minerale; also, my Gauloise cigarettes, my passport, my knife; my bread, cheese and sausage. The other bag, my pack, held my Travellers' Cheques, my jacket and change of clothes. It didn't seem to be there, the small bag. Where was it? At what point had it detached itself from me? I climbed back up and down the path, expecting to stumble across it—perhaps it had dropped when I fell over a boulder . . . I decided to climb back again in the morning and look once more. A further thought struck me. My passport had been in that bag. Suddenly I was a man without an identity. I couldn't even leave the country without it, or even change my Travellers' Cheques. I stopped and looked down the overgrown path and thought: this is the worst moment, the most dismal position I've been in. I'm too tired to think, it's too steep to lie down on the path, I've no tobacco, nothing to eat or drink. However, proceeding downwards, and considering that, at all events, it was quite warm, and it wasn't raining, I at last came to a sort of promenade. After a few hundred yards I came to a small hotel, closed for the night. I walked down the steps into a beer garden—a patio, chairs and tables; statues, vines, steps descending towards the gardens and beach below. I sat in a chair at one of the tables, wishing I had a cigarette from my lost bag. Still, when in doubt, I thought, change your clothes. I put on a collar and tie and my jacket. A man appeared from a doorway, rubbing his eyes with sleep, and approached me.

"Accommodation?" I enquired, getting up and walking towards him.

"Ah, non, non, tout complet—"

I explained in a French that developed somewhat remarkably in the face of necessity that everywhere else was closed. He was sorry.

"What do you suggest I do?" I asked at last—in English. The pathos of my situation seemed to get through to him. He considered. He explained with his hands—

"*Une* chaise—*deux* chaise—*trois* chaise—" he brought his hands together.

"Oh, thank you very much—I see!"

He wished me goodnight. I collected three chairs, and made a bench from them. Then stretching out beneath the vines, I went to sleep. I was now formally dressed, in a delightful garden—how suddenly different to the recent predicament. It was hot enough not to need a blanket, although it was outdoors. I was woken first by the sound of bare feet, and a figure in a bathing-costume padded across the patio past me at a run, leaving a trail of water . . . evidently taking a short cut from a night swim on the beach. The next time I woke and found a huge figure bending over me. I hardly dared move, but sat up slightly. The great bulk bent towards me—

"Accommodation?" it requested timidly. I was not so generous as my original benefactor. In my relief—

"Non! Non! Tout complet!" I waved him away.

Early next morning I was once more climbing the path up the cliff. At that time of dawning the picturesque effects were of a fantastic beauty; although considering the steepness of the cliff path it was surprising I hadn't plunged off it in the dark. I didn't find the bag. It was now obvious that I had left it on the train. I went to the little station, where the official was most unhelpful, explaining that the train had gone on to Italy, and in that case, as regards the bag—"c'est fini!" I had a little cash on me, and tried to buy supplies from a grocery, but was refused service before eight o'clock. An hour to wait. All at once, a train came in, bound for Nice. With inspiration, I leapt aboard. At Nice I became friendly with an American wanderer, but the acquaintance was cut short—I had to find my passport. On the platform, I asked an amiable, small-moustached young man where the lost property office was, explaining about my passport, etc. With great good nature he took me to an office, to a group of porters, and up and down the platform for some time, making enquiries. Meanwhile a huge train with a gigantic engine stood waiting. Nobody could help me. The young man shook my hand. He said he would like to go on helping me, but—he had to drive the train to Paris! Running to the engine, he jumped on—cheers from everyone, a wave, and they were off. I sat down to consider what to do next. The only solution was to search the stations of every nearby town on the line. I decided to go back and start at Menton. I bought a ticket. An hour or so later, having passed back through Eze-sur-Mer of dubious fame, I was at Menton. It was very hot. I bought wine, bread, meat and cheese and cigarettes; and feeling at least restored, (though increasingly shorter of money) cross-examined the station staff, with no luck. The only answer was to see the authorities about a new passport. I set off, in the increasing heat, down to the main street. Seeing a bank I pushed through an angry crowd and flourished my Travellers' Cheque book, without much hope.

"No, no, we are not paying out *anything*—!"

The angry travellers and holiday-makers were apparently in panic. It appeared that the international financial situation had collapsed, or something—all banks were refusing to change Travellers' Cheques in any case, and everyone was in a state of desperation. I made my way to the police station to ask where the consul might be, but was refused admission twice. Walking in for the third time, I ran past the official at the desk and found an upstairs office where a thin elderly man in a grey suit examined my motor-bike licence with interest and informed me that I would have to see the British consul in *Nice*. I returned to the station to wait for the train, and sat in a café opposite for about two hours drinking a variety of refreshing beverages selected from the list on the wall. Suddenly an inner voice seemed to say—"You're tired of all this nonsense. You can go and get your passport back now." I marched into the station; saw an inner room full of suitcases, and made to enter, with no particular scheme in mind. A large man in blue shirt and jeans sitting on a counter put out a leg to bar my way.

"Look," I said, "avez-vous trouvez un sac gris—"

"Avec deux bouteilles?" he said.

"Si. *Un* vin, *un* aqua minerale."

"Si. Et *un* couteau?"

"Si. Et un passeport—"

"Si. Et fromage—" He beckoned me to follow. We went through the station, round a corner or so to a shack down the line, in which various railwaymen were drinking, apparently, tea. Propping the door open was *my bag*, the two bottlenecks protruding from it. Everything inside was precisely as I had left it—or as it had left me. But there was still the problem of what to do next, as I could still get no cash. However, I had two English ten pound notes, a card in hand, in my hip pocket. I went back to the bank, and alone of the crowd, was able to get some francs. I at once bought a ticket to Newhaven, England; and then went down to the beach where I swum far out—keeping however a careful though blurred eye upon my clothes, identity, and packs on the shore. The night train took me, asleep on an upper berth, back to Paris. By late afternoon I had crossed the Channel and was on the bus to Brighton. Getting off at Black Rock, I walked down to the beach and swam far out. It was freezing cold and a dismal contrast to the Mediterranean of the previous afternoon.

Deciding to continue my roving life, I went on to London, staying with friends I had not seen for some years. I walked round with my watercolours, spending long days at work, drawing in parks and by the river, the heatwave continuing throughout October. Near Holland Park I found a pleasant tree-lined avenue with Georgian and Regency buildings that made a decorative Impressionist effect with the branches overhead and the early morning sunlight. I was looking for a suitable site to work from, and trying my sketching cushion on various parts of the pavement, when I became aware of the inevitable policeman.

"Excuse me, Sir, but just what *are* you doing?"

I explained, and asked if it would bother anybody if I sat down to draw a watercolour study.

"As far as *I'm* concerned, it wouldn't. But I have to be careful, you see—they're all foreign embassies about here—technically, I could run you in for obstruction if you were to sit in the way of the pedestrians. But, tell you want, I'll give the Nick a Buzz."

"A what?" He brought out his pocket telephone. "I've got a gent here—" with a wink to me—"is it in order for him to sit on the pavement to *draw?*"

A great amplified answer boomed through the air, like a voice from the gods. "No, it is *not* in order! He must apply to the *Home Office* for *Special Permission.*"

It was rather like a Victorian view of the world of the future. I tried to suggest that it was of no importance, that any other view in any other street would do

just as well . . . at this point a woman came up to hand in a purse she had found
. . .

"Excuse me—" the policeman extricated himself both from the distant authority and myself and examined the purse.

"You found it?"

"It was thrown down my basement—there's not much in it. . . ."

"You didn't take anything out?"

'Now would I hand it in if I *had?*"

"I'm just asking, because it *could* constitute an offence. . ." He wrote numerous notes, before escorting me down the road, evidently to see me off his beat. On the way he talked of art.

"Now that view there—" he said. "How would you set about painting it?"

"Well," I said, preparing to expand on my own subject, "It's rather like a Constable—"

"No; more of a *Corot, I* think," he interrupted.

"Er, yes, now you mention it, a Corot—"

"Of course," the policeman waved a hand towards the buildings—"Canaletto would be more the chap for all this—except that he would probably take liberties with the scene——move the buildings about—create one of his *capricci*—"

I gave it up and merely listened as we exited from the sacred road. At the last house a coffin was being carried out and put in a hearse. The policeman became quite excited. "Now, in a T.V. thriller that would be highly suspicious— probably full of machine-guns—" He rushed off to investigate and I managed at last to escape.

One Saturday afternoon, when the dust blew lazily across the hot sunny pavements, I thought of Richmond and the river, and the desire I once had years ago to paint riverside scenes there. I bought tubes of oils and turpentine at an art shop, and had some board cut at an ironmonger. Boarding the Underground at the floral station of West Kensington, having walked past the site of Burne-Jones' house in North End Road—now a block of flats—I was soon walking down to the sparkling river, where I painted a view of the bridge and the boat bestrewn water. I sat drinking bitter and smoking the last of my Continental Gauloise at a riverside inn, before calling on my old friend B. We hadn't met since I caught the mouse at dinner.

During the following weeks I went out each day painting the river, by heatwave day and overcast afternoon—or painting the sunset as it increased and deepened its reflection in the sliding water. I gave a talk to a local ladies' club, illustrated with all my paintings, and began to sell them; although at the talk a member of the audience got up and said: "I should like to draw the attention of those present that a perfectly adequate representation of this view may be purchased in the High Street for three and sixpence." When November at last made the weather too cold for oils, I worked at quicker water colours; taking them to the *Artist* magazine, renewing my old acquaintance there, and writing a series of articles, illustrated with my new work, on the art of pen and colour wash. I also wrote on etching, my inn-sign painting experiences, and other aspects of art. . . I took some trouble to exhibit my work, and the New Grafton Gallery sold one of my little panel heads of Renaissance girls for a hundred guineas; all these odd activities served to keep me wandering about in my peripatetic artist fashion. Early in '72 I was restoring some large plaster Eighteenth Century stucco plaques of classical figures for the Richmond Poppy Factory; a commission kindly suggested by my old master, the Inn-sign painter. It was pleasant to commence work at about 6 a.m., and to climb down from the ladders to enjoy a man-sized military breakfast among the ex-service veterans in their canteen, and hear their anecdotes. The plaster had to be applied in layers that required a day's drying between, so one could only at first work a few hours each day.

Later that spring I was painting again in Brighton, and apart from landscapes, worked in the good Mediaeval signpainting manner on the West Pier, painting signs for the shooting gallery and the Moonwalk. Sitting on the pier in the early morning sunshine, with paints all around, the half-finished signs before me, I enjoyed that strange half-nautical sensation one gets from the plank flooring, the masts, the flags, and the healthy salty breeze with the wavelets below pulling at the iron struts and supports. The shooting gallery signs required Western Bar-Room style lettering with figures of cowboys and sixguns; and the Moonwalk children astride rocket-ships. This sign was a huge board in Da-Glo colours that was for a short while placed over the main turn-style entrance. Unfortunately, after a few weeks, the equinoctial spring gales arrived. That night, the Moonwalk itself—a large bungalow-sized blown-up rubber balloon in which one could jump in ten-foot leaps—hence the *name*—was detached from its moorings in the storm. Ropes trailing, it was whirled in the air, away from the pier, high above the sea, and never seen again. Perhaps it went to the moon. The signs were taken down, and my work came to an end.

There had been a general, laissez-faire atmosphere about the whole episode; the stall attendants would tell me about the Clairvoyant—"never awake until mid-day, and always drunk from two o'clock onwards," and all about the resident sign-painter, who wasn't too happy about my presence there as a pencil-man. However, although he could, as it were, paint rings around me, he *would not* move away from the two styles of lettering (he did them very well) for ghost trains, amusements, whelks and mussels, and he had only one colour scheme, that he would not alter: red lettering and black lettering on white. He was probably correct in the assumption that this was the most legible; but mine was a compendium of rainbow, spectrum, Bonnard and Toulouse-Lautrec. At least, it was something different, if scarcely up to the professional.

In August I went with B. and other friends to Cornwall and painted views of a countryside I had not seen for many years. B. and I sat in the old grave-yards, painting and drawing the finely carved slate tombs, and visited the Cornish churches around us. We took rubbings with heel-ball on lining-paper of the florid pen-like inscriptions carved in the slate. The heel-ball was purchased from the local hardware shop, an ancient establishment that stocked everything one could wish for. Around the top shelves of the end room stood some seventy plaster heads, apparently cast from the distorted and twisted countenances of condemned criminal lunatics. Some were marked as if for phrenological analysis. The shop-owner told us the room had once been part of the town-hall, and these had been given to the town when the local prison closed; he had always kept them, and there they remained, high above the hardboard and do-it-yourself emulsion. The children of my friends would say: "If we're going shopping, can we go and see the death-masks?" in a matter of fact manner, as if suggesting a great treat.

One afternoon a friend and I visited a nearby traction engine rally and fair. We photographed the great traction engine "Hero" with its identical twin drivers—huge men with blonde beards and long hair, in the viking image. A small tent yet remained uninspected; outside, a lugubrious young man beat a tambor in a melancholy manner and announced a Magic Show within. We paid our ten pence and entered. A tall, stout, still youthful magician with beard, tall blue hat, porcupine quills and magic bag round him, smiled mysteriously and bemused us with his conjuring. He then announced he would saw a woman in half. A girl assistant was laid across a table, covered with a shield of tin, and a circular saw brought down to a slot in the metal. We all smiled in a superior manner. All done with mirrors, we whispered to each other, although there was nothing in the tent but us, them, the saw and the table.

"I'm glad *you're* here," the magician remarked to two nurses in the audience of seven— "you may be necessary in a moment. I wonder if you'd step back a pace or two, everyone—there may be a bit of blood flying about—"

Nobody moved; the saw came down through the slot, ripping the gumstrip paper the magician had just glued over it. Twice it descended and arose—the cover was lifted—the girl was unharmed. We emerged, like all the other sophisticates, jaws hanging open in yokel fashion, as they had from immemorial time whenever the fair came to the village. . . .

I was sitting on the grassy roadside one afternoon, painting a view of a group of cottages and the one shop that faced the gates of the drive of the house (once the vicarage) where we were staying. At intervals the tenant of the cottage immediately across the green opposite me would appear at her window, interested and curious. At last, unable to resist further, she came over to look at my work and have a few words of conversation. She next appeared some minutes later with a large tray of tea, scones and cake, which I thought it best to finish to the last delicious crumb—starving artist image—so as not to disappoint her, while she beamed from her window with a pleased sense of having helped humanity a little. I returned to the vicarage circuitously by travelling round the back of the church rather than let my new friend see me enter the gates immediately after the repast.

Afterwards, the painting was put on show in the village gallery. Unfortunately, the lady recognised it, and realised that I had not, as she supposed, made a pilgrimage across the moors to her vicinity.

"I velt zuch a vool," she confessed, "taking him all that to eat; and his tea were waiting for him indoors all the time!" However, I made a point of subsequently purchasing a good many supplies from the village shop she owned.

I chose a quiet Sunday morning to paint the church, forgetting about the arrival of parishioners for the 11 o'clock service. Slowly, as I limned in the quaint tower in its damp hollow at the foot of the valley, cars began to scrunch the gravel about me. I remained cross-legged on my cushion, an indifferent Buddha, or perhaps an apparent rebel against the establishment. The worshippers disappeared into the church—the bells ceased; a faint sound of melancholy organ and singing made the rooks caw lazily in echoes from the treetops. An hour or so passed by—my study was nearly completed. From the church came groups, individuals, chatting, enjoying the Sunday comradeship and satisfied that their weekly duty, or penance, had been observed. As conversation languished, the boots around me, that had previously ignored my activity in the dust, now turned towards me; the congregation were defeated by my pinpointed, active presence; they watched the evolution of the last sparkling brushstrokes that summed up and brought together the composition in a final burst of virtuosity I found impossible to suppress. . . .

"I see you've put in my feet," said the Vicar, noting that I had indeed sketched him as he stood at the porch—"I didn't think they were as large as *that*."

"And you've put in my old straw hat," quavered a very elderly clergyman (the vicar's father as it appeared) whom I had added as a final touch—"I've had it these ten years."

"And it's good for another ten," said a parishioner, with loyal enthusiasm. There was an instant silence and awkward embarrassment all round. It was a little too obvious to all that the old gentleman himself was nowhere near good enough for anything like another ten years, whatever the durability of his hat. Fortunately, however, he appeared not to have heard.

. . . . . .

A little after this expedition I returned to Brighton to undergo a surgical operation for the removal of an unfortunate item from my leg. After various appointments with doctors and experts I presented myself, as required, at the hospital, a new clean, light-filled palace resembling a luxury hotel or the waiting-room of an airport. I was directed to a small vestibule and took a seat.

"Seems quiet this morning," I said at last, to the nurse at the desk.

"Nine-five," she said, glancing at her watch— "the cut thumbs will be along soon."

"The what?"

"The restaurant accidents. They prepare their meals early—start before eight. Then about eleven, the ladder cases arrive."

"Ladders?"

"They fall off their ladders mid-morning. Get careless."

"What happens in the afternoon—anything?"

"The old ladies get tired after their lunch. Then they slip over—"

A small Chinese nurse, masked to the eyes and seemingly rather pretty, now poked her head round the door and said I would be next. At this moment a figure tottered up and sat heavily opposite me. He was in full chef's costume: check trousers, apron, waist napkins—the tall hat bobbed back and forth as the pallid chef, like a sorrowful clown, sat clasping a large and bloody dishcloth.

"Hurt your hand?" Of course one had to ask.

"One thousand and ninety-nine," cried the chef, in a sort of burst of passion. "One thousand and ninety-nine grape-fruit I've sliced in that machine since breakfast. The two-thousandth sliced my thumb off—it's all in here." He shifted the reddening towel. "I picked it up and bunged it on. . . ."

"I think *you'll* probably be treated before me," I began. The Chinese beauty opened the door, looked at the chef, and beckoned him in. Well; at least I was next. But round the corner came another young man, this time covered in oil, black grease and overalls, his hand wrapped in a blood-dripping, oily rag. It seemed *his* thumb had got caught by a spanner flying off an engine . . . I sighed and waited for the Chinese nurse to beckon the wounded mechanic, who was by now reading a children's comic in a listless, unseeing manner. The chef emerged, his thumb swathed in tight gauze, his tall hat missing.

"Twenty-five! *Twenty-five* stitches it took!" He announced. "They bunged the thumb in disinfectant, bunged it back and sewed it on again!"

At last, I found myself in, requested to undress and leave my boots outside the operating theatre. These were consequently visible to the waiting patients whenever the Chinese nurse opened the outer door to peep out. The boots stood there like sentinels—"Blimey," somebody said, "that's all they've left of some poor bloke—"

Needles were being inserted and a local anaesthetic given. The surgeon began to cut away, while I relaxed in the warmth; even enjoying all the solicitous attention.

"This is pretty well attached," the surgeon was muttering. "Tell me if you can feel anything—" He was sawing away, head down, as if engaged at his lunch at a café table. The sharpness of the scalpel reached me. Another shot of anaesthetic in response to a polite murmur from me that I *could* feel it, if it was of any consequence. At last, with a sigh, the surgeon announced he had removed the offending part.

"And now to open it," he cried, "and see what caused the cyst. . ."

"May I watch?"

"Of course." I sat up, while he moved the scene of operations (as it were) up to my lap. Our hair intermingled like fish footmen, the Chinese nurse, the surgeon and I bent over the minor postmortem. It was no use, however—it seemed to defy dissection. "The analysts in the laboratory can deal with it," said the surgeon at last. The nurse brought a small jar of spirit, labelled in a sinister, if appropriate way: "Michael Blaker"—and the surgeon picked up the object in his tweezers to deposit it in the jar. Unfortunately, it fell—rolled down the nurse's arm, and so to the floor. After we had all groped about down there for some time it was at last found and firmly secured in its bottle.

A week or so later I returned to the hospital to have the stitches removed. The surgeon approached me with a smile. "Good news," he said—"It's benign." I looked blank. It hadn't occurred to me it could have been anything else. "Benign!" he emphasised. It was no use. With a hopeless shrug at receiving so little response to his announcement, he went off to find somebody more interested, apparently, in their life and its continuity. In the next bay I could hear a nurse soothing a patient: "It won't hurt—your stitches will come out quite painlessly—" This comforting statement was followed by a series of heart-stopping groans and cries from the patient. I steeled myself, and detached my mind for an ordeal that proved in fact quite painless, in fact. Leaving the hospital at last, I observed the regulation young man slouching up the hill, hand wrapped in a bloody rag. . . .

.   .   .   .   .   .

My grandmother, now aged ninety-three, had always been a favourite model of mine, for etchings and paintings, since the *Swiss grandmother and child* of nearly twenty years earlier. One morning she began to climb up the staircase—I was standing at the top; she paused, lost her balance, and fell backwards over the banisters, floating down slowly (it seemed to me, watching helplessly) as if supported on a kind of horizontal cushion, until she came to rest in a corner of the floor below. Her head had hit the wall, and a long red trail ran down the wall above her.

Curiously, she was unhurt; nothing broken. She was indeed, very resilient and had survived again undamaged—being knocked down by a van the previous year. Indeed, her only known illness had been a rheumatic leg, which she claimed had been cured by a bee stinging her in the knee. Perhaps the goat-milk diet of her infancy had created this strength. As regards goats she remembered one of her uncles setting off to emigrate to Australia via Italy, and walking over the mountains from Switzerland with a goat before him, the milk of which would nurture him until he reached the port of embarkation.

Six months after the staircase fall, however, I felt impelled to draw her one Saturday morning. I made study after study, in charcoal, and afterwards we laid them out on the floor, and getting down with them on hands and knees, discussed the merit of each. This denoted her general agility; indeed, although

becoming older and older, and often saying, "Time I was shot," in a semi-facetious manner, she would still crack nuts with her teeth. On my objecting she would ruin her teeth in this way, she would say: "Well, what do I want to keep them for?"

Two days after the drawing morning my uncle phoned to inform me that my grandmother had died, with a sigh, on getting back into bed after a disturbed night. It seemed a mercifully unlingering manner in which to move away from this world. I felt I should like to see my grandmother once again. She had been removed quite quickly to an undertaker's establishment. By 11 o'clock I was at his address—a large barn-like structure, with a chapel attached. Entering through a door in the great gate that formed one end of the workshop, I found a small office, full of saw-benches and coffin-lids and elm planks. The undertaker suddenly appeared, in a large apron, wiping his hands on it. He seemed reminiscent of a polite butcher, paradoxical though such an image may appear . . . I asked if I could see my grandmother.

"See her?" he cried, in outraged astonishment at my indecent request. "Why, I've only had her forty minutes!"

Apologising to the indignant expert in embalming, I said I'd come back tomorrow. "She'll be ready for you about ten o'clock," said the undertaker genially, as if I was going to collect a bicycle with a mended puncture. "And will you kindly move that motorbike," he went on, with increasing irritation. "We can't get the hearse out with it in the way—"

Next morning I was again at the establishment. The chapel door was locked, but eventually the undertaker, now solemn and reserved without his apron, ushered me in. Two coffins stood on trestles. He removed a cloth from over the face of the first, and retired, leaving me with my grandmother. I heard myself saying: "Well, you always did have a good head." I studied her face for some time—a strange experience. The fact I had always found her so aesthetically satisfying meant I felt no shudder. The time seemed endless—as it was, for her—perhaps I was picking up the vibration atmosphere—and one had the curiously peaceful mind-state that occurs if one is *alone* with the dead. Two people with a corpse seems to me to constitute a kind of indecency. One cannot commune if other live persons are in the way. It is strange to stand by somebody who can neither speak nor wake, who isn't even there any more. To find one's own mind trying to communicate and finding only cold blankness is a disconcerting experience. Finally, I said: "What a waste!" thinking of all the experience and recollections of nearly a hundred years now lost—and turned to go; carefully avoiding bumping into the other open box behind in the dim grey light.

There was a dark alcove before the door of the ante-room and stepping through this I ran straight into a standing figure; with great shock to my state of mind, now soberly attuned to the coldness of eternity. It was of course, the undertaker, who had been waiting (impatiently, no doubt) for me to conclude my endless philosophising. For a while we grappled desperately, until he switched on a light and matters explained themselves. I felt he might have stayed outside, not lurked in the shades. However I left laughing, in high spirits at this readymade anecdote and thinking how much it would have amused the main figure in the—literally enough—case.

· · · · · ·

One morning in '73 David Wolfers, of the New Grafton Gallery, phoned me with a curious commission. Would I like to paint a copy of a Rossetti for a steamship? It sounded so strange an idea, yet so much what I would particularly like to do, that the request appeared somewhat dream-like. As usual when one's guardian angels have evolved a situation, everything began to fall into place—other angels leapt from the earth (or the heavens) to help. I visited the offices of the steamship company, where the director explained to me that each of their ships was named after a painter whose name commenced with an R.; this being the original idea of the Company President's wife who was an artist.

"We've got the Ribera, the Rembrandt; Reynolds, Renoir—" he explained. "The Raphael we *haven't* got. Our competitors in Liverpool who do poets as well as painters have already purloined *him*—" We seemed fortunate still being able to claim Rossetti.

By pure chance, the Royal Academy had arranged a large retrospective of Rossetti's work at this point—the first for ninety years. It was a beautifully designed exhibition—I had visited it earlier, having had a life-long reverence for the artist, the unique poet-painter. Each room was set out like a Victorian temple to an artist-priest—culminating in the final room with the great *Dante's Dream*, *Mariana*, *The Blessed Damozel* and all those other immense, enveloping, velvet women from whose panther-like embrace one would never have emerged, nor, it is possible, wished to. How Rossetti must have wished them capable of stirring from their langorous lethargy. But even Mrs. Morris was in a sense a figment of his imagination also. *Had* she been able to cross over to him in reality we should never have had these aching portraits, anyway.

The *Bower Meadow*, a lyrical subject of girls set against a landscape background (painted on the canvas many years previously in company with his brother Pre-Raphaelites) had always pleased me. A reproduction of it had in fact helped inspire my series of Renaissance/Pre-Raphaelite paintings of girls in idyllic settings during the late Sixties. To see this canvas in actuality was a pleasure and almost a mystic experience. The shipping company director now suggested that as he too had liked this picture the most of those on show, would it please me to make a copy of it?

"I don't want you to paint it if you *don't* find it pleasing—" he said. Explaining that merely to paint it at all would be an unexpected pleasure, I waited while David Wolfers arranged for me to paint in the Royal Academy, during the last weeks of the exhibition; from six to eight in the evenings, and from nine to one on Sunday mornings. A great friend from earlier days (the next angel to appear) now provided me with a room at her house, her easel, and transport to the R.A. with all the equipment. By chance, at nine o'clock on Sundays she sang in the choir at St. James's, Piccadilly, almost opposite Burlington House.

At last, the first Sunday morning arrived, and I was alone in the Royal Academy, with Rossetti's life work about me. Pulling all the great doors shut, and closing myself in, I paced through the exhibition—this gigantic studio I had been given, surely a unique experience for any lover of Rossetti. Around me were the immense works, glowing and sighing with suppressed ecstasy.

In an alcove was the plaster death mask of the artist, over which I bent requesting psychic aid, and hoping for ghosts. The only sensation that seemed to get through to me, though, was a kind of blurred thought: "I consider all this a great impertinence." However, I set to work at last, to the sound of the pigeons cooing on the roof above, like Hunt's *St. Swithin's Day* the other side of the glass skylights. Day after day, having waited until teatime, I took a bus to Piccadilly, and sat in the R.A. foyer until the public had finally drifted out. Then, from my private cupboard, I brought out my easel, table, paints, and the canvas. This gradually ingratiated itself into the graces of the elderly attendants. At first it was: "Going to have to work pretty hard to finish *that*, aren't you?" Then, halfway through, grudgingly: "It's not coming on badly, *really*—" Towards the end, when the last bare areas still to be painted seemed to stare out with time-challenging audacity, it was: "You're getting on very well. Think you'll finish it?"—"He won't unless *you* leave him to get on with it, Joe!"

Late in the evenings, I would have a word or so with the twenty-four hour Securicor guard who sat in the hall. One of the attendants brought him into the exhibition one night to show him the paintings.

"Look around, if you want," he said. "Don't mind *him*. He's just the artist." I continued quietly. Of course they gravitated over to my little camp, as children do if you don't look at them. "Yeh. That's good! *I* prefer it to the original. More colour. Mind you don't swap it over, though. We've got our eye on you. No, I *really* prefer it, I really *do*—it's *brighter*—"

He took the guard around the walls, explaining the character of Rossetti.

"You see, he painted the same woman all the time. Same face. Same expression."

"I *see!*" The guard screwed up his eyes to peer at Mrs. Morris in one of her incarnations. "They *are* all the same."

"*Course*, 'e never '*ad* 'er. She was Morris' wife—'is mate, see? But 'e couldn't get 'er out of 'is mind. Bloody *obsessed*, bloody *obsessed* with 'er, 'e was. Couldn't stop painting 'er."

"I can see how he felt—" the guard shook his head sadly.

"Mind you, she looks a handful! One of *those*—you know—"

"*I* know," the guard looked knowing. "Bit too *much* of a good thing—"

Before I left, the oldest custodian told me in a confidential manner that: "ever since we've 'ad these Rossettis here—you know 'e liked red-'eads—well, we've 'ad more red-'eaded girls in 'ere than I've seen in thirty years of exhibitions—and all these girls, they got their 'air done just the same as them in the pictures—"

There was a certain grandeur in ordering the great gates of the Royal Academy open on a Sunday morning in order for my friend to bring her car in to collect me at lunch-time.

"Let me know when she's due and I'll have them open, Sir—" and so they were, as I stood there on the steps. Lord Burlington himself could scarcely have asked for a grander gesture for his friends—especially as it all seemed to be automated.

However, it was only because I had won through. I always heard myself referred to as "bloomin' good artist, '*e* is," by the staff, as they pointed me out to their friends, as a sort of possession, like a dog.

. . . . . .

Rossetti's paintings seemed to conform to a conviction of mine, or a conclusion based on twenty-five years of gallery-peering, that genuine paintings talk to one like friends—fakes and school-ofs are cold distant strangers, full of pretence, whom one distrusts on sight. People portrayed in pictures—great pictures—should have a sad and saint-like appearance, apart from studies of children, who cannot be expected to—except of course when they become abstracted and seem to have absorbed a dead spirit from the past, an older spirit, that has momentarily taken them over. At such times, the faces of children have a look of maturity and somewhat incredible pathos, as if of a pre-consciousness of the melancholy of the future. It is such holy seconds as these that should be portrayed by the artist, with brush, or camera, or any other medium, provided he is willing to wait endlessly for the essential mood. . . .

Transience—Impermanence—Sadness. The battle of the individual for personal survival, which is of course beyond him in more ways than one. The most profound minds and intellects are, when just about to comprehend it all, snuffed out. Great painters, great composers—Schubert, who understood everything—constantly express the pain of loss, the loss of the moment—the lost moments of our place in time. And yet this individual consciousness of himself, that seems so valuable to the artist, is, we are often told, of no consequence to the purpose of nature. But why then, are no two leaves, no two rabbits, no two *artists* even, identical. . . .

In art, in painting, one cannot succeed, however, without forgetting one's self as an individuality. Detachment is all—you must become what you paint; live and breathe at the same pace as what you are drawing; become the person, place, object, as the cat becomes the mouse in order to catch it, to enter its time-space rather than her own, so that it is caught already before she even pounces—and it knows it. As that ubiquitous Zen archer must be the bow, the arrow and the target, and so can never miss his mark, being all things at once, so your brush, your magic extension of personality must unify all time, and make a monument of a moment. At least, it's a theory.

. . . . . .

One morning the *Artist* magazine phone me—Catriona McTurk, the new assistant editor, had been interested in a synopsis of an article I had sent in—on painting dogs—and wished to commission me to write it. I discovered later that this was mainly because my notes had been typed, and were quite legible. In view of later developments canine and otherwise, this was somewhat of a premonitory commission. I set about borrowing portraits of dogs I had made and even borrowed a dog or so in order to paint a new portrait or two. I painted a Maltese terrier and an English setter. Eventually, my study of an elderly spaniel appeared on the cover of the magazine in full colours, which was a pleasing tribute to my liking for animals.

Chapter 9

One day, on the Isle of Wight, I was marching over Freshwater Down in the steps of Tennyson, and seeming to see his tall silhouette, with the great black caricature of a hat that we may see in Carisbrooke Castle now stilled behind the glass front of the museum case. One thought of him sending up the skylarks into the fine blue of the sky. I came upon Gatcombe church during this expedition—one of many made to places of literary and artistic interest. In fact, what can be more romantically enjoyable than a Victorian literary pilgrimage? The events, places and people we trace may be of national import, or merely village notoriety; but one story is as good as another when all are but dry bones like autumn leaves—

The pleasant whirr of the lawn-mower welcomed us into the churchyard, as it tidied the spaces between the tombs—tidying a little too conscientiously, we thought, in some ways; the hedge parsley that makes white lace along the banks of paths, that gives a poetic delicacy to old graves, the white stars of stitchwort, and the pink crane's bill—all had been cleared away. No tufts of grass stood up about the base of tombs, retaining a Dickens illustration romanticism. The old lichen, even, seemed to have been polished off the stones, leaving them with the revolting starkness of newly erected memorials, uneasily recent memento mori.
. . .

One plant alone seemed to flourish, to have been spared the enthusiastic holocaust. Bank upon bank of wild garlic grew undisturbed, milk-white chandeliers on light green stems. The old gardener, getting off his machine, spoke to us as old gardeners will.

"We 'ad some visitors the other day; they picked great armfuls of that garlic to take home. I had to laugh! They dropped it all pretty fast even before they got in their car!"

Inside the church was a marble effigy, in the centre of the nave: a young officer, laid out full-length like a crusader. The gardener leant across the stone recumbency of the figure; the morning sunlight filling the church haloed the gardener's face.

"I remember," he said, "when *he* was a boy. Used to ride down here from the house on 'is bicycle and talk to me. Used to follow me round. One time, 'e come off his bike, I recall. . . ."

Inconsequential predictable recollections, stories that led nowhere, like life—except to the heroic image here before us, vicarious body of the martyr. . . .

"But what happened to the *nose?*" I said, observing it was defaced away exactly as if Cromwell's desecrating minions had been at it.

"A lunatic done that," said the gardener. "A mad woman. Escaped from custody, got over here from the mainland, and went for it with a hatchet."

At last, a story! And, of course, melodrama! No subtle nuance here; no underplaying; no Katherine Mansfield shades of suggestion, no Gwen John deft toning always just below the level of irrevocable statement. . . . And what was the reason for her actions, this maniac? What had led her to the effigy? Chance, or determined malice?—what was the cause of her madness?—but of course, like all real-life stories, there is never a neat ending, never a theatrical twist, only a lame tail-off, only supposition.

. . . . . .

I was walking along Shaftesbury Avenue one lunchtime; an ordinary crowded shopping morning. Two young men ahead of me, wearing white shirts, jeans, baseball boots, all at once fell upon a large middleaged man, dragged him to a doorway, and beat him to the ground. The blows were silent, unaccompanied by the crashing noises they produce on film soundtracks. The passersby blinked, paused—we were a kind of gaping half-circle of irresolution. The two youths, having successfully carried out their reprisal, or robbery, or whatever it was, turned to escape. The crowd backed away either side hastily, leaving me with my back against the fence preventing pedestrians entering the road. The assassins ran forward like panthers, and leapt the fence, one either side of me, like two gazelles. A glimpse of them running between the cars and buses, with practised ease, and they were gone—all in a moment so quickly can such things be accomplished that are outside conventional behaviour.

Yet another story with no twist: I was on the Underground to Richmond, at about seven o'clock in the evening. Some half a mile from our destination, the train was seized with a chill shudder, and stopped. Repeated attempts to start the motive power failed. The six or seven people in the carriage, each until now in the private shell of their thoughts, looked into each others' eyes. Wry grins. The mutual companionship of the damned. Time went by. Half an hour. An hour. Another hour. By now the girls were chatting together—the men had gathered at one end where we discussed the chances of getting the doors open and walking down the line. The guard, a pleasant young man, gently forbade us to do this. At that point, a middleaged well-dressed woman—well-dressed in that sense of being dressed to suit no contingency whatsoever—fell into aggressive hysterics, shrieking and swearing at our ever-apologetic guard.

"If you want to fight somebody," said a tough-looking beautiful girl, her appearance presenting an aspect of up to the minute suavity, "fight *me*. It's people like you who cause all the bloody trouble in life." She gave the guard a protective smile. The men grinned. A quiet black woman continued to read her paperback novel, imperturbably. At this point, after almost three hours of maroonment, the train lurched forward. Three minutes later, the doors opened at Richmond station. Everybody made for the platform. The black woman looked up and put away her paperback. We were once more strangers on the Underground. Looking at nobody, we continued the course of our respective lives—three hours late for them.

Sitting in the stalls of the Colosseum in St. Martin's Lane, at an opera, the following occurred. The interval was just ending, and the audience were beginning to settle once again, when an elderly-middle-aged man next to me, who had been looking over his shoulder for some while, suddenly took courage, turned round, leant across and tapped the gentleman behind him on the chest.

"Franz!" He said.

Franz gave a start—his wife gasped—Franz stood up—

"*Heinrich*! Is it possible—"

Franz's wife had stood up as well. Heinrich's wife was grasping her hands. The four of them, with the slight inconvenience of the row of seating between them, and the heads of other members of the audience close by, effected a joyous reunion.

"But what *happened*? You *escaped*!—" Franz was eager to learn the full history of the newly re-discovered friends.

"Yes—in '37," Heinrich explained, as the lights began to dim. By now, however, everybody around was much more interested in this extraordinary meeting than in the next act.

"We have not seen each other since the 'Thirties, in Germany!" Franz explained to those about him. We all leaned forward with eager interest. "The best of friends we had always been—"

The audience passed the information along the rows. "Always the best of friends." The orchestra was striking up.

"Such friends," Heinrich was beaming—"we thought you *must* be killed—"

"Thought he *must* be killed," the audience repeated to one another.

"We also thought—" Franz and his wife sat down as the curtain rose. With occasional reassuring glances over their shoulders, Heinrich and his wife, like the rest of the audience, settled down to the entertainment; but for a while, nobody's thoughts were with the unfortunate Lady of the Camelias; we were all back in those terrible Thirties.

About this time, in 1972, I became interested in enamelling, and set about acquiring a small kiln from the Crafts shop in Macklin Street. My main interest was in *painted* enamels, as a method of a more permanent technique for small portraits. However, at the shop—an enthusiastic mecca for enamellers, a place where the interest of the craft made it like the headquarters of a cult, I was instructed as to what to buy, and advised to visit the exhibition of the Society of Enamellers, then being held at the Alpine Gallery in South Audley Street. Carrying my purchases, I made my way there, and proceeded around the exhibits. I had been told particularly to study the work of a certain enameller. I did so—something about the pose of his Madonna subject, set in her decorative border, gave a little shiver of recognition; that child—the hair, the hand—of course! It had been copied from *my* etching of a mother and child, reproduced in an article on etching I had written for the *Artist* magazine. It was a strange kind of full circle to make in my enquiry into enamelling procedure. It was perhaps, something of a compliment, though a little cavalier.

Looking at the silverpoint drawings in the British Museum, finely hatched pale survivals of the working drawings of the 15th Century, I felt a desire to work in the same manner. A short piece of silver wire, filed to a point, and a sheet of paper laid over with a wash of gouache: these, it seemed, were the necessities. I took a bus to Hatton Garden and enquired of a jeweller where I could buy silver. I was directed to a vast emporium further up the street. Inside this building were long queues—shabby students in patched and torn jeans and old t-shirts—impeccably dressed Orientals—middle-aged ladies bundled into consciously careless clothing—all sorts. I joined the end of the shortest line. Peering ahead, I could see a table behind the counter stacked with rings and coils of a brass-like metal. Occasionally the girl serving would chop some of this with a mechanical cutter and pack it in a plastic bag, like a quarter of sweets. There was now but one person ahead of me.

"Half a pound of such and such a grade—four ounces of another—"

The bags were put before him.

"That will be ninety pounds for that one, and a hundred and eighty for the other," the girl informed him, as if he were buying cheese at the grocers.

At last it was my turn.

"I want a small piece of silver wire—about two inches—"

The girl fixed me with a stern look as if I was wasting her time deliberately.

"I'm afraid Sir, this is the *gold* counter—"

I never did get round to making my silver-point masterpieces.

I met a rat-catcher in London. In a neat overall, provided by the municipal authorities, he passed a pleasant morning chatting as he chemically fumigated the meeting of walls and floor with an anti-cockroach fluid, the meanwhile discoursing enthusiastically on Jack Russell terriers, the old days, and selling the rats for barbarous (and I hope illegal) Saturday afternoon gambling sessions, i.e. how many your dog could kill in a certain time against the others.

"But there's only one way to kill a rat," he said. "Pick it up quick by the tail and dash its brains out. . . . Yes—I've had a rat shoot up my trouser-leg—

quick as a flash. You don't go mad—you just gently shake it down again—then he won't bite. But some people! When they phone you and say—I've got rats as big as rabbits swarming everywhere—well, they've seen *one*, maybe *two* normal-sized ones. It's the natural tendency to exaggerate. *Thousands* of cockroaches—*Ten*. 'course, some people are funny about rats. Don't like them at all. I had a call—to get rid of the rats from one of those big West End hotels. The rats had made a nest in the fireplace pillars—people around all day and they inside taking no kind of notice! But hotels! That's where you find 'em! They had a wedding lunch all laid out the night before, in one place I was called to—the rats got to it first, though! There was some patching up to hide the traces, I can tell you! There wasn't time to get it all prepared again! The chef worked overtime with the icing! A good thing the guests didn't known about it! The table was just a mass of rats, an hour before! But I could tell you some tales about hotels and vermin. Vermin and hotels! But *this* place. The manager called me round. Get rid of those rats, he said. Big bold strong feller, he was—a V.C., as well, from the war, if you like! Well, I had to prise open the wood pillars by that fireplace, and the rats leapt out every way. One up my trouser-leg, like I told you. One of the others made for our friend. Well, V.C. or no, he was up on that table in a flash, terrified: 'Don't let it near me!' I tell you, everybody's afraid of something, and for a lot of them it's *rats*. . . ."

Perhaps because I have always liked animals, dead or alive, I have not myself any dislike of mice or rats. I actually enjoy the proximity of small furred animals a good deal more than that of human strangers wedged against one in an Underground carriage, though I have known a melancholic girl so lonely that she used to go round the underground circuit in the rush hour, crushed against strangers just for company.

I was standing in the centre of a country lane when I heard a crackling in the hedge, and a large rat climbed down, as if from a ladder, walked across the road to inspect me all round, nibbled the toe of one of my boots, and then loped off up the lane, unhurried, going from side to side like a questing dog. I have several times had weasels come out to watch me painting in a wood, coming right up to the hardboard in their curiosity, leaning back, their feet out, like puppies ready to play.

· · · · · ·

I was passing the Italian Travel offices in Regent Street one morning when I noticed a fine poster of Masaccio's *Expulsion of Adam and Eve from the garden of Eden*. I had always liked this, and had a small and inspiring reproduction of it (as opposed to my usual custom) framed on my studio wall. Entering, I asked if it was possible to obtain a copy of the poster. I was directed downstairs towards the publication office. Staircase followed staircase—down into the bowels of London, crisscrossed with passages. Beyond, one realised, were sewers, Underground railway, even unknown and forgotten Mediaeval passages, no doubt. I took several wrong turnings into dusty bare-bricked passages leading ever downward, but at last came upon a small bright fluorescently-illuminated room full of metal racks stacked with pamphlets. A small neat Italian with a black moustache greeted me politely. "I help?"

"Yes," I said, "I wondered if you could sell me a poster—"

He waved his arms furiously as if to magic me away entirely—

"I will sell you—*Nozzing!*" His eyes flashed.

"Oh!" I was taken aback—"well, in that case—"

He prevented me leaving, with a disarming smile, full of warmth, his arms held out as if to embrace me—

"—I *give* it to you!"

Reassured, I paused.

"Which?" he requested. "Which? Which is one?"

"The Masaccio."

"*Forget* it!" All eyes and fire, he was shouting furiously.

Thinking I had somehow come upon some national embarrassment, I attempted again to leave, but he prevented me.

"They send us only the one—for the window," he explained, in silken tone. "But *why*," he went on, "do you *want* the poster?"—with increasing suspicion, and darkening brow—"for what *reason* can you want it?"

"I'm an artist—and I admire his work—that's all!"

"Excellent!" he applauded me. "I will give you a Filippo Lippi!" Which he did; and it hangs in my studio yet.

Being commissioned to paint watercolour drawings of Exmoor, in the bitter cold of a fresh and sunny October, I visited sheepfarmers and conservationists, sat out among the heather—the colour brilliant but not really art—and at one point observed the stag hunt on the hill opposite . . . a little line of Dance of Death figures, horses and hounds against the sky. I hoped they wouldn't find their quarry, certainly. Just then, a large red deer stag came through the wood, ran up and down, and eventually crossed the road—we had stopped to watch him—directly in front of us, and slid away between the trees to our left.

"Brow, bez, tres and tine," I said, rather knowingly. Two workmen who had been occupied with picks and shovels looked across.

"Nay," said one: "Brow, bez, and tres."

"You're lucky to see *'im*," said the other.

"Ay," said the first." They'll be zum music when they find *e*'s away."

.   .   .   .   .   .

My old friend A. had moved to a town in the north, and invited me to stay there in the spring of '73. As I had arrived at Euston somewhat early, I listened to the music that rather pleasantly filled the new covered reception area, and boarded a fast train that took me to the town in question as early as two in the afternoon. I found my friend not in when I telephoned from the station, as he was expecting me later. It was a hot afternoon in early spring, but shouldering my pack, I set off up the long dusty street from the station. The only person approaching, in this quiet after-lunch atmosphere, metamorphosised, as it came nearer, into a bus-conductor in full regalia; tickets, machine, satchel, everything. This good angel, happily placed in my path, gave me elaborate directions; which I soon forgot, however. After more time had elapsed I paused at a small second-hand bookshop, the kind of place that always has some treasure among the shelves of forgotten one-time bestsellers. Naturally, I went in. The little old lady owner was in somewhat of a confusion.

"Art? Books on painting? Yes, I'll try to look you out something. I'll have to leave you a moment or two—you see, the window fell out, and I'm having some new glass put in—"

It was quite true that the little bow-window was being fitted back into position by two carpenters outside. Feeling I could not wait, however, I silently left without bidding her farewell, as she seemed so engrossed with the situation. In about an hour or so I discovered the right bus at last, having been sent from one stop to another by various helpful people. The conductor-driver looked puzzled. "Macaulay Road?" he said. "It's a place I've heard of, but I can't seem to—"

"It's near Tennyson Avenue," I said.

"Up Rupert Brooke, turn sharp into Shelley, and out through Wordsworth," said a lady behind me.

The driver looked relieved. "*Shakespeare* estate!" he cried. "Of course—now I remember."

Off we went. At long last I arrived. My friend, now at home, was surprised that I had discovered my way through the tortuous jungle of suburbia, of curving crescents and location-defeating shopping centres. After a cup of tea, A. said he wished to drive back into the town for a T.V. set that had been repaired. I agreed to accompany him, and we drove back in—it was a pleasant luxury to recognise areas where I had waited, or paced through with my heavy pack, so recently.

"There's a place I'm sure you'd be interested in near here," said my friend, pulling up. He led me into a little book-shop. A repaired window was just receiving its final touch from the workmen. The old lady proprietor, with a sigh of relief, bade them farewell, and turned to me.

"I'm awfully sorry to have kept you waiting" she said, "now—books on art, wasn't it?"

As regarding second-hand bookshops, A. selected a book from the shelves outside the front of one establishment, took it in and handed it to the assistant. The assistant looked at it dispassionately, ran his finger up the spine, flicked through the pages, and said: "I can't give you more than half-a-crown—"

"But I'm not *selling* it," A. protested; "I'm trying to buy it from the sixpenny rack outside. . . ."

In '73, I was in Scarborough; and from there, having photographed the grave of Anne Brontë, and visited G. F. Bodley's church filled with works by Morris and Rossetti, set off through the fog and mist to the moorland home of the Brontës at Haworth. Fierce walls of millstone grit; grey, sharply cornered little houses. The cobbles up to the old village and the church were still remarkably archaic—in the churchyard, water dripped from the wet headstones, a living poem by Emily Brontë, and the rooks cawed in the two pines Charlotte had planted on her wedding morning. In the parlour, where stood the couch Emily had died on, or refused to, bravely standing up to die, I felt only Charlotte, without the others—I felt her walking into the corner, the angle of the wall, fastening her eye on the line from floor to ceiling as the one line to hold to, and saying over and over, "What shall I do—what shall I do—" to herself. Later, I discovered that when she returned from Scarborough, leaving Anne dead in the churchyard there—when only a few days earlier they had stopped on the way to see York Minster—enthusiasts to the last!—Charlotte wrote: "Once in the parlour, I waited for the agony that must come"—The house, redolent of Brontë atmosphere, set in Heathcliff fog, was more intense even than one had imagined. It was incredible to be in the actual place where they had written those birthday letters to themselves—where Emily had written that astounding book I had come upon when I was ten, with such impact upon me. This house where those people had lived, their lives so well documented that one knows their very thoughts, year by year, in each room—so well documented that we know them so much better than they knew themselves—we think. I photographed the pine trees from the window of Emily's little room upstairs—thinking of them writing Gondal books there on the floor when it was their playroom—amazing! Later, I painted a portrait of the three, using reproductions to work from—Charlotte by George Richmond; Anne by Charlotte; and Emily by Branwell (the profile study). This last was so gratifying to paint from, so full of character, that one feels he was a better artist than his reputation or even his technical accomplishment suggests.

By contrast, some months later, on a warm June morning, I entered Jane Austen's home near Alton. A neat, red-brick, delightful residence; again with that curious sense of having been a shell for genius, though not full of ghosts like the Brontë residence. But, after all, what a setting Haworth was for writers and artists.

. . . . . .

Returning one day to the site of the Brighton Art School—now an immense new streamlined edifice, I stood in the foyer—my head on a level with the old floor of the original etching room. About *here*, was where we used to stand chatting in the hall—in the mind, in memory, one could see the coloured light shining through the war memorial window—one thought, once, such things were sacrosanct, secure forever! Almost, the harmony of hammering could be heard from the silversmiths' workshop. . . . Where had it all gone, that which had such reality, such a sense of tradition? Old men, past students, would call in and remember their own day—one was to have done the same, in turn—but no; I stood in a lonely glass and concrete replacement—a functional part of a functional box; where, on screens, an exhibition has been put on show of *relics*, as from another planet, depicting the history of the original college. The Victorian period was immediately the most interesting, as being of course, the most *able* . . . art was actually difficult, then, requiring intense application. There were amazing stump drawings in charcoal—that style of life drawing so denigrated by critics and writers on art in their defences of modern movements that certainly in hindsight, need some defending . . . ah! Suddenly, here is *my* period!—or one of them. A drawing by that remarkable student Hussein Abbo, circa 1958—I recall when he drew that—up to the right, a bit to the left—that's where the long bench of the etchingroom was, where that concrete pillar stands now! The drawing is yellowed, rather torn—I remember it on *white* paper, newly bought from the office, pinned on a board, while the bees drift through the open sash window, and Brighton is full of Regency lanes, and not a hint of a tower-block or a shopping complex. That was the day he etched the giant prawn—or he made it so, on the plate. He bought twelve, and ate eleven, and then set up the last, and made this extraordinary analytical etching of it.

Now! Here's a drawing by another of my near-contemporaries, and a photograph that looks a good deal more out of date than the art work. All that life, those jokes, anecdotes, vital discussions—all those talented potential artists—are recalled by but a few foxed scraps; dead leaves. I met nobody familiar in this chill tomb that had replaced the temple of living memory. Was I myself but a projection into the future from my real self, safe in the past, still in that more real world of yet only fifteen years ago, a world of steamrollers, steam trains, gaslights on country stations, narrow roads; a world uncrowded, where individuals came in ones instead of dozens. And yet, what had it all meant, the fevered energy of those forgotten people? There now stood here a temple set up by the devotees of a new race, whose aims and ideals were totally different—but just as valid, presumably. . . .

I turned to go—there was, in fact, one familiar item. In a glass cubicle in the centre of the plastic and white cement of this frozen world, was the same caretaker! Forever immured, with telephone to hand, his eye upon all who entered. Once, he would have been smoking a cigarette, reading his paper, down by the fire in the boiler room. I went closer. It *was* the Same Caretaker! I couldn't cross the gap of the years. I left, a stranger to him, as he was a stranger to his new era.

In the autumn of '73, I became interested once more in making etchings of and on the Brighton Palace Pier. The Victorian Baroque of its domes and cast-iron fancies—a firm structure concealed under frivolity, like perhaps the Victorian age itself. Rigid supports disguised as airy nothings—the place had always inspired me; but now, all at once, they seemed part of another age in very fact—a living dream, something that might soon disappear. All at once, one felt the pier itself should at once be preserved in a museum. To walk on the wood decks, looking between the slats at the passing waves, should have been by now only a childhood memory. I had recently taken a number of pier photos for a friend who was writing a comprehensive work on the history of the Seaside; now, I went on board again with my plates and etching needle. A warm sunny afternoon in October; the last of the visitors drowsily in deckchairs—I saw the pier afresh; not as a familiar part of the town, known all one's life, but as a survival. Every curious wooden arch, semi-eastern column—the profuseness of pierced decoration that had drawn on all schools for its design, seemed like work from a dream. I kept saying to myself—this *can't* last long—a fire—a chance match, such as had put pay to Waterhouse's Hove Town Hall, and the unique old Bedford Hotel, might carry the pier off—it would become only a faint memory of the years it had owned. Even the view of the coast behind me had changed—the multifloored flats rising above the town gave the suggestion of filmic New York, the Hudson River, rather than an evocation of Regency days.

Generations of art students had drawn the pier, the boats, the old capstans. In the early Sixties the famous 'Town cap' had been chopped up while I was *actually drawing* it, by corporation workmen. The relevant authority (it seemed) had one day visited the sea-front and been appalled at finding so untidy a relic from the past, with no present function, as the fish market had been cleared off the seafront after a visitor had complained, apparently, that it smelt of fish. The fishing boats had inevitably dwindled in number subsequently. "We can't touch the other capstans," the workmen told me: "they're privately owned; but this is the Town Cap, so we can chop it up." And they did so, while I made drawings of its demise, as I had so often made drawings of its unusual presence in a serene retirement. By '73, the final rotting fragments of the only capstan left had, with the new interest in conservation, been carefully restored and returned to the beach, in response to an elevated and informed new public opinion . . I continued my work on my plate . . .

"I don't think you've paid," the deck-chair attendant was saying.

"I'm sitting on my own deck-chair," I explained.

"I can hardly charge you for *that*, I suppose," he admitted . . .

I finished my etching. The part I was drawing, the strange steamboat architecture, the swelling curves, had become microscopically clear to me, as if they were being revealed in their completeness at last, in all their inner substance. When a person, place or thing does this to you, take heed; you are to lose, or to leave them, very soon.

An iron barge clanked by the pier jetty. Part of the ironwork was being dismantled for repairs, and the rusty pieces thrown in the barge. "That jetty," I thought, "receives the force of the gales from the south-west—its repelled them for years—let's hope they rebuild it soon—"

A week or so later, in a storm, the iron barge, left tethered, was forced into the weakened jetty, which crumbled, and smashed across the pier supports.

These, meant to sustain force from above, not from the side, buckled; and down came half the marvellous woodwork I had been etching—the oriental arches sagged, knocked off balance. In such cases one feels either all inspiring buildings should be drawn before they fall down; or else that one puts a curse on them by one's very exercise in that field.

. . . . . .

I had been working away quietly for some six months, seeing very few people, developing my work and ideas. From the large canvases and small panels of girls and flowers, lyrical Fifteenth Century subjects, I was progressing to more monochrome treatment and increasingly more dramatic themes: *The Martyr—The Victim*. No concession to twilit colours, flowers in the dusk, now. A stark backdrop: a certain cruelty—no prettiness. Children, cats, roses, arbours and lawns all in abeyance. The weeping girls seemed to weep over real tragedy now, not poetic regret at nothing occurring in their lonely lives. In treatment, a neo-classic solidity had taken over; heavy shadows, accented lights, had replaced the simplicity of the early Italians.

At this period I was also using my old interest in taxidermy; as through a friend who knew of this predilection, I set up a number of groups of small mammals for a museum service for schools; the preserved creatures—my

speciality being moles, shrews and mice—being mounted on a block with natural vegetation. The specimens would be borrowed by the schools for the purposes of study and drawing, rather like a public library. The creatures I was required to preserve were usually found dead on the roads; and on one occasion a lorry-driver brought to the museum a white mole—a beautiful pale orange animal—that he had found on the main highway; presumably pulling his lorry to a swift and immediate halt. The white mole was kept on ice until I could be contacted, and then rushed to me by special delivery, and certainly was a beautiful animal.

My painter friend now invited me to stay in London with her family. This would also give me the opportunity to work from her young daughter, one of my favourite models. As I waited at Victoria, a coach backed into a taxi near me, crushing the bonnet. Out jumped the drivers; an argument commenced with me in the middle—my friend's arrival saved me from further participation, however. We were to look round a succession of studios open to the public. Accompanying us was an older lady. Unfortunately, on a pavement in Hammersmith, the lady fell heavily; and we were obliged to call an ambulance. The next day we made a visit to the hospital; on leaving, our over-wrought nerves were entertained with the names of the wards, bracketed in pairs on the wall as we descended the staircase. Jenny Lind was paired with Lord Leighton; Sir Joshua Reynolds with George Eliot; Henry James with Charlotte Brontë. As ,we read more and more of these oddly-assorted couples we became more and more amused. At last, in a state of weakness, we arrived at ground floor level, only to be brought up, no doubt as a salutary corrective, with the shock of reality.

Four dispassionate men in white were standing round a stretcher on wheels; porters waiting, posed immoveably like a group sculpture. On the stretcher, head exposed, eyes closed, white face, black moustache, like a recumbent warrior, a young man. The tableau seemed to possess the significance of a dream; but no doubt artists see such events subjectively so.

I was, one autumn evening, baby-sitting for my friend B. and his wife. Off they went, for a pleasant evening at the theatre. I remained in the quiet house, the children asleep in bed. Of course, they awoke as soon as the door closed, and demanded refreshments. I went to the gas stove—turned the switch—lit the oven. But, on turning it off, the switch flew to pieces in my hand, and projecting bits of spring and plastic flew about the kitchen. As I couldn't turn off the gas, it seemed best to leave it alight, although the stove became rapidly overheated. Eventually, by putting together the remains of the broken switch, I turned it down to a small flame. At this point I heard water pouring down into the garden terrace. The cistern washer had evidently given way, and water was soon flowing into the lower rooms from the flooded patio. With repeated unsuccessful attempts to contact gas board and plumber I turned on the television, for a little distraction. There was a bang, and the set blew its fuses. When my friends arrived home, full of the performance they had enjoyed, I was obliged to bring them down to earth violently, and the next few hours were spent trying to set matters right—to no avail. The next morning, the house was a mêlée of gasmen, television mechanics, and plumbers trying to repair the damage of that evening's tenancy.

But my existence of intense work upon huge canvases, coupled with a wandering life of visiting sympathetic friends and patrons was about to alter. . . . Presumably, there are some days and events that possess a pre-ordainment; as if some central agency, tired of seeing one ambling vaguely about (or so it must seem) decides to propel one into a situation where decision is paramount.

March 21st, 1975. The anniversary of my grandmother's birthday—the first official day of spring; and as a further marking of the date, the day when I first met—unofficially—Catriona.

The object of my excursion that day had been the yearly presenting of three works before the selection committee for the Royal Academy summer exhibition. I joined the queue at the familiar back door, shuffled along the familiar chill stone vault, flanked with huge sculptures evidently rejected from past exhibitions, and too heavy for anyone to ever move again, and handed my three pictures to the familiar porters whom I had watched slowly age, submission day by submission day, over the past thirty years . . . from anxious young apprentices to head foremen, or so it seemed. I then joined the anonymous crowd of dispersing artists who continued to shuffle through the galleries of Bond and Cork Street, anxious to see what was new in the gallery world. Lightened of the demanding responsibility of those three pictures all hearts were lighter.

Nonetheless, I among them all was still encumbered. I had conveyed my pictures on a trolley, which still carried my plates, watercolours, paper, drawing-board, sleeping-bag and other accoutrements of a wandering and artistic existence. The trolley always seemed to have a life of its own, bumping into passersby, veering irresponsibly into traffic and usually demanding apologies to someone. In fact, when a wheel finally came off it at Victoria station one day and flew into the path of an oncoming train, it was perhaps a relief. However, on this particular occasion the trolley (still intact) seemed to lead me—via the Westminster Public Library, where we lingered as long as possible—straight to the Tate Gallery.

This building has always seemed to me to be a kind of perennial home, in spite of the continual changes in arrangement. One has seen so many exhibitions there in the always lively atmosphere, and has so many recollections connected with it over the years. I have seen the brand-new frames become old and discoloured; I have seen the gleaming gold brass head of Osbert Sitwell by Dobson fall from its trolley (another trolley) while being moved by porters and bounce its way down the gallery. We picked up the sacred object, and I dare say no one knew any more of the matter. It seemed all right. There was at one time on view a large sculpture by Lynn Chadwick, an enormous green and corroded metal wishbone like a bird in flight, that held a chunk of quartz at one end as a counterbalance, the whole teetering on the apex of a metal stand. It was a favourite trick of the young artists, cultural hooligans, or what you will, to wait for the attendant's boots to cease their echoing tread, and then to pull one end of this dangerous grotesque violently downwards, so that the wishbone rocked and leapt on its tripod. How the art-lovers scuttled for safety, as it careened about! But in these luxurious days the floors are all carpeted, and the tramps no longer sleep all day in the high box pew benches of the Sargent room.

I entered the Tate Shop—now a whole gallery given over to books and posters and publications. There, at work, was Catriona; rather like a Tissot etching; long black dress—fringed hair looped, bunned and cascading—rather like one of my etchings. It was imperative to paint her, and an arrangement was at once made. It did occur to me at that moment that I had indeed been summoned to the Tate that day, and it would be marked on the memory as a signal-post of existence.

Etchings were created, paintings were made, and Catriona's flat in St. John's Wood began to fill with my works. The rooms were of a Gwen John austerity—a small window looked across to large and comfortable artist's houses, of a Regency-Victorian date and style. They had all been artists in St. John's Wood, in the old days—many still were—and every house seemed to have a giant studio at the back. This one was no exception. Downstairs, built into the garden, and over a haunted garden room of sinister, low-ceilinged aura, was a studio large enough to hold a London omnibus. It had once been occupied by Sir Arthur Streeton, the noted Australian painter. Previous to him, the house had been the home of one of the St. John's Wood Clique; and a book kept in the house told of their work and festive gatherings here. Calderon, Marcus Stone—it had been a very haven of the late Victorian anecdotalists and their return-to-Regency subjects. They had decorated the room on the floor below the flat with murals in a flat semi-Mediaeval pre-Byam Shaw kind of style that they favoured when involved in decoration—a sort of enlarged book illustration. These had regrettably been painted over at some point (although previously photographed and reproduced in the book), but some of the distemper had fallen off, and one could see a little of the murals, and an eye that knew enough could get some idea of the originals, as the image of a dinosaur can be constructed so to speak from one toe-bone.

The house belonged to an elderly recluse, tied to the house by crippling and twisting arthritis, who pulled herself around the lower floors on sticks; her head in a mobcap, and dressed always in nightclothes and blue dressing-gown— which was convenient, as she spent most of her time in bed. She had character, and even charm, and would talk for hours about her more active times, and her childhood—she had attended dancing-classes in company with Elsa Lanchester in her teens, but had moved away from a potential theatrical career to follow Gurdjaev's philosphy. He seemed a troublesome prophet, battening on his followers; but she, like others, never minded that, and viewed his faults with indulgence. She had given funds to various philosophical enthusiasts with which to build temples, and spoke endlessly about them—one would be summoned into her bedroom to hear the saga often.

As I painted so much in the house, she began to be interested in the canvases, although she made me move a nude of Catriona from the staircase as it "would not be good for the plumber to see it," perhaps with reason. She kindly offered me the use of the great studio, and Catriona and I cleared it up a little; which was to say we created some floor space. There were some good paintings on the walls—a Frances Hodgkins, a Paul Nash, and others of the period. I painted a full-length of Catriona in a check dress and straw hat, in blue with china plates on the wall behind, and in a fur-collared and cuffed coat that I found particularly inspiring. But it was difficult to give one's attention both to art and

to conversing with Miss X. as she lay in bed in the adjoining room, and eventually the art work moved back upstairs to the flat. Besides which, the studio was filled with curious obelisks of cardboard boxes, stacked a dozen or so high. All were unopened, and were all purchases from London stores delivered to the house over the last forty years, the unopened fruits of Miss X.'s shopping expeditions during her active period. They went back in time as the obelisks descended, and thirty years of fashion had been preserved, carefully wrapped in tissue—as sent—for no one ever to see, or wear. We looked into a box or so: silk underwear, hats, gloves, purses, a feast for the Victoria and Albert. I wonder what happened to it all.

Catriona at this point was a critic on the *Arts Review* (the famous *Art News and Review* of my youth) and between her spells at the Tate we frequented private views and exhibitions—after which the night would be given to writing it up, and I would take it down to the magazine offices in the morning. Once, when Catriona was ill, I reviewed the show in her stead—with the agreement of the *Arts Review*—and remembered how much has to be said in a small space, and how concise one has to be.

Nearby, around the corner, was the once colonnaded garden where Tissot had painted and etched and photographed the pale and beautiful Mrs. Newton: perhaps one of the saddest love stories in art, but given less attention because of the suspicious mistrust the English have always had for a foreign artist who is both good and apparently too fast a worker—can he be really *sincere*? Rossetti is never doubted—but then he was as English as roast beef, really—could one imagine *him* participating in the Commune? Tissot was too different—went his own way, did just as he pleased; took up with society when he wished, and dropped it without a qualm to be with Kathleen Newton. It would not do. I often looked at this house, and peered up the drive to what one could see of the famous garden. It had been subsequently taken over by Alma-Tadema, and altered a good deal. However, on the suggestion of Miss X., I made an etching of the visible part of the building.

Curiously, Catriona had once worked at the Conduit Street galleries, so I presumably had at times handed my R.E. exhibits to her. We now attended P.C.C. evenings, and she was able to renew acquaintance with the gallery. As we returned to St. John's Wood, the zebra crossing opposite, in front of the recording studios, was usually being photographed whenever one walked over, day or night. This was because the Beatles in their heyday had been photographed on it for a record sleeve, and this quite ordinary site was now holy ground, visited by foreign tourists presumably from all parts of the known world.

In the large studio there were also a number of framed drawings made in one line by Miss X.'s brother. He had gained some reputation with them in the Twenties, and can be seen featured in old volumes of the *Studio* magazine. It had, indeed, been a marvellous century, as Miss X. was fond of saying.

That summer of '75 it was incredibly hot; and while Catriona was at the Tate I roamed about St. John's Wood painting 24×20″ impressionist pochades on board. I painted the Parisian-style tree-lined boulevard effects, naves of foliage meeting over the road, and sat on the pavement with my gear around me immortalising corner after corner. This hill was a pleasant oasis between Maida

Vale and the Finchley Road. Catriona would return in the evening to the cool heights of St. John's Wood; the Morris Dancers would perform outside the Hero of Alma, and the warmth of a London summer night filled the air. I made many new etched plates, particularly of the nearby Bell Street and Church Street, off Edgware Road. Here was a wealth of subject and interest. Both streets were markets; Church Street for much of the time was lined with barrows and stalls, and Bell Street on a Saturday was a mecca for junk and antique enthusiasts. Never mind the fashionable Portobello Road, where the tourists go and the stall-owners know more than the value of everything. Here they knew the value of nothing; or, if they did, they were the more eager to shift it all by lunch-time rather than demand a large price. Early Saturday morning we would cut through the streets towards the barrow and stall-filled Bell Street, like hounds on the scent feeling the thrill of the chase indeed. What rare piece of china, what fine etching was to be ours today? With what treasure would we be struggling back to the flat in an hour or so? This impossible-to-predict immediate future, in a world full of shops of predictable stock, is the drug-like lure for the market addict. And Bell Street was a fairly rough lode-stone. As the stall-owners unpacked their boxes from the backs of Morris Travellers, the well-dressed vultures from St. John's Wood pressed about him, elbowing each other mercilessly. The stall-owners, out of Dickens, the clothes seeming to have grown with them rather than having been put on (like Phiz's illustrations) disclosed Victorian everyday china from newspaper wrappings, plate by plate, and the waving arms seized the pieces and filled the vendors' palms with silver. I bought a fine tureen, blue and white, decorated with linear passion-flowers printed from engraved transfers; and slowly I added to a subsequent collection of such plates and bowls—then quite reasonably priced: in fact, given away. Flowers and birds decorated these pieces—beautifully drawn and engraved natural history studies, with strange sudden rectangles and circles and lozenges cutting across them, a legacy from Japan that had crossbred into the Pre-Raphaelite detail, much as Whistler and Albert Moore had affected Rossetti, and vice versa. Bell Street was over by lunchtime, when the sunshine of early morning was giving way to a drizzle about to set in for the day. The unsold pictures and frames were by now standing in puddles against the nearest wall, heaps of near-rubbish, the stall-owners giving them surreptitious kicks, hoping that the glass might break and so give them the chance to regard such stock as no longer viable, and to save themselves the trouble of throwing it all into the back of the van again. I have always considered that any treasure I find I am meant to find—that it will wait for me, because, pre-ordained, it has to; and my competitors' eyes will all day be blinded to it as they pass by. I have acquired most of my best finds at the end, rather than the beginning of a market. Many a gold frame plastered with flowers and loops, a tinted Victorian photograph only just hanging in, with the shards of fractured glass hanging out, have I bought for a few coins, and spent the rest of the day restoring and remoulding, cleaning away dirt and dust, and giving it a new life.

My horde of these painted photographs increased, and even my knowledge of this so far uncatalogued art form. Today I find they are being priced as oils—sometimes higher—and as they are in fact unique this is perhaps right. I found many prints—one, a large Axel Hermann Haig, an R.E. at one time considered much too overweight. I thought so too—but who is one to judge? One is also at the mercy of the prejudices of one's time; the thing to do is to buy it, and wait. A year or so ago an exhibition of his revalued etchings and watercolours was held at the R.I.B.A. Books were published; articles written. I saw at once *that*, after all, he *was* a vital figure—the etchings were not weighty at all. Perhaps they were not *profound*, precisely, but they were on the way. Perceiving it was more valuable now, my Haig went into a more impressive frame, and it increases in authority daily.

A feature of the Bell Street market was a stall-owner whose approach to the public was one of raucous insult and fury—swearing obscenely at all who requested the prices of his goods; rushing like a madman to tear from the hands of prospective purchasers the treasures they had plucked from his stall. Pint after pint of beer was brought to him by a family of ruffianly sons and nephews, and he became worse and worse. Yet sometimes a sale was made and he would seem even affable as he helped the successful purchaser—at some skyrocketed price—load up a piece of rubbish into a waiting car.

My interest in antiques, our life of supper parties with friends and expeditions into outlying parts of London now necessitated that our income be increased; and I began to tour the print galleries that were just now—fortuitously enough!—beginning to proliferate. This concept of bins of mounted, plastic-covered prints, through which a customer might browse at leisure, was catching on; and a living might be made with some luck—or, at least, a pound or so. Some galleries were not interested in my work; some were. My plates were in the main of Brighton and Sussex subjects: beaches, elaborately drawn piers and old wooden bridges. I had always drawn the precious relics of the days when (as Oscar Wilde said of the galleon-decorated maps in old geography books) engineering projects were actually paintable. However, it was pointed out to me clearly and incisively that monochrome etchings, however painstakingly delineated, would not sell. Colour, was what the world wanted today, etc., etc. Colour, was all they bought. Did they? *I* didn't. Nor did many people I knew. Nor did most painter-etchers of the old school favour it. Colour, to a painter-etcher, had been traditionally anathema. However, the whole new modern school of printmaking went in for colour wholesale. My own approach, was admittedly, unmitigatedly Nineteenth Century; but that was what I liked . . . I was not going to change, because I only wanted to draw what I saw, and what I saw was seen with the eyes of that period, even when I inserted a contemporary car into a plate.

"Why not colour them as you colour your watercolours?" said Catriona. "Or, like the Eighteenth Century aquatints—gentle, delicate washes—" I commenced to do this; but my colour for a long while remained somewhat assertive.

I liked Anthony Gross's pen and watercolour the best of all the recent pen and wash tradition, and his fierce yellows, greens and oranges were always a pleasure to me. However, my tints increased in delicacy as time went on, and I began to sell from the bins in the print galleries. So much so, that I needed to spend several days a week printing, and a good deal of the rest of the week hand-colouring, pressing, signing and editioning. In order to keep all this going, I had to go down to Brighton and use my press at the back of the old basement studio where my large canvases were stored. I have often commenced printing at mid-day, and gone on until four or five o'clock of the following morning, the floor littered with drying proofs.

It is a fascinating business, printing and marketing one's work. A book must be kept of the state of the editions, and account books and lists and stocks of the galleries who have your work on consignment, or to whom you have sold editions or part editions—but it all takes time, and constant eyestrain is endemic.

I set to work on ever more new plates—Bell Street, of course, and subjects around London—the Embankment, Edgware Road (not a frightfully popular subject) and a plate of the Duke of Wellington's Cortége vehicle in the crypt of St. Paul's—again not a run-away(!), but interesting, and an ideal subject for the medium. I bit these in the somewhat primitive wash-basin in the tiny convenience at the St. John's Wood flat; it is amazing where one can work if one has to. I etched the drinkers outside the Church Street pub on a Saturday morning, and the Bell Street vegetable stall presided over by a muttering apple-cheeked old crone with the face of Marghareta Tripp. Occasionally I still had time for an outdoor study in oils—a view of the Hero of Alma and the old post office, perhaps, or a street scene near the Underground Station. Sometimes passersby would ask how much a painting cost, but were usually offended at the sum quoted. Curiously enough the public will accept the price if the artist is not present. If he is actually at work on the canvas they feel he must be swindling them unless (it would appear) they do their best to knock down his price. On the other hand an old lady once bent down and dropped twenty pence into my watercolour saucer, with a sympathetic murmur of concern.

Every etcher without a press conveniently to hand sooner or later considers converting a mangle. Of course, it will not work unless you are content with a very small print, or plate; but the etcher always wants to print something too big for his machine. Old mangles have the wooden rollers worn uneven with constant damp and usage, and require turning down with a lathe. If you try to print too large a plate, and screw down the pressure, the castings of the gearing will break, as they are not made for that kind of work. As one only discovers all this by obvious experience, I looked eagerly for a mangle in the market, which I could then drag up to the flat and convert. At last, there was one staring at me—in good condition, painted red and green, and even with near-perfect rollers. "They usually buy them to convert into a bar for drinks," the young man informed me, and offered to bring it round that afternoon, if I helped him.

An hour or so later I returned to the now empty street to find that his premises were none other than Old Charlie's—he being some sort of relation to the mad old man. The old lunatic foamed and roared predictably, despite the fact that I had already paid for it; tried forcibly to prevent us removing it, and finally claimed rent for storage from the time I had bought it in the morning. At this we both shouted him down, and hoisted the incredibly heavy machine into the lorry, and then by slow degrees got it eventually up to the flat—here it stayed, unused and unconverted, until we finally left; upon consideration there was no space for the full equipment necessary for the working of an etching shop up in the flat. Enthusiasm had clouded, as usual, logic.

At this point Catriona suggested that we buy a three-wheeler car, as I had a motor-bicycle licence and therefore was qualified (officially) to get into one and drive away down the street in it—whether or not I had ever driven one before. This seemed to be the answer to problems of late-night travel—it would save rail fares to Brighton, etc., etc. Surely a second-hand one might be bought cheaply, just to use for a few years. Everyone knew that old beat-up cars would run forever—good old bangers, nothing like them . . . always provided you let them alone, and didn't go trying to improve them . . . we searched through the advertising columns—and again one learns what not to do only after one has done it—decided on a dealer rather than a private owner, as therefore one would feel more confident he would be selling one something in good condition.

Before I could go to look at this vehicle, however, I had to go once again as an out-patient for a minor operation. On the appointed hour I took my seat in a dismal hall full of waiting patients. As usual, none of them looked particularly ill; in fact I recalled that the last time I had visited the doctor's I had found my neighbour from across the street sitting next to me.

"Well! How are you? Anything wrong?"

"No, no! Nothing whatsoever! And you?"

"I'm fine—very well indeed—" and so on.

The hospital had once been a workhouse; and still had some of that atmosphere, as if the height and proportion of the walls and wards had been especially designed to impress the poor and lowly with both a sense of their own ignominy and their duty to respect a benevolent autocracy that had provided them with such a haven.

By chance, all the younger doctors were on strike, and the senior surgeons had taken over their duties, treating these lighter cases that were presumably not their usual sphere.

"Well, take off your shirt—"

It occurred to me that he might as well—while about it—attend to an injury on the sole of my foot that had (in fact) bothered me ever since I was seventeen. The result of a sand-blister, it had never healed, and would re-open if I wore Wellington boots, gymshoes, or went swimming. It had been a painful inconvenience I had always borne—doctors approached had said it would go away; and as Balzac says, voiced the opinion that it was nothing to worry about when they had no idea what it was.

"I said remove your shirt not take off your socks, man!"

But despite this irascibility, the surgeon agreed to look at the second difficulty after he had settled the first.

"Turn over and lean on your arm," he ordered, preparing the injection.

I had to explain that this was impossible, as a week or so before, after carrying a number of frames from the market, my right elbow had swollen into an enormous Housemaid's knee full of water, and showed no signs of diminishing.

"Good God! the man's one mass of troubles! Just look at this will you?"—he called two associates. "Do you think I should drain it?" He asked. "I should just about think so," said one.

"I'll deal with the foot first." He took the syringe to my waiting sole. "This is going to hurt—" It certainly did—it felt as if it was going through me and out of my ear. Pain made me dumb.

"*Good* man! And what is your occupation, Mr. Blaker?"

It appeared he was an enthusiast for the etchings of the English School. The interlude inevitably ended on a note of friendship and equality that had not characterised its commencement, and I hobbled away wreathed in bandages, my arm bound and fixed, tight and immobile in its sling.

A day or so later it snowed, and walking down the street I slipped, fell, and somehow rolled under a parked lorry, where I stayed wedged under the wheels. The bound arm prevented me moving free, and the sense of incapacity and cold produced a total depression, until a pedestrian appeared who hauled me out. I continued towards South London, where I was to inspect the celebrated Reliant three-wheeler, which I at last discovered in a street of small garages, each with its complement (but no compliment to the establishment) of apparently scrapped motor-bikes and three-wheelers. The one I had come to look at had a broken door and was half full of rainwater.

"'Course, I haven't had no time yet to *fix* it, but it's a good car."

This seemed dubious, but with all these assurances I was induced to agree that the vehicle should be delivered when repaired, driven over by the mechanic, as obviously in my bound-up state I could not collect it myself. Eventually, however, the day came when I could remove my bandage and sling, and consequently no longer be an object of compassion to the world, even when I bumped into them. But, to my horror, the arm was rigid, immoveable, a paralytically static right arm. Only the fingers answered the commands. A fine situation for an etcher who has to turn a press! But day by day it eased a little, until with a mighty effort one could tell it to raise itself above the head, and even comb the hair. Soon after this the three-wheeler arrived—suspiciously enough on the back of a lorry. It was hastily rolled down to the ground, and the lorry sped away. Little seemed to have been done to the machine, but to a certain extent it was working—just. I got in, but had quite forgotten the few lessons I had received in a car as a boy. We succeeded at last in starting the engine, and I edged along the road, lurching and bumping and grinding the gears, while other cars lurched as wildly to avoid me. Down to Maida Vale I went, and along Kilburn High Road, all among the buses. It was here that I went over an obstruction and ripped off the exhaust pipe, which trailed behind, clattering. I left the car in a free-parking zone, and went off to seek a new silencer. We lived in a parking meter zone, and the runway of the house was daily occupied by Miss X.'s cook housekeeper, who drove up every morning at eight; so here was yet another problem.

My attempts to fix the new silencer, by working under the car all day with spanners, were not very successful; but I discovered a mechanic who said he would fix it. Most garages will not touch a three-wheeler, regarding them (somewhat justifiably) with a kind of abhorrence; and the specialists tend to be proud but sensitive regarding their charges. However, the new silencer was fastened by late evening, but now the engine refused to start. Considering the advances of modern science, moon rockets and the like, it is extraordinary how often every car-engine refuses to start, or "makes a funny noise" that it won't make when the mechanic arrives . . . the mechanic fixed a tow rope from his car to mine, and prepared to transport me to Miss X.'s house, in the hope that we might find a parking place nearby. We set off, to my surprise, at top speed. The wet black dazzling light-reflecting surface of Kilburn High Road flew beneath the wheels—the rain crashed against the windscreen. My lights and brakes—surprisingly—were working, but it seemed to me, as I avoided traffic and the rear bumper of my assistant's car by the merest lick, that this was probably not only my last essay at driving the car, but on earth. There seemed no possibility of anything but a lethal conclusion to the journey, given the night, the speed and the circumstances. The tow rope pulled one out of true when it tautened, and left one floating and swerving whenever it slackened. As I had no communication with the madman ahead it seemed to go on forever. It was only my second journey in the car, and only the second time I had even sat in a car driving seat for over thirty years, and then I had never been on my own.

Suddenly, swerving unexpectedly round a corner, the lunatic stopped, and we got the wreck onto a piece of waste ground. I wanted no more of my assistant; but the next day, with the carburettor unflooded, we started the car quite easily.

Eventually I succeeded in learning to drive; mainly by taking the car out into the thick of the most involved traffic I could find. I drove down Edgware Road to Bayswater so that I could negotiate Park Lane; and at Hyde Park Corner I would spend the morning going round and round the Quadriga arch, while speeding lorries and bus-drivers leaned from their cabins to curse and hurl abuse. But at last I could negotiate all these hazards with thorough knowledge, sliding into the right lanes by day or night.

I would drive to Brighton and back, knowing every hole in the badly filled-in roadworks in Streatham and Brixton, and often prefer the circuitous Red Hill road to the boredom of the motorway. We made some epic journeys when the weather improved—to Ipswich, to look at some inns whose signs I was to paint—a commission gained through the New Grafton Gallery—and another to Manchester; where the reality of the Lowry-Salford scenery, the smoke-covered black church and red-house landscape, was a revelation of aesthetic interest as great as the city Art Gallery with its fascinating plunder of Pre-Raphaelitism.

As I had prepared three portraits of her to send into the Royal Academy, Catriona decided to revive Show Sunday, that day when painters invite their friends and patrons round to inspect their entries; and we arranged a Sunday lunchtime gathering. In the event—fortunately—one of the paintings was accepted and hung on the line: a study of Catriona at a window with a still-life of fan and recorder on a nearby table. I was able consequently to mingle with my fellow-artists at the varnishing day party. No one was varnishing except the aged Alan Gwynne-Jones, who had got his picture off the wall and appeared to be entirely repainting it.

The summer of '76 was as warm as the previous one, and I not only added to my stock of landscape studies, but gave lessons to a lady amateur painter, going out to picturesque sites at Hampstead or the nearby Regent's Park. I made the mistake, however, of insisting that a landscape sketch belongs to that day and hour, and any landscape painted in situ that takes more than three hours to complete is not a correct transcription of the occasion, and therefore valueless, as all the tones and light will have altered. The lady amateur wished for strong and corrective criticism, and would have preferred to work up the same motif through several sessions. Teaching, though fascinating, is a dangerous business. One has to re-analyse one's approach—retrieving back from the sub-conscious into the conscious all the knowledge and experience you have acquired and carefully forgotten so that the picture comes naturally as if remembered. It is constructive to the pupil, but retrogressive to the teacher. It is no use developing a conscience when you paint a picture—you are not paid extra for signs-of-hard-work and duty-done and pulling-it-through.

. . . . . .

My prints were now at Zella 9 in Fulham, one of the first galleries to open for the purpose of selling contemporary prints—and one where the new young artist, if of good standard, was as welcome as the well-known and famed. Up to the Seventies, it had been extremely difficult for younger artists to make their way, as galleries tended to stock only the well-known, and the interim period was trebly hard for the ex-student. Other galleries took my work, and I began to send to galleries outside London as well. I needed new subjects, however, and new images to show. In August we set out for Paris. A small boy who had often stood watching me paint in St. John's Wood was astonished to see me walking along an empty deck towards him—I was no less surprised myself at

the coincidence. All he could find to say was "Are you going to do some painting?" In fact, I was going to etch. I carried a satchel of grounded plates, which had to be shielded from any excessive heat, or the beeswax ground would turn to a lard-like consistency—this could be doubly distressing if they had contained the expedition's work already needled in.

One is not unusual as an artist in liking the roofscapes of Paris—but there they are, and why not use them? Chimneys emitting black puffs at intervals like surreptitious smokers—amazing vistas of corrugated iron and balconies and pieces of half-timbering filled in with bricks and plaster—irregular iron railings . . . the window of your room will always give you a subject; and then there are the different effects of the time of day and the weather to give you further pictures. We went to Barbizon, climbing the extraordinary rocks in the woods, and looking at the untidy studios of Millet and Diaz as if they were chapels of one's faith; which is what they are indeed. We visited Versailles, where I had once sketched the Petit Trianon nearly thirty years before; but all seemed different, changed; the other way around. One felt it was as weird as had the ladies who saw the famous ghosts; and Marie Antoinette's village had a haunted atmosphere indeed. The Rodin museum alone remained precisely as it was—a perennial source of inspiration. The Carrières and the Van Gogh *Tanguy* and the Renoir sketch were still in their same places, reliable to the end. We visited a fish restaurant in Montparnasse where I enjoyed a delicious crayfish; and was intrigued by a couple at a nearby table who each sat before a plate containing nothing on it but a large crab staring back at each diner. A picture entitled "Dual confrontation," perhaps . . . I etched the gardens behind Notre Dame, where black-garbed old ladies sit looking into the past, while little girls in pink play near them as the aged did once themselves—a good subject for artists, the actors taking all parts over the years . . . later, I made a larger studio etching of this scene, including an elderly man on crutches.

One morning we caught a train to Chartres, intending to draw and etch the cathedral; but in the event we were more taken by an old laundry, whose sign romantically proclaimed "Blanchisserie des Trois Moulins," and apart from admiring in the dark of the cathedral the lights of the windows like rubies and emeralds displayed on velvet, spent the greater part of the day down by the stream etching our more basic and humdrum choice of motif. I have always been interested in the typographical elements of a landscape—or more usually, perhaps, a townscape. A board with lettering on it not only creates an associative idea in the mind, but gives all the attraction of decorative art to coincide with and offset nature—or the buildings; all of which latter seem to stem design-wise either from a Classic, Gothic or Cubist source. (We may add to that, I suppose, the peasant craft aspect in a landscape of picturesque utilitarianism, the kind of design, totally adapted to purpose, that built boats and timber-framed houses.) Lettering itself, of course, is also designed within these styles—except possibly the last, ethnic one. The symbolic nature of an inn-sign in a landscape—originating in the knight's emblem hung outside his pavilion—also gives this extra point and interest to a scene; and to my aesthetic, a scene of nature where the hand of man is nowhere evident is not only lacking in scale, but full of terror. As a child, I would look eagerly from the London–Brighton train at the reassuring sign, standing in a field of cows, that advertised—I think—Paint. Two white-overalled workmen, cut out like dummy-boards, carried a plank with the lettering emblazoned. This element of advertising was, in those days, somewhat feared—perhaps with reason. I recall a Strube cartoon showing Dickensians in a coach proceeding down a road totally flanked with hoardings. "And when, Sam, shall we be in the heart of the English countryside?" "Hunless my heyes deceive me Sir, we are already in the heart of it." But then, the posted bill on the wall, from the Lautrec of the Nineties to the Mediaeval woodcut proclamation, has always been a part of the life of man—even the inscriptions of the Egyptians; and although there is truth in the statement (of whoever made it) that Piccadilly Circus would be a wonderful sight if you couldn't read, perhaps, if you can, the suggested images give even more of interest—to the sociologically inclined, at the very least.

We continued, on our return, to Edinburgh; it was my first visit, and I photographed Catriona by the Greyfriars tombs in the very places where long ago one sunny morning Hill and Adamson had set the models for their own immortal moments. Only the level of the ground had strangely altered.

"I'm not dead yet, I'm still in me clogs," an old drunk was saying—"Will ye tell me where is the Medee—eval part of the town, where all the boys is drinkin'?" We went to Glasgow, to stand at last before Whistler's *Carlyle*—an ikon for the devoted.

Back in London I went to the Print Collector's Club lecture and heard of George Mackley's illness—sadly, he would no longer be able to engrave. The meetings and lectures were a great pleasure—we had Charles Wheeler to speak, and many others of interest and celebrity in their fields. R. T. Cowern was of course a member of long standing, as were Andrew Freeth, Paul Drury, Harry Eccleston, Wilfred Fairclough and many others—each one holding office, dedicated to the Society and with whom it was a pleasure to meet and talk. The R.E., as Malcolm Osborne had inferred, was a microcosm where etchers and engravers could find that they were not isolated phenomena, but were each one of a select band who all spoke the same language.

. . . . . .

About this time I again took up the painting of fish still-life subjects, buying prime examples regularly from a stall in Church Street. Here one could acquire the oddest creatures—Australian sunfish, frog-faced red gurnets, and of course the artistically ever-popular but none the less interesting for that, the magnificently gilded Venetian richness of the kipper, the gleaming Velasquez treasure-chest silver of the herring, and the glittering diamond and green emerald-backed Manet mackerel. Each would make a meal after the sitting (as great a mouthful as the previous sentence, perhaps) and this was a further advantage. I painted these canvases with total directness, using thin paint at first, and ending with palette knife for scales and light reflections. I had worked

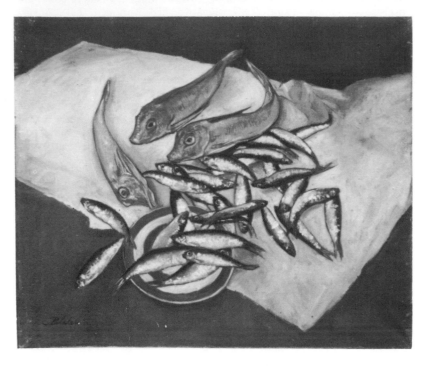

at this approach in my Twenties, but had not continued with it. Fish are some of the most exciting of motifs; and I used my studies to compose a five by four foot composition of a whole fishmongers' slab with them all arranged, like a midnight sky full of glittering stars. It was perhaps not surprising that such a conceit should have been subsequently refused by the Royal Academy.

One day, when staying with friends in the country, I was sitting in a lane etching, with my back to the passersby. I heard a footfall. I wore the long hair of the period, and was wearing also a widebrimmed straw sketching-hat. "Excuse, me Madame—I wondered if—" I turned, and he fled at the sight of my beard. It was the local eccentric, a harmless but apparently persistently amorous old lunatic.

I had some paintings in the summer show at the New Grafton in Bond Street, and had the pleasure of seeing a nude of Catriona hung between a Duncan

Grant and a Vanessa Bell—still life pictures of colour, strength and vigour. It is not always that one may have such an advantage of comparison, and much may be learnt from it. I painted views from the flat of the street below, copper autumn leaves filling the greyness of the streets with out-of tone colour. I painted views of Miss X.'s house, and more studies of the nearby shops, corners, and roofscapes.

The three-wheeler now showed signs of mechanical degeneration; I sold it and bought another that appeared by its outer shell to be of superlative quality; but inspection by an excellent new mechanic I had discovered (or who had discovered us, broken down in the Richmond Road) showed that the chassis was not only corroded to a lace-like consistency, but that these faults had been covered with ordinary sticking-plaster and then painted over. Consequently I was to drive it only towards its final grave, with a strong possibility of this also becoming my own; while my original three-wheeler, which I had sold to an amiable old gentleman who nurtured it along at about fifteen miles an hour is probably running yet.

I continued to use the car, however, on quite long runs—delivering and collecting etchings from out-of-London galleries to save time and money postage-wise. I was driving one night towards Lewes from Brighton, on a road I had known (with various vehicles) from childhood onward. Cars whizzed towards me, a constant stream down the hill as we came up to Lewes. Faster cars overtook me . . . my left rear wheel caught the edge of the suddenly protruding pavement; I hadn't seen it, and had been dazzled by oncoming traffic. The car leapt in my hands like a bucking rhino, out of control—a frightening sense of its power, as if willed by a sudden-developed mind. By a fortuitous chance, the other side of the road was momentarily empty of advancing vehicles—the car sprang about madly, every which way, while I turned the wheel this way and that—behind me, cars screeched to a halt. Then we were suddenly all still. No damage had been done—except to everyone's nerves.

I had experienced a great many difficulties in learning to drive the three-wheeler at all. "Get over to the side before you kill yourself and us as well—" an overtaking police car bellowed at me as we tore down the North London Ring Road against the one-way traffic. This had been due to a poorly labelled entry from a side-alley, and this explanation was accepted; but I was twice chased by irate vehicles—once by a lorry, who screamed: "How you passed your test I'll never know"—and subsequently on a country road in Gloucestershire, when I was forced off the road and had to leap the car up onto the grass verge—for what apparent insult to my pursuer I did not know.

One day I bought a strange machine, rather like a small H. G. Wells space craft, about the size of a large typewriter. This contraption was in an antique shop in Maida Vale, and was a kind of ancient electric sandwich toaster—café-sized. I was in two minds about using it—it looked lethal. I was just coming past St. John's Wood church when a police car drew up. "Hold it!" as the driver spoke, two other constables leapt out and surrounded me. "Now—very carefully—and don't move! Put that thing down . . . steady, now . . ."

"It's only a toaster—a sandwich toaster. . . ."

"A WHAT? Blimey—you had us worried—we thought it was a device. . . ."

It was at this point that I decided finally, the time had come to alter my appearance from that of a French Romantic c. 1840, with flowing hair and beard (in fact, quite fashionable for our own mid-Seventies) and adopt a style not only suave but anonymous—or at least unsuspicious.

The Brick Lane market was one of our Sunday expeditions (here the car was useful for conveying acquisitions home) and the crowds at this archaic site were sometimes almost too dense to force a way through. The deserted ruined houses were filled with stalls and barrows—one went through roofless courts, Pompeii-like—old shops filled to the brim with apparent rubbish—strange characters warming themselves at braziers of glowing coal—comforting cheap restaurants on the perimeter of this netherland, with old-fashioned meat, potato and gravy lunches, or traditional pies and plates of whelks. Puppies in deplorable condition were offered persuasively for sale from under coats to the sentimentally kind-hearted . . . who were asked to regard these living entities as potential Xmas presents rather than life-time responsibilities. "Sandwishes" proclaimed a stall whose commodities one hoped were more reliable than the spelling. . . . We purchased four Victorian wooden kitchen chairs—which we still use, painted bright yellow—and variegated plates and dishes and books. Our collections continued to grow apace. I commenced to draw memory impressions of scenes that had got into my eyes on such expeditions, and eventually consciously set about training the observation to remember shapes and colour and images for this purpose—drawing without a pen or paper, so that it came back later, from this re-recording.

.   .   .   .   .

I had my frames made by the celebrated J. T. Burns, whose kindness and enthusiasm was unbounded. A picture framed by Mr. Burns turned into a work of art if it wasn't one before. He acquired a nude of Catriona from me, had some of my work hanging in his show-room workshop, and reproduced it in his book *Framing Pictures*.

One November day we drove to Henley; on the way back the car lights failed and we had to continue lightless, through a snowstorm. On another long drive a schoolboy helped me move the stalled car into the yard of a small theatre, from which the rehearsing cast subsequently came out and gave me the essential push to re-start the engine. But it was obvious that this could not go on . . . the ventriloquist was in the hands of the dummy. The engine eventually blew up in the Malvern Hills just as we were starting it one frosty Boxing-Day morning. After a subsequent repair I took a morning train ride from London to Malvern and nursed the car back through the January night all across England, from the flooded roads of Upton-on-Severn to the sleet of the final stage from foggy Woodstock. It was not the kind of experience that made one wish to drive again, and shortly afterwards, after a final trip to mid-Sussex and back without lights or handbrake, I slid it into a breaker's yard, handed them the log-book and tip-toed away. I have never driven since, nor wish to despite suggestions that I should have lessons and take a driving-test.

Catriona, whose usual art medium was pastels, had also taken up etching, and her prints were being stocked at various galleries. A friend of hers now arranged an exhibition of my work at Bedford College at Regent's Park, and my fellow-painter L. kindly took me to Brighton in her car to where many of my canvases were stored, and we conveyed them to the hall of the College. The resulting effect was of great interest to me—it is always of great value to see a selection of your work hung up away from the context of where it has been produced. I selected my more restrained and monochromatic portraits and prints, and sold quite well, including one painting to the College itself. At the nearby Regent's Park church both Catriona and I exhibited in the yearly art exhibitions, and I met Hans Feibusch, the famous mural painter. As students in Brighton, we had been advised to look at his work, both in Brighton and Arundel. A vibrant, typically energetic octogenarian artist, he was at work upon a large sculptural figure to stand outside the church. Nearby the flat in St. John's Wood were several interesting houses where artists had lived, apart from the great studios and the Tissot residence. We visited one that was open to the public in order to sell off the recently deceased sculptor's equipment and works. He had fallen from favour in his old age—the saddest of experiences for an artist, who has no time left to wait for his reputation to revive with a swing in fashion. His wife and unmarried daughter, with a large house they could not keep up—spacious and high-ceilinged, a sculptor's dream,—were surrounded with carvings, maquettes, easels and stands and accessories, a weight of acquisition that nobody wanted, but to which they felt an inescapable obligation. They were not English, and he had been one of those obliged to flee as a refugee and start again in a new country, leaving behind the goodwill of half a century's efforts; few have the strength and resilience to build themselves up twice.

I discovered, curiously, that a painter who had been quite a well-known Brighton artist—and in fact been in the same class at school with my mother—had once rented the flat in Miss X.'s house. The establishment, with all its artistic connections, was to have a preservation order placed upon it; and to celebrate this a party was held to which St. John's Wood local residents attended. Miss X., mob-capped and dressing-gowned as usual, enjoyed this party from her bed, while visitors permeated the house and studio, admiring the works of art.

One day, looking into a dealer's who regularly bought my prints, I was presented with an old portfolio that he had acquired in an auction lot from a gallery that had sold up some years before. It bore my name, and was the very one with which I had trudged around the galleries thirty years before, with it full of pen and wash work: precious never-to-be-repeated works of youth, carelessly thrown off, with an energy that later works envy and emulate but cannot possess.

I was, however, now painting with a different, more concentrated energy some new large works, intending to submit them for the next Summer Exhibition of the Royal Academy. Friends had been pressed into service as models for a *Raising of Lazarus*; such albeit self-indulgent subjects are favourites for painters. Another subject painting was of Catriona in the kitchen at a table with a lamp, and reading a letter—enacting the part of one whose love has jilted her. These two epics, together with the multifish painting, were framed and sent off via Gentle Ghosts, an interestingly named firm of carriers whose vans would arrive from nowhere at a moment's notice—and of course at a price—but who were extremely useful. We had enjoyed a Show-Sunday party as usual; but this time they were all rejected—one cannot always be lucky—and I had to go down and collect them. This time I carried them all back on foot, with a cord around them suspended from my shoulder. I felt that rejection did not somehow warrant the same luxurious mode of travel as had the outward journey.

I had several commissions to take me away from etching, printing and colouring; and these were welcome interruptions to my unceasing work. One was a portrait of a Dalmatian, which on Catriona's advice I made to fit into an oval shape against a silver background. This was to be hung in a decor of grey and white, with glass-topped tables and black upholstery, so that the sitter himself would echo in his own harlequinade the contrasts about him. The second commission was to paint another Rossetti copy, this time the wonderful *Ghirlandata* in the Guildhall Collection. Applying for permission to make a copy in oil, I was given every help. I arrived at the Museum at an appointed hour. "You'll have to give me a bit of help, Sir," said the man in the peaked cap, leading me out into the street. "We don't keep everything on the spot. We've got things stored all over London." We entered a modern office, and at a nod, a door slid open and we descended a staircase. As with the Italian Tourist office, a few yards below the surface and you are back with London's ten thousand years. Deep in the brick vaults we entered a long Romanesque tunnel. Here, resting on a board floor lifted slightly from the stone, were pictures upon pictures—like a glorified and enlarged Bell Street market collection. Massive gold frames, voluted to the point of a carrier's despair—enormous paintings, portraits, sea-battles. . . . "Now, she's here somewhere . . . *Yes!*" We lugged her out—there she was. The hand of Rossetti himself had painted this—a picture I had stood before at the R.A. show as she hung in state on the walls, her eyes fixed always a little beyond the spectator, seeing—what? The man in the peaked cap was leaning on the great frame as it rested sideways on the floor. "First of all we've got to get her up the stairs." It was a problem, but we managed it, and out of the door into the street. Fortunately, it wasn't raining.

"Best if we carry her flat . . ." One at each end of the five by four foot frame, the custodian leading, we set off through the traffic, *La Ghirlandata* face upwards. Suppose a brick—or a falling safe—even a suicide?—should choose that moment to drop from the sky . . . and here were we below. "Steady at the back!" We had stopped at the traffic lights. It brought back days of the three-wheeler. Cars obligingly made way for us. It seemed a long journey, but at last we had arrived. "The best place for you would be the changing-room, perhaps, Sir . . ." We propped her up against a wall, supported on a low bench. All about were the blue and purple robes of the liverymen and the ceremonial robes of the Guilds.

"You won't be disturbed . . ." I got out my canvas and brushes, and set to work. After about a week the critical grunts of the doormen (as before) turned to a certain grudging admiration—"Well, it's turning out a bit better than I would have thought—" Another week, and they were staunch supporters, partaking of the progress—"Seen our artist, then, have you?" People would stroll in and sit and chat from all strata of the establishment. At last it was finished. "Won't be the same without you, Sir—no, that's all right. Me and my mate will take her back."

It had been extraordinary, once more spending the day with Rossetti regularly; following his hand, comprehending his approach (or even his assistant's) as only a copyist can—as only a copyist sees. It was different to the picture being on the wall of the gallery, as in my last essay. This time I was responsible for it—not to let it slip; to check it as one left and arrived.

"So long as you're not going to leave the copy and slope off with the original?" They all quipped the good old joke in turn. But my canvas was going to Morris's Red House, where Rossetti had spent so much time (and where several of my Fifteenth Century panels hung); and I went back to the flat to paint more contemporary (or somewhat Rossettian near-contemporary) portraits of Catriona.

On my forty-ninth birthday I woke early, after dreaming of walking on a vast Egyptian fortress wall, very flat—a raised stone plateau; the dawn very clear, the sky blue to palest orange-yellow. One could smell the flower-scented morning. The sea beyond was calm and grey. I thought of early paintings I had made—of the Leicester Galleries now closed. Of Oliver Brown saying "this is my son who is joining the firm." Of watching his career span over the years. Catriona and I walked that day through St. John's Wood to Primrose Hill, and down Parkway, where I had sold a tortoise to the pet-shop in 1959 for four shillings. We had found it wandering in a wood, lost, with a hole drilled in the shell, and a string trailing. In 1952 one could buy there a pair of flying foxes for seven pounds ten shillings. Inside the pet-shop was a large and dangerous-looking bird-eating spider, as large as one's hand. Subsequently, it seems, this creature had a strange history. Someone, as a sinister joke, bought it and sent it in a box through the post to a family who opened it all unsuspecting. Oddly, and with remarkable lack of panic, they managed to recapture the creature without injuring it, and returned it to the same pet-shop. This we later read as a news item. But it was no wonder that the spider had an air of exhaustion about her, as if anticipating all the inconveniences to which she was to be subjected.

. . . . . .

When I first came to St. John's Wood, Catriona had taken me to see the church nearby. On this site had once stood St. John's hunting chapel, in a clearing in the (St. John's) woods . . . one could still see it, almost, by closing the eyes and concentrating, but it was heavy work. Inside the present church the Victorian tiles, alabaster and mosaic locked it into its period—a marvellous place. As we stood side by side in the empty chancel inspecting the reredos, the organ had all at once and unexpectedly broke forth, and the inevitable conviction came upon me that we would be married on that spot. And so we were. It was after one Boat Race day opposite Price's Candle Works that we decided to become engaged. This was a fine excuse for an engagement party, and subsequently we crossed over to Paris on the night boat.

Shortly before this major decision, Catriona had bought a small bicycle. I occasionally rode this, and was going fast up the Kilburn High Road when I missed the pedal, and came off over the handlebars. A following bus swerved to avoid me, and the passersby hauled me to the pavement and administered to bruised spirit and cut hands and knees. Feeling rather sick I wheeled the conveyance back and put it in the garage, from where it was subsequently stolen. I think, like Jim Hawkins when Long John Silver decamped from the Hispaniola with one of the bags of treasure, we were all pleased to be so cheaply rid of it, as they of him.

In Paris we stayed near St. Cloud, and I etched two plates there that I felt particularly happy about: *Paris Café* and *French Breadshop*. They seemed a step forward—light and direct and not over-weight. In the park at St. Cloud I was much fascinated by a curious little kiosk. The almost pathetic hopelessness of a coffee stall adding a frieze of pierced fretwork and the slogan: "Café de Félicité" did seem in fact actually to succeed in its aim, of seducing one into the sphere of picturesque romance and—almost—the world of Watteau embarkations.

Perhaps it was a mistake to stop for dinner at Dieppe, with the intention of boarding the midnight boat. Unfortunately, it appeared, we had been misinformed, and this had been withdrawn. We walked up to the station to see if we could sleep in the waiting-room. The station official said we might make ourselves at home, but he would have to shut us in after midnight until the morning. However, during these discussions Catriona became locked into the ladies' convenience, and we were obliged to hunt up screwdrivers and jemmies in order to take the lock off the door and release her. This experience was unnerving, so bidding the station farewell we strolled back past the reflecting lights in the harbour—where I made a hasty small plate: I am a believer in taking half an hour off from the exigencies of a given situation—and subsequently passed the night close to a hot-water pipe in the corridors of the Customs House. It was a different, newer customs house to the old yellow shack in which I had passed the night thirty years before; as one often does, I wondered how many people I was: a different one in the same place, or someone in a different phase of the same place's existence? But it was rather cool, despite the hot pipe, and I got tired of philosophising, and went out to draw a night scene of the waiting ferry. At eight o'clock we were allowed on board, and returned to London, where I bit my plates in the sink as usual.

Our wedding-day approached; but first we were witnesses for the wedding of two great friends nearby. Us two potential grooms went about the London suppliers, from Burns and Nathan to Pro-Nuptia, trying on various Victorian or modern black and grey suits, top-hats and waistcoats, with a view to hiring something interesting in which to get married. In the event, we both succeeded in building up a wardrobe of borrowed articles from willing friends. The girls, of course, enjoyed their own outings for apparel—we grooms spending most of the afternoons in tea and cake houses—and Catriona eventually selected an off-white, puffed sleeve dress, with a broad-brimmed hat—later I painted a still-life group of the hat, gloves and bouquets together with her favourite much-immortalised black umbrella.

After the first ceremony, we awaited our own event. My chef friend S. and his wife made our cake, in the form of a three-decked castle, with small marzipan animals inhabiting it. We designed a souvenir hymn sheet reproducing a page from a Victorian calendar page. I went to the St. John's Wood church bazaar, and bought some giant frying-pans—"Somebody's setting up house"—the stall-owner guessed.

One morning about this time, she being unwell for the day, I volunteered to look after a friends' nearby greengrocery. Acquainting myself with the prices, receiving the day's supply of fresh vegetables, cutting off the rotted bits of yesterday's, chopping down the withered parts of old chicory, celery and so on, I even began somewhat authoritatively to alter the prices of one or two articles. I put the old corncobs at bargain prices to tempt the public . . . The sense of power can go to your head—particularly when somebody buys an article that looked from far tempting ten minutes ago before you worked on it.

A long queue soon formed and I was succeeding quite well; but the churchwarden appeared, took an apple, put the money in my hand, and said, as they will—"I only want *this*—It's the right price—" All calculations concerning my current customer flew from my head. I went to pieces—couldn't pick it up again. The queue, sensing this, and that I had lost power, broke rank, each demanding to be served for "Only a pound of tomatoes—" "You see, I *really am* in a hurry—" "I honestly only have two minutes—" I stood blank . . . "Who *is* he?" "I don't know—he's not a regular, I *know*—" The suspicions and mistrust grew.

With decision I seized pencil and card, got back the first customer, and remarshalled the situation—almost. The next day my friend was back at work. "We had an absolutely extraordinary person in here yesterday," the customers told her. "He was absolutely *hope*less!"

We decided to go back to Dieppe for our honey-moon, and booked a couple of weeks, paid for in advance. After buying the wine and paying for the other expenses we were fairly low in funds. I sped around the galleries, gathering up any cash owing me, and converting it quickly into francs. However, by the day of the day of the wedding I had only about eight pounds left in the world in hand, so to speak.

The wedding day was bright and fine. I went along early to the greengrocery to get a carnation buttonhole. The owner's father, who was sitting in that day said: "You can have the carnation free, if you're the artist bloke."

Back at the house, the guests were beginning to arrive. I met my prospective brother-in-law at the door, resplendent in tails and top-hat. "Well, I think I look better than you," he observed regarding my jeans and t-shirt.

Shortly afterwards, while I was changing in the midst of a welter of bridesmaids, one of the guests arrived with a crate of pies he was donating to the festivities. "I say," said my imminent brother-in-law, putting his head into the bath-room where I was helping Catriona on with her dress, "the caterer's arrived, but he won't go away and is sitting down comfortably!" "Well," said Catriona—"give him a drink!"

Having changed, I went along to the church, waving to the greengrocer's father. The church was nearly full, but I had to select a best man due to some previous confusion. It took a while, as I kept seeing people I knew as I walked amongst the pews on this best man quest; but having deputed the willing participant, I got to my place shortly before Catriona's procession entered to progress up the aisle to the music of *All people that on earth do dwell*.

We were married by an old friend, Dean Milburn, Master of the Temple, which was a very pleasant experience, with the church full of music, and the pews behind closely packed with the living ghosts of many of the people one had met in life up to that moment.

Down the aisle we walked, to Handels' *Arrival of the Queen of Sheba*, admonishing each other not to go too fast; outside, I took many photographs, and appeared in many others. Then, back to the flat; and the great castlecake was cut and the bottles of wine opened, and the party commenced.

Painters, etchers and illustrators talked with doctors and barristers, novelists, teachers, architects—arts and sciences were well represented, but all deferred to the highest manifestation of art present—that of the Chef. Late in the evening, after it was all over, we cleaned up the flat and went round to our friends for a meal.

The next morning we set off for Dieppe. It was strange to be sitting in S.'s galley on board the Newhaven Ferry so soon after seeing him cutting up his cake for the guests; now, in full chef regalia, hung with knifes and equipment, he brought us glasses of wine, plates of delicacies, glasses of brandy. We had docked for some time before we realised we had arrived, and set off with S. for a nearby bar to meet some Dieppois friends who ran it. Finally, we parted from S. and walked round to the promenade to our hotel. Thirty years before G. and I had come to one of these hotels—but as the only room available had been on a floor half of which was falling into the street, and the place was full of sailors happily and drunkenly carousing with their girl friends, we had sought quieter and more reflective accommodation. The hotels were quite changed now— almost too restored—"out of existence," as Ruskin would say. All character had departed from the interior decor; but the roofscape view was the same, and I made an etching of this the next morning, the air having a strange bitter scent I connected with boyhood at Brighton, and which I at last identified as burning coal from chimneys in the near-frosty chill of an early autumn morning.

Dieppe no longer possessed the run-down old fairground booths near the dock; the cliff caves were boarded over, and no waving children greeted the steamers from them; no rabbits (happily) sat with the vegetables on the onetime Sickertian shop stalls, to be poked and treated like ripe pears—although on a country walk we were asked the way by a boy with a black and white buck in a basket who was worried he would not deliver it in time for a dinner; but there was still much of more pleasant picturesque interest in the town. On our one evening on the way back a month or so earlier we had not sufficient time to look further than the dock area; but now we investigated outwards, etching and drawing the churches, and admiring the mediaeval St. Jacques and the great carved primitive angels within.

We found the sailor's church on the cliffs, full of ship-models; and watched the dredger far below, working away as had the *Foremost Prince* at Newhaven years before. We enjoyed above all the art collection in the castle, particularly the paintings of Jacques-Emile Blanche. This artist, treating both Brighton and Dieppe with equal sympathy—both favourite towns of my own—belonged to the era of my Swiss grandfather, when the paddle-steamers ran regularly between the two resorts and there was great mutual connection. Some of that old connection seemed to exist still in a few restaurants—although there did not seem to be so many "Café Brighton," or "Café Palace Pier," as formerly. The way a linen table napkin was folded reminded me of my grandparents, and the way in which one might sit eating within sight and sound—more or less of the sea—brought the two towns together—although Dieppe has her back to the sea, it is true.

The faded photographs of the Raid, and of the prisoners huddled together—possibly some were our erstwhile neighbours of that period—were still displayed, rather tattered, as an attraction on the dockside. They seemed to be yearly becoming decades further back, joining as ancient history the Fourteen-Eighteen and the Boer wars—one day to become even Romantic; fascinating as the Napoleon-Wellington times—horror and fear degenerating into the merely picturesque; and in comparison with true savagery the picturesque must be regarded as mere.

We took the bus out into the countryside of halftimbered farmhouses, etched and photographed and made a special pilgrimage—the concept is attractive—to find the J. E. Blanche museum, which was part of a village town hall offices. We looked with interest at a great mural he had painted in the local church; but he excelled more in the direct transcriptions of memorable bits of seaside towns, or in the portrait of a friend who was also a person of achievement— Beardsley, or the great portrait in the Dieppe Castle Museum of fellow-painter Fritz Thaulow, another immortaliser of Dieppe. Blanche is superior to the great Impressionist painters in that he is not so tied to his own dogma—he is not too grand to put his interest in the subject first. The greatest artists simply use the world as their vehicle—they can't help it. Personal interest has to dissolve in the universality of their genius, and a broken fence or tree, the Battle of the Nile, or the nearest girl with an apron means just as much or as little to them as their dearest loves and the objects of their deepest emotions.

On the beach, we joined in the traditional pastime of waiting to watch the packet-boat arrive. I nearly came to a sad end on these very ill-fated beaches of history. Two plump middle-aged men were attempting to launch a small boat, outboard motor attached, in which they had loaded fishing-tackle, refreshments, bottles—all the happy equipment for a day's expedition. It was, however, a little too cool, too much end-of-season, the sea too choppy, and the boat kept being swept back. With recollections of my own difficulties in such situations, I put down my etching plate, and went to help. One of them got in, but too far aft. We pushed him out, just between two incoming waves, but he forgot to take the oars and row, and a third, larger, wave overturned him and the boat on top of us in the shallows. A hail of body, boat, and the out-board—happily, true to its nature, it didn't start—fell all around—I scrabbled wildly to get out of the way. Miraculously, except for a heavy bump or so from the gunwale, nobody was damaged. The sea was full of tackle, bottles, bait, rods—and, I had lost my glasses! But I saw at that moment a glitter more glittery than the rest of the pebbles as a wave receded for a moment, and I sprang into the surf—by a kind freak of chance it was they—unbroken. A short-sighted person has only one real preoccupation that he has learnt to place before all other considerations! The two fishermen were far too depressed at the soaking of all their sandwiches to even thank me; perhaps they even blamed me—but I crawled away up the beach in my wet clothes, and sat etching all the afternoon in my shirt—my underclothes, trousers, socks and shoes spread on the stones in the weak sunlight to dry. I thought how slight a hold we have upon our fragile-fated selves; and it is as well to think twice before going again to help somebody accentuate their foolhardiness.

We much enjoyed our bottles of wine and coq-au-vin and moules marinière in what became our favoured restaurant. It was patronised by old people who came in wearing their slippers, and we would stay until half the chairs were on the tables, and the ginger and white cat crawled up to sleep there on high. We went to Rouen and sketched and etched. Under an archway a trio of Sousaphone, banjo and one clarinet were playing *High Society*.

Back at Dieppe we saw a fight among fishermen on the quay. It was stopped by a six-foot high gaunt fish-wife out of the French Revolution, and the defeated one, dodging, suddenly dismantled his opponents' stall and threw it into the harbour, with a sort of vicious enjoyment. We saw a porpoise at the water's edge, which vanished as we looked at it. We discovered the ivory-carving tradition of Dieppe, and one of the last workshops; and we returned to London when the season suddenly ended—all the visitors left overnight, and we travelled back in the galley of the *Senlac*, well victualled by S.

. . . . . .

We arrived back to find a good few cheques for prints awaiting me, but Miss X. was more bed-ridden than ever, and somewhat depressed at our long absence. It seemed she had come to rely upon our presence in the house, which was not unnatural; but we felt it was time to look around for other accommodation. We nearly moved to a flat at Hastings, and once considered the offer of another nearby, advertised as rent-free in return for "some help." Deciding to give this a try to see how much this help intruded time-wise, we arranged a week. Catriona was then stricken with flu, so I took on the lone experience of being a valet myself. But my prints, particularly my new Paris set, were becoming increasingly successful, and time was beginning to necessitate being proportioned out carefully.

Galleries were now approaching me, and I had no longer the need to take my portfolio on the gruelling round artists know so well. The "some help"—to albeit exceptionally pleasant people—in the proposed flat was, in effect, a kind of endless slave labour. I met the last incumbent. She was an aging, crushed mid-European lady, one of those whom life seems to have selected to humiliate. She was just moving out, and said she couldn't stand it any more. The first duty was to wash the breakfast dishes, plus last night's dinner and cooking relicts. Then, mopping the kitchen out fully. Tidy away the innumerable toys of the two small children, vacuum-clean the house, and dust and polish all the furniture and pictures. Next to make the beds and pick up and fold all the various clothes that the master seemed to have found neccesary to fling about the floor of his dressing-room. Soon, I would have sold him to the sans-culottes without a qualm. The bath was, of course, to be cleaned, and all fittings. After all this, there was some time off; but I was expected to clear up after lunch. In the afternoon there was a suggestion that the garden needed some attention—in the event I pruned and tied so that the subsequent summer should have seen a good show. Later on the children demanded songs and amusement at the piano—it was a full-time job, and the most exploited week one could have experienced. Of course, I didn't give it a week; a couple of days seemed fair, but the family were genuinely surprised at my rejection of their offer. They didn't thank me, or even offer a remuneration, but seemed merely put out. "How annoying! We must try for someone else—" said the Master as I left.

Miss X. at this point dropped a teapot into her lap and scalded herself so badly that she never rose from her bed again. I got her into a dry night-dress and called the doctor, and a permanent nurse was engaged.

Increasing difficulties consequent upon the age and illness of our landlady made it more than ever imperative that we should soon move. More space, in any case, was needed for the increasing amount of work I was involved in. Catriona continued to work part-time at the Tate Gallery. On going down to the Tate to see her, three bottles of wine were found in my pack upon the obligatory inspection at the door. "You realise we shall have to confiscate these sir, don't you?" said the guards; but it was merely the English sense of humour, as they knew who I was. That is to say, of course, Catriona's husband.

An interesting experience of this period was attending the wedding of the daughter of my old master Louis Ginnett. I was probably the only person there who had known the bride's father. She herself was by coincidence connected with Catriona through a mutual friend. I seemed to see Mr. Ginnett there all through the ceremony. We continued to look for flats—inspecting converted corridors and minute attics that the owners of the houses fondly hoped might furnish them an income. Shared facilities including kitchens, and exorbitant rents at short notice terms did not make much appeal to one. Next door to Miss X. lived Lilian Somerville, who had done so much to make contemporary art a vital part of British life from the war onwards through the medium of the Arts Council and associate bodies. We spent an evening with her, looking at her great studio flat filled with large abstracts by William Scott, Pasmore, Peter Kinley and others of that period. A memorable canvas was a surrealist picture redolent of the Thirties, which she admitted was a work of her own.

A conjointure of circumstances now permitted us to seek a house, rather than rent a flat. We searched throughout Clapham and Streatham, where there was a 90% grant available; but we had many possessions, and inherited furniture was choking the flat and the floor below at Miss X.'s house. There was no time to wait for a house to be rebuilt around us. Day after day we roamed the streets and estate agents of South and North London; we nearly bought a flat at Finchley; we developed an extensive knowledge of all the Italian restaurants in these areas; and it being January, we were continually looking at property in the darkness of a London wintry teatime. Catriona, applying decisive methods, sent for sheaves of estate agents' lists of property for sale from all over the Southern counties; we looked even as far afield as Worcestershire. But by narrowing down the size of the property relative to the price, Kent was found to be the chief choice, and of that county there were large houses in Ramsgate. We went to several attractive mansions, but the distance from London seemed too great. In those days, it had not seemed I might be able to work entirely by post—and then, of course one had friends and social interests in London.

Finally, there evolved therefore the Medway Towns—full of available property, very inexpensive at that time—before the property boom which brought them up to the general level of prices—and near to London. Rochester, moreover, was like a village—or a cross between a county town and a village—with river, castle, and cathedral. We decided to spend the February days in a search for a house there.

This strange, seemingly inland port, redolent of Dickens—an attribute that was soon to be realised even more fully—appealed to us at once upon arrival. The only competitor still with us was a rather small house in Greenwich; and this stood in a street whose subsidence was so marked in walls and pillars that it was only too obvious—although the residents seemed oblivious to this fact—that the river was biting away the foundations deep below ground.

I had once made an etching at Shoreham in Sussex of an old barge with the name "Rochester" white on the black of the stern. This seemed almost prophetic; it had been treated with such emphasis, as if I had been trying to tell myself something . . . eventually we came to Beresford House—a spacious (it seemed before all our varied books and bits and pieces were brought in) Victorian style terrace dwelling. We had a survey made—and were so put off by the apparent dereliction, woodworm, dryrot and so on prevalent, that—unused to this business—we assumed it must be about to collapse, and so withdrew our offer. But after some thought we made a new and lower offer, which was accepted. The back garden was a derelict mass of rubbish—evidently a godsend to the street in general, as the lack of a back fence created the availability of a rubbish dump for old planks and rotting vegetation all the year through. There was no indoor convenience, and no wash-basin; there was a broken sink in the scullery, and an old bath upstairs with a broken geyser. There was no heating, except open grates—beautiful Victorian fireplaces in every room.

Before we left London we went along to the R.W.S. galleries to a demonstration of methods evenings. Michael Fairclough and Michael Chaplin were printing—other members engraving, laying grounds, biting plates. It was to be one of the last evenings before the removal of the R.E. to new premises. Many things were changing. I sent my two best Paris etchings into the R.A., and Catriona sent three. We cleared the flat ready for the removal men to pack everything into tea-chests. As a last expedition we visited our favourite restaurant in Finchley Road with our best friends—it was a favourite venue for mid-European emigrés, apparent intellectuals, reserved and mysterious. On the way home the snow was falling through the lamplight onto the open pink flowers of a cherry tree. The next day we visited the London Zoo; something one had not done for twenty years. The snow fell from the grey sky, and nothing was about except the penguins. All was altered: a brave new Zoo. But where was the famous old Lion House, where the great cats would sprawl like tabbies in the sunshine, close to your ear, listening to the human conversation? And feeding time within, when we lined up on the tiers of stone steps to watch the black panther pacing up and down, and listened to the roaring and the crashing as the bars were slid aside and great carcases of meat thrown within . . . all was gone. Cages of a concentration-camp era replaced the cosy Victorian approach, that had made of the animals domestic pets. Now, the world wished to see them travelogued, as in the Wild. Through a glass screen, we queued in the cold to peer at the beasts pacing their field of grass, wearing a drab path away just as if it had been the inside of their old cage. They had been told they were wild creatures, who loved nature. De-humanised, they were left only with that most inaesthetic of vegetables to the artist—turf. Boring in the country, deplorable in an urban setting—*grass*. The penguin pool, once the pride of the moderns, the harbinger of Things to Come, was paradoxically, the only part of the old zoo seemingly remaining—shades of the posters and Julian Huxley—the penguins spun around as of old, but the elephants were invisible in their strange dwelling, and all about was desolation. We went into the cafeteria—empty except for a depressed attendant, who swept at our table with her damp cloth in the best Joe Lyons tradition. It was here, in the dream-world of the Thirties—on this spot—that we had sat at a linen-clothed table; my mother with a bucket of ice by her side cooling the bottle within—waiters in black and white, palm trees and an orchestra—excited talk—sunshine and music . . . my grandmother's cousin the manager, bringing us personally delicacies from the extensive menu . . . an ordered world, enthusiastic, the Zoo a new success, and all knowing it . . . outside the elephants walking, loaded with children. And now the small mammals had been banished to the Twilight world. Beware of the pickpockets said the notices everywhere, and they no longer meant the monkeys. And the monkeys were no longer available Not to be Fed. Where was the Chimpanzee who so enjoyed a cigarette-end—picking it up with his lips, up side down to show off—smoking and inhaling, carefully stubbing it out (to our surprise) before it burnt his fingers, and asking for another . . . No smoking in the monkey house now. . . .

The weather was ever more wintry. Heavy snow was forecast. It was April the twelfth. We had tea at Fortnum and Mason's—a kind of symbolic gesture—we didn't usually. The next day the carriers drove off with all our material, moveable world. We followed in a taxi, to Charing Cross Station. As we turned the corner, past the Beatles' zebra, we noticed that the trees were different. Their branches had all been clipped, no longer met across the roadway, and St. John's Wood no longer looked like Paris.

Chapter 10

We approached Rochester that morning as official residents—no longer merely potential first-time buyers, as the agents' phrase has it. We were now to be dwellers "up Delce" the area above the High Street. It was only later, talking to an elderly resident in nearby Jackson's Fields, that I learnt about the origin of this name. Apparently one of Duke William's successful army, John de Delce, was given this section as his post-Hastings reward. The Delce, I was told, had once had its own regalias, mace and crown. They were made of wood—the Delce had the right to hold its own trials, and so on. I had not heard of this elsewhere; but when the shadowy informant had disappeared back through the mists "up Jackson's" I wonder if it were the Lord of Delce, still walking—albeit in cloth cap and overcoat.

It was strange to be a resident in this Dickensia town of Rochester, the High Street lined with half-timbered buildings, the odd floating jetties on the river that rose and fell with the tide . . . no local Whistler seemed so far to have realised their artistic possibilities. They were wonderful survivals, but no one had seen them as picturesque—it is true that they were exceedingly difficult to draw . . . it was all rather like an illusion, as we had hardly heard of the town only a few months before. On our arrival we went to our house and waited outside for the van with all the furniture and china and pictures to arrive. We had been obliged to hire forty tea-chests to accommodate all the books. As we waited, the snow fell faster.

The van arrived, the forty boxes were emptied and placed in the garden. The world of the artist, the portfolios, easels, canvases, the furniture, china, frying-pans—all the history of the London flat in portable form was here—"You've left your tea-chests," we reminded them.

"They're yours—you bought them." "We thought we'd hired them." "We don't rent tea-chests. We sell them." As they drove away we looked out at all the neat wooden cubes filling the yard. Abandoning for a while the freezing cold of the house interior, we went down to the High Street to an old-world tea-shop; just the predictable kind of place one would expect to find. You stepped down into the shop, the bell tinkled, the great burning logs in the hearth threw up sparks, and black-jacketed boys from the King's School entertained their girl friends with tea and scones. Outside, an occasional car or bus crawled through the snow. This was before the traffic was diverted from the High Street and before the great burning logs ignited the mantel-piece, and were subsequently replaced by a gas-log fire.

After tea, a stroll along the street—so quiet and parochial after London, even the relative peace of St. John's Wood High Street, the great studios and the tree-lined avenues—along to the Gordon Hotel, where we had very sensibly previously booked a room for the week, in order to acclimatise ourselves at least in comfort. To wake the next morning to Cathedral bells and breakfast in the painted panel room was a transmutation to a previous century.

By day, we worked on our house; we had a lorry come to take away the garden's rubbish, and an aged pensioner, a Mr. Johnson, built a high brick wall and a gate. We compared very favourably now with those of our neighbours whose separation from the back lane was at best composed of brieze blocks and at worse of bedsteads. We took up all the planks of the rotted kitchen floor, and went down to the tarred four by fours sitting on brick piers with a piece of slate sandwiched to prevent the damp rising. The joists *above* had rotted, from the damp penetrating from the yard outside. It seemed that the take-away water pipes under the ground had been broken years before, and generations of emptied baths had poured water steadily into the foundations. However, they seemed unaffected. We applied for grants and in due course and with perhaps no more than the usual delays and difficulties with builders—who always had first to oblige an apparently more useful client elsewhere—eventually got a new roof, yard, and other improvements.

A bomb had dropped opposite in the war and demolished two houses (since rebuilt) and the blast had cracked one of the roof supports and run down over the back to affect the bathroom wall. All this was put right, and Mr. Johnson and I climbed about on the sloping tiles inspecting brickwork. Mr. Johnson, quite happy at this dangerous elevation, discoursed of the pleasures of a steamer trip from Sheerness to Ostend "with a Disco all night through," but I was not so happy as he with the slanting surface and the drop beneath. We never were tempted to try the Disco trip, either.

With gas wall-heaters inserted, and the gas and electric company cutting holes and runnels all over the fabric, we papered and painted to cover their tracks; and Catriona removed the Chinese lacquer-like layer of white paint from the mantel and fireplace in the parlour to reveal white marble and glazed Victorian tilework. The parlour was the grand part, with a bay window and elaborately corniced ceiling. The degree of decoration grew less impressive as one moved kitchenwards, and even the door panel possessed one less chamfer as one left the room tailored for Company. The middle room acted also as a corridor, and the removal of a piece of boarding in the kitchen revealed a fine range, sealed up many years ago, but with all the necessary pieces and accoutrements carefully placed upon it, as if awaiting this resurrection, like the furnishings in a Pharaoh's tomb.

The large cellar was to be the etching workshop, and here my old Kimber press was conveyed and set up. We mended most of the broken windows, and cut holes in doors and inset others. We made a latticed gate for the yard from strip wood painted white, and put up myriads of shelves. A heater was placed in the bathroom, and plug-in radiators provided extra heat to assist the picturesque but somewhat unpredictable coal fires. A new sink was supplied to the kitchen. By and large, all these improvements did not take more than about five years to achieve finally, but for many months, awaiting promised grants and builders, we shivered in the wintry periods. The woodworming was however an early job; and we moved valuable possessions from room to room as masked men with jets and cylinders soaked the house with fuming chemical. It was difficult to survive for a week or so, but we hoped it was even harder on the wood beetles. Large carpets were acquired in the Saturday market, or from "Wally", Rochester's favourite second-hand dealer whose shop was on the Banks near to the Tattoo Artist. Almost every youth who came to carry out some mechanical function in the house was tattooed extensively. It was a particular Medway trait.

Catriona visited a local garden suppliers, and returned home with a number of dry sticks that eventually turned into a large and variedly flowering mahonia, a pear tree that grew pears after seven years, a japonica, and a broomstick that became a cherry tree higher than the house after eight years, and full of succulent sweet red cherries. The garden, with white decorative iron chairs and round table, the trees, and the roses (a legacy from a previous inhabitant) eventually gave the once rubbishy yard the atmosphere of an oasis of Edwardian beauty and culture.

For some time Catriona retained her part-time work at the Tate Gallery, and I would go up with her, and etch views of the Embankment, or beachcomb at low tide. Below the Tate, the shore was littered with broken pieces of blue and white from the one-time Vauxhall Potteries. Otherwise I built up my postal connections with galleries increasingly farther afield, so that I worked constantly. All about were new subjects, and I roamed Rochester plate and mirror in hand (I etched from the reflection, so that the resulting image was the right way round) and sat about the waterfronts from Strood and nearby Upnor to Ship Pier and the Sun Pier at Chatham. The Francis Iles Gallery in Rochester began to show my prints, and have always been of tremendous help in every way; their twice yearly private views great local events for the fortunate invitees.

The Royal Academy opened, and we discovered that Catriona was accepted and hung well—all three of her etchings—while my two Paris scenes hung nearby. Here was returning to London as successful artists with a vengeance! We were able to attend the private views and varnishing day and meet again all our friends in the art world. Such days mean a great deal to artists whose lives are inevitably lonely, as one requires time and solitary concentration to accomplish anything at all. Our prints prospered in the Exhibition—red stars appeared in profusion—every moment another seemed to appear. The summer was spent in printing and colouring and sending the orders off to the purchasers. Soon, the post office knew well our daily parcel-laden arrival. At the close of the Exhibition Catriona had sold sixty prints, and I ninety.

Running across Cambridge Circus, I stepped on a large man-hole cover in the centre of the roadway. This has been taken out and poorly replaced. I trod on the far side, which tilted down—as I began to descend, the other edge, tilting the other way, hit me from behind and fortuitously threw me out again, onto the road, where I was helped up by passersby, unhurt apart from various cuts on shins and knees. A curious experience, and possibly a warning to look at the ground beneath your feet rather than dream of the stars. . . .

I continued to etch out-of-doors, to paint more of my large landscape pochades on board, and to take up again my pen and watercolours, there being so great a wealth of potential subject. The Vines, with the avenue of trees altering across the seasons—the Cathedral from all angles—the Castle grounds. At Ship Pier, small boys fished all day; and workmen out of Rembrandt sculled their boats, standing up, with one oar from the stern, back and forth across the water as they had done since boats began. There were derelict steamers, the hulls of rotting barges—endless material. I made a series of the Delce lanes, that interconnect between the back yards; each house had a mast in the garden, up which two lines of washing might be hung, in nautical fashion, to flap away high over the garden. Here were fine etching subjects. I was working away when two old people appeared. They paused. "Doin' a survey? Shockin' isn't it?" "Well," I said, "it has character."

"Character! Well, it's got that all right!"

Down at the Saturday morning junk and antique market, which we never missed, I asked a stall-owner "Do you mind me looking?": "Your looking is my living, Sir."

A friendly black and white cat (called Wellington) adopted us as cats will, and provided some indoor subjects. We bought an Edwardian front door from a man who was replacing it with a modern one. "It's going to cost you," he warned us. "How much?" "Well—say a *pound*?" Everywhere in the Delce, with its history of hard times, we found this sense of people wanting you to save your money and not waste it. They would hardly let you buy anything—"Oh dear, I'm afraid that's going to be at least fifty pence—" Everything could be bought in the Delce—wood, bricks, cement, paint, board—a timber yard along the street. Supermarket, Indian shops open all round the clock, eight a.m. to eight p.m. all day and every day, Sunday and even Xmas day. "If we *are* closed, just give the door a knock." Fish and chips along the Delce Road; Take-away Indian curry five doors up open every night to one a.m. Off-licence, butcher, undertaker, greengrocery (along the street in that order)—all requirements catered for . . . it was a Hogarthean effect sometimes to see the varied races; turbanned elderly Sikhs, old ladies that could have been in my earlier pictures, shoppers, Dickensian workmen. . . . Two tophatted mutes lifting a coffin above the crowd to place in the hearse—Eighteenth Century London. . . . I made many pictures, in my earlier formalised manner, from such inspiration.

Nearby there was even a sheet-metal works from which I could buy an eight-by-four foot sheet of ten gauge zinc for etching. For a slight extra fee, they would work out the most economic way of cutting it into the varied dimensions I required. "It's not in much demand anymore, though—used to use it for roofing extensively, but there's no call anymore." "What *do* you use it for, then?" "Well, you were lucky with this lot—the order was cancelled. It was got for lining Pakistani coffins—they send them back to Bangladesh, you known—"

A Victorian church was being demolished nearby, and we went down and bought—for the usual pound or so—a number of classic fragments: capitals, bits of rope-moulding and archway. An obliging van was found to bring it home, and we set up these classic ruin motifs among the trees in the lyrical garden, now a masterpiece of space creation, considering how much was now in it.

I regularly took plates to London to continue my series. I was etching at Hammersmith Bridge, an area for oddities, certainly. An old woman of about 100 stopped and offered me a tomato—"Your throat often goes off," she said. Which was true enough, as it happened. A middle-aged drunk appeared, at the happy point, weaving along. "Mon-thassa *real* work of art, I'm telling you!"—with an air of immense seriousness and self-importance—"I'll look at it again when I come back." This said grandly as if he were going to purchase it for the Tate Gallery. Later, regrettably, he did come back. It's always the only thing they remember. He began to stop every passerby to make them look at my work, as if he was my partner and acting on my orders. "Look at what he has done only with *Scratching*." He even stopped passing motorists who slowed in the traffic—"I must show it to *this* gentleman—"

Outside Rochester there were walks of interest, if one took a bus to nearby Cuxton or Sole Street. We could go by train for convenient short distances, and walk to the Dickensian Leather Bottel at Cobham for lunch. Once we were taking a short cut by some immense strawberry fields. I bent down to tie a shoelace. I noticed in the fields that continued into the valley below a gesticulating figure. Two men then leapt into a Landrover and roared up to me in a cloud of dust.

"Were you eating those strawberries?" I wasn't. "We saw you bend down, you were against the sky." I was tying my lace. "Well," with relief, "that's all right, if you *haven't* been eating them. They're all sprayed with poisonous pesticide—you can see the notices. . . ." Indeed, all around were boards with skull and crossbones and the word *Strawbs*—an interesting variant on the pub-sign and hoarding communication in the landscape motif to which I was so attached.

Opposite our house was the Mason's Arms, a corner public house with a white balustraded Edwardian railing along the top. This rather pleasant feature unfortunately finally fell off soon after we arrived; but the landlord, Mick, had another interest for us—his labrador, Whisky. An aged, roaming old collie, lame in the hind legs, got at her a few weeks before he finally passed on; but he had obviously been impelled by fate to be the means of providing us with our dog, Sweep. Mick said we could choose a pup, and not knowing that one chooses neither the quiet one who won't mix, nor the over-boisterous show-off, we selected the puppy whose characteristics combined both of these faults. Consequently he was a difficult, highly intelligent, self-willed animal, although goodnatured to a fault. The fault was in kissing any passing child with an all-encompassing lick—not always to the pleasure of the mothers who had read a great deal of anti-canine literature, and did not realise that saliva is essentially antiseptic. Sweep would tear any piece of card or paper—or his own bed—to pieces, with a concentrated ferocity. A piece of bread held forgetfully in your hand would be torn away, and you would get a good bite with needle teeth into the bargain. He tore half of Catriona's dress off her in the garden; and wallpaper off the walls by the roll. He had only just succeeded in getting born, by the expedient of, while emerging, kicking in the head of the litter-brother behind him—a forgivable action, given the circumstances.

Who would have a dog? That is the end of your freedom, although you didn't known you had any until you so lost it. You must get back: he must be let out/be fed/have his walk/will be upset/anyway, goodbye. What are your successes as an artist now? Your eminence at having made a few pounds in cultural connivance? Here is an end to your vanities. They won't wash with him. I want my walk and where's my ring? (Ear-splitting barks. My god, the neighbours). Now for the injections, the boosts, the endless visits to the vet, the ears red and inflamed, the next injection, come back for the next four days each evening for treatment, the pills, my god the expense. This will make you appreciate the Health Service—suppose you had to pay as much for *your* medicaments? Yes, keeping a dog makes you think, for a change. You're not in the cosy sphere of aesthetics now. You won't philosophise on your walks.

You'll hope he won't commit some offence to embarrass you. As for guests to the house! Who would have thought so many people were terrified of teeth? And why do dogs always go to those frightened people? Worried, hospitable, they edge up to reassure them with a wide toothy smile. Why do the myriad books on the fancy never tell you of what dogs really do? The mounting of anyone and anything, the marking of every new place, indoor and out? "Well, I think we'll just leave him outside in the car anyway." Oh, was the window slightly open, and the car in the shade? And when *did* we last let him out. . . .

Ah; but now addicted, you even decide to get another, as well! This time it was a finely-bred pedigree. Maltese Toy Terrier. Not only the smallest breed, but for some reason—"Well, we didn't want to breed from him or show him"—probably the smallest dog in England—or the world, halfway between a guinea-pig and a rabbit. With the spirit of a lion and the inclination to attack Alsatians, stealing around the back to select a good piece of leg, pausing, fitting the teeth carefully, then, *bite* . . . but the large dog thinks he is a puppy, and therefore that a ferocious and defensive motherdog is just around the corner. Sweep, however, comes to aid the little dog, and the fight is on. Dragging them apart, you find that all the blood comes from the largest dog having bitten his own tongue. The children all around the swings are crying and screaming, the owners vie for taking the blame for it all, and another walk is—nearly—over.

Hero, the Maltese, with his high forehead and huge mental capacity, is of course the cleverest animal in the world. And how many words they soon know. Everything has to be spelt out between the humans in the end. Sweep learnt to catch a ring thrown high in the air, with an energetic enthusiasm that no other dog up Jackson's could—or more sensibly wished—to equal. An accidental somersault was developed into a further trick to order—spinning in the air as the ring is caught, from a lying-down position. This always caught the crowds as well. Then the lying down and refusing to move on the walk from the house until asked if he likes "Fish and Chips?"

"Bit of obstinacy, there," a neighbour rather unfairly comments, seeing the first part of this result of intensive training.

The Maltese, as a motif, appears in very many paintings from the earliest times, as this old and undiluted breed is a symbol of faith; and most pictures prior to the aesthetic movement could be read from left to right symbolically. I invented a Renaissance joke about the Maltese. A famous princeling orders a huge picture from some Raphael or Leonardo. It must have all the trappings—still life, angels, Madonnas, Crucifixion, Deposition, Flayings, Martyrdoms, all the subjects, and set in one great Marriage at Cana—the artist works day and night—at last, the great tableau is wheeled in, groaning upon the stretcher with the weight of so much imagery. The princeling contemplates it, says nothing. "Do you like it, and please you Sire?" It's all *right*," says the princeling—"but where's the Maltese?"

As the dogs grew, we attended many of the summer festival and carnival days in the nearby villages, where there was always an exemption dog show. On gala days, Sweep might be taken home with a rosette at his collar, for the dog with the Most Appealing Eyes, or the Dog the Judge would Most Like to Take Home. But eventually, although we had enjoyed the timelessness of these summer events, we were disappointed that usually some pedigree would sweep up all the prizes, and felt that the mongrel classes should have their own events, and exclude the superior dogs. Hero, of course, could enter the upper class category, but he trembled with fear so much, and showed off, tail down, to so little advantage when being handled by the Judge, that it seemed pointless to enter him. On all these days I of course built up a huge file of visual reference, and produced whole series of small plates on varying outdoor aspects. These I found were much desired by people who liked my larger plates, but had no room for them. The small etchings were eagerly collected and can of course fit into any corner. I etched rain, snow—our first real winter in Rochester was one of heavy snow, and I went out with plate and mirror and worked at a series on the spot, a useful variant of effect on the familiar subjects.

We took Sweep to Brighton on one occasion, but the seaside never does seem suitable for dogs. Following a thrown ball, he hopped over a breakwater, only to fall ten feet down the unsuspected drop the other side. However, recovering, he saw a large piece of iced currant cake in the distance and rushed over to gnaw at it. On catching him up, we found that (as he had) it was not cake, but a sea-worn piece of masonry in the very semblance of that illusion. This might suggest that dogs are sometimes neither colourblind nor only actuated by scent. The yellowish mortar was exactly like cake; and indeed we now keep the stone upon a plate with a knife, in our kitchen, and many visitors have licked their lips with unrewarded anticipation.

On one walk Sweep leapt for a small red rubber ball we had unwisely bought him. It disappeared. He looked round, surprised—where was it? Lodged in his own gullet! He began to look a bit dazed, as well he might with the air supply cut off. Fortunately he stood still. Opening his mouth, I could feel the top of the ball deep down. The books said, force an obstruction further down—but then, suppose it still stuck? With no reference to his feelings, I thrust my hand down into his throat, which happily seemed to stretch, and just managed to get a finger or so round the ball. A few minutes later he had forgotten all about such a narrow squeak—which was about all he could utter in fact for some time afterwards.

Sweep was not free of varied crimes—basically of negligence and carelessness, both on his part and our own. Taking my eye off him for a second in a newsagent's I discovered he had marked a whole case of of paperbacks newly arrived. Honesty demanded I pay for any even lightly affected, and I arrived home with twenty pounds' worth of copies of *Orgies of Ancient Rome*.

On another occasion, in a restaurant, the owner kindly brought him a dish of scraps. With some horror, I then noticed a large trifle on a stand nearby. Half-gone, and with tooth indents, it told its own story. I was obliged to take the smile off the kind restauranteur by telling him, but restored it by paying for the whole of the expensive trifle. We then somewhat shocked him by eating the half remaining.

I exhibited some of my low-toned portraits at the Royal Society of Portrait Painters exhibitions over these years; but eventually gave it up as I did not wish to concentrate on that line. I showed at the Royal West of England Academy, and was later elected an Associate. I painted a number of pictures using the subject of the Vet's waiting room—one had ample time to practice the memory trick, and I made whole folders of memory studies. I exhibited some of these paintings in the R.W.A. and heard a lady say to her friend: "Oh do come and look at this—you won't like it."

Our next door neighbour was an elderly man with an ailing wife who did not long survive. He had worked all his life on the Short Sunderland Flying-Boats. These marvellous images of my youth—I have seen them land at Brighton in the shimmering blue sea of the Thirties—were designed and manufactured at Rochester, and half the labour force here were employed by them. To imagine these great silver fish wheeling about and descending like swans into the Medway is a picture that seems one with the galleons and men of war. The last flying-boat left (a dodo paradoxically of the air) flew in about 1984. We went to see her, now hauled ashore and in a large shed in the dockyard. Archaic and strutted, she looked simply old-fashioned, something off a cigarette card—could she have ever flown to Australia?

I painted not only versions of the life about me, but in a reflective mood all manner of subjects—some I had painted before and lost or destroyed; some I had meant to paint but never done so. I painted my grandmother, as a child, being shown by her grandmother the fierce wooden carving in the centre of the Swiss village church, of Christ being hammered on the Cross. (I have seen this frightful image myself). "See what the bad men are doing," my grandmother had been told, and never forgot it. I painted a canvas of an enthusiastically friendly Sweep making a leap at the mutes carrying a long box out from the Delce undertaker early one morning—this happened, and they laughed at this strange onslaught with Mediaeval humour. I painted a scene of a market in Paris—chicken being treated with insensitive callousness and simply stuffed into a plastic bag, alive, all among the other purchases. I would call this a real horror subject; not Dracula Frankenstein romanticism, but real absence of thought and feeling. This kind of picture, which makes a point, is a different kind of picture to one that is only concerned with tone, colour, atmosphere, and all the rest of it. A picture with a point to make—even an angry objection to state—is still not literature; it should at the same time be painted with a due awareness of all the abstract principles of picture-making, or it won't make its point anyway, but will be only absurd. Art has many dimensions, but one has to be careful.

.   .   .   .   .   .

A visit to some relatives staying in Broadstairs necessitated us taking the dogs with us, to which they did not object. We also had with us a third dog: Tina, Sweep's particular friend. They had met one day at Jackson's, and seemed to recognise each other on sight. The two owners, surprised at this, conversed on the subject of the difficulties of holidays, and at once a plan was made, and kept to ever after, that both should be available as a refuge for each other's dogs, on a moment's notice even, if mutually convenient, and in any case for planned regular vacations. As the dogs always delighted in each other's company, and seemed to regard the other's house as a second home, this arrangement worked well. Tina was black with a white front, quite typical of the local cross—in addition, she had an interestingly Doberman style in ears, of great character, that I have tried to paint accurately time and again. The bitch's nature is entirely different to that of the dog, as they actually seem to want to obey you. On the occasion of the Broadstairs expedition we spent a day on the sands that was not without incident. We bathed, and the two dogs splashed happily, working up an appetite. While we were drying ourselves, Sweep observed the nearby camp of a family at present in the sea. There sat—deserted—deck-chairs, towels, thermos, baskets—and packs of sandwiches ready for their return. Suddenly, Sweep was at the sandwiches. We got him away, gathered up what was left, repacking them and hoping no one would notice. It seemed crueller to tell them, see them put off their lunch, made unhappy. They all

returned, wet and boisterous, and the Sweep-disturbed delicacies were munched with cries of enjoyment, while we tried to look the other way. Just then, up came an irate dog-hater, who accused Sweep of unpleasant and anti-social habits on another part of the beach. Sweep advancing to make friends, the dog-hater struck at him with a tennis racket he was holding. Of course, there was no real danger—he couldn't have hit the agile animal, but I thought it necessary to object; so the beach was presented with the image of two snarling humans, slowly and carefully backing away from each other as they muttered imprecations, to the embarrassment of their respective friends and families.

. . . . . .

One afternoon we carelessly locked ourselves out of the house, and decided to ask the local police to help us. A young constable and a police-woman kindly came around, but to our naïve surprise appeared to carry no magical skeleton keys. However, after we had scaled the back gate through the over-hanging foliage, Catriona succeeded in entering the house through a dog-flap I had cut in one of the panels of the back door. "Don't you wish you could do that, Jane?" said the young constable to his confrère—or consoeur—but she forebore to reply.

At the market, among all the clutter and rubbish, there was always a treasure to be found somewhere. Catriona came upon a drawing by Will Owen, illustrator of the W. W. Jacobs stories of the crews of tramp steamers. It seemed he had attended the Rochester Art School, and some relative must still have remained in the area, for the drawing to appear on a stall. I found an oil of the Twenties, with Matisse's *La dance* painted in the background with a sophistication that proved the painter someone of note: but absence of any documentation makes all attribution a matter of hazard. A large Landseer engraving of his famous black and white Newfoundland subject was a pleasurable find. At one stall the copy of a Watts allegory—not too badly done, and almost of its period, took my eye. Supposing that such information might be of use to the stall-owner—even elicit some grateful thanks for my expertise, perhaps—I pointed to the canvas and said: "Watts' Love and Life."
"*I* don't know, Mate!" said the stall-owner—"'how should *I* know?'"

Now and again our house became so crowded with various frames, Edwardian doors, railings, excess works of art and so forth that the only solution, in order to even move about, was to rent a skip—a great yellow iron bin—to be dumped outside, and in which we could happily hurl all our excess belongings. What a temptation it is! Everything goes in—it is surprising one really needs anything, there are so many things you can do without. Why did one acquire all this rubbish, if you can't even recall what it was once the skip goes off? Within an hour, or so, anyway, the skip will be picked clean by others eager to load themselves with your cast-offs. I threw away a number of old proofs from a catalogue of my pictures. Two down-at-heel idlers were carefully going through the pages.

"'E's an artist, then, what lives 'ere—"

A long pause, and even longer look at the work.

"Not very good though."

I gave a number of clothes that no longer fitted me to the local Oxfam shop. Chatting to a friend in there later, I mentioned that my old suit was hanging on a peg close by us.

"Well, Michael," said my friend, "I'll be saying goodbye—" he shook the sleeve of the suit jacket and departed.

On one of our walks we came upon a house violently on fire, the upper floor roaring tongues of flame from the front windows. At the rear, an old man, somewhat drunk, was looking out of the back window on the same floor, while two or three people in the garden tried to open the door of a garage in the yard. "There's a ladder in it," cried one. Eventually we got the door open; there was the ladder, but padlocked to the wall! It was like a dream of continual inadequacies. We tried every way to loose it, but it was no use. We were still at it when the fire-engine, with its own ladder, arrived to save us all the trouble. Out next door neighbour had an adult son of reduced intellect; as we sat in the garden, or sipped our wine at the decorative iron table under our tree, he would stand in the garden, tall, thin and expressionless, a tireless and disturbing spectre at our feast. Eventually, still staring, he would get a kitchen chair, and arranging it carefully, still without taking his eyes off us, he would sit down, and continue staring. One night, there was a terrible crash as if a wardrobe had fallen two stories; then the sound of an ambulance. We got up to offer help, but it was unnecessary. He had either fallen, or thrown himself, down the stairs; but it was the end of him.

The atmosphere, compared even to the life in St. John's Wood, was one of village-like closeness. One evening the lights failed all over Medway; and for a while we could only think of the poor blind lady—well over eighty—who lived four doors up; would she need help? Until of course, it occurred to us. We did wake up another old lady, who, coming to in the dark, was more upset than if we'd let her sleep through it. As regards the blind lady, one of our neighbours said it gave her the horrors to see the blind lady cooking on a gas ring. "Surely there *must* be someone up there," said our neighbour—"there *must*. Otherwise—"

The mangle had come with us from London, and now I at last converted it to a press, for one glorious moment. I had made a large plate of the Café de Tribunaux at Dieppe—the favourite subject of Sickert and others: curiously, not at all typical of France or a port, but being an Austrian Chalet-type beer house in style. However, Sickert had made it typify Dieppe, so—as with the Beatles' zebra—I too had seen it through the eyes of art and romanticism, and made a studio plate of it. My Kimber press would not accommodate the width, so I had the rollers of the mangle turned smooth, fitted a bed, and tightened the

Michael Blaker

pressure; the castings of the gearing snapped. With difficulty, I found a workshop to weld the pieces together, and tried again. A perfect print! One more try, and the main casting snapped across the weld. It was hopeless; but I had at least the one print. I sent it to the Royal Academy summer exhibition and it sold thirty-five of the edition, which I had printed by a professional. But the mangle had proved its worth, and in the end had shown a profit over all that exhaustion and difficulty. At least, I think so. The print was also reproduced in the Royal Academy Illustrated, which pleases an artist.

It was suggested to me by a print firm at this time that I might undertake a commission for them, and a day was set aside for a meeting with the committee who would consider the many points of the scheme, which would involve the preparation of a whole edition for some large sum. I did not particularly want to do it, as it sounded like a good deal of labour, and I would prefer to work through my editions print by print. A whole edition can be tedious. However, at the relevant hour we presented ourselves at the door of a heavily fortified office. I say we, because for some strange reason Sweep had to be present; possibly the exigencies of the day meant that he could not otherwise have been fed or let out.

Inside, I apologised for the mongrel's presence. There were some raised eyebrows, as it was all meant to be terribly impressive and very high-powered. We all filed up to a board-room, and the celebrated members of the board—at least, they looked as if they felt celebrated—took their seats, in an impressive hush broken only by Sweep's continual whining. "Now, what we have in mind, Mr. Blaker, is for you to visit this site—probably need to stay there for a few days, but you'll be able to afford that out of the substantial fee—" "I'm very sorry," I said, getting up, "but I'm afraid my dog is eating your wastepaper basket—" It was true; he had nearly reduced the wicker to shreds, spreading it all over the carpet . . . "Perhaps you wouldn't mind if I fed him," I said; "he may settle down." They waited, pencils tapping, through the tedious, bark interrupted ceremony of opening the can of Pedigree Chum. Eventually we got down again to the equally tedious commission—we were interrupted by a wild cry—"Stop him! They're *precious*!" Sweep was sniffing, with a kind of eager interest, as if about to devour them also, a stack of signed limited edition photolithos (if you can fairly call a photolitho a limited edition, which by its term presupposes a print taken manually from a limited-life plate by the artist or an equivalent hand-printer). "They've only just arrived," someone wailed—"they've got to go out tomorrow—oh get rid of him, get rid of him!"

"Well," I said, getting up, "perhaps we had better leave it for today! Perhaps you'd like to get in touch with me if you want to proceed with the idea—" I was glad to leave, and fortunately, not surprisingly, they never did get in touch with me.

With our interest in dogs, we always visited Crufts, and got much good material subject-wise. The owners seemed to suit their dogs . . . the two went together; and the poodle people were totally different to the bull terrier fanciers. I made several pictures and one very large composition on this theme.

Feeling the need of a form of transport for excursions into the neighbouring countryside, Catriona took driving lessons, eventually passed her test, and bought a Morris Traveller. In 1982 I also branched out somewhat, and took over the editorship of the *Journal* of the R.E.; the founding editor, Charles Bartlett, wishing to pass it on. I was made a co-opted member of the R.E. Council and began to enter more fully into the life of the Society, helping to hang exhibitions, and participating in demonstrations of methods of print making at the various new communal days that both the new Gallery at Bankside and a new and enthusiastic younger organisational department encouraged. The new premises were formally opened by the Queen, and the ceremony had much of a local village flavour about it, with the Queen raised on only a small dais, and being very much a part of the crowd of artists present. Charles Knight, the watercolourist, was there, who had taught me at Art School, and whom I had not met for many years. It is admirable how much the Queen has always been so close to the public as a presence. I remember when she was a princess going round the corner of our street and seeing her being photographed in the centre of a group of officers outside a hotel, she being the Honorary Colonel, I believe. Then, riding over to Lewes on my motorbike, finding a small crowd of children waving as the Queen and the Duke emerged from their car. I have seen her in processions along Victoria Street with visiting Monarchs in carriages—one seems many times to have waited for the moment when the Royal car approaches. At Rochester she unveiled a plaque and opened the new formation of the High Street in 1984, going over to talk with a young artist—somewhat of a local personality—and accepting a painting from him. Her official entourage tried to hurry her onwards; but no, they kept talking away, laughing and chatting. If one can have this conception of her busy personality, no doubt others have it also; and the suggestion must be that the time she gives to her public is almost all-encompassing.

We were fortunate that almost immediately opposite our house—just round the corner from the printer where I had the Journal produced, and adjoining the Mason's Arms, was the garage workshop of Gypsy Dave Norman (he wrestled professionally under this title) always ready to restart the Traveller at a moment's notice, to service it and to see to M.O.T. welding, and all the other ills that such old wrecks are heir to—slowly, the car was nursed along; although finally it seemed best to pass her along the line, as the fabric of her chassis was beginning to resemble a leaf skeleton. Also, having parked her one day on a hillroad near St. Margaret's field, we were surprised on returning with the dogs to see a flash of blue in a shrubbery; and found that she had run down hill in our absence, avoiding both the gateposts of one house and the front door and bay window of another in order to bury herself sensibly in a grove of elder trees. Reversed out, no damage had been done whatsoever, though she might well have careered round a corner and down a street, gaining momentum the while, to who knows what cumulative tragedy.

Almost at the same time as we arrived, Rochester began to reorganise herself. The first Dickens Week was evolved, in which we all dressed in Victorian costume; and for four days or more every shop assistant, including the post office staff, dressed in high collars and frockcoats and long dresses. Events were held, theatrical performances and street entertainments abounded, and we joined in all the processions, meeting the special Dickensian train from Victoria, and permitting Hero to join in with us, the crowds lining the route giving him a special cheer—particularly when he left the procession violently at the Star Hill junction to attack a dog in the crowd.

In addition to this participation in the yearly festivities, we acted, one year, in a production of *Great Expectations*. I, as Compeyson, had nightly to be shot (in a variation of the plot for the sake of the theatre), making my escape from the stage as the lights were dimmed. One evening when they were not, my exit as the body revived was greeted with derisive laughter; however, one learns to survive such moments. We were in a Dickens Quiz on the local Radio, (in which I impersonated Mr. Jefferson Brick, the scurrilous journalist) and a panel of Dickens experts had to guess our identities before an audience in the Corn Exchange. Catriona joined an Experimental Theatre Group, and we painted scenery, wrote songs, acted, and made the artefacts for other productions, including a Dada figure and a Venus de Milo made of sugar for

Tom Stoppard's *Artist descending a staircase*. We also lent a good deal of our Victorian collections for another production, at the King's School. Catriona was dressing the set; and it was extremely strange to walk about these recreated rooms full of objects that belonged to different times of one's life—all set in a house one didn't know—another dream made manifest. We busked in the street in Victorian costume, playing a selection of Victorian songs such as *Granpa's Waltz*, from old songsheets bought in the market. The profits from our bucket of coins—quite a heavy load, and taking many hours to count into separate bags of the correct coinage for banking—we donated to the Battersea Dogs Home, receiving a courteous and friendly letter of thanks from the Director. We also performed in other Charity Concerts, with recorder and guitar, or recorder and piano; my old jazz band experience being a useful asset. Catriona, having given up etching for music, was now a piano accompanist and recorder teacher at the school at the end of the street; and even I was called in to give some advice for a school committee of children involved in a publishing project. "Have you all voiced an opinion regarding the choice of designs?" I asked them. "All had a go," one of the boys obligingly translated for their benefit.

As we stood in the street, busking, a large Continental container lorry pulled up. It contained nothing but bunches of chrysanthemums—hundreds of them—and each of these large paper-swathed cones held twelve other more conveniently proportioned bunches, also wrapped in paper. The driver impassively descended, moved one of the enormous cones from the truck, and advanced upon us, presenting the bouquet to Catriona with Italian gallantry. Returning to the lorry, he drove off, waving gaily. We stopped a passing Victorian soldier in a red tunic, and asked him to distribute eleven of the bunches to the Victorian beauties parading. Consequently, as we played, the street was increasingly decorated with the colourful blooms borne by the promenading ladies. There seemed to be flowers everywhere in the end—a non-diminishing abundance of them.

Catriona sung in the Rochester Choral Society, whose productions at the Cathedral were grand affairs for the town, with all seats filled. The Cathedral as a concert hall and venue for such events was full of atmosphere, and I would attend rehearsals and sketch from the shadows of the Norman columns or pulpit as the afternoon light faded and the leader lectured his choir for the evening performance. It was rather like being back with John Greenwood in the Grammar School hall on a November afternoon. The Orchestral Society joined with other choirs in a massed musical event at the Festival Hall; and as usual I was an eager fan.

When painting scenery for a play at the Medway Little Theatre I was of no sort of use. But Catriona's stunning vista of Exmoor under snow received its own personal applause as the curtain rose. Although willing to help, my own vision seems to prefer a smaller canvas, as it were.

We discovered that an earlier resident of our house was a composer, Percy

Whitlock, who was born in Chatham in 1903, and died at Bournemouth in 1946, where he became borough organist. His particular achievement was a long and much admired organ sonata in C minor that he wrote in 1938.

This kind of historical association is always pleasing. Curiously, the house had never before been owned, only rented. Originally built by a local stonemason as an income source for his daughter, the rented-out condition had been the reason for the original fireplaces—even the range—not having been destroyed. The local village character of the Medway Towns was sustained in their accent and manners of expression. At a boot fair on the Great Lines an old lady said to her grand-daughter: "*Lo*, 'Ginia aintcha growed evensin las *Sad*-dy."

．　．　．　．　．

In 1979 we were in Paris, where I made a whole new set of plates, using a mirror to reverse the image. I etched the Lapin Agile, the famous bar where the cubist painters and others had foregathered. Now, it still remained like the part of an old village. Painted and repainted, tourist thronged or not, Montmartre remains full of picturesque elements and corners. I see no reason to stop using the place as an inspiring subject—I have been doing so for nearly forty years; and the buildings remain much the same on their hill, although the view below is spoilt with square blocks inspired by the very cubism developed in the rural heights and cosy studios of this eminence. No doubt the very elevation of this section of the city has contributed to the artistic production—there is something elevating, obviously, about elevation; and although no real painter, it is true, wishes to be associated with the mere nonsense produced in the Place de Tertre, the actual scene is of people, houses, and details—what more could Rembrandt himself want, as he stands there with his etching-plate? The day and the view is yours to take.

I etched some rather different aspects to my more usual approach of objective recording: an old man turning the handle of a children's roundabout in the Bois de Boulogne seemed an allegory of oppressed futility—or what you will; at least it seemed to have something of more than the moment about it. Another large black and white plate was of a mother and child by the horror images of the ghost train in the fair in the park at St. Cloud. I see no reason why one should not paint horror images, if they come to one. They are the other side of the coin to the sunshine. Nevertheless there is no reason to suppose that an artist who takes the subject of violence is protesting against it. Horror and violence may be the only things that can sufficiently impress his jaded vision into seeing. Goya must have enjoyed those marvellous but appalling etchings of his; they represented not his abhorrence but his sadistic pleasure—the horrified attraction that draws the crowd to a street accident or would to a public hanging. We appear original, perhaps, mainly due to tiredness and lack of

concentration as we grow older—we are not so like those who have impressed us; a lack of conviction has arisen in us in the perfection of these artists we have previously taken as our models. Perhaps we are irritated that we have been so impressed at all by works that we now believe we can equal or even surpass, and we begin to assert ourselves. This is perhaps why artists cannot believe in religion. Traditionally, they have created all the visual equipment for making people Believe. They are the Backstage crew. If the artist believes in the religion he paints he may consider himself divine or divinely inspired while producing it, and the result might be a very bad picture. When artists do have this conviction, they are subject to a vanity that spoils their work. Possibly, religion is mainly a real comfort to the artless—in more ways than one. To the complex it is just one more thing to worry themselves about—but perhaps, after all, there is a certain comfort in that.

I etched another inspiring Paris scene—a corner or junction of streets, and on the side of a building the fading painted advertisement still remaining—a peeling fresco from aeons ago—Chocolate Menier. I made, subsequently, several larger paintings and etchings from this subject, including a favourite motif of a little old lady with a long stick of bread under her arm, and her hair still in the Japanese combed-back style of the Nineties—the style my grandmother always kept, and one which has now perhaps finally and at last faded from the streets and the world. I had carried some twenty grounded plates with me on this trip, and filled them all—standing in the street, or posing Catriona on a railing before a Metro entrance—news-stands, kiosks, bits of the everyday world—these are the best subjects. They mean something to everyone—everyone sees them and everyone relates. And then, I happen to like detail, whatever it is; it does not have to be significant in itself—merely put there by the hand of man, and the more carelessly the better, as far as I am concerned, *so long as it is there!*

Near the somewhat horribly remodelled and rebuilt part of the city that had once been rundown but at least what we like to think of as Parisian, we came upon the studio and gallery of the sculptor Bourdelle, with the rooms still as he might have left them—dusty, old sinks, modelling stands—he might have just stepped out for a moment. And then, the great gallery of his work presented in a formal setting adjoining. The French, as with the Rodin Museum, are good at this sense of living atmosphere. In the Museum of Modern Art there was at one time a reconstruction of Brancusi's studio, complete with the endless column and his old bed, upon which my companion sank with a sigh of relief, being told at once by an indignant custodian to remove themselves from the exhibit. Imagine the Yellow House still surviving at Arles, and a Van Gogh museum next to it—what a mecca for pilgrimage! It is almost worth rebuilding it facsimile.

In 1980 we made an etching expedition to Lake Como, and I discovered a different kind of subject altogether—villas, placid lake—even palm trees and exoticism, and the languid charm and restaurants of Bellagio, where I made several plates. We discovered one or two antique shops, and were discussing the chances of interesting acquisitions with the owner. "No, there is not much in Italy," she said. "My husband he goes to London for much of our stock." We were a little disappointed at this, but said we knew the London markets well, and had been patrons of the Bell Street market. "Ah yes—my husband is at Bell Street this weekend."

The plates resulting from these sorties in France and Italy became the stock for our own subsistence for the following months, and my time was mainly taken in printing, colouring and marketing. The details of business, letters, filing, accounts, took much time and as always took up the moments so essential for not only the actual contemplation but the making of new subjects.

We drove one day to the Thames Barrier in order to obtain details of craft for a commission that I much enjoyed. Both Catriona and myself boarded a strange flat motorboat, the driver in a kind of well beneath us. In this we chased various craft in order to obtain a satisfactory view of them. Both the driver and I by an odd chance were wearing identical black and red striped t-shirts, which gave us the appearance of Gilbert and Sullivan pirates. On this occasion we did not take Sweep to give the final touch. In 1982 we obtained bicycles and set off from Rochester one wintry day in September on a camping trip, tents and sleeping bags and cooking utensils hung from our machines. Catriona had organised the whereabouts of the farms and campsites where we might stay, and the first evening was spent in a windswept dusk; the rain beating down, an oak tree swaying above us, and Catriona, in a black plastic dustbin sack to cover her, frying the supper on our gas-cylinder stove. Next morning we struck camp early, and skimmed down the hills into the Weald of Kent, where in the lyric complacency of late summer we looked at village churches, bought flagons of Biddenden cider, stayed at a campsite ringed with orchards and vineyards, and visited Sissinghurst, where high in a tower was of all things the very machine used by Leonard and Virginia Woolf when they founded the Hogarth Press. On our tour we took a loop around Kent, at the back of Hythe, proceeding through mysterious valleys towards Canterbury. Once, on stopping to retrieve my cap, which had fallen off, I felt an eye could be upon me, and looking up, saw that the hills at the entrance to the valley made ideal look-out towers. Surely, at this point, I would have been the perfect target for the Saxon or Roman sentry who must have at some time sat there. Canterbury was a fit end for this wheeled pilgrimage, and on our return we were unwilling to live indoors, and set up camp in the garden, continuing to live like nomads. This very much worried Sweep (back from Tina's) who stayed in the bedroom indoors, although Hero insisted on sleeping under canvas with us, presumably for the purpose of defence. Subsequently plates resulting from this tour were extremely useful to us: Wealden cottages at Smarden, and old houses sunk in the excess of vegetation of late summer; windmills and oast-houses, and all at their best, we had seen from Tenterden to Faversham.

Our expedition the following summer was also a camping one, but this time

by means of the Morris Traveller. The original model had been sold to a young couple who did not object to its state, but only wanted it for the season. We felt somewhat guilty only a week afterwards to see it abandoned by the side of the main London Road, but subsequently discovered that the fault had been rectified. I had been unwell that year over a fairly long period by reason of falling down stairs; and muscular pains in my back had frequently locked me immobilely so that I could barely move on waking, and hardly walk. Printing was abandoned for a while and I got no better as summer progressed. Eventually, with dogs, tents, water-colours, and plates unused for weeks, I was put into the front seat of the Traveller, and we set out for Suffolk, every lurch of the car seeming to shake my head off at the condyles. At the conclusion of the Dartford tunnel it was necessary to throw a fee of fifty pence into a receptacle. The officer in charge stopped us. "And it will be a pound each extra for those dogs," he said. We groped for the money, but he waved us on: "I was only joking!—have a good holiday . . .!"

Once into the warmth and countryside of picturesque Suffolk, and my spirits began to improve. Groaning tended almost to cease, and I forgot even to complain. We found a campsite, and Catriona put up the tent. To sleep on the hard ground was so much of a purgatory that it cured me; I was able to move more easily than for weeks past by the next morning; I even took up my watercolours and made traditional style attempts at the somewhat unpromising subjects of vivid blue tents and touring cars—tinting them, however, in sepia. The dogs enjoyed walking—or running—and rolling in the mud in Sudbury meadows, while I stayed by the river making wash drawings where Gainsborough had worked before me . . . all this soon restored me, and within a week I was setting up tents and pitching them and fully recovered. There was a wealth of new material to be gleaned here, and such a harvest-style expression is the right one. I sat in the stubble near Dedham, with Constable's black elms about, and did much work at Flatford Mill, the surroundings of which still demanded and received artistic attention. We got to Norwich, where I saw an inspiring exhibition in the museum, of the Dutch influence in etching on the Norwich school. I at once made some plates happily influenced by this Rembrandt—Hobbema—Ruisdael—Crome—Cotman aesthetic. Indeed all about were the actual sites of the works of the English masters, and we were even encamped in what had been Cornard Wood.

Catriona had recently given her lecture (illustrated with slides) on the work of Gainsborough, both at the King's School in Rochester and to the Tunbridge Wells Art Society. I had made a small version of the famous showbox and the glass oils, the whole illuminated by interior candles and diffused with screens, as in the original. The talk had been a great success wherever given; and to visit the haunts of the painter—and indeed his house—was a bonus to our trip.

On leaving the Sudbury site we had driven to a strange and almost haunted place set among trees that were like an oasis in a great plain. We approached down old concrete roads and runways. This had been a Battle of Britain aerodrome . . . were there not ghosts here, to those who knew or remembered? Certainly the camp had a military-like discipline to the rules posted everywhere; and here we were nearly brought to a halt in our trip, if not career. While fixing a new can of gas to our stove, it was incorrectly punctured; and a stream of highly explosive liquid gas poured forth, vaporising slightly at ground level. Some nearby Dutch campers fled for cover—it appeared they had seen something of the sort happen before. Very luckily we had not yet lit our second gas-ring, and no other lit flames were nearby—what good fortune. With the contents hissing over me, I ran the sixty yards along the lane nearby with dynamic speed, and hurled the can to the centre of a pond, where it hissed and bubbled, and the moorhens fled. The Dutch couples' subsequent reminiscences inclined us towards the good old camp-fire with twigs for future expeditions; it seems the cloud of vapour ignites and rushes along at ground level, in and out of tents, exploding as it goes. . . .

Sweep, having enjoyed himself so thoroughly running in the meadows and splashing violently about in the Gainsborough shallows, now developed a sore on his back that gave him the appearance of an uncared-for stray. A vet was found, and we were once again in the familiar setting of the waiting-room. A large fibre-glass panda stood oddly among the patients, a slot in the top requesting contributions, and posters of close-ups of otters and badgers smiled down as if conscious of their conservation. There entered a lady with a labrador puppy, which took one look around and rolled on the floor in a fit of terror. Every other dog there at once took on a look of perfect obedience and disapproval. The puppy—as fat and pinkly repulsive stomachwise as a piglet, rolled and squealed, until the owner, profuse with apologies, retreated with it, not to reappear. Subsequently I made a painting of this; a companion to another vet subject wherein a large Alsatian was led in, this time paralytic with apprehension, and scarcely comforted by Hero taking the opportunity to assert himself vociferously, albeit from the safety of Catriona's lap.

At another campsite, this time oddly on a race-course, we again experienced the flatness of Norfolk. It was unexpected; and we returned to the more lyric settings of Suffolk, and an idyllic camp named the "Moon and Sixpence," where we could swim in a lake from a sandy beach, and sit on the grassy banks like the Seurat figures on the Grande Jatte. Here I was well into a pen and watercolour phase.

Out painting again in Rochester I was watched for some while by some small girls from a nearby caravan. They were accompanied by a villanious-looking Alsatian who sniffed at me suspiciously. Continuing slowly to wield my pen I ignored its baleful red-eyed leer. At last the smallest of the tinker children asked me if I would give her one of my brushes. "Take no heed of her, Sorr," said the older softly. Then: "Is it the black muck you're painting?" (I was in fact trying to render the effect of golden light emanating from the foreshore in the glory of a Turnerian morning).

"Yes," I replied, "but it looks pinky-yellow, doesn't it?"

Ignoring this, the girl said, with Realist acumen: "Why do you not draw the white can?"—it was sitting in the immediate foreground.

"Because it's too much of a detail—too large—no need to notice it in such a broad view—"

"Oh, but you *should* put it in!" Looking closer at my picture. "Did you *make* that sky? Did you *make* that boat?"

They all three continued, patiently, to watch my progress, the alsatian's nose jammed suspiciously into my ear the whole time.

Adventures come to one on the foreshore. I was etching the *Kingswear Castle*, the veteran steamboat, as she lay at Ship Pier. The steam was curling from the funnel, and a man rowed over and asked if I would like to come aboard. Down in the engine room the great fire was glowing. She was, apparently, the last coal-fired paddler in service left in the world. What an experience—to be in the bowels of the last of the megatheriums! In a moment, with a shovel or so of coal, steam could be put on, and away. I sketched the annual arrival of another large paddler—but diesel-driven—on her annual visit to the Medway. How she tore along as one drew, round the bend of the river and up to Rochester Bridge—then, in no time, she was back, coming at one head-on; showing the surprising width of her beam. She sped by, the decks lined with cheering children. A quieter, sadder effect I etched was the wrecked hull, rusty and green, yet with still all her fittings somehow hanging on, of the Dunkirk veteran the *Medway Queen*, towed to her last berth with a hopeful optimism that she might one day be resurrected even after years submerged in the mud of the Isle of Wight. I had myself seen her funnel protruding down in that river valley, years before. And once, far away in those romantic Thirties, I had travelled to Ryde from the West Pier on the *Waverley*—lost, in turn, at Dunkirk like the other paddlers, the *Brighton Queen* and the *Brighton Belle*. I had photographed the *Normandie* on that occasion, as she steamed out of Southampton." The *Medway Queen* safely made seven rescue trips, but the *Brighton Belle* hit a submerged wreck, the *Medway Queen* rescuing her passengers. The *Waverley* was sunk after a battle with enemy aircraft and with great loss of life.

. . . . . .

Being now editor of the *Journal*, I rather wished to find a copy of my previous publication the *Art Gazette*, of the pre-history period of thirty and more years ago. Unfortunately, I had carelessly neglected to preserve a copy for the future. However, as I had providentially deposited copies at the British Museum Reading Room at that time, there they must still be; so armed with my reader's ticket, I presented myself at the familiar circular setting. It was some time since I had been there, but I noticed particularly the radiating lines running down from the centre of the Dome, that I had once made the leitmotif of a semi-abstract painting of the scene. I decided to repaint this, as it came back to me—I had painted over the original long ago. Most of an artist's work goes this way, if it isn't bought or persuaded away from him. He is bored with earlier work, and only the next picture excites.

I looked through the catalogue. There it was, sure enough! I set about disinterring this Pharaoh from his long tomb—I had all but forgotten the procedure, but on the appointed day returned, and was handed the now carefully bound copies. How strange it was to re-read it all in this timeless padded setting. Here were the features on young artists—how young they looked, indeed, in the photographs—scarcely developed, surely? The sound of the milkman's cart in Bond Street was in my ears—the scraping of the wheels on the curb as the horse followed his master obligingly from door to door, keeping up while bowler-hatted businessmen early for work produced the occasional apple. Imagine a horse drawn milk-float in London today! One of the young artists was now a professor at the R.A. There, at the back, were the adventures of William Bloodstock, in his adventures through the artistic metropolis . . . this was good stuff. I determined to resurrect this idea for the Etcher's Journal; only now it would be the diary of an old artist—both had been and would be myself transmogrified. I hoped the new diary would not altogether lack the bright and observant character of my earlier incarnation. . . .

I bore the volume to the clerk responsible for duplicating, and asked to have a copy of every page. Reverently he handled the binding. "I'm afraid that's not possible," he said. "This is fragile, and has been carefully sewn and bound. Any copying might result in flattening and possible serious damage. I'm afraid the Conservation Department would never allow it. I'm sorry, Sir."

I was in a mind to say that it was my own magazine; and if it came to that, I used to have your job. But what was the use? I went out, leaving the past to bury the past—or, at least, carefully to preserve it.

. . . . . .

In a blustrous north-west wind that all but carried portfolio, bag and parcel of canvas and stretchers (I had been to Russell and Chappell) over the railing of the footbridge into the swishing water, I got across the Hungerford Bridge on my way to visit the Topolski studio on a Friday open day. It was low tide below, and a lone figure on the long pebbly beach below the Festival Hall kicked at the pebbles. The rushing tide broke upon the bridge piles, and the thin hair of the mouth-organ player on the steps waved wildly.

Down below, on the door of the studio was a note—drawing-pinned and crooked but still in place—it said "Other Arch" but in fact I met the returning Feliks and a little crowd of devotees as they crossed over the zebra.

"You have come to Visit?" he said. "You are welcome," and I followed them into the huge cave hung with gouache and emulsion figure paintings—heroic-sized images reminiscent of the lively figures peopling the books of drawings—the *Three Continents*, the *Russia in War* and all the others. But here were Punks, Rock-singers, people of this day—the wild fashions of the present, such a boon to artists. "First put down all your bags," said the Master—"get relaxed."

The others departing, Feliks sat down on an upturned box. "You have brought some drawings to show me?" All around were cans of paint, brushes, paper. Many of the pictures hanging from the roof seemed to have been painted on great sheets of proofs from pages of books on his own work: the texture, close-up, was composed of tiny Toplolski drawings making an extra contribution to the over-all effect.

Feliks looked at my memory-sketches. "Drawing from memory," he observed, "leads to clichés and preconceptions—predictable shapes are used in place of the unexpected ones of reality." It was a good point.

As he spoke, the great west window was illuminated with brilliant sunlight, diffusing through the whitewashed lower panes. It was replaced with blue-black shadow, the hail of rain, and the thundering of the trains from Waterloo to Charing Cross above, as they regularly punctured the conversation. We discussed the visit I made over thirty years earlier to his studio by the canal in North London; the one he had so long tried to protect from eventual demolition by the developers.

"Possibly you are the last living survivor of those times," he said. "You are an antique. What were you doing then?"

"I was running a small gallery, but had to give it up in the end."

"It couldn't have cost much to run in those days. Didn't you have that kitchen-sink gallery nearby?"

It was interesting, to talk of those times, and it was quite true that such times themselves were now, indeed, antique.

. . . . . .

At the conclusion of the Falklands War we went down to see the return of Chattam's own ship, the *Endurance*. It was a grand and actually emotive experience and occasion. The sea sparkled green and choppy, all eyes strained to see her—"There she is!" Helicopter out-riders. Steady and dignified she sailed in, sailors to attention immoveable on the decks. It was like the return of a ship from facing the Armada—an old-world event, perhaps one of the last.

. . . . . .

The Delce, being a series of Edwardian terrace houses—Victorian in style—running from the shopping centre of the Delce Road, constitutes a village community centred on the church. The church itself is more of a modern lean-to of little architectural interest, and many bemoan the absence of the giant Victorian edifice that once stood near by, and was demolished a decade ago. The new style of church has perhaps this advantage over its august impressive forebears, that it does not swamp the congregation with that Victorian sense of spiritual dominance which, after all, was largely the effect of the art work in the choice of sculptured reredos and other fittings. I am myself a great admirer of such artifacts, but they can be more than a little depressing in a community centre, and the Victorians did carry on about themselves, dead or alive. As regards Death where is thy Sting, the new churches would seem indeed to be in every way more constructive, provided the modern roofs continue to keep the rain out. Another excellent innovation in the modern church is the absence of the pews. In early times—as witness Rochester Cathedral still happily pewless—the large area of enclosed floorspace in these community buildings was used for multivarious activities. In the new Delce church, the seats can be put away, and the space employed to accommodate a bazaar, a barn dance, a party, or whatever secular activity is of use to the parish, the community and the church. Artists, who keenly paint Madonnas, Crucifixions and the like, will usually disclaim an enthusuiasm for Belief—"I'm not religious *myself*, of course—" Whether this may be true or not, they usually have a keen interest in churches, and church matters, and seldom let a church go by, (as it were) without entering and inspecting the fabric. One is, of course, no exception to this professional trait; and one enjoys the church activities.

Catriona, singing all day in the choir on Sunday, sees of course more of the inner life—even the true nature—of church and congregation; and those who sit in the front seats even at the services have little knowledge of the varying opinions that may have engulfed even the most recent practice. Yet, harmony prevails from the small child, the newest member, to the useful presence of experience in the octogenarian bass.

The new spirit in the Church is very marked in the Delce. An ancient Baptist chapel has become a Sikh Temple, owing to the large number of immigrants who live here. Indeed, we are spoilt for easy living here. Directly across the street we have an Indian shop where we may purchase groceries every day in the year, from eight to eight, including Xmas day—"and if we *are* closed, just knock on the door." We can buy bread, pastries, even croissants, of all things, and we have a Take-away curry at the corner. In Rochester High Street (but a few minutes' walk away) we have Dr. Barnardo's and Oxfam shops wherein the Rochester residents find their apparel, and to which it is returned when they tire of it. Also, we have the Pizza restaurant, the Italian delicatessen, the French bread shop—one might be in Paris, so many pedestrians are armed with bagettes of a morning—a Belgian chocolate and coffee house, second-hand bookshop, and a High Street carefully restored to Victorian and Georgian splendour with street lamps, paving stones, and timberframed houses replaced in their entirety, rescued from their tendency over the past thirty years to imitate Clapham, and having been caught in time, re-established to a county town prestigiousness. And our Health Centre is next to the Delce church.

Back in the Delce—where the local patios for a farewell is a universal "see you later"—we sometimes participate in a multi-racial evening at the church. Rows of elderly turbanned Sikhs with beards or large moustaches sit, arms folded, in the back row, as pinkly plump ladies perform Scottish dances—but after all, does not Kipling tell us that the Scots and the Gurkhas are brother-regiments? After the reels, a group of Indian girls perform their classic dances, with saris and strange half-hopping hesitant steps. Later, as they chat among themselves, we interrupt their unknown tongue to compliment them—"Oh, pleased yer liked it!" They can speak Delce as well; and Up Delce we have our own argot. The turbanned owner of the timber yard welcomes one with: "Hallo me old mate me old son, what'd you like today?"

At the Troy Town school, where Catriona is piano accompanist and teacher of the recorder, we have a mixed bag of types that cannot be anything but wholly admirable for integration. At the end of term or Xmas concerts the recorder groups play at advanced or elementary levels, having eagerly practiced through their morning break-times. The Xmas stories are well enacted with so great a variety of races to select from for the characters—and Black, Indian, Chinese and White give a remarkably convincing cast for Joseph, Mary, Knights, Saracens, jugglers, tumblers, court musicians, or whatever you please. On occasions such as the Rochester Sweeps Procession on May Day, when the High Street is packed with spectators, and the Morris Men—no effete aesthetes these, but Macho Pagans of ferocious aspect—dance and beat batons, the Troy Towners are out in full force. Troy Town abuts Delce, and is again but an area of a few streets. The Morris Men are arrayed in hay and straw covered top-hats or Billycocks, white hose and green jackets—one has a headed rabbit skin adorning his hat—another a whole head-dress of a boar's head, with which he proceeds to bite at a friendly policeman's helmet. The officer remains friendly, and the young Headmaster of Troy Town beats his tamboured stick of bells upon the ground—he also is top-hatted, and picturesquely attired—Catriona conducts, and the Troy Town children, dressed either as sweeps or apparent candidates for Victorian angel pictures, produce lively mediaeval music. Following this, they sink, exhausted, upon the green—"Can I lie down, my back is killing me," says one small infant, whose back cannot be more than twelve inches long at best. The others collect for a new bass recorder: "Spare ten p. for the new Bass'corder—" Along comes the sinister living tree, the Jack in the Green, spinning and dancing, eerie reminder of pre-history.

At the Delce Church we have a German evening—we are twinned with a German town, and they are here for the week. Catriona's pupils make music, and others of the congregation and the famous choir also entertain. The back of the hall, however is still full of lively chatter, as somebody has broached the beer and the wine a little too soon, perhaps. . . .

"The next song," the lady singer announces, "is 'Gather ye Rosebuds while you may'—I think this means to take your chances while you have them—that is to say—"

"I think you'd better get on with it," said the Vicar.

I, looking, perhaps rather tired, am introduced to a local cleric.

"Are you in work?" he enquires, with an almost Victorian sympathy for a possibly potential victim of the current cuts and lay-offs.

"I'm rather tired of work at the moment," I reply (I have indeed been printing for two weeks); "and I was demonstrating all day yesterday—" This was at the R.E. display of craft and techniques at the Bankside.

"Ah," says the cleric, with deep understanding—"*political*, I suppose?"

It seems a shame to disabuse of him of the happy image of myself as a banner-bearing agitator, and I feel quite ashamed of being an artist, and even in demand . . . I explain my profession.

"An *artist!*" says my friend, with even deeper sympathy—"Ah, yes, I *see*—"

It is quite true that such an admission does nothing to gain respect. One invariably sees the phrase beginning to form on the other's lips—"Famous when you're . . ." But one forestalls it quickly with: "Artist—printmaker-*technician*, that is, of course—" and their brows clear with relief and they stop worrying about you.

Our curate has gone to be a missionary in the head-hunting lands—he was, and is, a remarkable man, a little below middle-age, and of a mystic temperament yet tempered with a propensity for reciting Stanley Holloway monologues—an old fashioned custom that seemed refreshingly new. On Good Friday the congregation parades—led by the Vicar, choir, and a donkey—from one parish to the next; and on Guy Fawkes night a large bonfire burnt a sinisterly real effigy on the church lawn, cheering as the figure clutched and writhed in a truly distressing manner, while I sketched with frantic haste at this unusual aspect of the occasion.

The jumble sales, like all jumble sales, seem to attract a far larger congregation than are ever in church, and we come back from them with a large number of the books we donated the previous year, or so it seems.

. . . . . .

I commenced this book by admitting that I have always liked cheap printing—the Ben Day tints, the screens of coloured dots over outlines—the ordinary strip cartoons that are more and more evocative of their lost era as time goes by, until at last they are the only real memento of it. Real art is too timeless and of all time, and deliberate social reportage too self-conscious to be sufficiently permeated by the period it is recording. Looking at some Steinlen Gil Blas litho illustrations that I had bought—c. 1890—I discovered a pleasure in the ephemeral newsprint paper itself, that is made almost deliberately fragile—it only has to last a week, yet despite all, these had lasted nearly a century—perhaps the last few of its issue, like the one frog achieving maturity from a million tadpoles. Oddly, they increase in authority hourly—minute by minute, as every second takes the browning fading paper nearer to dissolution; strangely, the actual ink is probably indestructible.

I have often spent days scouring old bookshops for such items; one such quest I made was for Pip, Squeak and Wilfred annuals. This apparently immortal set of characters, splendidly drawn by A. B. Page, are eagerly sought after in these later days; not by the children for whom they were drawn, but by the children become adult; indeed, old—searching for the one-time trivia they originally discarded, and eager to pay an antiques price now in place of the half a crown for the annual or a penny for the Daily Mirror in which the trio daily sported.

I had bought an original drawing by William Radford, cartoon-strip artist of the Twenties and Thirties, but had not yet found an original A. B. Payne. No one kept the originals in those days—they were discarded—they had done their work when photographed for the block. I searched through Charing Cross Road and into Cecil Court, where I did in fact secure a Wilfred annual, with an enclosed game printed on card, still uncut within the pages. Some child had only been allowed to read this volume on special occasions. It must even then, to some family, have represented an expenditure as relatively high as the sum I had just paid today. "It will be worth something one day. Look after it!" And they had. Later, in a cellarful of such ephemera of every kind, magazines of all eras, newspapers with headlines that had once signalled whole countries free of thralldom—now collectors' pieces in a cosier circumstance—I found a Pip, Squeak and Wilfred saucer. Once sixpence at Woolworths, but no longer so. In a glass case, at a price I did not wish to approach. But I wish I had; for where may be its peer?

A little later, as if it was anticipating my demands, I saw an advertisement concerning some original drawings of the three for sale, and was able to acquire two examples. They were the last ones in the set that showed *profiles* or three-quarters of all the characters; naturally no one wanted Pip's back view, or Auntie disappearing in the distance, or out of the picture; or only Wilfred's (albeit significant) ears.

Sitting in the train on the way home to Rochester, I heard the following conversation from never-seen people. I wrote it down as it was being spoken. ". . . The only time I've ever felt really scared in a train—and I've never forgotten this—we were near Tonbridge; there was a whoosh; and a bullet hole appeared in the glass opposite, and another above my head in the woodwork. I sat there for twenty minutes, just thinking, it couldn't be. If I'd been standing up . . .! There was no one else in the carriage—no one I could talk to. I'd been reading the Guardian at the time and suddenly I looked down, and the headline said 'New Big Bang Theory'."

. . . . .

I had been to a private view at the West of England Academy at Bristol; and had re-met old friends and acquaintances I had not seen for many years. However, I arrived back at Bristol station to catch the Inter-City for

Paddington, but after an hour of encouraging messages from the driver and a sense of increasing immobility, the final statement was relayed; "I'm sorry, Ladies and Gentlemen, but I have to inform you that this train is—a *Failure.*"

One felt that it meant a great deal more to himself and British Rail than us, and that he would probably never be the same again. We were advised to go to Platform 7 where a special new train would be laid on for us. At once, panic! Everyone got up at the same moment, fighting for hats and coats—card games were broken up, on the instant . . . in the new train, the lady opposite had two dachshunds. "Under the *seat,*" she kept commanding them. Out they came, every time. I volunteered the information that I was usually taking Sweep for a walk at that time of day.

"Only—some people don't *like* dogs in the carriage," she confided. I thought of Sweep once falling between carriage and platform at Salisbury, and only being saved by the lead . . . pulled up again like a fish.

"I can see you're one who prefers animals to people," said a talkative old person, turning her attention to me as I patted the Dachshunds.

"I certainly don't like people much," I said absently, at which all the people except the old lady suddenly laughed heartily. . . .

On the last day of summer I watched from Strood Pier the last trip of the season of the *Kingswear Castle*, whose engine room I had looked at earlier, the last coal-fired paddle-steamer . . . the sun had broken through, dispersing the cold commencement of the day, and creating the illusion of a June morning. Just recovered from a severe cold, and my first day out, I had phoned for a taxi and sped to the pier, where the gangway looked like a Boudin with all the people waiting on it for the arrival of the little ship. In this final apotheosis of the season, one could almost sense the final apocalyptic conclusion of the Victorian age of steam . . . The water was like slowly moving treacle in the golden early rays—then tick-tick!—tick-tick! Here she was, coming round the bend! It was all Tom Sawyer and Huckleberry Finn again, and the Mississippi. Where else could one have found such an occasion? Brown smoke poured from the funnel of this delicate-seeming tea-kettle and her gentle lines seemed frail; the decorative paddle-wheel housings, the rails and seats, all seemed scaled to a more Victorian, more diminutive people than our contemporary giants. But all got aboard. "Not got a ticket?" cried one jovial officer, to a passenger: "Well, better a passenger without a ticket than a ticket without a passenger!" A contemporary touch appeared when a voice spoke from the bridge: "I have been informed that a blue Volvo ashore has all its lights on. Would the owner like to disembark and switch them off? I will stay the ship for two minutes." A figure broke from the crowds, up the gang-way, along the little pier. Re-embarked, the *Kingswear Castle* began to move away from the pier. "Tick-tick!—Tick-tick!" she was rushing along, now, a mere silhouette of funnel, smoke, heads, a black reflection below among the gold sparkles of the sun on the water. It was rather like seeing people off into outer space, and when she had rounded the bend there was only sunshine and silence and the slightly disturbed water, and I was alone on the pier.

In connection with the *Journal* I visited the Imperial War Museum, an amazing place indeed, strangely archaic in that most of the exhibits are of so recent a time—indeed, in many of the visitors' memories. This makes it even more of the past, for nothing is so far back as what has only recently gone out of date. Nevertheless, more recent developments in the field of battle—so to speak—have caused these now ancient eras of World Wars I and II to have become the subjects of a revival of interest in them. They have—regrettably in some ways—become *romantic*; thus defeating Wilde's hopeful dictum that war would go out of fashion when it ceased to be picturesque.

However, having acquired some photographs of Nevinson etchings after his paintings—pictures that I have always liked both for their design and for the sympathy and feeling flowing through them which is even intensified by the cubist futurist sharpness, I enjoyed the Sargent Jagger retrospective. Here was the sculptor of the Artillery monument—the recumbent soldier and the standing figure with bat-like cape spread wide like Dracula, that have always intrigued me from the seat of innumerable bus rides round Hyde Park Corner.

Further on, in a series of upstair rooms, were the galleries of the War artists' pictures from the 39–45 period. I stood by these oils, pen and wash paintings, drawings—here were pictures by my teachers—Leslie Cole's scenes of the Siege of Malta—Dorothy Coke's Home Front recordings . . . if you've known the artist, the picture almost takes second place, even though it's like some of their old clothes hanging there. Your masters are closer to you than your relations—they seem to be standing there in the afternoon mist with you. Shaking off a slight depression, I leave the building, buy some postcards, and go out under the shadow of those Surrealist Naval Guns into the wastes of Lambeth . . . it is cold and wintry as usual, and only a few tourists huddle over the tables of the snack bar.

But summer at last appears, and we are off to Salzburg and Vienna in the grand chase for subjects and inspiration. The result of a perusal of some fifty travel brochures and whole shelves of the geography section of the public library, until one feels (like Pooter) that it might as well be Broadstairs as usual after all. Yet, the decision is at last made. A few days before our departure I go down to the bank to collect some schillings I have ordered. At the cashier's window two other customers seemed very eager to peer at me as if they knew me; it appears at last that they have recently purchased some of my prints . . . we talk about etching, while the doors are being closed: it is half-past three.

"I'm sorry to hold you up," I said to the cashier.

"I don't know what I would do if you were holding me up," he said. "Give you all the money in the till, probably—" But all was organised at last, and on a Monday morning, we set out. The recent reports from Austria and indeed from all Europe (us included), had been of gales, severe flooding (particularly in Austria) and a continuation of the freezing August weather that had been ruining everyone's summer since the end of June. It is curious how at every manifestation of any facet of the weather it always breaks all known records of any year of the past century. How perennially surprised the authorities always are! Did they really keep records all those years, or merely hold parties on that Air Ministry roof which seems to have been so useful a barometer for all conditions.

Once at Dover, we entered the grey white-horsed waves; but as if magicked especially for us, they subsided in a moment; the sun appeared, the water became a sparkling travel-poster green, and the view mirrored the memory of that archaic advertisement I use to look at while sleeping in the old waiting-room at Victoria among the tramps. At Ostend we have the luxury of a first class cabin; and while this precludes the literary material that might evolve from the Dickensian repartee of sharing a six-tiered couchette carriage, it is a good deal more comfortable.

However, before discovering our reserved cabin we do indeed spend some time in a carriage talking to an American father and son who have just passed three weeks wading through Europe; but this weather warning is dispelled by the increasing heat of the night—summer has come upon us for a few days at least, and we roar across the frontiers –the thrilling early morning mist discloses tempting vistas of trees and river and lakes, with Turner's sun rising through the mist at irregular intervals. This endless morning atmosphere— always like the creation of the world—fascinates me as I lean from the window at stations and see the German lettering—only previously familiar life-long in films as suggesting fear, the S.S., *The Great Escape, Night Train to Munich* and other provincial images for one who has unaccountably never travelled here before.

Salzburg, approached via scenes of chalets that are better than their predictable image, is like the tropics; and at last one can breathe (I like the heat and its dizzy relaxation effect, and I like working in it). Our hotel is of old world quality; rather homelike with its antiques and pictures and painted furniture. Outside, Salzburg appears to have been created especially for the etcher, and within seconds I am at work with pen and watercolour, needle and plate. Beneath the Mozart statue a young man is playing a piano; an extraordinary Van Gogh bridge and kiosk at the riverbank nearby demands etching; in the great blinding glare of the platz horse drawn carriages come and go—there are no cars—all views are visible—cafés, people, shops, souvenirs (a passion of ours) all that a landscapist of the social scene could require. Behind and above, a backdrop of mountains and trees; but I am not a tree and stone man. Give me a hoarding, a church door, a passing mongrel, an old lady and a man with an ice-cream barrow; there you have your picture. Not that I have always eschewed the Impressionist glories of nature; but you have to have the gypsy and his cart, or the passing shepherd, to give it point and life—even to set it in Time—as I have often proclaimed in these pages.

I etched the fountain and its Bernini horses—it appears to have come via

Rome and the Piazza Navona—I draw the carriages as they move, avoiding (or being avoided expertly by them) as I stand too close, in the way. Near the Mozart birthplace, which we regard as the shrine it is, and which is partly the reason for our choice of city, a bearded pavement artist is drawing a portrait of the Master in pastels in the centre of the roadway. This is on the colossal scale, and is slowly being covered with coins thrown by admirers. To remove them will necessitate redrawing the portrait tomorrow; which will again attract the crowds . . . everywhere there are buskers, young people with clarinets and violins; music students with a high standard of quality.

We are intrigued by a woolly sort of shortlegged poodle that walks about near our hotel. Its name, oddly, is Robby, and it gets into the drawings. I etch in the castle, after we have climbed to the summit, ignoring the funicula for the sake of the varying views en route. On the battlements an Italian family are trying to place their youngest child into the wide mouth of a kind of mortar, in order to photograph him. The sisters smooth his hair neatly, while he screams with dismay, supposing (not unnaturally) that he is about to be propelled high in the air over the town. This makes also an interesting sketch. In the blue evening in the Platz are many people, well-dressed, with the typical jacket falling lapel-less from one high button, for the men; and puffed-sleeved dresses for women; evening dress abounds, as the concerts are under way, and there seems to be a permanent musical festival. We ride around and through the picturesque streets and squares in an open carriage.

In Vienna, to which we eventually proceed, we are driven to our hotel at about ninety miles an hour by a young man in bathing trunks who not only drives his taxi without hands—so to speak—but also appears to be reading a novel at intervals as well. Our room is on the top floor, and an ancient art nouveau lift conveys us up and down to it. The hotel is being redecorated into an atmosphere of Edwardian tastefulness; our room is still (so far) in its previous fashion phase of teak veneer and modernity; however, by our next visit here we shall be back in the true ambience for visual comfort. But never mind; there are plenty of tables and surfaces to use for pen and watercolour work, and I draw away hours into the night recreating scenes from memory before they should fade. The weather is still of heat wave temperature, and we go out at once to look at the great cathedral, restored from a state of almost total destruction. Again we find in the pedestrianised main street an atmosphere of relaxation; more horses and carriages of even greater elegance, and a variety of character in the buskers that would out do the anticipations of any eager Mayhew. We sample the giant ices in the cafes, with their immense side-dish of whipped cream, and favour particularly "La Dame Blanche," with its hot chocolate sauce, cream and ice-cream. I also ordered a pot of tea (English to the last) which somewhat puzzles the waiter. "Now—you pour it on the ice-cream—?" he says. A young man of stocky appearance stops in the middle of the street, pauses, and launches into an operatic aria. We find, upon conversing, that he is in fact English. Next day he has found a bassoonist to accompany him. A group of young Chinese or Japanese violin and cello players are excellent, and we spend many hours listening to all these performers. Eventually we find ourselves at the Strauss statue, and indulge in the obligatory gesture of being photographed and of photographing other couples. We enjoy a meal in an open restaurant under trees—curiously, a French café. The trees sparkle with little lights; the green-painted lattice apes Montmartre in the Nineties rather successfully, and we are intrigued by two sounds from opposing directions—one seems like a mob rioting. "Oh, that's the wrestling," said the waitress (from London). Catriona goes off to investigate the other sound, which is more like the Vienna Woods, and returns to take me to the dancing round the corner. Here, below the terrace of a palatial building, on which long tables are crowded with people drinking, is an open-air dance floor and a pavilion. More tables are below the steps, and waitresses dash here and there bearing in one hand wide trays laden with quart mugs and glassed refreshments. Joining the dancers, we waltz through the warm night, the orchestra playing madly, the drinkers applauding the dancers.

Later, we succeed in rediscovering our hotel by means of a useful map; and thread our way through Third Man streets and courts back homewards.

The next day, finding a small area of the mainstreet free of immediate buskers, we decide to set to work. Catriona has her recorder, and I hold the music as a stand. We begin to do quite well; groups of people pause, clap, add coins to my hat placed on the paving. Gathering up our profits (subsequently spread—apart from lunch—among the other performers) we set off once more and see the superb special exhibition of Secessionism, which includes painting, music, history, film, design . . . here are Klimt and Schiele, of course, but also other artists unknown to us, and even a reconstruction of the Beethoven room. We meet a couple who congratulate Catriona upon her playing earlier in the streets, and go to see the Mozart statue, with great treble Clef in red tulips in the flower bed beneath it.

Our meals are often of a so-called bowl of soup which turns out to be a vast stew of varied meats with giant and delicious dumplings. We sit about at lunch for some hours, and discover the cream pastries made of ground nuts instead of flour; we experiment with more ice-creams, and in fact indulge gourmet-wise on every possible occasion. We sit at the café tables out of doors, and in romantic old inns particularly preserved as such to tempt us in . . . but at last, the weather changes, and it begins to rain. Early Sunday morning, in what seems an untypical drizzle, we set off to the Mozart house only a street or so away. Few visitors have arrived, and one might fancy Him in residence. The inner courts of these houses, with the balconies diminishing to the small square of open sky as they go upwards, so that the area admits little rain, are ingenious. On leaving we heard music in the silent rainy streets—it appeared to be Beethoven, a full orchestral rendering. Following the sounds, we came upon a fireman, with traditional crested helmet and oilskins, playing a hose upon the side of a house, while all about him the tumultuous music filled the air. What a country! They even put out fires to Beethoven! But through the arch, crouching beneath the water, umbrella aloft, comes a hunched figure. Could this *be* Beethoven? Something said it was. He was followed by a car bearing a camera and crew. It was, of course, a film production; and as if the weather was not bad enough in itself, the fireman had been hired to simulate still more rain. Apparently the genuine article does not register sufficiently when photographed.

The sun appearing after lunch, we took a tram—having no knowledge of the language it was almost impossible at first to acquire the simple information necessary in order to buy tickets—and after indulging in pancake soup, giant dumplings, and more Dame Blanches, visited the Belvidere collection of Austrian painting; and here one's eyes were opened to a whole new school—a history of art—artists one had never even heard of—it was like being born again and being presented with a new Tate Gallery. And one thought one had seen everything. . . . It had come upon me, slowly enough, that there was an excellent tradition of watercolour drawing here in Vienna—topographical scenes of the streets and buildings—stemming, it seemed, from one Rudolf Alt and his descendants and followers. How much one can discover in a few days! This tradition—his work was in the Albertina, where I bought a poster reproducing one of his oils—was to be seen in reproduction, as postcards available in every tobacconists—true fame, and what is better, true appreciation . . . the approach was used by other, relatively modern etchers. We saw in a print gallery—the kind one is familiar with, bins full of etchings and engravings by contemporary artists—the colour aquatint etchings of Eidenberger; and we bought a monograph on his work. It was a popular tradition; it was one to please the visitor to the city; I felt it close to my own approach, and being inspired worked far into the night on my memory sketches.

Being about to leave on the night train, we paid a last visit to Mozart's house. Two old ladies with brooms went up the narrow street and vanished under the lamp through the archway—it seemed unchanged from time past. We sat eating and drinking at an old inn and then taxied to the station, to find we had made a mistake, and our reserved sleeper had left two hours earlier. However, we still possessed our first class tickets, and so could make our way towards Ostend by way of various trains, and in a first class compartment. This setback only served to make the journey more interesting, as they often do. We were soon comfortably settled; I made an etching of Catriona as she lay asleep; and with books and drawing the night was a relaxed affair. At intervals frontier guards would call in with peremptory knockings and much noise to inspect our passports—again much *Night Train to Munich* atmosphere—a little disconcerting to the dozing British Provincial, who thinks for a moment that Michael Redgrave and Margaret Lockwood are about to plunge in seeking sanctuary—and at last we were at Cologne, where I wandered down to the river—and then perceiving that the Cathedral was in fact next to the station, went over to walk round it. The Gothic severity seemed to reproach one, after the swirls and gilt of the Baroque that we had become used to enjoying. All in Vienna had been basically exuberant; all seemed preserved carefully, as well—except the ruined Secessionist Gallery, which we made a point of going to see. The once golden dome was only just holding together, like a half-blown dandelion clock—the walls were grey, a tramp slept on the grass; the Charioteer sculpture was of course presumably indestructible; but an optimistic note was suggested by planks and cement mixers and such builders' material, that seemed to have been gathered there very recently indeed—such as that very morning; so no doubt the final expression of Austrian art may yet be symbolically and factually recreated.

Our boat from Ostend approached Dover through and towards the sunset; a twinkling palace of a ferry gliding through the night, as they had sat in the evening off Newhaven during my early fishing trips, magically hanging on the luminous water, Whistler and Turner combining—what a thought; and one to make Ruskin shift uneasily in his catacomb. At Dover the station platform was unswept—the peeling hoardings sprayed with ignorant and pointless slogans— the vandalised amenities, the air of *Huis Clos* suggested despondency and apathy; the absence of any authority or information, and the fact that we had been taken on and off three buses from the docks to get here, all gave the impression that we had returned from the piping days of peace to an apparently wartime utilitarian austerity. However, all is grist to the artist, or should be, remember, and you must keep reminding yourself of this, or all is lost. But roll on next summer, and the carriages of Salzburg.

. . . . . .

Exhibiting at the Royal Academy it was interesting to see the work of senior artists of accomplishment and pundits to the young, whom I had shown in my exhibitions when they were students. Yet, one goes on, working at pen and wash as one has always done. Did anything ever really happen? Is anything happening now? Are we in a continual state of shock by the events of the moment hitting us? Is time but a continual state of shock? Take Milliais' *Chill October*, a huge studio picture in effect, but painted out of doors, a real piece of time—herein lies its hypnotic quality over hundreds of imitators. It is a brilliant use of—nothing at all. There is a linear base to all Millais' work, even in the marvellous late paintings, which art critics once dismissed in toto by falling into the trap of judging the picture by its story—the very element they have always taught us to despise. This linear base is always present in thought, even if not put in; like an off-beat in a band that is silent, but to which everyone is playing.

In every great picture there is some vital point that holds one, not always immediately apparent, but present. Have you ever suddenly become aware, in a hedge of flowers and foliage, of the unwinking eye of the Deadly Nightshade berry, black, shiny and malevolently attractive, daring you to pick it, and realise that it has been staring at you unwinking all the time?

. . . . . .

It occurs to me that I have said little about the actual technical details of the art and craft of etching—perhaps because they come to one, by now, as second nature. Nonetheless, the physical work of etching is hard; it is full of essential steps that must not be skimped. I have written a good deal about the methods and my own approach, in all sorts of fields of art, for the *Artist Magazine, Leisure Painter,* and *Pictures and Prints.*

I have also written a considerable amount concerning my happy experiences with the Royal Society of Painter-Etchers and Engravers, and these may of course be found in the pages of the *Journal,* where accounts of the activities of the Society, and my own personal impressions, may be found. The *Journal*—including past numbers while they last—may always be found at the Bankside Gallery; and if disappointed the interested and enthusiastic may consult the catalogues of the British Museum Reading Room, where copies are deposited; and if preserved as carefully as my early essay in magazine publishing they should be available for research for some time to come. There are many outstanding and important members of the R.E., foremost among whom is, of course, the President, Harry Eccleston, O.B.E.

"It's Harry who has kept the Society together," Joe Winkelman, the new vice-president, said to me once, and he was right. Joe himself, like Harry, gives unstinted time and effort to the R.E., and the members should be aware that without this kind of energy and dedication from its officers the Society would fade away, become moribund, and lose the respect it has now built up—particularly—after its move from Conduit Street to Bankside. Guided by and managed with the endless enthusiasm—and patience—of the Director, Michael Spender, and his staff, the Gallery has become a centre both for the R.E. and R.W.S. that is perhaps a unique one in London, being affiliated to no one else, and running their joint affairs in a harmony that is essential to our mutual progress. The various Council members who deliberate the elections of new members, hang the exhibitions, and encourage participation in art events, deserve no less commendation for all their efforts. Both Societies, also, have Friends Schemes that provide considerable advantages for those joining them.

Wishing to be able to print some of my larger plates myself, I ordered a Harry Rochat press—a fine and solid construction. Mr. Rochat himself brought it along and set it up. He had asked me to provide some sort of table support, as it was a bench model, but shook his head sadly when he looked at my attempts. "I'm thinking of *you*," he said. "I don't want to feel responsible for all that weight collapsing on you. Where's your nearest timber yard?" Happily, it was round the corner. In no time Mr. Rochat had calculated, ordered, driven back with the wood, and constructed a support. The press gives excellent results, and the workshop, with presses and wheels and ironwork everywhere, looks rather like the engine room of a paddle steamer.

In 1985 I sent in three etchings to the R.A. and was fortunate enough to see them all hung and to sell out an edition of nearly two hundred from one plate. This enabled me to continue publishing. I had commenced earlier that year with a small monograph of my etchings from 1947 onwards—a sort of portmanteau exhibition. My time has become more and more involved with printing and designing for publication, with reviewing and collecting contributors for the R.E. *Journal*, and with writing An Etcher's Diary. It was the encouragement from those who enjoyed that contribution to the magazine that suggested the writing of this autobiography, which I hope has been of some diversion for the reader who has achieved this point.

Michael Blaker

Other Publications Available
from the
Beresford House Press
include

Michael Blaker—Etchings
published 1985

Michael Blaker—Paintings
published 1986

Each book has over 70 B/W full page monochrome illustrations in an attractive paper cover format 192mm×135mm.
Both available at £3·75 each post-free from the publisher.